CHR, LV (April, 1969)

Within the limits of a review it is impossible to do justice to the wealth of material contained in this massive volume of Jean Favier. The book also includes a number of useful tables and graphs as well as appendices listing the collectors for Avignon and Rome. The complex financial details make for difficult reading. *Les Finances Pontificales* is not for the general reader, but a careful study of its contents is essential for the specialist in papal history.

JOHN E. WEAKLAND

Ball State University

William Courtenay, Archbishop of Canterbury, 1381-1396. By Joseph Dahmus. (University Park: Pennsylvania State University Press. 1966. Pp. vii, 341. $8.50.)

The medieval archbishop of Canterbury ruled one of the largest provinces in the entire church, a province so large, in fact, that in the days of Archbishop Lanfrank the popes began to fear the rise of a powerful patriarch in the West. As metropolitan and, after the Norman conquest, as primate of England, the archbishop of Canterbury was the natural leader of the English bishops and the king's most important agent or opponent in the affairs of the English Church. As a result the office was held by some men of outstanding ability and its fortunes loom large in the history of Church and kingdom.

The activities of the archbishops of Canterbury have been the subject of some splendid monographs, most importantly of I. J. Churchill's *Canterbury Administration* (1933) and F. R. H. Du Boulay's *Lordship of Canterbury* (1966), and a number of the medieval archbishops have found recent biographers: Pecham (Douie; 1952), Theobold (Saltman; 1956), Anselm (Southern; 1963), Augustine (Deanesly; 1964), Thomas Arundel (Aston; 1967). To these can now be added Professor Dahmus' volume on William Courtenay, archbishop of Canterbury from 1381 to 1396.

Unlike some of his brilliant predecessors, whose accomplishments transcended their work at Lambeth, William Courtenay's achievement lies in what he was and did as bishop and archbishop. In fact, in many ways Courtenay was a typical prelate of his age and his career mirrors the trends of the late medieval English Church.

As a descendant of Edward I and the son of the earl of Devon he obtained the see of Hereford by papal provision at the age of twenty-eight and was "a prime example of the aristocratic bishop" at a time when bishoprics more than ever became the preserve of the aristocracy. When he lobbied for the king to wring funds from Convocation he appears as the Crown's servant first, a role which his successors notoriously could not escape. His most significant acts—the condemnation of Wyclyf's teach-

ings and the suppression of Wyclyffitism at Oxford University—brought him face to face with the anticlerical and evangelical revolt which would tear apart the medieval Church. Even his will reflects the problems of the Church by providing for 15,000 masses for his soul, the kind of multiplication of religious acts which characterized late medieval piety and aroused the wrath of the Reformers.

In his biography of the archbishop Dahmus gives us first two chapters on Courtenay's background and on his career as bishop of London; this is followed by five chapters on Courtenay's prosecution of the Lollards and his metropolitan visitations, subjects which the same author has treated at greater length in his *Prosecution of John Wyclyf* (1952) and *Metropolitan Visitations of William Courtenay* (1950). The rest of the book consists of a chapter on Courtenay as bishop and one on "Courtenay and the State," followed by a final evaluation and thirty-five pages of translated documents from the archbishop's unpublished register.

The author offers a careful and interesting account of Courtenay's career, his discharge of ecclesiastical duties, and involvement in the political issues of the day. It would be hard to differ with his assessment of the archbishop as an able, prudent, and conservative prelate, who shied away from innovation but worked for reform, defended the prerogatives of Canterbury, and tamed Wyclyf's followers at Oxford with moderation and magnanimity. Professor Dahmus regales us with many an interesting episode from the registers and the chronicles, but the entertaining detail soon leaves the reader thirsting for some generalization. This, when given, is judicious and persuasive. The biographer of a medieval prelate obviously has to follow a path largely determined by the kind of sources which happened to survive. Since the registers of the archbishops of Canterbury have little to say about the activities of the archbishop as a territorial magnate, the reader will find next to nothing in this work on the temporal possessions of the archbishop, the management of his estates, his household, property, and manner of life. Thus this book lacks a dimension which lends a great deal of interest to Margaret Aston's recently published biography of Courtenay's successor, Thomas Arundel.

Seton Hall University   BERNHARD W. SCHOLZ

The Register of Thomas Langley, Bishop of Durham, 1406-1437, Volume V. Edited by R. L. Storey. [The Publications of the Surtees Society. Volume CLXXVII for the year M.CM.LXII.] (Surrey, England: William Dawson & Sons Ltd. 1966. Pp. ix, 197. £2.13.)

As Dr. Storey explains in the preface, this volume presents the remaining folios of the register of Bishop Langley, Bishop of Durham,

William Courtenay

Archbishop of Canterbury

1381–1396

WILLIAM COURTENAY
ARCHBISHOP OF CANTERBURY
1381–1396

by
Joseph Dahmus

The Pennsylvania State University Press

University Park and London 1966

Note on the Spelling *Courtenay*

The most common variants of William Courtenay's surname in contemporary documents are *Courteney*, *Courtenay*, and *Courteneye*. I have discovered no fourteenth-century support for the spellings *Courtney* and *Courtnay* which appear on occasion in more recent writings. "Register G," the register kept by the monks at Christ Church cathedral, is not consistent in its spelling of the name and employs both *Courteney* and *Courtenay*. So do the scribes that kept the archiepiscopal register. While the spelling *Courteney* appears most frequently in fourteenth-century manuscripts, including the archiepiscopal register, *Courtenay* is almost as popular and it is the spelling the archbishop chose for his seal. (For a description of the seal, see Baigent, "On the Prelates of the Courtenay Family," *Collectanea Archaeologica*, I, 236–238.) For this reason I have adopted that spelling.

❧{CONTENTS}❧

❧{1}❧

COURTENAY'S EARLY CAREER

John of Gaunt was furious, and with good reason. Though he was England's uncrowned king (1377), he was being bearded by the youthful bishop of London, William Courtenay, who dared challenge his protection of John Wyclif. "You trust in your parents," he thundered at the courageous prelate.[1]

This dramatic incident emphasizes the eminence of the Courtenay family, an eminence the historian Gibbon helped enhance.[2] Gibbon traced the Courtenay name from the court of Robert Capet to the kings who ruled the short-lived Latin Empire of Constantinople but rejected as monkish legend the story still current in Edward III's day that the English Courtenays were descended from Prince Florus, a grandson of Louis VI (d. 1137). As the first of the English Courtenays, Gibbon designated a French knight, Reginald (Renaud) by name, who lost his ancestral home in France to Louis VII but gained Henry II's friendship and through Henry the hand of a Devonshire heiress. The Devonshire Courtenays between this Reginald and Hugh, the grandfather of our William Courtenay, served their own fortunes while serving those of England. But the family's real distinction originated with Hugh, who established the family's fame in 1335 when his prowess earned him from Edward III the earldom of Devon.

Hugh's son, also a Hugh and second earl of Devon following his father's death, contributed to the family's fortunes by marrying Margaret whose father was Humphrey of Bohun, earl of Hereford and Essex, lord high constable of England, and whose mother was Elizabeth, daughter of Edward I. These two, Hugh and Margaret, were William's father and mother. With earls, therefore, on both paternal and maternal sides of the family and himself a great-grandson of Edward I, William Courtenay was not wanting in those favorable circumstances which have frequently provided less talented aspirants distinguished careers in church and state.[3]

William Courtenay, the fourth son of Hugh, second earl of Devon and his wife Margaret, was born in the family's manor house at Exminster, a small town four miles from Exeter, in or about the year 1341, and was baptized in the parish church of St. Martin.[4] Of his early education which he must have acquired at his father's house, we know nothing. He entered Oxford probably at the age of seventeen or eighteen, and took up residence in Stapledon Hall (later known as Exeter College) which Bishop Stapledon of Exeter (d. 1326) had founded for students of his diocese.[5] That Courtenay chose to apply himself to the study of law was nothing unusual at a time when the study of law was popular, particularly with young men like William who could hope to find careers for themselves in church or state.[6] For one with William's aristocratic connections, this was a particularly reasonable ambition. He completed his degree in law in 1366 and is described as both "doctor of laws" and "doctor of civil law."[7]

William's ordination to the priesthood probably came in 1366 when he was twenty-five years old,[8] although his introduction to ecclesiastical life had come long before, at the age of fourteen, when he was instituted to a canonry of Salisbury.[9] This canonry was but the first of a number of benefices which the powerful influence of aristocratic relatives such as William Bohun, the earl of Northampton, and the Black Prince brought Courtenay. By 1366, when Courtenay's ordinary, Bishop Grandisson of Exeter, required an accounting of him, he was enjoying an annual income of more than one-hundred pounds from one canonry in the diocese of York, two canonries in Bath and Wells, and three in Exeter.[10]

On June 10, 1367, Courtenay entered upon his long and full career when his election as chancellor of the university of Oxford was confirmed under protest by John Buckingham, bishop of Lincoln.[11] Whether of Courtenay's own doing or by accident, the element of controversy which here marked Courtenay's introduction to public life was seldom absent during the more than twenty-five years of active life which lay ahead. The circumstances which attended his appointment as chancellor were these. Upon his election by the university as chancellor on June 4, Oxford commissioned John Shepey, professor of civil law, and Adam Plumpton, master of arts, to carry official announcement of this action to John Buckingham, the bishop of Lincoln, whose confirmation was necessary since the university lay within his diocese. The emissaries presented themselves to Buckingham at his manor of Buckden on June 10 and handed the bishop two letters, one which deputized them as the university's proctors, and a second which requested the bishop to confirm Courtenay's election.

John Buckingham, a young bishop hardly ten years Courtenay's senior, was in his sixth year as ordinary of what was the largest diocese in the province of Canterbury. Whether he decided to use this opportunity to affirm his position vis-à-vis the university, or whether he wished to demonstrate his competency to administer his extensive diocese, a competency which had been questioned when the pope had been asked to confirm his election as bishop in 1362,[12] Buckingham chose to demur. What disturbed him, so he informed the university's proctors, was the absence of the chancellor-elect Courtenay. "Why has not the one you selected as chancellor come personally as have his predecessors in times past?" the bishop inquired. The University's deputies replied that the bishop was in error, since newly elected chancellors had not always presented themselves in person to receive episcopal confirmation, but had rather handled the matter through agents much as Courtenay was now doing; furthermore, that among other reasons why Courtenay could not come in person was the heavy expense such a trip would have entailed the university.

Buckingham in turn denied that chancellors-elect had not always appeared in person to secure confirmation, and he declared he did not now propose to begin confirming any one in his absence. In the end he relented, however, and announced that he would permit himself to be persuaded by their earnest entreaties and the excellent character of the new chancellor to confirm him; but he protested that such action on his part was not to be considered a precedent. Under no circumstances would he ever again confirm any chancellor-elect who did not appear in person. On June 10, 1367, Courtenay was accordingly confirmed as chancellor.[13]

This was the first of several occasions when Courtenay and Buckingham brushed elbows, and it is possible that this early encounter may have contributed later to occasional coolness between the two.[14] The incident did prompt the university to take steps to eliminate similar embarrassments and expenses in the future, and an appeal was made to Rome to relieve Oxford of the obligation of securing the bishop of Lincoln's confirmation of newly elected chancellors. The university explained in its appeal that deputations sent to secure the bishop's confirmation "every second year" had frequently to seek him out in distant parts, at great expense and hardship to themselves, while during such periods when authority was suspended "the wicked sin with impunity and our entire university founders about deprived of rector and head. . . ." Pope Urban sympathized with the university's plight and issued a bull dated November 8, 1368, which exempted Oxford from the obligation of ever again securing episcopal confirmation for its chancellors-elect.[15]

Even though Oxford officially expressed its gratification over the selection of a man like William Courtenay for chancellor who was "refulgent with the blood of kings,"[16] unofficial opinion must have been more reserved. For if Courtenay had so early given evidence of any particular talent, either administrative or academic, which might have recommended him for his post, there is no suggestion of this in contemporary sources.[17] Since Courtenay was no more than twenty-five or twenty-six years old at this time, we can scarcely do otherwise than view his appointment as motivated more from interest in the young man's fortunes than in those of the university. The election of men like Courtenay reflected, therefore, if it did not contribute to, the low academic estate of Oxford during these years.[18]

If Oxford was pleased with the election of Courtenay to the office of chancellor, that satisfaction was not shared by the friars who were in attendance at the university. It so happened that Courtenay's election took place shortly after an appeal from Oxford and Cambridge had led parliament to intervene in the long-standing controversy between the friars and the universities. Shortly before Courtenay's election, parliament had ordered the universities to curb their hostility toward the friars and to repeal certain statutes which they had enacted with a view of forcing conformity upon the mendicants: to abrogate, for instance, the rules that all students must be eighteen years of age and that only those who held master of arts degrees could enjoy the privilege of lecturing in theology.[19] The friars for their part were enjoined from employing any bull they might secure from Rome to the prejudice of the two universities or any of their members. All future disputes between the universities and friars were to be brought before the king and his council, the inference being that they were not to be taken to Rome.[20]

Just how Courtenay came to provoke the anger of the mendicants is not known, nor do we have any way of ascertaining whether the complaints of friars against him were related to their recent disputes with the universities which had prompted parliament's intervention. All we have is Wood's brief statement that in the late spring of 1367 the friars were about to appeal certain grievances they had against Courtenay to Rome when "the king sent his Prohibition to the contrary."[21] If Courtenay had given offense to the friars during his short tenure as chancellor, that might explain in part their willingness to support Wyclif on the occasion of the Reformer's first encounter with Courtenay in 1377.[22]

Courtenay's two-year term as chancellor proved uneventful. The university enacted several statutes dealing with judicial business, but what part Courtenay had in their enactment, if any, is not made evident. One statute instructed the proctors to appoint judges to sit during the long vacation to hear causes and appeals. Heretofore judges had presided only during the regular terms, but the pressure of increasing business necessitated the change; furthermore, should the eligibility of so many judges be challenged that an insufficient number remain to handle the business, the proctors were empowered to select as many as were necessary from among the least objectionable of those challenged.[23] Another statute sought to regularize under pain of excommunication, imprisonment, banishment, or loss of privileges, the proper procedure to be observed in handling appeals pertaining to civil and spiritual matters terminable within the university: from the ruling of any of the chancellor's deputies appeal must be made to the chancellor; from his decision to the congregation of regent masters; from this judgment to the whole university of regent and non-regent masters; and from their verdict, finally, to the king in civil cases, to the pope in spiritual.[24]

BISHOP OF HEREFORD

Courtenay resigned as chancellor of Oxford about Easter (1369)[25] and two months later was proposed as successor to Lewis Charlton, bishop of Hereford, who died on June 24. The cathedral chapter had elected Thomas Brantingham,[26] a canon of the cathedral, upon the death of the bishop, but Courtenay's patrons interposed, forced the quashing of Brantingham's election, and secured Courtenay's appointment instead.[27] That the preference of the Hereford chapter went unheeded should evoke no surprise, since "elections to bishoprics in the fourteenth century tended to be hardly less of a formality than in the Church of England at the present day."[28]

Courtenay had resigned his office at Oxford more than two months before Bishop Charlton's death, and he and his patrons were probably waiting for such an episcopal vacancy to appear. One may wonder why they did not bide their time a while longer since the bishop of Exeter, John Grandisson, was 77 years old and could be expected to pass on within a short time. Grandisson's death would have left the larger and more important see of Exeter available where the Courtenay family influence was unrivalled. Grandisson did, indeed, die a month after Bishop Charlton of Hereford, and while there still remained time for Courtenay's patrons to push him for that see, nothing was done.[29] Perhaps the bishopric of Hereford, like the chancellorship of Oxford, was intended simply as a stepping stone to something more important, which function it could serve as adequately as Exeter. In any event, a formal dispensation was granted by Pope Urban V to clear the way for Courtenay's consecration, and on August 17, 1369, a papal confirmation of his election was extended "inasmuch as by the study of letters and other virtues he had supplied the defect of his age . . . and had shown himself as prudent in spiritual matters as he had been circumspect in temporal."[30] He was consecrated on March 17, 1370,[31] and on March 19 the king ordered the temporalities of the see delivered to Courtenay "whom the pope has appointed to that bishopric . . . and whose fealty the king has taken on his renouncing all words prejudicial to the king or his crown contained in the bull of appointment."[32] He was enthroned as bishop on September 15 following and made his profession of obedience before Archbishop Witlesey at Lambeth Palace on November 13.[33]

During the five years Courtenay served the diocese of Hereford, he appears to have engaged in nothing beyond the routine duties incumbent upon any ordinary. One might express surprise at the large number of ordinations which are recorded in his register, a circumstance due principally to the extended absences of Bishop Brantingham from the neighboring diocese of Exeter. Brantingham held the office of treasurer and since his duties kept him in London a great deal of the time, what was more natural than that he should ask Courtenay, his episcopal neighbor, to handle such episcopal duties as ordinations for him.

On several occasions Courtenay journeyed over to Exeter upon Brantingham's request to take care of these ordinations, doing so five times at Tiverton and once later at Cowick when he was bishop of London.[34] Courtenay's mother lived at Exminster, just a few miles from Exeter, and filial devotion must have eased a task perhaps already lightened by the satisfaction of presiding as bishop in "Courtenay territory." The fact that Brantingham asked Courtenay to take over these responsibilities and that the latter was willing to do so should dispel any notion that friction might have developed between the two men over the manner Courtenay's supporters had nullified Brantingham's election to the bishopric of Hereford. Except for a few months in 1384 when their friendship was strained over Courtenay's insistence that he had the right as archbishop of Canterbury to visit the diocese of Exeter in a manner Brantingham considered untraditional,[35] they appear to have always been on the best of terms.

Although Courtenay's five years as bishop of Hereford proved uneventful from point of view of his responsibilities as diocesan,[36] it was these years which ushered him into the troubled waters of politico-ecclesiastical affairs in which he was destined to move until his death twenty-five years later. Whether by choice or compulsion, becoming enmeshed in politics was a common experience with many medieval bishops. A few like Robert Grosseteste (Lincoln) of the preceding century and Thomas Brunton (Rochester) of the fourteenth did succeed in holding to a minimum the intrusion of political matters upon time which should have been preempted by diocesan business, learning, and prayer. But for the majority of bishops, church and state were so closely intertwined and the business of one so often the concern of both that it would have been unrealistic for a bishop to have expected to live only the life of an ecclesiastic.

Because of their training and education, the prominent position they held in medieval society, together with their generally greater reliability and loyalty (they could not found a dynasty), bishops were ordinarily preferred by kings to members of the lay aristocracy for important posts in the government. As one modern scholar has aptly expressed this fact of English politics in the later Middle Ages: "if you want to find out about the fourteenth-century bishops, you will do well to start by looking at the index to Tout's *Chapters in the Administrative History of Medieval England*."[37] Beyond these considerations, other factors which brought bishops out of their ecclesiastical roles into public life included those never-ending disputes over judicial competence in criminal matters and jurisdiction in civil disputes. The bishop might even invite the assistance of the government in order to compel unrepentant and obdurate excommunicates to make their peace with the church. Finally, in fourteenth-century England all bishops took their places in parliament as lords.

Then about the middle of the fourteenth century a new trend appeared in the character of English bishops which brought the episcopacy and politics still closer together. This was the appearance of the aristocratic bishop. Not that sons of the aristocracy had seldom become members of the English hierarchy prior to this time—they were actually no more numerous under Edward III than under Henry III[38]—but it was only after 1350 that they attained so prominent a position as to be counted an influential element in political life.[39] Even then it was not so much in numbers that the aristocratic bishop made his presence felt as in the eminence of the sees he occupied: Canterbury, York, and London.[40]

These new bishops, though political appointees, were unlike the civil servants to whom the younger Edward III had given bishoprics. These earlier bishops of Edward's had received bishoprics in recognition of loyal service to the crown or to reduce the cost of government. Their work had already been done or, if the crown expected more, it would continue to be performed in the role of faithful administrators. The new bishops, because of their family connections, were expected to fill a much more vital role, which was to bolster an unstable crown or enhance the hopes of some politically ambitious aristocratic faction. The trend toward the aristocratic bishop, therefore, reflected the growing insecurity which was to characterize English political life from the period of Edward's declining years until the close of the Middle Ages. William Courtenay, son of the earl of Devon, now bishop of Hereford, soon of London, and finally of Canterbury, provided a prime example of the aristocratic bishop.[41]

Courtenay's introduction to the politico-ecclesiastical arena came on the issue of a royal subsidy. The occasion was October

1373 when Edward III requested parliament to grant him a subsidy. Under pressure of mounting costs of government and of the war in France, such requests were coming with almost annual regularity, although they had not yet assumed so regular a character that parliament could not protest them as irregular and excessive, if not unjustifiable. Because tradition, sanctioned by papal canons, frowned upon the state's taxing the church, the ecclesiastical lords were excused from parliamentary consideration of requests for such subsidies, although they were expected to give them the same degree of consideration in convocation. And by the middle of the fourteenth century, this had become little more than an empty courtesy, for the "clergy were generally willing to make a virtue of the necessity which lay upon them; they never, or only in rarest cases, refused their tenths when the parliament had voted its proper share."[42] After its usual show of reluctance, the fall parliament of 1373 voted the crown a fifteenth for two years and hopefully attached the provision that should peace with France intervene before the payment date, the grant would not be made.[43]

Convocation which met at about the same time at St. Paul's demonstrated even greater resistance than had parliament to the government's demand for a subsidy; at any rate, their opposition appeared the more marked in view of their customary willingness to follow parliament's lead without more than nominal objection. After Archbishop Witlesey had excused himself on the plea of illness and Bishop Sudbury had assumed the chair, Robert Thorpe, the royal chancellor, and Richard Scrope, the treasurer, presented the government's demand, namely, a subsidy of 50,000 pounds. The clergy protested the magnitude of the demand and announced their inability to raise that amount. They argued that these repeated royal demands for money had all but ruined the English clergy, coupled as they were "almost every year" with demands from the pope; which "intolerable yoke, were it removed from their necks, they could more easily come to the assistance of the king in his difficulties."[44] Nonetheless, after this expression of dissatisfaction, convocation proceded to vote the king a tenth.

That the pope's demands for financial assistance were anything so large as the crown's, even the most harassed bishop in convocation would not have insisted.[45] But the bishops knew that whereas protests against royal demands were largely futile, protests against those emanating from Rome would find a sympathetic ear at Westminster. Furthermore, all bishops would have protested the practice of papal provisions and reservations as a constant source of irritation since it involved a loss of revenue for them and at the same time constituted interference in the administration of their dioceses. Just the year previous, for example, the pope had extended to William, bishop of Carpentras, his nuncio, permission to "confer forty benefices, with or without cure of souls, reserved or not to the pope, which may fall vacant during his mission to France or England."[46]

This sort of curial interference the English episcopacy had come to expect and of itself it would not have precipitated the open revolt in convocation. What did cause convocation to erupt was the papal demand for a charitable subsidy. This may have been the tacit purpose of the embassy the pope announced to John of Gaunt as early as April 1371, which he was sending, so he explained, to assist the duke in his laudable efforts toward ending the war between England and France.[47] This embassy consisted of two cardinals, Simon Langham of St. Sixtus who had been archbishop of Canterbury, and John of Sancti Quatuor Coronati. The fact that "some prelates and councillors [had] presumed to hinder the same" from entering the country, even though Simon was an Englishman, as the pope complained in letters to the king and to several bishops (including Courtenay), suggests the probability that it was pretty generally known in high places that the unofficial objective of this embassy went beyond the establishment of peace.[48]

What it was became officially clear from the letters the pope sent to King Edward, to Cardinal Simon Langham, and to a number of bishops early in 1372, when he informed them that William, the bishop of Carpentras, was coming to England to raise a subsidy. The pope asked the king to induce the prelates of the realm, "who alone of all Christendom do not do so, to come to the help of the pope and the Roman church, which is the king's mother church."[49] The pope's letter to the cardinal carried instructions that he support the efforts of the bishop of Carpentras in persuading the king and prelates to "come to the help of the pope and the Roman church in this their great necessity."[50] The pope reminded the bishops that they should be most ready to aid the pope and be willing to convince the other ecclesiastics to "pay a fitting subsidy, such as had been imposed on and accepted by France, Spain, Almain, and almost all of the Christian world except England. The pope bids them consider that the clergy of England, unlike the clergy of other regions, has not been wasted and desolated by wars."[51]

The bishop of Carpentras, the papal emissary, reached England at the beginning of April, and in the presence of Cardinal Simon Langham explained the pope's urgent need for financial assistance. He must have convinced the assembled prelates of the reasonableness of the pope's demand, for in July Gregory issued formal instructions concerning the subsidy: the province of Canterbury was to pay over to the papal collectors a tenth for one year, the first half of which was to be turned over by Easter, the second part by Michaelmas. While the subsidy could be expected to produce in excess of 100,000 florins, the pope would be satisfied with that amount as Innocent VI had been on a similar occasion some years before.[52]

If the papal emissary had been able to convince Cardinal Langham of the justice of the pope's demands, other bishops felt differently, and a "number of ecclesiastics, at which the pope marvels," were able to prevent the entrance into England of the papal letters, and the Carmelite friar bearing them was promptly seized and clapped into prison.[53] It so happened that John Buckingham, bishop of Lincoln, together with several royal justiciars, were under papal summons at this time to come to Rome. In May 1373 their problem became linked with the question of the subsidy when the pope wrote Edward and agreed to postpone his processes against John and the royal officials. He asked the king in return not to show favor to the "many ecclesiastics of the realm [who] rebel against the pope's orders, especially those touching the bestowal, even upon cardinals of the holy Roman church, of canonries and prebends and benefices, and those touching the subsidy asked for against . . . Milan . . . and to liberate a Carmelite friar who has been arrested by royal officers whilst carrying papal letters touching the subsidy."[54]

Was Courtenay among the bishops who had succeeded in blocking entrance of the pope's letter? In the absence of anything but negative evidence, one can only speculate. The pope had written him, together with other bishops in July 1371, to request him to use his influence with the king in order to obtain a safe conduct into the realm for Cardinals Simon and John over the opposition of "some prelates and councillors."[55] Early in 1372 when the pope again addressed letters to several bishops, urging them to "induce, as best they can, the remaining ecclesiastics of the realm to pay a fitting subsidy,"[56] Courtenay was not among those approached. Was this omission simply an oversight or was Courtenay among these "remaining ecclesiastics"?

The query concerning Courtenay's position is not idle speculation. For no sooner had it been agreed in this fall convocation of 1373 to give the king his subsidy, than "William Courtenay, then bishop of Hereford, trusting in his rank and family, for he was the son of the earl of Devon, rose courageously in the midst of the synod, and announced in a loud voice (*alta voce*) that neither he nor the clergy of his diocese would give anything until the king had provided a remedy for these mischiefs (*calamitatibus*) which the clergy had for so long been enduring."[57]

What prompted Courtenay to make so outspoken a protest against papal exactions? Had he been casting about for an opportunity to make his presence known among the bishops into whose company he had just recently been introduced, to put himself in their good graces, and to advance his ambition to become one of their leaders? He could not have chosen a happier issue than money demands by which to accomplish this. It would have been a rare bishop, indeed, who would not have shared his repugnance for financial levies, whether they emanated from Rome (Avignon) or from Westminster.

At first glance, one might suppose that it was the crown Courtenay had in mind, for it was his share of the subsidy convocation had voted the government that he threatened not to pay.[58] This was surely not the case, for Courtenay knew as well as the other bishops assembled there, that such rebellion would have been an empty threat on their part, since the crown had effective means at its disposal to force uncooperative bishops into line. Courtenay had himself experienced the effectiveness of such means just the year previous when the crown had ordered his temporalities seized, together with those of other delinquent bishops in the province of Canterbury, for failing to pay over to the exchequer the entire amount convocation had voted earlier that spring.[59]

Apart from personal ambition which may have stirred Courtenay there can be little question that he made his protest in the hope of enlisting the support of the crown in his and his fellow bishops' resistance to papal exactions.[60] That this is precisely what happened makes this suggestion the most likely explanation, particularly since Courtenay was still smarting from a personal encounter with the papal curia over financial demands it had made upon him. Just three years had passed since his consecration as bishop and hardly a year since he had finally satisfied the curia for the heavy charges it had assessed him for approving his election and consecration. So heavy were these charges that though he was the son of a wealthy earl and enjoyed a sizeable income of his own, he was obliged to beg the camera for an extension of time in meeting its demands. The papal chamberlain had granted such an extension, but with the warning that were the entire balance not paid by the feast of St. John the Baptist (June 24), not only would he be held for the unpaid balance but also for the 499 gold florins, 27 shillings, and 11 pence he had already paid over.[61]

No doubt other bishops gathered in convocation with Courtenay in the fall of 1373 must have nursed sore memories of similarly heavy curial charges which they had been assessed on the occasion of their elections and consecrations. The heaviest item among such charges was ordinarily that of annates. Because the pope had experienced less difficulty collecting them than a direct tax, they had a tendency to grow over the years. Recurrent protests appear in the parliamentary rolls of the fourteenth century against their excessiveness.[62] Consequently, any attack Courtenay might make on papal demands, whatever the particular nature of those demands, was certain to enlist episcopal support.

In answer to Courtenay's protest, the crown promised that it would seek concessions from the pope concerning the "intolerable yoke" of which the bishops had complained. In April 1373 the king sent an embassy to Avignon to discuss papal demands for the charitable subsidy, together with the usual issues of provisions, reservations, and summonses. In the ensuing negotiations at Avignon and in 1374–1375 at Bruges, the papal representatives conceded nothing in principle that would have limited the pope's right to make what provisions and reservations and to issue what summonses he chose, although they did promise that the curia would be more moderate in its employment of such rights in the future. On the issue of the charitable subsidy some concession was also made. It was finally agreed that the English clergy would contribute the sum of 60,000 florins, with the payment of the remaining 40,000 florins being made contingent upon the establishment of peace with France.[63]

In the fall of 1374, to go back a bit, Pope Gregory wrote

to the Black Prince, to the king's envoys who were about to leave for Bruges to continue Anglo-papal discussions, to Sudbury, and to Courtenay, urging them "to foster peace and concord between the Roman church and the king. . . ."[64] That Courtenay was the only bishop other than Sudbury thus appealed to suggests the probability that the curia had come to consider him the most influential member of the English hierarchy next to the bishop of London.[65] Courtenay's bold attack in convocation on exactions, whether royal or papal or both, had apparently had the effect of bringing him forward as a new leader in politico-ecclesiastical affairs. His family's position, more aristocratic than that of any other English bishop, his friendship with the Black Prince, and Edward's advancing age, all recommended him to the papal curia for special consideration. It appears, furthermore, that Courtenay did not long continue in the role of an insurgent, for in the letter noted above the pope took the opportunity to acknowledge the good efforts the bishop had made in behalf of the papal cause.[66]

Courtenay's consecration as bishop of Hereford in 1370 brought him to the threshold of English religio-political affairs; the protest which he voiced three years later in convocation against papal exactions projected him into their midst. Both events constituted vital steps in his career. Without the rank of bishop, he would have remained unknown, for only the extremely brilliant or exceptionally pious priest could hope to rise above obscurity, and Courtenay was neither unusually brilliant nor unusually pious. Once bishop, however, the way to influence and fame lay open, although few fourteenth-century English bishops ever went far down that road. Most bishops in similar circumstances would have been content to live out their careers in the relative isolation of Hereford, but not Courtenay. Ambition spurred him on and what he might have lacked in other qualifications on his way to greatness, his lineage more than compensated for. A like protest against papal exactions by a similarly youthful bishop but of common parentage would have evoked only an indifferent response from the gray-haired prelates in convocation who listened to Courtenay with respect.

Why then did Courtenay rise in convocation to voice an attack on the papal curia? Hardly because of any personal rancor he might still have been harboring toward the curia for the heavy expenses his consecration had cost him there. These expenses were probably no heavier than those other bishops had experienced and Courtenay should have expected nothing different. Furthermore, after this one outburst against papal exactions, there is no more antipapalism in Courtenay's record. Three years later, in fact, an irate government censured him for his loyalty to the pope.[67] The picture of an ambitious, paternalistic prelate emerges from the relatively impersonal documents which trace Courtenay's long career from his election as chancellor of Oxford in 1367 until his death in 1396. His protest in convocation in 1373 may have been the action of an ambitious young man, of a youthful prelate who had his eye on places higher than Hereford. Or it may simply have been the normal act of a young man in whom the combination of aristocratic origin and educational background had produced a spirit of proud independence. This much at least is quite clear from the sources: Courtenay at no time during his long career ever displayed evidence of timidity or subservience.

{2}

COURTENAY AS BISHOP
OF LONDON

THE POLITICAL SITUATION AND HIS ELECTION

In May 1375 William Courtenay was translated to the see of London. The death of Archbishop Witlesey the preceding June had opened the door to Courtenay's promotion, for Simon Sudbury's moving to Canterbury had left the great see of London vacant. Courtenay's advance to London was perhaps the most crucial step in his career, for it greatly facilitated, if it did not assure, his later translation to Canterbury.[1]

The diocese of Lincoln exceeded London in size, that of Winchester was far the wealthier, but no episcopal see rivaled London in importance.[2] It was the oldest diocese in England next to Canterbury itself, and if Augustine when consecrating its first bishop in 604 could recognize London's preeminence at that time over other communities, the passage of seven centuries had established London beyond question as the center of England's political life. Even in ecclesiastical matters, because the English crown had always assumed a positive voice in the external affairs of the church, it was inevitable that London's leadership in politics would lead to that city's eminence in church matters. That fact was reflected in the archbishop of Canterbury's preference for his Lambeth manor across the Thames from Westminster to his palace in distant Canterbury.[3] By the late Middle Ages Paris was no more France than London was England.

Contemporary men of influence in church and state affairs must have generally accepted Courtenay's translation to London in 1375 as logical whether they approved of it or not. Those opposing it could find little beyond Courtenay's youthful thirty-four years to press as an obstacle, and the danger of delivering the leadership of so important a see into the hands of one so inexperienced. If this objection was raised, Courtenay's advocates could have been counted on to remind the young prelate's critics that the proximity of the archbishop of Canterbury at Lambeth would serve as an effective restraint upon Courtenay's possible imprudence, furthermore, that Courtenay's aristocratic associations had already provided him a degree of political and ecclesiastical awareness which a man of more humble origins would have taken considerably longer to acquire.

It was Courtenay's aristocratic character that brought him promotion to London in 1375. True, he had served two years as chancellor at Oxford and for approximately five years as bishop of Hereford. But what kind of record he left in either place is not known. Only a superlative performance on the one hand or manifest negligence on the other would have attracted the attention of contemporary chroniclers.[4] The silence of these scribes suggests that the level of Courtenay's performance as chancellor and bishop lay somewhere between these two points. That he was actually promoted to London and that subsequently as archbishop he demonstrated real talent as an administrator, give one reason to suppose that by 1375 he had already provided evidence of some ability along these lines. This much one may certainly say, and this is all that need be said to account for the rise of a man of the aristocracy who enjoyed powerful friends among the nobility, namely, that Courtenay had made no important enemies, none in England at any rate.

The one act of Courtenay's which the sources single out as bearing possible significance in assessing his acceptability as a candidate for the see of London in 1375 was the protest he had voiced in convocation two years earlier against papal financial demands. This had been a bold act and one which could easily have had important consequences for his career. By it Courtenay must have enhanced his acceptability to the English hierarchy, to the lay aristocracy, and to the crown, all of whom would have generally agreed with him on the problem of papal exactions and have applauded his courage for raising the issue. This protest must, conversely, have displeased the pope. Yet in terms of influence Courtenay had gained more than he had lost. For in the fourteenth century appointment to a see as important as London lay almost wholly within the crown's prerogative: the king would pick the man whom the chapter at St. Paul's would elect and the pope at Rome (Avignon) would approve.[5] Had Courtenay remained unalterably hostile after making his protest in convocation, the pope might conceivably have blocked his election. But if Courtenay was ever basically antipapal, he did not long remain so, and Pope Gregory in his letter to Courtenay in the fall of 1374, a short year after this protest, was already acknowledging the bishop's good services in the papal behalf.[6] It must, therefore, not have been a great surprise to Sudbury to receive a letter from Gregory dated September 9, 1374, that expressed, first, the pope's prerogative to translate Courtenay to London, then the information that he had "diligently" discussed his qualifications with his councillors, and because of his distinguished record at Hereford, was translating him to London.[7]

The people of London probably endorsed Courtenay's promotion with enthusiasm, whatever the measure of consideration the crown may have given their reaction in its selection of their bishop. Still, other things being equal, the crown would have preferred to please the people of London. These constituted its most proximate, numerous, vocal, and wealthy citizens. The crown may have known that Londoners would have approved the fact that Courtenay had never been outside the country and that, unlike Sudbury, he had never served in the papal curia. That Courtenay had never practiced law also stood in his favor at a time when lawyers were objects of pretty general aversion.[8] Even Courtenay's aristocratic lineage would have pleased many Londoners. Their bishop was to be much more than a spiritual father. In an age when church competed with state for prior claim to the individual's allegiance, they expected their bishop to defend their rights against all enemies: against the crown, the aristocracy, and the papal curia, and to champion their demands. And who could do this more effectively than the son of an earl and a great-grandson of Edward I who had already proved his mettle in convocation in 1373 when he challenged papal exactions?[9] Finally, in an age traditionally dominated by the aristocracy, many Londoners would have felt that, for the post of lord bishop, only a son of the aristocracy was to the manner born.

The critical factor in Courtenay's promotion to London in 1375 was his political acceptability at that particular moment. A year or two later he might have been denied this promotion, for by that time John of Gaunt's will in politico-ecclesiastical matters had become preemptive. In 1377 the duke would probably have insisted upon a man more of his own choosing. In the spring of 1375 the political situation favored Courtenay. Though the Black Prince was in his last illness, he had still more than a year to live, and so long as he was alive he could be counted on to advance the career of his former protégé. Edward III's power of leadership, his honor, and his popularity had progressively declined since the death of Queen Philippa in 1369.[10] By 1375, between his growing senility and his worsening health on the one hand and the charms of the mercenary Alice Perrers to which he had succumbed on the other, he remained but a shadow of the Edward of Crecy and Bretigny. Yet until the complete breakdown of his health late in 1376,[11] he was still king, and until that breakdown he would be inclined to follow the voice of the Black Prince, rather than that of Gaunt if and when these two were in disagreement over a question of episcopal preferment.

Apart from Courtenay's early years when the Black Prince proved himself a powerful patron, it was with Gaunt that his career was most closely associated, so a word now about the duke. In a period of unusual confusion as were the seventies,[12] Gaunt remains a particularly puzzling figure. Not the least cause for the uneasiness of a scholar who seeks to unravel the confusion of the last quarter of the fourteenth century is the duke himself: a protector of John Wyclif despite his own belligerent orthodoxy;[13] an "anticlerical" foe of Bishops Wykeham, Brantingham, and Courtenay, yet with strong friends of his own among the hierarchy; England's unofficial regent from late 1376 until some time after 1381, whose dominating influence, however, while a very real fact, was seldom clearly compulsive nor even often discernible. Through his marriage to Blanche, the heiress of Lancaster, Gaunt acquired a great name and the largest fortune in England, and he used his wealth and position to stock the government and church with his men.[14] He began to take an active interest in political affairs possibly as early as 1371.[15] He only assumed a prominent position after his return from France in the summer of 1375, however, following a disastrous military campaign that he had commanded and peace negotiations at Bruges where he had headed the English plenipotentiaries. Then whatever his earlier ambitions might have been, the fatal illness of his brother, the senility of his father, and the minority of his nephew, the future Richard II, pushed him logically into first place in English political affairs. His enemies, and he had many,[16] accused him of usurping the authority of his father and conspiring to unseat his nephew. Modern writers clear him of both charges and counter rather with commendation for his sense of loyalty: loyalty to his brother, to his aging father, to his nephew, to all men, indeed, whom he liked or who were in his and in the government's service.[17] That the duke may also have had the insight, rare among Englishmen of the time, to favor a realistic settlement with France,[18] counted in his favor. These "credits" the historian must search for. Manifest, on the other hand, is evidence of Gaunt's lack of greatness in political affairs, although even a more capable leader could hardly have hoped to do more than muddle through the impossible situation created by an empty treasury, a losing war, a senile king, and the prospect of a child king's succeeding in the near future. The seventies were years of political turmoil, years of indecision and rudderless government, which spawned "those political movements and party combinations which continued throughout the next fifteen years."[19]

A glance at these movements and combinations is necessary since Courtenay's career became intimately involved. The oldest group, so traditional and nonpolitical that it may not be proper to distinguish it from the government itself, was composed of members of the chancery, exchequer, and other branches of the administration. Old household officers, usually bishops, headed these different branches, while professional civil servants staffed the lower offices. The majority of these servants were recruited from the ranks of the clergy, although in the late fourteenth century the common lawyer began to make his appearance. The atmosphere in the government remained, however, predominately clerical. William Wykeham, bishop of Winchester, headed the chancery, and Thomas Brantingham, bishop of Exeter, administered the exchequer in 1370, a situation which was not considered unusual.[20]

This clerical preponderance in the government was both traditional and logical, for until the later Middle Ages only members of the clergy commanded the necessary legal and linguistic skills to handle the business of administration. Monarchs, too, normally preferred a bishop to an earl or duke as head of a department, since a prelate was less likely to permit family ambitions to interfere with his devotion to the crown.[21] Double reason had the financially straightened monarch for preferring a bishop administrator, for the bishop's diocese would support the prelate while the income from benefices would take care of his staff.[22]

Because this was the kind of government that had conducted the crown's business for a generation or more, it enjoyed the support of the Black Prince and normally the confidence of Edward. It could not have been otherwise, for this was the age before "governments" and ministries depended upon parliamentary majorities.

A break came in 1369. After an eight-year lull, the war with France reopened, followed by a series of English defeats in France and a French attack on Portsmouth. Overnight a relatively self-satisfied, confident England was faced with "military disaster and . . . increasing economic exhaustion."[23] The slow, quiet strategy of Charles V had finally borne sudden fruit, and in 1371 England awakened to the tragic realization that the days of Crécy and Poitiers were no more and that great effort and cost would be required to rectify the situation.

In its search for someone on whom to pin the responsibility for this sorry development, what was more natural than for parliament to hold the crown's councillors to blame and to demand a change of personnel? Because the immediate targets of this attack were the chancellor and treasurer, both of whom were bishops, older scholars, in an effort to identify this opposition, have labelled it an anticlerical party. True, there was a tinge of anticlericalism in the air, against the papacy at least. The failure of the statutes of provisors and praemunire of the fifties to curb papal reservations and provisions had engendered some anticlericalism, and Pope Urban V's attempt in 1365 to collect the arrears on John's tribute had sharpened this. A measure of this hostility touched the English clergy, and commons petitioned parliament in 1371 that the temporalities of the clergy be appropriated for war purposes.[24] While this proposal scarcely received serious attention, the crown did bend to the opposition to the extent of replacing Wykeham and Brantingham in March 1371 with laymen and handing the privy seal over to a layman for the first time in its history.[25]

There is danger, however, in employing so modern a term as anticlericalism to describe the motivation behind the move in 1371 to reduce clerical influence in the government. This opposition did not stem from that basic hostility toward the church, not uncommon in the history of modern western Europe, which would restrict ecclesiastical influence to areas narrowly spiritual.[26] Its objective in 1371 did not extend beyond the exclusion of bishops as heads of departments and the wider employment of common lawyers rather than clerks in the lower offices. Further-more, the opposition of men like Gaunt (when he joined this group) to the use of bishops in the administration was apt to be selective. Certain bishops, not all bishops, should be excluded.[27]

Only Wyclif objected to the "caesarean clergy" on princi-ple, although his concern did not spring from anticlericalism. He feared politics would debase the church, not that churchmen would misuse the state. Because the war with France was going poorly, because the pope was French, because his bishops were holding the highest offices in the government, why should there not be voices demanding that these prelates be replaced with laymen. Laymen could prosecute the war more vigorously and laymen could be punished for negligence and malfeasance. Fur-thermore, Gaunt who was now assuming the responsibility for prosecuting the war might quite properly insist that his men replace those who had been, and still were, in charge of the government and its operations.[28] Finally, among others demanding a change in administrative personnel were a few scoundrels who hoped to be able to work their knaveries with greater immunity under a new and inexperienced government.

It was this last group which supplied the most prominent members of this anticlerical or, better, new court party. There were Lord Latimer, the king's chamberlain, for example, the London merchants Richard Lyons and John Pecche, and Alice Perrers, the king's mistress.[29] Together with a scattering of simi-larly corrupt courtiers and officials, these constituted the unsavory element in the court party, the respectable element being represented by common lawyers, several northern lords, and southern bishops.[30] Toward the end of 1375 Gaunt emerged as the unofficial leader of this "band of nobles and knaves,"[31] and in his wake shortly after appeared the spare figure of John Wyclif.

The clerical party, on the other hand, if it harbored as varied and as sordid characters as the court party, gave less evi-dence of this to the chroniclers whose sympathies were solidly with them under any circumstances. A clerical party could count on the neutrality, if not support, of those lords who were not exercised over the reverses in the war and who were reasonably content with conditions at home. And its very clerical nature assured it the cooperation of a majority of the bishops as well, including that of Wykeham, Brantingham, and Courtenay. Countering the tacit leadership and degree of identification which

Gaunt afforded the new court party was the prestige of the Black Prince which the clerical party enjoyed.

That Gaunt and the Black Prince were generally on friendly terms during the seventies[32] points up the danger, however, of attempting to define very sharply the membership and objectives of either group and of thereby creating the image of two sharply opposed factions. In any event, whatever the degree of hostility among the associates of the Black Prince and Gaunt, the two royal brothers could themselves have had little difficulty agreeing that Sudbury, the friend of Gaunt, should move up to Canterbury, while Courtenay, the protégé of the Black Prince, should be elevated to London. The promotion of the two bishops appears so logical, indeed, that one is surprised that negotiations required almost a year to complete.[33] Courtenay was translated to London on May 12,[34] consecrated on September 12,[35] and provided the temporalities of the see on December 2.[36]

COURTENAY AND THE FLORENTINES

If there were any who had questioned Courtenay's maturity when he was being considered for the important see of London, they would have found their apprehensions confirmed by one of the bishop's first public acts. The affair into which Courtenay blundered concerned citizens of Florence, principally merchants, who had taken up residence in London where they were quietly making money for themselves—and for the crown[37]—only to find themselves suddenly caught up in the backwash of a war in far-off Italy between the papacy and Florence. The chroniclers are brief and their usual nonanalytical selves in describing the origin of the trouble, although it is possible that they were not aware of the complexity of the factors which had preceded the pope's action.[38]

These chroniclers content themselves, in any case, with a detailed account of the grisly manner in which the citizens of Florence had tortured and murdered the papal emissary who had come to negotiate a peaceful settlement and of Pope Gregory XI's harsh retaliation. Not only did the pope excommunicate the Florentines and place their city under an interdict, but he also extended the force of his anathema to apply to all Florentines wherever they might happen to be living. They were to be despoiled of their possessions, debts owing them were to be repudiated, and countries were ordered to bar them entrance. A concession modified somewhat the bull's harshness. Those Florentines who wished to do so could remain unmolested in the countries where they were residing, provided they made their homes there permanently and provided they lived there as bondmen to some lord.[39]

Such was the nature of the pope's anathema. Harsh though it was, it would probably have passed unnoticed in England and the Florentines have continued about their business in London without molestation, had it not been for Bishop Courtenay's precipitate interference. It so happened that the pope sent his bull denouncing the Florentines, not only to the king but to Courtenay as well,[40] who as bishop of London would have been the logical prelate to see to its promulgation. And Courtenay, with the imprudence of a child and without clearing the matter with the crown, proceeded to publish the bull forthwith (*non segniter*) with all solemnity at Paul's Cross.[41]

It is not clear from the chroniclers whether the Londoners, upon hearing Courtenay's announcement, proceeded to give the pope's bull their enthusiastic cooperation by pillaging the establishment of the Florentines, something they would have been most willing to do papal sanction or no.[42] The chronicler merely writes how, in terror either of what was already happening to their possessions or of what they feared would surely happen, the Florentines appealed to the mayor who took them and their plight to the king. "Are you *our* men" asked the king. "We are indeed," they answered. "And we," replied the king, "will protect you," which he did by ordering all goods that might have been seized to be restored to them and by taking them and their possessions under protection of the crown.[43]

Courtenay had not long to wait for a summons from the crown, and Thomas Brantingham, the chancellor, promptly cited him to appear at the chancery to explain his part in the episode. To the question why he had had the audacity to publish the pope's bull in defiance of the statutes of the realm without first consulting the king or his council, Courtenay could only answer, "Because the pope commanded" it. This explanation did not impress Brantingham, bishop though he was, and he directed Courtenay to choose between the forfeiture of his temporalities and retracting in person the statements he had made at Paul's Cross.

This would have been a humiliating task even for a humble prelate, which Courtenay was not, and it was only "with difficulty" that he prevailed upon Brantingham to permit him to have his commissary do the retracting for him. So it was Courtenay's deputy who addressed the people at Paul's Cross, telling them that "my lord said nothing here about an interdict" against the Florentines and that it was surprising how they could have made that mistake, "you who hear so many sermons."[44]

The episode concerning the Florentines does Courtenay little credit. That he should have published the pope's anathema without first securing permission from the government seems incredible, particularly at a time such as the seventies when the crown was so sensitive over papal provisions, reservations, appeals, and bulls. And it is so out of character, the act of an impulsive man, not that of the level-headed prelate and administrator Courtenay proved himself during his long years as archbishop, that one would like to deny his part in the affair were it not for the positive character of the evidence. It is true that Courtenay was not one to avoid controversy, as he would demonstrate shortly in his clashes with Gaunt over Wyclif and over the violation of Westminster Abbey.[45] But in these two instances, as invariably in other controversies in which he found himself involved, Courtenay dealt from strength, with reason, right, or tradition on his side. Never before nor after did he leave himself so vulnerable as in the incident concerning the Florentines.

Why did he act so imprudently? Did the receipt of a papal bull directed to him personally deprive him momentarily of his sense of reality? Or did he wish to use the occasion to prove his loyalty to the pope, should the curia have had doubts about his fidelity after his challenge of papal exactions in convocation of 1373? Or did he simply wish to gain the goodwill of the Londoners, which he very probably did with his act? Not one of Courtenay's contemporaries has a word to offer in explanation, and Courtenay least of all, who probably hoped the affair would be forgotten just as quickly as possible.

THE GOOD PARLIAMENT

What helped take people's minds off Bishop Courtenay and the Florentine affair was the work of the Good Parliament[46] in 1376 and Gaunt's efforts to neutralize this. Considerable excitement stirred the people that spring over the coming parliament, not so much because there had been no parliament since 1373 but rather because the crown, despite its grave need for revenue, had avoided convening that body since 1373 lest it provide popular discontent a forum. This discontent was widespread and affected most classes, born as it was of a variety of causes: high prices, a trade depression, bad harvests, a recurrence of the Black Death, and inept leadership and corruption in high places to which universal consent attributed the military setbacks abroad and the bankruptcy of the government at home. By 1376 the pressure of financial need left the crown no longer any alternative, and on April 28 the parliament summoned in February opened its sessions at Westminster.

The aging king made one of his last public appearances when he welcomed the assembled lords and commons in the opening session. After that it was his son, Gaunt, who represented the crown. This was unfortunate, even though necessary,[47] since many members of parliament were inclined to associate the coming of evil days with the emergence of the duke. His presiding presence would serve to arouse, not mollify, their sensibilities. So rather than consider the matter of a subsidy which the chancellor had urged in his opening address, once commons had withdrawn to the chapter house of Westminster Abbey to hold their discussions, they proceeded to voice a bitter attack on the government. Actually they leveled their assault less on the king's ministers and officials as a group than on individuals in the government who, they believed, had misused their positions to defraud the crown of funds which would otherwise have sufficed for its needs.

Scholars have credited the commons in this Good Parliament with exhibiting considerable maturity. They gave early evidence of this by selecting Peter de la Mare,[48] a knight of the county of Hereford, to act as their "speaker." In the hope of enlisting the support of the lords for the demands they might wish to make upon the government, commons decided to seek the assistance of a committee of peers to meet and advise with them. This request de la Mare carried to the lords, who accepted the suggestion and formally authorized the twelve men nominated by commons to consult with them. These twelve included four bishops, four earls, and four barons, and among the four bishops designated was Courtenay of London.[49]

The political convictions or loyalties of the twelve councillors varied. Houghton, the bishop of St. David's, for instance, was a friend of Gaunt, Courtenay of London the reverse. The most that can be said of the views of a number of the others is that they were undefined, if they had any.⁵⁰ This explains the lack of hesitation on the part of the lords in appointing the committee. The twelve were to provide counsel of a general kind to commoners, who, as de la Mare explained, were unschooled and needed guidance. Because the twelve lords must generally have shared popular dissatisfaction over the manner certain corrupt officials had been conducting the crown's business, they could be expected to agree in the main with the demands of the commons.

These demands were both punitive and constructive. Commons brought charges of malversation against Lord Latimer, the king's chamberlain, and Richard Lyons, a London merchant, who was a member of the king's council. Similar charges were made against several other courtiers, while Alice Perrers, the king's mistress, was accused of drawing several thousand pounds a year from the royal treasury.⁵¹ Commons demanded that the two men be imprisoned and that Alice be barred from the court. They then requested, through de la Mare, that the king's council be assisted permanently by a group of nine lords, this council to consist of three bishops, three earls, and three barons. All important business such as the grant of feudal revenues should have the approval of this "continual council," while four or six of its members were to be constantly in attendance at court in order to scrutinize matters of lesser importance.

This last request might suggest at first glance a limitation upon the royal prerogative reminiscent of that forced upon Henry III and Edward II. Such was never the intention of the commons. They were entirely willing, they assured Edward, that he select the nine members of this council and, what was more important, that the authority of the council should never contravene the freedom of the king's principal ministers in the conduct of their business. Edward agreed to the establishment of the council and, perhaps to gain the good will of the commons, graciously accepted the nine peers they had recommended. The three bishops appointed to the council included the three most prominent prelates in the kingdom, that is, Sudbury, the archbishop, Wykeham, the bishop of Winchester, and Courtenay. The king also agreed that Latimer, Lyons, and other corrupt courtiers be deprived of their offices and punished and that Alice Perrers, whom he protested he had never realized was the wife of his trusted lieutenant in Ireland, be removed from court. Her promise to leave Edward alone, Archbishop Sudbury and his attendant bishops swore to force her to abide by under pain of excommunication.[52]

The Good Parliament, up to then England's longest parliament and, in the opinion of many of its members, the most successful, held its last session on July 10. That fall Gaunt proceeded to undo its work through the instrumentality of the great council which he summoned to Westminster in October. No longer would he follow an ambiguous course in political affairs. If he had not already identified himself with the court party, the acts of the Good Parliament led him to declare himself openly as its leader. What had driven him to this step had been the "insolence" of the Good Parliament. Despite generous concessions on the part of the crown, parliament had been most niggardly in voting money,[53] the prime purpose for summoning parliament in the first place. Instead of considering the government's desperate financial needs and satisfying these, it had spent most of its time attacking his father's appointees and his father's mistress, and had attempted to perpetuate its interference by saddling the administration with a council which would keep it under surveillance. Unless such parliamentary arrogance were suppressed and those men punished who had encouraged such arrogance, there would be an end to royal government and to traditional kingship.[54]

For a few months Gaunt had everything his way. Now that the Black Prince was dead—he had died while the Good Parliament was in session—there remained no one able to oppose him.[55] He ordered Latimer and most of the courtiers who had been condemned to be released and, in fact, made Latimer his chief lieutenant. Perhaps to silence any objections his father might have raised over such summary defiance of parliament, he ordered Alice Perrers to be brought back to the court, with not a word of remonstrance from the bishops who conducted themselves "like dumb dogs not able to bark."[56] Peter de la Mare was thrown into prison and Bishop Wykeham was summoned before the great council to answer to charges of the same kind of malversation with which he and others had attacked Latimer.[57] Though Gaunt overruled his associates and permitted Wykeham to have the assistance of counsel, composed of Courtenay and six sergeants-at law,[58] Wykeham's judges found him guilty as expected, declared his temporalities forfeit,[59] and forbade him to approach within twenty miles of the court. Since Wykeham had left the chancery more than five years before, Gaunt's attack must be viewed as less a punishment for that prelate's real or alleged misdoings than as a warning to him and more highly placed prelates like Courtenay not to interfere in the duke's handling of the government. Archbishop Sudbury, incidentally, was neutralized by means of a grant of lands.[60]

Gaunt blocked possible opposition among the lay lords by forcing the earl of March, his principal opponent there and de la Mare's lord at the same time, to resign the office of lord marshall, which office he promptly turned over to Henry Percy, earl of Northumberland, in order to gain the favor of that powerful baron from northern England. He assured himself of the support of the royal family by confirming the dower and rights of the Black Prince's widow and by creating his son, Richard, prince of Wales. His youngest brother, Thomas of Woodstock, he appointed constable of England. Meantime the great council had declared all acts of the Good Parliament invalid inasmuch as that parliament had been an illegal assembly from the start. This move nullified among other of its actions the creation of the continual council. And the relatively cooperative parliament[61] which met in January 1377 ratified the restoration of Latimer and the others who had suffered at the hands of the Good Parliament, and denied a request of commons that de la Mare be released from prison.

Only convocation offered any opposition. It convened February 2 in a most uncooperative mood. What had aroused the anger of the bishops was the pressure parliament and the crown had placed upon them to vote a subsidy and to do this without delay; otherwise, they were reminded, parliament would be needlessly protracted and the kingdom suffer injury. Several days previous to this, four bishops, among them Courtenay, had protested in parliament against the proposal to tax the clergy, for they "wist not for what cause they shold give tenthes and graunt subsidies . . ."[62] When commons indicated that they might hold up making any grant of their own until the clergy had decided what they would give, the bishops protested that the clergy "is of such auctority and so free that the lay folk ought not to judge them, neither to medle with them, but would if they list neither promise nor give any thing, doe what they would."[63]

A second source of convocation's anger was the enforced absence of Wykeham who had been forbidden to come within twenty miles of the court. The assembled bishops agreed that they would not accept his absence. The majority of them considered the charges brought against him as fraudulent and designed as much to frighten them into quiescence as to punish Wykeham. Even were Wykeham guilty, he was surely no more guilty than Latimer who was now back on the royal council. Such was the reasoning of the assembled bishops, and particularly of Courtenay who had acted as Wykeham's counsel and who had more reason than anyone else to view Wykeham's fate as a warning to himself. Upon Courtenay's urging, therefore, that they consider the attack on Wykeham as an attack upon themselves and upon the church, they announced that they would not take up the business until all members were present, inasmuch as the business concerned them all.[64]

This resistance did not altogether please Sudbury, for he found himself in an impossible situation: defending Gaunt on the one hand[65] while being the spokesman of the wishes of convocation on the other. His own failure to summon Wykeham he sought to excuse on the plea that the king had forbidden the bishop of Winchester to come to Westminster. But excuses and the possibility of arousing royal displeasures did not break down the resistance of the prelates. Sudbury had finally to adjourn the meeting and take the matter to the king. Since Edward wanted money above all else, he readily granted the archbishop permission to summon Wykeham. Both convocation and the king were happy over the outcome. The bishops welcomed Wykeham into their midst as a conquering hero,[66] while Edward got not only the subsidy he had asked for but the satisfaction as well of specifically excluding Wykeham from a general amnesty he extended at this time, the occasion of his jubilee, to all criminals save only to traitors and murderers.[67]

{3}

COURTENAY AND
WYCLIF: ST. PAUL'S

Several scholars have discovered a direct connection between Gaunt's attacks on the Good Parliament and Wykeham, on the one hand, and the summons Sudbury and his bishops issued John Wyclif at this time to appear before them at St. Paul's to answer to charges of heresy on the other.[1] The temptation to find such a connection is understandable. Prelates like Wykeham and Courtenay were not only bishops but politicians as well. In what way could they better embarrass the haughty duke who had been badgering them than by arraigning his clerk Wyclif?

Two points militate against an easy association of these developments, however: first, the probability that the case against Wyclif had long been preparing, from some time before the meeting of the Good Parliament at any rate; second, the fact that Archbishop Sudbury, who must be counted a friend of the duke's, could have blocked, or at least delayed, Wyclif's summons had this been issued purely as a maneuver to embarrass Gaunt. But before discussing this problem more fully, it may be profitable to take a glance at Wyclif's early career and his first introduction to the duke.

The reader who desires an understanding of Wyclif's place in the public life of late fourteenth-century England would do well to approach his subject with these considerations in mind: that Wyclif was never anything more than a priest; that the gulf in importance between priest and bishop in the late Middle Ages was fully as enormous as it is today; and that, as a consequence, Wyclif would have been as weak and defenseless in a contest with his ecclesiastical authorities as an ordinary commoner. Without the protection of the duke of Lancaster, Wyclif would no doubt have suffered effective, if not painful, suppression. Without the duke's favor, too, he would probably not have enjoyed the liberty to carry on the extensive writing program which brought him fame in the sixteenth and post-Reformation centuries. And a final consideration—it was this posthumous fame that has prompted sympathetic writers to magnify Wyclif's importance in his own day. During Wyclif's lifetime most Englishmen never heard of the man.

Exactly how early in his career Wyclif came into the service of the crown remains in doubt, but whether it was as early as 1371 or only several years later makes little difference so far as his association with Gaunt is concerned.[2] His principal assignment prior to September 22, 1376, when he received a summons under the privy seal from Gaunt to appear before the king's council—in fact, the only formal assignment of which there is any record—came in July 1374 when he was appointed to a commission to treat with a papal delegation at Bruges over the problem of provisions. No significance need be attached to this appointment. As a clerk casually employed by the court, this was the kind of assignment one might expect him to receive, and the chronicler refers to him not by name but simply as a "master of theology" who accompanied the commission.[3] What he contributed to the discussions at Bruges is not known, nor do we know why he was not reappointed to the commission in 1375 when it resumed its negotiations.

If there was some special reason why Wyclif had been appointed to the commission in 1374 and, further, some reason why he was left off the second commission in 1375,[4] these might shed light on Gaunt's motives in summoning him to Westminster in the fall of 1376. Since the sources suggest no reasons, scholars have generally taken the position that the duke ordered Wyclif to come to London because he felt he could use a man of Wyclif's anticlerical leanings.

The basis for this analysis is a double one: first, the reasoning that if Wyclif was critical of the church at this time, which he was, at least in its acceptance of a wealthy and "Caesarean clergy," that must have been the reason Gaunt wanted him; second, the testimony of Walsingham, the monk of St. Albans, our principal source, who is quite frank in linking the duke to Wyclif's anticlericalism. The first line of reasoning has a plausible ring, namely, that Gaunt sought out Wyclif because of the Reformer's hostility toward the church. For the duke had probably endorsed the replacement of Bishops Wykeham and Brantingham in 1371 with lay officials[5] and was surely behind the disgrace of Wykeham in late 1376.

Yet this reasoning has nothing beyond these incidents to sustain it, and they of themselves are too isolated to be sufficient to tar the duke with anticlericalism. For if the duke did approve of the removal or discrediting of these prelates, his motives in so doing were personal or political. They did not stem from a general hostility toward bishops or even toward bishops holding high office in the government. His most trusted adviser was Bishop Erghum of Salisbury, while in 1377 he had two friends, Bishop Houghton of St. David's and Bishop Wakefield of Worcester, appointed chancellor and treasurer respectively. Additional evidence to refute the charge of the duke's anticlericalism is provided by the generosity he showed the church during his lifetime and by his own unswerving orthodoxy.[6] True, he did protect Wyclif and he did block his punishment at the hands of the ecclesiastical authorities. Still Gaunt's sympathy for Wyclif did not extend to the Reformer's views. If the duke ever showed any interest in these, which is unlikely, he must have considered them at worst misleading, never heretical.[7]

As for Walsingham's testimony, perhaps the less said about this the better, for "in no matter affecting John of Gaunt can the testimony of the monk of St. Albans be accepted. The only question is whether this chronicler was a malicious liar, or greedily credulous of any story which pointed to the hidden hand of the duke."[8] Walsingham accuses the duke of plotting to gain control of church and kingdom, which objectives he could not accomplish without first corrupting the church and destroying the liberties of London. It was to aid him in debasing the church that he had recruited Wyclif, and Wyclif would make a willing ally, so Walsingham declares, since he had been attacking the church for some years already in anger over the way he had been deprived of a benefice.[9] Surely preferable to this imaginative narrative is the simple explanation that Gaunt, now de facto ruler of the kingdom, summoned Wyclif to Westminster because he had need of his services, and of those of other clerks as well, to help with the business of government.[10]

Certain scholars will insist, however, that Wyclif's anticlericalism, whether known to Gaunt or not, had actually little bearing on the summons received from Sudbury and the bishops. They maintain that it was principally convocation's hope of embarrassing Gaunt, not the silencing of Wyclif, that provoked

their summons. Gaunt had been responsible for Wykeham's banishment and had been conducting himself in a wholely autocratic
fashion. He must be humbled. Upon what evidence or reasoning
do these scholars base this view?

There is, first of course, the source of the summons issued
to Wyclif and its timing. The same convocation summoned
Wyclif as had protested Wykeham's absence. Since Gaunt himself was beyond attack, scholars argue, why should not the bishops wish to attack him where he was vulnerable, through his
"heretical" clerk? Persuasive though this argument appears, these
other considerations interpose themselves and render it most
doubtful: that this was the first time convocation had met since
Wyclif had begun to disseminate his controversial views; that
had that body convened a year earlier, they would probably
have issued Wyclif a summons at that time; that if Wyclif was
to be examined, it was high time that such action be taken (witness the chiding the bishops received from the pope three months
later for their negligence in silencing him earlier);[11] finally, that
Sudbury would scarcely have made himself a partner to a maneuver which had as its principal objective the discomfiture of
Gaunt. The chronicler laments, indeed, that it was only with
difficulty that the bishops, notably Courtenay, were able to rouse
Sudbury to action. "Wherefor (although somewhat late) the
bishoppes beynge moved, wakened the archbishopp, there father,
as out of a greate sleep, and as a myghtye man drunken with
wyne."[12] The chronicler would not have written in this manner
had interest in summoning Wyclif been no more than two or
three weeks old.[13]

A second basis for the charge that interest in humiliating
Gaunt was what motivated convocation in summoning Wyclif,
and a more convincing one, is the dramatic appearance Wyclif
made at St. Paul's the afternoon of February 19. Wyclif
came, not a solitary figure in black clerical attire, but "with
the greatest pomp," in the midst of a group of powerful nobles,
preeminent among whom were Gaunt and Henry Percy, the
new marshal. Had Wyclif come alone, the temptation would
be less great to propose political motivation as inspiring his summons. That he came escorted by several important lords, including the hated duke, would appear to make that charge
uncontrovertible.

This much can surely be said in support of the above
interpretation, namely, that the duke must at least have been

convinced the attack on Wyclif was motivated from malice toward himself. Were not the bishops indignant over his, the duke's, treatment of Wykeham? And what, on the other hand, was there heretical about Wyclif's views? So a display of power should sober the prelates, while the four friar theologians he invited to accompany Wyclif, each of the four representing a different order, would effectively give the lie to any charge of heresy. Since his clerk was orthodox, the motivation behind the summons must be political, and he would answer in kind. Entirely different, incidentally, were the circumstances attending the summons issued Wyclif a year later upon instructions from the pope. Here there could be no political motivation present, and the duke's interference to save his clerk was, accordingly, so subtle it was scarcely discernible.[14]

That the duke was convinced the bishops were striking at him through his clerk Wyclif, however, does not give modern writers the right to make that assumption. They base their position on Walsingham, but it is Walsingham at his weakest. The chronicler, in writing of the duke, is his usual partisan self, but when he describes how the duke and Henry Percy had long been commending Wyclif for his knowledge and sincerity, he is undoubtedly using hindsight to blacken the case against Gaunt and Wyclif. Percy had not joined the duke before the fall of 1376,[15] and it is unreasonable to assume that either Gaunt or Percy would have had sufficient interest or have taken the time to notice Wyclif's views prior to the summons from convocation. And to suggest that it was to punish convocation for its inaction in the matter of the subsidy that Gaunt had urged Wyclif to attack the church is equally unrealistic, since hardly more than two weeks elapsed between the opening of convocation on February 2 and Wyclif's appearance at St. Paul's on the 19th. We do know that Wyclif had been preaching his views already for several years,[16] and we have the words of Walsingham that it took some prodding to get the hesitant Sudbury to act. Since there is no good reason to believe that either Gaunt or Percy had much interest in Wyclif's views prior to the summons from convocation, reason recommends leaving the matter there. No one need doubt, of course, that bishops like Courtenay must have entertained an unholy satisfaction in pressing the charge of heresy against Wyclif because of his association with Gaunt.

In the mid-afternoon of Thursday, February 19, 1377, a memorable incident in late English medieval history took place

in St. Paul's, London. The occasion was Wyclif's appearance
before the bishops gathered in convocation to answer to the summons he had received. His expected appearance had attracted
a large crowd. Defendants on their way to trial customarily
arouse the curious, and Wyclif was no ordinary defendant. He
was a priest. He was charged with heresy. He was a royal clerk
and a personal appointee of the duke of Lancaster who at that
moment was the most disliked man in London. And rumor had
it that the duke would be accompanying Wyclif in person.[17]

Gaunt had never been popular, but the events of that
morning had left him the most hated man in London. During
the session of parliament that morning when he had presided,
a bill had been proposed, no doubt upon his recommendation,
that would have transferred the government of London from
the hands of the mayor to any captain the court might appoint.
Among other changes "which manifestly nullified the liberties
of the city and threatened injury to the citizens," the bill would
also authorize the marshal of England to make arrests in the city
of London just as he could elsewhere in England.[18] Since the
real power in the court was the duke, he would be the man
who would appoint London's captain. The marshal who could
arrest anyone the duke might want arrested was Henry Percy,
the arrogant lord from the north. Little wonder a crowd was
on hand!

So great was the concourse of people that Wyclif and
his party had difficulty forcing their way through the throng
into the church and through the nave toward the Lady Chapel
where the questioning was to take place. As noted above, Wyclif
did not come alone. With him were the duke and Percy, and
"several others who hoped their rank would overawe the timid,"
together with four friars who were accompanying Wyclif at
Gaunt's request.[19] They would provide Wyclif counsel in the
coming interrogation, although Wyclif's companions assured him
he would need no assistance, since, opposed to his learning, the
bishops would appear "almost illiterate." Nor had he to fear any
assault from the people crowding around since he was being
protected on all sides by so many lords. The chronicler continues
his narrative as follows:

> Because the crowd of people was hampering the progress
> of the lords and of John [Wyclif], Henry Percy presumed
> upon his authority as marshal and began to order them
> about in a most deplorable manner. When the bishop of

London noticed this, he warned Percy not to exercise his authority in the church; and he declared that had he known earlier that he would so conduct himself there, he would not have permitted him into the church. Whereupon the duke flared in anger and announced that he [Percy] would exercise his authority there whether the bishop liked it or not.

When the group had reached the chapel of the Blessed Virgin and the duke and barons together with the archbishop and bishops had taken their seats, Henry Percy directed John [Wyclif] to be seated as well. "For," said he, "he will have much to answer and will have need of a softer seat."

But the bishop of London protested sharply against his being seated: that would be contrary to reason and justice, for he had come there as one cited to answer before his ordinary to the charges made against him, and as long as the interrogation required, that long would he stand.

Whereupon Henry Percy and the bishop exchanged bitterly abusive words and the crowd began to stir. Next the duke [joined in the altercation] and he and the bishop strove to outdo the other in hurling reproaches. When the duke saw that he was not prevailing, his face became inflamed and he assailed the bishop with repeated threats and swore that he would humble his pride and that of the entire English hierarchy as well. And he added: "You trust in your parents, who will not be able to assist you, for they will have enough to do defending themselves." His parents, that is, his father and mother, were indeed of the aristocracy, being the earl and countess of Devon.

For the sake of truth the bishop protested. "I do not put my trust in my parents," he replied, "nor in you, nor in any man, but in God, who is not one 'who trusts in himself.' "[20]

Then the duke muttered under his breath: "Rather than endure this, I should take him by the hair and drag him out of the church." When the Londoners heard this, they raised a very great clamor and swore that they would not suffer such injury to be done to their bishop; they would sooner lose their lives than have their bishop dishonored in his church or be dragged with such violence from it.

The chronicler then explains how the crowd was already in an ugly mood over what had happened that morning during the session of parliament, and he concludes his description of the incident with the lament that because of the mutual contumelies of the duke and the bishop on the one hand and the fury of the crowd on the other, the devil would find a way to preserve his own, that is, to save Wyclif from harm.[21]

One must assume that the meeting broke up in uproar and that the duke, Wyclif, and party made their way back out through the church as best they could, midst the jeers and insults of the crowd.[22] One may also assume that the man who had been tagged as the principal figure in the affair, namely Wyclif, had remained silent throughout the episode and almost forgotten. What should have been a theological exchange between Wyclif and convocation had degenerated, even before it had commenced, into a row between the duke and the bishop of London. And this was not an entirely preposterous development. At that moment those two hostile, strong-willed men were among the three or four most influential lords in the kingdom, each strong in his own right and strong, too, as representatives of the two groups striving for control in the government. From our point of vantage, Wyclif overshadows the duke and the bishop. In London, in February 1377, the two wrangling lords completely shut out the Reformer from view.

One regrets that the crowd rioted and broke up the meeting. It would have been interesting to learn what the decision of the tribunal might otherwise have been. Would Wyclif have admitted to a view which convocation would have condemned? And if convocation had ordered Wyclif to recant such a view, would be have done so with such puissant champions as the duke and Percy in attendance? Is it possible that Gaunt welcomed or even planned some such development as a quarrel between himself and Courtenay which would disrupt the proceedings and prevent the handing down of an adverse judgment which he could neither accept nor reject? A year later under circumstances somewhat similar, he prevented that eventuality by forbidding the bishops to pass formal judgment.[23] Here in early 1377, with Edward still alive, he could not speak with such authority. A last reflection—would Wyclif have been able to convince his episcopal judges of the substantial orthodoxy of his views, with a little assistance from the four sympathetic friars? He presumably was able to do this a year later.

The quarrel between the duke and Courtenay brought about a breakdown in the proceedings, for the bitterly partisan crowd would not endure the insults and threats Gaunt cast at "their bishop." Gaunt's harsh words were the proximate and principal cause of the rioting. Had the proceedings moved ahead smoothly without altercation between the duke and Courtenay, a decision of some kind would undoubtedly have been reached. It is possible that had no bills been proposed that morning in parliament to deprive London of its rights, and had the crowd not entered St. Paul's with aggravated feelings against the duke, there would have been no riot. But this is improbable. The Londoners had never liked the duke, and their dislike of him had turned to hatred as they saw his star rise with the failing health of their idol, the Black Prince, and as they witnessed, too, his successful efforts to undo the work of the Good Parliament. No doubt they would have raised a storm over the duke's insults at the expense of "their bishop" without the added provocation of that morning's developments in parliament.[24] For Courtenay was as popular with the Londoners as Gaunt was unpopular. The events of the following days would reveal the great respect they had for him,[25] and a year later they would beg Pope Urban VI not to go through with his intention of creating Courtenay a cardinal, "thereby depriving the citizens of his personal influence."[26]

The incident at St. Paul's did not end with February 19, for the Londoners did not let the matter drop there. The next morning, Friday, found them still angry and fearful over the developments of the preceding day: angry over the treatment of Courtenay, fearful over the bills proposed in parliament which threatened their liberties. All the stories they had heard about Gaunt's ambitions to be king appeared now only too true. If the duke could march into St. Paul's and browbeat the bishops assembled there, what could stop him from attaining his goal? So Friday morning the leading citizens of the city gathered to discuss ways and means of thwarting the duke's plans. While they were deliberating, two lords, Sir Guy Brian and Walter Fitzwalter, walked in. They had been adherents of the duke at one time, but being large landholders they had been alienated by his ruthlessness.[27] Some of the citizens were for manhandling them and ejecting them forcibly, but Fitzwalter quickly convinced them they had come as friends. They feared Gaunt's designs as much as did the commoners, he told them, for the duke's autocracy would mean the end of everyone's liberties. Fitzwalter reported, in fact, that the liberties of London were even at that moment slipping away, for Percy had already arrested a Londoner and was holding him prisoner in his home beside Aldersgate. Unless an immediate stop were put to such presumptions, there would be an early end to their rights.[28]

The group lost no time in further discussion. Each grabbed what weapons he could find and all rushed out, headed in the direction of the marshal's house. When they reached Percy's residence and found it locked, they broke down the doors, released the prisoner, and celebrated their victory around the burning stocks that had secured him. They could not find Percy, which was fortunate for the marshal. He happened to be dining with the duke at the home of John Ypres, the duke's steward. The chronicler states they had not yet finished their oysters when several of the duke's attendants burst in with the news that the mob was seeking them. Gaunt jumped up from the table in such a hurry that he barked his shins. Both men hurried to the Thames, grabbed a boat and hurried to Kennington in Surrey where the widow of the Black Prince made her home.

Meantime the mob had left Percy's home and, not knowing that the duke had fled, headed for Savoy, the duke's palatial home just outside the city. On their way they met a priest who asked them the cause of all their hurry. They explained that they were looking for the duke and Percy and that they planned to force them to release Peter de la Mare who was being unjustly held in prison by Gaunt and the marshal. Whereupon the priest had the imprudence to say Peter de la Mare was nothing but a traitor and that he had richly deserved hanging for many years. The mob beat the priest so unmercifully that he died a few days later.

Courtenay got word of the mob and its designs while at dinner. He hurried off immediately toward Savoy and reached it in time to save it from destruction. He reminded the crowd that their behavior, bad enough at any time, was particularly reprehensible now since this was the holy season of Lent. Upon his promise to secure them full satisfaction for their grievances if they would but give up their destructive plans and go home, they left Savoy alone and turned back to the city. But as they passed through the streets of the city, they relieved their feelings toward Gaunt by reversing his arms wherever they found them.[29] They also beat up a retainer of the duke whom they found wearing his lord's badge. The duke's other subordinates discreetly hid their badges.

Courtenay's intervention undoubtedly saved Savoy from

destruction. He may have even saved the duke's life.[30] Did the
bishop's intervention lead to an improvement in his relations with
the duke? Probably not. A proud man like the duke may have
even resented his adversary's assistance. Ten months after the
incident at St. Paul's, Wyclif again found himself facing an episcopal tribunal. This time Gaunt kept himself well behind the
scenes, but there was no mistaking the bluntness of the message
his emissary carried to the bishops. The prelates, one of them
Courtenay, were not to pronounce judgment against the
Reformer.[31] Then in the summer of 1378, on the occasion of
the violation of Westminster Abbey, both men would again be
at each other's throats.[32] It would require time, and a good bit
of time, before their animosity would diminish to a point where
their relationship would become almost normal.

What part Courtenay took during the next few days in
mediating the quarrel between the citizens of London and Gaunt
does not appear in the chronicler's account. The bishop had
promised to secure satisfaction for their grievances, and he undoubtedly was among the bishops who are occasionally brought
into the narrative, but he fails of specific mention. The princess
of Wales was first to make a move toward peace. She was popular
with the Londoners, and it was to her house that the duke had
fled. This made her the logical one to attempt a reconciliation.
The citizens with whom she conferred, however, were less interested in peace and peace offerings than they were in demands,
and their demands were that Wykeham and Peter de la Mare
be given fair trials. These demands got them nowhere, so they
delegated a group to seek an audience with the king. This committee did get in to see the king in spite of Gaunt's efforts to
block them. There they told the king of the bills that had been
proposed in parliament and added that they had been presented
in the king's name. For the riots they acknowledged regret, but
denied any part in their authorship. They were the work of
malicious men, the kind that can always be counted on to make
trouble in any crowd.

The king was heartened by their visit. He assured them
that he did not want their liberties curtailed, in fact he would
they were increased if this was necessary, and he was certainly
not behind the proposals laid before parliament. His assurances
greatly relieved the Londoners, for they feared the riot had provided the duke the justification he needed for demanding a
change in the city's government. Meantime lampoons ridiculing

the duke began to make their appearance in the city, which infuriated him, and he appealed to the bishops to excommunicate his libellers. This the bishops hesitated doing for fear of angering the people, even though the civic leaders of the city approved of that step as a means of placating the duke. Finally, the bishop of Bangor, not Courtenay the bishop of London, came forward and issued the sentence of excommunication against any person who might so defame the duke.

When parliament reconvened a few days later, the duke and Percy thought it prudent to make their way to Westminster by back streets and with armed escort, so as to avoid possible ambush. Parliament proved reasonably cooperative. Commons voted a poll tax and agreed to the restoration of Latimer, Lyons, and Alice Perrers. The lords, however, refused to ratify the restorations.[33]

The duke was far from satisfied. Upon his insistence, the king summoned the mayor and aldermen to Sheen, there to meet with him, the archbishop, certain bishops, the duke, the king's other sons, and many notables. Sir Robert Aston, the king's chamberlain, addressed the Londoners in the name of the crown. The purpose of their coming, he told them, was the king's desire for peace between themselves and Gaunt. The king felt they merited censure for the riots and the indignities suffered by Gaunt, and he suggested that it would be prudent for them to place themselves at the mercy of the duke.

The Londoners for their part denied that they had any part in the riots. The riots were the work of people who possessed neither property nor money and, therefore, had no fear of any possible fines. All they would promise to do would be to speak to the people about the advisability of making satisfaction. They themselves would pay no damages. As the meeting was breaking up, the king suggested privately to the city's representatives that as a peace offering to the duke they lead the citizens of the city in a solemn procession to St. Paul's, carrying a wax taper on which were engraved the duke's arms, and place it before the image of the Virgin where it would burn perpetually at their expense. But when the people were called together and asked to approve this plan of appeasement, they refused point-blank. The upshot was a very small procession, with only the mayor and aldermen taking part.

Such a sorry procession only annoyed the duke further, and he objected specifically to the way his coat of arms had been impressed in the candle. Such a ceremony was ordinarily reserved for honoring the dead, and he was still hale and hearty. When the Londoners explained that they had only done what the king had advised, he refused to be mollified, but kept complaining that they knew what he wanted. This prompted one of them to ask: "Does he want us to acclaim him king?" This they declared they would never do. In the end, the mayor and aldermen resigned and others were elected in their place, and both sides to the dispute thought it prudent to accept this as a solution.[34]

Before closing the book on the Good Parliament and its aftermath, mention might be made of Wykeham. The chronicler tells us that in despair of ever recovering his temporalities by means of the courts, he had finally turned to Alice Perrers, the "king's mistress, who could do anything she wished, and there was no one who could oppose her." The chronicler wonders about the ethics of the bishop's action, but rationalizes it as being good since it benefited both diocese and church. He observes, too, that as the gospel of the unjust steward suggests, Wykeham in appealing to Alice was only making use of the mammon of iniquity. Perrers was willing to plead for the bishop—he offered her gold—and the king ordered Wykeham's temporalities restored forthwith. The duke could only swallow his anger and wait for a later time to get his revenge.[35]

{4}

COURTENAY AND WYCLIF: THE LAMBETH TRIAL

The case against Wyclif did not end with the fiasco at St. Paul's in February. Three months later, on May 22, 1377, Pope Gregory XI issued five bulls against the Reformer, three addressed to Archbishop Sudbury and Bishop Courtenay, one to King Edward, and a fifth to the chancellor of the university of Oxford. The pope knew nothing of the effort made at St. Paul's to silence Wyclif. He upbraided the prelates for their negligence in offering "no resistance that we know of" to the Reformer's activities. A commentary on their negligence was the fact that the Roman curia had learned of Wyclif's heretical views before any opposition had been provided them in England.

One may question the justice of the pope's action in censuring both Courtenay and Sudbury. Courtenay had never been one to ignore or run away from responsibilities, however distasteful they might be. He had been among those prodding Sudbury to take action on Wykeham's behalf against the open opposition of the duke, and he was probably principally responsible for the summons issued Wyclif to appear at St. Paul's. The pope may have been aware of Courtenay's courage, and it was perhaps only the need for addressing his instructions to Sudbury and Courtenay jointly that caused him to link them in the matter of negligence. To have officially singled out the archbishop for censure would not have been politic. Furthermore, the pope addressed his words of criticism to Sudbury and Courtenay in the name of all English bishops in general. If blame for negligence was to attach to any one individual, however, the most culpable man was Sudbury the archbishop.[1] Next would John Buckingham, the bishop of Lincoln and Wyclif's ordinary, come in for censure, and then the university of Oxford. Only in fourth place might Courtenay merit some reproof, since Wyclif, according to Walsingham, had been going about London sowing tares. Yet Wyclif's connection at court made the matter too weighty for any single bishop; only convocation should initiate action. And that had been done in February.

There is no record of any correspondence between Pope Gregory and Bishop Buckingham over Wyclif, and this is curious. As Wyclif's ordinary, Buckingham would appear to have been the logical person to bear the onus for past inaction, the logical person, too, now to undertake an investigation of the Reformer's views. Wyclif had been spending most of his time at Oxford, it is true, and Lincoln's episcopal jurisdiction over the university remained hardly more than theoretical.[2] But Wyclif was still pastor of Lutterworth and Buckingham had not been unaware of his existence. Several years earlier he had questioned Wyclif concerning the income he derived from his different benefices.[3] Why did he fail to make any queries on the far more serious issue of heresy? Buckingham may have used the excuse that Wyclif had disseminated no questionable views in the diocese of Lincoln, only in the halls of Oxford and in London. Or he may have considered Wyclif too dangerous a person to confront in view of his associations at the court. This fact Pope Gregory must also have appreciated, for he delegated Sudbury and Courtenay, the two most powerful prelates in England, with the responsibility of bringing Wyclif to bay. And he felt it wise to send a bull to Edward to acquaint him personally with the dangerous theories of his son's clerk.

In his bulls to Sudbury and Courtenay, Pope Gregory said he had his information concerning Wyclif's errors from "many trustworthy persons." Such a reference might fit any number of people: travelers, pilgrims, monks, even bishops and lay lords, whose closer identity the pope might have wished to avoid. In one of Wyclif's rare personal asides, he considers the source of the pope's information, rather misinformation he called it. From his none too clear allusion scholars have drawn the name of Thomas Brunton, bishop of Rochester, as one of the pope's informants. Brunton was a Benedictine who had spent several years in Rome and had maintained a correspondence with the curia after his return to England.[4] Monks such as Brunton had good reason to seek Wyclif's disciplining. They had borne the brunt of his attack on the wealth of the church, while their rivals, the friars, had basked in the sunshine of his praise. Nothing would have pleased them more than to have their tormentor punished.[5]

In the preface to the first of his three bulls addressed to Sudbury and Courtenay, Pope Gregory painted a sad contrast between the vigilance of earlier English churchmen who had always shown themselves most zealous in plucking out the first signs of cockle, and the negligence of the present group who sat about idle and inert in the face of manifest heresy. For John Wyclif, a "professor of holy writ—would he were not a master of errors!"—was, by reliable information, preaching falsehood. Among his perverse teachings could be found some of the detestable views of Marsiglio of Padua and John of Jandun which had already been condemned as heretical. For their failure to do anything about suppressing these doctrines of Wyclif, they "should feel ashamed." They were now to act with dispatch, if not both of them, then either of them,[6] and secretly conduct an investigation of doctrines attributed to Wyclif, a copy of which was included. If their inquiry should establish Wyclif as their author, they were to imprison him, seek a confession from him, and send this, other writings of his, and any other statement he might have made, in all secrecy to Rome, meantime holding Wyclif in prison until further notice.[7]

The second bull to the archbishop and bishop considered the possibility of Wyclif's going into hiding once he got wind of what was afoot. In that event, they were to cite him to appear before the pope within three months when he would be questioned concerning his views. In the citation notice which they were to have posted in Oxford and wherever else Wyclif might be expected to be, he was to be warned that judgment against him would be made were he found guilty, whether he answered his summons or not.[8]

The third bull instructed Sudbury and Courtenay to secure the assistance of learned scholars who were orthodox and well-schooled in the scriptures, in the task of convincing Edward, the king's son John, the princess of Wales, other lords, and the royal councillors, that the propositions attributed to Wyclif were heretical, that they attacked the holy faith, and that they also carried a threat of destruction to the state. They must impress upon them their duty as Christian lords to aid in the extirpation of these errors. Unless the government could be persuaded to cooperate in this matter or at least assume a neutral position, Gregory knew any efforts he and the English hierarchy might make would be wasted.[9]

In the bull Gregory addressed to the king, he admitted the futility of the church's efforts to silence Wyclif unless the crown gave its blessing. Of Wyclif's heterodoxy, he assured Edward, there could be no question. The pope referred to "very many trustworthy persons" who had informed him of Wyclif's heretical views and how these views expressed opinions of Marsiglio of Padua which John XXII had already condemned. Because of the pope's responsibility to God for the preservation of the faith, he had commissioned Archbishop Sudbury and Bishop Courtenay to question Wyclif concerning his position on the propositions attributed to him, a schedule of which he was enclosing. If the bishops found him guilty, they were to imprison him "on our authority" and to send his confession, if they could extract one, together with other incriminating evidence to Rome. Since the archbishop and bishop would require the good will and cooperation of the crown in carrying out their commissions, he earnestly begged the king to extend them this.[10]

Gregory sent the fifth of his bulls to the chancellor and university of Oxford. He rebuked them sharply for their negligence in permitting tares to grow, to mature in fact, in their institution, one his predecessors had given such rich privileges. Because of their negligence, one John Wyclif had been able to preach his heretical views there with complete freedom, views which threatened the very existence of church and state and which included some of the condemned doctrines of Marsiglio of Padua. The pope directed the chancellor and Oxford, under threat of the loss of their privileges, to suppress the teaching of perverse doctrine at the university, however subtly its error might be concealed, to seize Wyclif and to turn him over to Sudbury and Courtenay, together with any other scholars in the university community who might be infected with similar errors and who would refuse to recant.[11]

The schedule of nineteen heretical propositions attributed to Wyclif which Pope Gregory enclosed with his bulls, consisted of the following:

> 1. The entire human race without Christ does not have the power simply to ordain that Peter and all his successors exercise political dominion over the world.

2. God cannot give civil dominion to a man in perpetuity, either for himself or his heirs.

3. It is impossible for man to devise charters which guarantee perpetual civil inheritance.

4. Anyone who is in that state of grace which finally justifies, has not only the right to, but in fact possesses, all God's gifts.

5. Man can bestow temporal or eternal dominion only ministerially to a natural son or by choice to one in Christ's school.

6. If God exists, temporal lords may lawfully and meritoriously deprive a delinquent church of the blessings of fortune.

7. It is not for me to consider, but for temporal lords to investigate, whether the church is in such a state or not; and if such be the case, they are to act with confidence and to confiscate her temporalities under pain of damnation.

8. We know that it is impossible for the vicar of Christ to declare anyone fit or unfit simply by means of his bulls, or by means of his bulls, his will and consent and that of his college.

9. Only that man may be excommunicated who is first of all and principally excommunicated by himself.

10. No one may be excommunicated, suspended, or persecuted with other censures to his injury except in the cause of God.

11. Malediction or excommunication can only bind if it is used against an enemy of God's law.

12. Power from Christ or His disciples is not demonstrated by excommunicating one's subjects, particularly for refusing temporalities, but the contrary.

13. Christ's disciples have no power to exact temporalities by means of censures.

14. If the pope or any other person claim to loose or bind in any way, it is not possible by the absolute power of God that he does thereby loose or bind.

15. We must believe that only when he conforms to the law of Christ does he loose or bind.

16. All should believe that any validly ordained priest has sufficient power to administer any of the sacraments, and,

consequently, to absolve any contrite person from any sin.

17. Kings may deprive those ecclesiastics of their temporalities who habitually misuse them.

18. Whether it was temporal lords, holy popes, or the head of the church who is Christ, who endowed the church with the goods of fortune or favor, it is nevertheless lawful, under the circumstances indicated, to deprive her of temporalities in proportion to her offense.

19. An ecclesiastic, even the Roman pontiff himself, may lawfully be rebuked by those subject to him and by laymen, and may even be arraigned.[12]

The five bulls were unusually long in reaching England. Although issued May 22, 1377, it was only the late fall that mention is made in England of their appearance. Walsingham says the bull Gregory sent to Oxford reached the university but a few days before Christmas.[13] Wyclif first learned of the pope's condemnation of the nineteen theses during the fall session of parliament (October 13 to November 28). He mentions that the bishop of Rochester came to him in great excitement to inform him of the pope's action. Since a matter of such importance could hardly have been kept from a bishop, particularly one who probably had a personal interest in the matter,[14] one may assume some six months elapsed between the day the bulls were issued and the day their presence and contents became known in England.

Under normal conditions it should have required no more than two months at the most for the bulls to reach England. What then was the cause of the delay? Some weeks may have been lost in Rome and the bulls held up there after they had been sealed. Travel conditions must have been unusually poor at the time; otherwise how account for Gregory's ignorance in late May of convocation's attempt that preceding February to question Wyclif at St. Paul's. It is entirely possible that when all five bulls reached the archbishop's office, assuming all five were delivered there,[15] that it was thought prudent to hold up their publication for a few months. Edward had died in June and the government was without a recognized head. Until Gaunt had established himself or had been appointed regent, or some other kind of regency had been established, the announcement of the bulls might serve to aggravate a situation already delicate.

Furthermore, the character of the regency might determine the manner the papal bulls would be carried out. Had Gaunt been deprived of all influence, for example, the hierarchy could have moved against Wyclif with considerably more freedom.

Sudbury and Courtenay may have agreed to delay publication until parliament had adjourned or was on the point of doing so lest possible sympathy develop for Wyclif and this further complicate what already promised to be a difficult assignment.[16] They had reason to fear some unfriendliness in parliament. Gaunt's supporters there might have rallied behind Wyclif, let alone others whom he may have attracted.[17] As it was, parliament did enact a statute requiring all foreign priests and monks to leave the country by February. The income from their benefices which they had been accused of using in France to defeat English arms was to be diverted to war purposes in England so long as the war lasted.[18] In that kind of atmosphere some sympathy might have been generated for a man who proposed to take wealth from a corrupt church. Prudent voices may have recommended delay.

Trevelyan and several older scholars even maintain that Wyclif addressed parliament in the fall of 1377, the very time the papal bulls were being brought into England. They have him speaking in defense of the condemned propositions before the assembled lords and commons.[19] These scholars base their position on a document preserved by Netter which carries the caption, "Libellus Magistri Johannis Wycclyff Porrexit Parliamento Regis Ricardi Contra Statum Ecclesiae."[20] Recent scholars, on the other hand, dismiss the document as spurious for a number of reasons. They maintain that Wyclif would not have presented a defense of the condemned propositions before the fall parliament of 1377 since notice of their condemnation may not as yet have been received; that to have done so a year later in the parliament of 1378 would have been too late; that there is no reference to any such speech in the rolls; that Wyclif in his writings fails to make any such claim.[21]

It is difficult, however, to dismiss as spurious one of the most important documents printed in the *Fasciculi,* "a collection of original sources," so says a modern scholar, "which has few rivals in the fifteenth century."[22] Netter, the author of the *Fasciculi,* was an eminently responsible person and one who was closely associated with a number of men who had known Wyclif intimately.[23] How could he have made the mistake of identifying something as a speech delivered to parliament when Wyclif never made any such speech? Netter probably made no mistake. The mistake is that of later scholars in mistranslating the rubric introducing this speech. Instead of translating the word *Libellus* as *speech* and the word *Porrexit* as *delivered* in an oral sense, *Libellus* should be translated as *pamphlet* or *memorial* and *Porrexit* as *delivering physically*, that is, disseminating or circulating. Translating the caption in this way would mean that Wyclif circulated a pamphlet among the members of parliament in the fall of 1377 in which he attacked the church. So much can be supported; that Wyclif ever delivered a formal speech can not. For it is quite probable that when Wyclif learned from the bishop of Rochester during this session of parliament that his propositions had been condemned and that he was about to be seized and imprisoned, he immediately prepared a defense of his views and circulated copies of this among his friends there present. This would have been the act of a prudent man, for Wyclif should have realized, after what had happened at St. Paul's earlier that year, that with the pope now arraigned against him as well as the English hierarchy, it would take even more than Gaunt to save him.

The papal bull reached Oxford, as indicated, a few days before Christmas. The authorities there were divided as to what action to take. To the horror of the chronicler, some of the masters were in favor of sending the papal emissary packing, without accepting the bull. "How seriously had the present procurators or rectors of the university degenerated in prudence and wisdom from that of their predecessors is clearly evident from this, that having learned the reason for the appearance of the papal emissary, they were for a long time undecided whether to accept the papal bull with honor or to dismiss it out of hand."[24]

There was not only Oxford's pride which rebelled at the presumption of any authority, even that of the pope, to censure it in matters of theology where it considered itself preeminent. There was also the presence in the university of many masters who had been Wyclif's associates for a long time. Several of these had known him for more than twenty-five years.[25] While the austerity of Wyclif's disposition might have proved abrasive on occasion, any attack from the outside would have closed ranks regardless of personal differences. Evidence of this solidarity was the decision of the masters-regent judging in favor of Wyclif's orthodoxy a few weeks later.[26]

In the end those voices which recommended carrying out the pope's instructions prevailed. Yet this action, while removing the danger of papal censure, left the university squarely in defiance of the law of the land. For English statute forbade the imprisonment of any subject at the direction of the pope, and this was precisely what Pope Gregory had ordered the university to do: to seize Wyclif and turn him over to the archbishop. The congregation of regents and nonregents took counsel along with Wyclif, and "because it appeared necessary in the opinion of the university to do something in view of the pope's command, a certain monk, the vice-chancellor, asked and ordered the said Wikcliff that he keep himself in the Black Hall and not leave that place since he wished no one else to imprison him."[27]

What might have passed as a kind of informal house arrest proved more serious than anticipated, and the vice-chancellor was subsequently arrested on order of the crown for daring to "imprison" Wyclif upon the pope's order.[28] The government's action in ordering the arrest of the vice-chancellor is significant. Its action made it unmistakably clear that no ecclesiastic, not even the pope, would deprive Wyclif of his rights as an English freeman without the consent of the crown. The crown could have quite conveniently ignored Wyclif's confinement on the pretense that it constituted no real imprisonment. That it chose to intervene provided the pope and the English hierarchy a blunt warning that no action would be tolerated that impinged upon the life, liberty, or property of any Englishman, lay or clerk, orthodox or heretic, without the permission of the crown.

That this was an axiom of English policy Pope Gregory had still not learned, despite the crown's having taken punitive action on several recent occasions when he had ignored that fact. From the language of his bull to Edward it is clear that the pope had never relinquished his right to order the arrest of any Christian on his own authority. While he must have accepted as a painful fact his inability to accomplish the imprisoning of Wyclif and his citation to Rome without the crown's cooperation, he was careful not to ask Edward's permission, only his assistance. So he wrote: "we have . . . directed the archbishop of Canterbury and the bishop of London . . . to investigate the preaching of the said propositions and . . . if they find such to be the case [that is, if they found Wyclif guilty of preaching them], they shall have the said John . . . incarcerated on our authority. . . . Since, therefore, the said archbishop and bishop are known to require the favor and assistance of Your Highness in the prosecution of this matter, we request and earnestly beg Your Majesty . . . to deign to extend in this prosecution . . . the protection of your favor and assistance. . . ."[29] The pope's language is respectful, but this appeal to Edward is for assistance in prosecuting Wyclif, not for his permission to do so. Should he have been able to accomplish Wyclif's punishment without formally asking the crown's permission, he would have established a useful precedent. This the crown would not permit.[30]

On December 18, in compliance with Pope Gregory's orders,[31] Archbishop Sudbury sent a mandate in his and Courtenay's names to the chancellor of Oxford concerning the issue of Wyclif's orthodoxy. He instructed the chancellor to call together professors "expert in holy scripture and who think correctly and holily in the catholic faith," and have them secretly investigate in what manner the 19 propositions singled out by the pope were being maintained at the university. He was to report to the archbishop "everything you have learned or think concerning the above," and to do so without hiding behind "sophistical words and curious constructions of terms." The chancellor was also to order Wyclif to present himself before the archbishop and bishop, or their commissioners, at St. Paul's on the thirtieth juridical day after receiving the citation, for questioning on the propositions.[32]

Sudbury did not direct the chancellor to imprison Wyclif. The pope had not specifically ordered this in the preliminary stage of the investigation. He had asked the prelates first to verify the fact of Wyclif's responsibility for the propositions. Once convinced of his authorship, they were to imprison him. But Wyclif's investigation was their responsibility, not that of the university.

The chancellor carried out the archbishop's instructions promptly although perhaps not to the letter. The chronicler does not say whether the investigation was conducted in secret as Sudbury's mandate had specified, nor that only "orthodox" masters were selected to pass judgment on the 19 propositions and the issue of heresy at Oxford. It appears that all the masters-regent in theology were asked to scrutinize the propositions and to pass upon their validity individually. And it was on the basis of their individual reports, that the chancellor announced their common judgment, namely, that while the propositions sounded poorly to the ear, they were orthodox.[33]

At some time before March 27, 1378, Wyclif appeared before Archbishop Sudbury and Bishop Courtenay at Lambeth. No more specific date may be suggested and March 27 is nothing better than the *terminus ad quem*. The only useful date the sources reveal is the chronicler's statement that the trial took place before Pope Gregory's death. So there is no means of ascertaining whether Wyclif actually presented himself within the 30 juridical days of receiving his summons or not, although one may assume he did.

Why did Wyclif present himself at Lambeth rather than St. Paul's as the archbishop's mandate had indicated? The chronicler offers no explanation, probably because he felt none was called for. The archbishop made his home at Lambeth and it would surely have been more comfortable to question Wyclif there in February or March than in cold St. Paul's. The change to Lambeth may have been the result of pressure from more prudent voices who objected to bustling St. Paul's for the trial of Gaunt's clerk, particularly after what had happened the year before at that church. It is also possible that the report from Oxford that largely cleared Wyclif of the charge of heresy recommended a reconsideration of the matter. Since Wyclif's views were ill-sounding, not heretical—if one accepted the judgment of the Oxford theologians—and therefore dangerous only to the ordinary public, reason advised that the examination be conducted in the relative privacy of Lambeth. The move to Lambeth would also reduce the danger of Wyclif's sympathizers among the London populace from attempting to disrupt the hearing.[34]

Precious little do the chroniclers have to say about this second confrontation between Wyclif and his episcopal inquisitors at Lambeth, and that little is confused. The confusion arises from the failure of the reporters to distinguish between the two occasions Wyclif was (or was to be) questioned: a first time at St. Paul's in 1377, a second time at Lambeth in 1378. The confusion is understandable, so closely did the one meeting follow upon the other. This much appears reasonably certain concerning the Lambeth trial: that hardly had Wyclif's examination gotten under way than an emissary from the queen mother was announced, a Sir Lewis Clifford, who "pompously forbade" the prelates to presume to pass judgment against Wyclif. Although considerably shaken by this intrusion, the bishops proceeded with their examination, only to have a group of Londoners force their way into the chapel where the inquiry was being held, and there voice their sympathy for Wyclif in an effort to disrupt the proceedings.

The intrusion of the commoners, while annoying, was not a critical factor in influencing the bishops in their handling of Wyclif. The injunction from the queen mother was a different matter. Condemnation of the man himself was now out of the picture, which fact must have forced a less hostile line of questioning. If at all possible, the bishops in the interest of the prestige of the church and their own as well, must avoid reaching a position in their questioning which would have left them no choice but to condemn Wyclif. The report from Oxford made it easier for them to do this, for there the theologians, as indicated, had judged the theses orthodox even though ill-sounding. Since neither Sudbury nor Courtenay could claim to be theologians and would, in any event, have had to depend upon their assessors in judging Wyclif's orthodoxy, the temptation to be guided by the Oxford report must have been compelling.

And Wyclif, too, appears to have met his questioners halfway and have made their task easier by qualifying his position on several of the theses. In the introduction to his *Declarationes*, a sort of apologia which he appears to have presented at this time, he protested against the distorted interpretations of his views that "children" had carried to Rome, which he was now presenting in the proper sense in which they should be understood, a sense established directly on scripture and the writings of the church fathers. If his views were still judged unorthodox, he continued, he was most willing to repudiate them, "submitting myself humbly to the correction of Holy Mother Church."[35]

In several instances, the "clarification" of his position, which Wyclif contributed in the *Declarationes* and presumably for the instruction of his judges at Lambeth, had the effect of transforming what had been wholly unacceptable theses into largely innocuous statements. Proposition number 6, for example, would have permitted lay lords to confiscate the property of a delinquent church. In the *Declarationes* Wyclif dismisses this as an unreasonable position. Only upon authorization of the church itself might the civil authorities seize the temporalities of a delinquent church. Again, proposition number 16 would permit priests to administer any sacraments and to absolve any contrite sinner. In the *Declarationes* Wyclif limited the priest's ability to do this to cases of emergency.[36]

The chronicler adds his indignant corroboration to the charge that Wyclif qualified his position on several of the theses in order to convince the Lambeth tribunal of his orthodoxy. He deplores the fact that Wyclif was able to deceive his judges, which, he says, is precisely what he did. For "if they [theses] are taken directly in the sense in which he maintained them in the schools and in his public sermons, they without question breathe the pravity of heresy. For he did not qualify them with any kind of circumlocution when he put them into the ears of the laity, but nakedly and openly, as they are above described, did he preach them. . . ."[37]

The judgment of the Lambeth tribunal was, accordingly, different from what the bishops had originally boasted they would give. At least the chronicler has them boasting before the trial got under way, that they would deal with Wyclif in the manner he deserved, regardless of who might support him.[38] The chronicler's words may be true, and it was to prevent such an eventuality that Clifford made his appearance. Whatever the mind of the bishops before the trial, they dismissed Wyclif in the end with instructions "that he was not to discuss such propositions any longer in the schools or in sermons, for fear of scandalizing the laity. . . ."[39] The *Eulogium's* brief observation of the trial read: "And the said W[yclif] proved those conclusions to be true in the presence of the archbishop of Canterbury and the bishop of London."[40]

A regrettable aspect of the Lambeth trial, from point of view of the historian, is the absence of any official report of the proceedings in the episcopal registers or a discussion of the incident by Wyclif. One might expect to find a record of the trial at least in Sudbury's register,[41] but there is none. The absence of a record may be significant. It may suggest that the judgment given at Lambeth was not to the hierarchy's liking, and not being to their liking was not recorded, nor for that matter considered final. Or Sudbury and Courtenay may have considered the final disposition of the problem the pope's responsibility, since it was Gregory who had ordered the action taken.[42] That Wyclif has nothing to say about the trial or the decision of the bishops is not surprising.[43] Wyclif wrote voluminously on matters concerning theology but hardly a line about himself. And here in the Lambeth trial, if he did actually qualify his position on several of the condemned theses, he would have had all the more reason not to break with his practice of avoiding personal allusions.

The decisive factor in the Lambeth trial was the order from the queen mother enjoining the bishops from passing judgment against Wyclif. The appearance of her name startles the reader. Not only was this her first incursion into public affairs[44] but almost her only one. Apart from this passing reference in the chronicles to her intrusion at Lambeth, she appears to have been content to remain nothing more than the mother of Richard. Why then did she take this one occasion to interfere? Did she have a personal interest in protecting Wyclif? Very probably not. There is no evidence of any such sympathy. As for Clifford, even if he may have become a Lollard twenty years later, he came to Lambeth as a representative of the queen, not in his own right.[45]

So the search for a reason behind Joan's action carries inevitably to Gaunt, the man most concerned with preventing the condemnation of Wyclif. Gaunt was still the most powerful man in England after the death of Edward, despite the success of parliament in reducing his authority.[46] The duke's relationship to Joan, his sister-in-law, was warm.[47] It was to her home that he had fled the year before to escape the London mob after the riot at St. Paul's, and if Joan had ever entertained any suspicions regarding Gaunt's designs on the throne, the coronation of her son in July, which was arranged with the blessing of the duke, must have completely removed these. Gaunt's painful experience at St. Paul's warned him against intervening openly. The most logical alternative was working through the queen mother.[48] Sudbury and Courtenay, particularly the latter, would have been more inclined to respect an order from the Black Prince's widow than one that had come from the duke directly. There is, finally, the possibility that Gaunt had reason to believe Wyclif's sympathizers among the London populace would intervene to save Wyclif provided he kept his hated visage out of view.

With respect to the critical problem Wyclif's theories and his association with Gaunt created, the Lambeth trial marks the midway point between the violence of St. Paul's and the quiet disposition of the issue by the great council some months after the Lambeth episode. Lambeth proved nothing more than a stopgap. Courtenay, and probably Sudbury, were not satisfied with the settlement the queen mother's injunction obliged them to accept. Surely the pope would have found it even less tolerable. There was no king on the throne who could have forced pope and hierarchy to live with Wyclif whether they liked what he said or not. There was only a boy-king, the twelve-year-old Richard, who scarcely knew what was going on; a powerful duke probably a little uneasy over his protecting a priest whom the pope considered a heretic; and influential bishops who, under prodding of the pope, demanded some better settlement than the Lambeth judgment that they could accept. Wyclif himself did not count in the final disposition of his problem, neither did his sympathizers among the commoners, however many these may have been. If they had been able to force their way into the chapel at Lambeth, they had not been able to stop the trial. And the more influential element in London was probably behind the prelates.

The third and final step toward a solution of the problem that was Wyclif came some time after the Lambeth trial of March 1378, probably later that same year, when the great council ordered Wyclif to cease discussing his controversial theses. The injunction that body placed upon Wyclif could hardly have antedated the Lambeth trial since its mandate was probably more inclusive than that given Wyclif by Sudbury and Courtenay. On the other hand, the council's action must have followed within a few months of the Lambeth trial, since only theses drawn from Wyclif's earlier works on dominion were involved in the order, not the more radical views which attacked the church, the papacy, vows, and transubstantiation that began to appear in Wyclif's writings during the years 1378–1380. The council's order, furthermore, was issued during the first year of Richard's reign.[49]

What prompted the great council to take action regarding Wyclif remains a question. It may have been prodding from Courtenay who as a member of the "continual council"[50] was in a good position to exert pressure. Sudbury and Courtenay must have resented the manner their hands had been tied at Lambeth, Courtenay because he suspected the hand of the duke, both prelates because they considered the injunction from the queen mother an unwarranted interference in ecclesiastical affairs by the secular authority. While they had been able to enjoin Wyclif not to discuss his questionable views any longer, they could do nothing with Wyclif himself, nor could they have any assurance that he would abide by their instructions since as Gaunt's "clerk" he apparently enjoyed immunity from ecclesiastical censure. Finally, Sudbury and Courtenay might have insisted upon a more satisfactory settlement than that forced upon them at Lambeth since they could expect a marked increase in the number of Wyclif's followers, once word got around that the Reformer enjoyed the protection of the court.

The great council may have taken up the problem of Wyclif on its own initiative since Wyclif had become the center of controversy and a source of unrest. Next to actual invasion by a foreign power, medieval states viewed few developments so seriously as the rise of popular unrest or violence, and the English government was no exception. Almost with the speed that small blazes turn into forest fires, could isolated islands of dissension mushroom overnight into grave threats to the throne since there were usually ambitious or dissident noblemen about who were anxious to exploit them. Men like the vagrant priest Ball were causing trouble,[51] and a crown already grown sensitive about religious controversy[52] could only view the bitterness engendered over Wyclif with apprehension. Already a riot after the incident at St. Paul's, now a mob breaking into the chapel at Lambeth! What Wyclif preached was a matter of indifference to the great majority of lay councillors. That he stirred dissension and conflict with his preaching was, on the other hand, quite a serious matter.

The order the great council issued Wyclif to discontinue his attacks on the church came not as a formal directive by the government—something Gaunt would not have permitted—but under circumstances which are puzzling even if convincing.[53] The order is found at the conclusion of a document recorded by Netter in the *Fasciculi Zizaniorum*. This document carries the rubric, "The answer of Master John Wyccliff to the question noted below put to him by the Lord King of England Richard II and his great council, the first year of his reign." The query is of a theological nature and reads: "whether in view of the critical need for its defense, the kingdom of England might not lawfully withhold the treasure of the kingdom lest it be turned over to foreigners even though the pope were demanding this under penalty of censure and by virtue of obedience." Then follows Wyclif's reply, consisting of a lengthy denunciation of the papacy and a stout justification for withholding the money. Next comes the wholly unexpected statement: "And here silence was imposed upon him [Wyclif] concerning the above by the lord king and the royal council."[54]

The activities of the papal collector Arnold Garnier prompted the council to ask Wyclif about the propriety of withholding money from Rome. For several years Garnier had been chafing English sensibilities with his zeal in collecting the charitable subsidy voted the pope in 1375, together with the usual first fruits and fees for papal dispensations and privileges. The principal victims of Garnier's zeal were the clergy and hierarchy, although once the gold had been collected, it was the crown that suffered most anguish over the thought of its shipment to Rome when there was such dire need of it at home. That Wyclif was consulted on the question of withholding this money was only normal since he was a clerk in the crown's employ. From the impersonal tone of the query put to him and the general character of Wyclif's reply, one must conclude, too, that Wyclif was not the only clerk the great council consulted, nor was there any implication in the query that the government would be guided by his counsel. Had the reverse been the case and had Wyclif alone been requested to render an authoritative decision, it would be difficult to deny the claims of Wyclif's modern admirers who have insisted that the Reformer enjoyed great influence in government circles. It would also be difficult to explain why the council, upon hearing Wyclif's *Responsio*, would have bluntly ordered him to speak no more of such matters, and, in addition, have blandly authorized Garnier to proceed with his collections.[55]

Wyclif's *Responsio*, which like most of Wyclif's writings is a fairly lengthy document, reaffirms in the main the views given expression in the 19 condemned propositions. Wealth and political influence had so corrupted the church, so Wyclif affirms, that they, not the service of God, had become the concern of the papacy and the church, while ecclesiastical censures such as excommunication were being employed to advance those goals. Because of the papacy's manifest deficiencies, it had forfeited the right to English gold, and the crown should withhold this and do so without any fear of censure. Substantially these same arguments run through the 19 propositions. When the crown, therefore, forbade Wyclif to discuss *"the above* [views]," it was, in effect, shunting him off the precise area covered by those propositions.[56]

Why had the council ordered Wyclif to cease his attacks on the church? There were two principal reasons. One was the interest of the pope and the English hierarchy in having Wyclif silenced. This was probably the stronger of the two reasons: it had, at least, the more vocal support. Given English government's relative insensibility to papal pressures, the pope of himself could have accomplished little. But since the views of the English hierarchy regarding Wyclif coincided with the pope's, together they could exert a great deal of pressure. For the "Caesarean clergy" whom Wyclif had denounced and antagonized seldom numbered so many and such influential bishops as at this particular time. They included Sudbury, Courtenay, Brantingham, Wykeham, Houghton who was the chancellor, Wakefield who was the treasurer, and Erghum who was Gaunt's trusted adviser. Both inside the great and continual councils[57] and outside as associates and friends of the lay lords, they could make their influence felt. The three last named bishops, Houghton, Wakefield, and Erghum, were, in fact, Gaunt's friends.

These bishops could not accept the Lambeth settlement Gaunt forced upon them, that is, unless the council affirmed the order the bishops had given Wyclif at that time, which was, not to speak further of those matters outside the schools. This was probably the nature of the demand the bishops made upon the crown, and this was what the great council did. For in ordering Wyclif to be silent on these matters, it meant that he was not to preach them, neither in public nor at Oxford. He might still propose them as academic theses within the halls of the university. This much license the bishops had also left him. It is, consequently, safe to view the action of the great council as complementing that of the bishops at Lambeth. In return for the willingness of the hierarchy to accept something less than a formal submission and silencing of Wyclif, the crown agreed to place an unofficial injunction upon his preaching. "And here silence was imposed upon him concerning the above by the lord king and the royal council."

The second reason that led the council to silence Wyclif was its concern over the unrest his views were stirring up. How sensitive it felt on this score is revealed by an order the royal councillors issued probably at this very time to John de Acley, a Benedictine monk, who had been delegated by his order to refute certain charges brought against the possessioners. The councillors had countermanded his appointment and had inhibited him from engaging in controversial debate, either to "support or oppose" certain views.[58] While it is possible that the controversy Acley had been selected for concerned the friars with whom the possessioners had a long history of friction,[59] it is just as likely that Wyclif had been his target.[60] If the latter was the case and the councillors had forbidden Acley to engage in an exchange with Wyclif, then an order to Wyclif from these same councillors, that he put an end to his controversial preaching, is exactly what one would expect. All controversy was bad whatever its argument.

Courtenay must have taken a prominent part in the Wyclif settlement. His interest in the matter was great. As bishop of London he had a direct concern with the issue since a good number of Wyclif's followers were scattered about London. Twice had Courtenay, in company with Archbishop Sudbury, attempted to silence Wyclif, once at St. Paul's and a second time at Lambeth. The pope had sent Courtenay a personal mandate in which he outlined a complete and final disposition of the problem. If Courtenay's behavior in the Florentine incident was any indication, he could be trusted to honor the pope's instructions concerning Wyclif as far as this was possible. There was, finally, Courtenay's personal dislike for Gaunt. No doubt, the association between the duke and Wyclif sharpened the archbishop's determination to silence the Reformer.

Courtenay's position, influence, and associations assured him a powerful voice in the discussions among the royal councillors who were seeking a settlement of the problem that was Wyclif. His aristocratic background and his presence in London, over against the relative passivity of the common-born Sudbury, had made him the most powerful bishop in the country by 1377. The Good Parliament had selected him as a member of their advisory committee and as a member of the short-lived administrative committee which was to advise the crown. In the autumn of 1377 he served as a member of the nine-man committee which was delegated to maintain a continuous check on the great officers of state.[61] During the period, 1377–1378, therefore, when the great council silenced Wyclif, Courtenay was a member of the most powerful group in the government and its most influential prelatical representative. Under the circumstances, there can be little question that his views were presented and considered during the process of hammering out the compromise ultimately agreed upon.

Was Courtenay willing to accept the compromise over Wyclif, namely, that the Reformer be effectually silenced, although only unofficially? The documents suggest that he was. Neither as bishop of London nor as archbishop of Canterbury does he appear to have made any attempt to arraign him again or to place further restrictions upon his freedom.[62] Even in the course of suppressing Wycliffitism at Oxford which Courtenay accomplished immediately after his election to Canterbury, there is no indication that Wyclif was himself personally involved.[63] Had the duke died or had he lost his influence during those years, Courtenay might have reopened the issue. But the duke and his influence outlived Wyclif, and the Reformer died unmolested in 1384 in the relative obscurity of his parish at Lutterworth.

The duke, too, honored the settlement worked out by the royal councillors in 1378. It happened some two or three years later that Wyclif ran afoul of the chancellor of Oxford for his attack on transubstantiation. While Wyclif must have desisted from all public preaching as ordered, the seriousness with which he had pressed his views on transubstantiation at the university must have aroused the concern of his superior. For Berton, the chancellor, appointed a group of university theologians to examine Wyclif's statements on this mystery and upon their judgment condemned two of his statements as heretical. Much to the chronicler's horror—and the modern reader's wonder[64]—Wyclif appealed the chancellor's condemnation "not to the pope or to the bishop or to his ecclesiastical ordinary, but as a heretic he appealed to the secular authority in defense of his error and heresy—he appealed to King Richard. . . ." But King Richard was still but a minor and, in any event, the duke claimed Wyclif as his responsibility. So Gaunt hurried up to Oxford and warned Wyclif to abide by the chancellor's order.[65]

Who was not partner to the Wyclif settlement was the pope. He did not, however, renew his instructions to Sudbury and Courtenay that they continue their efforts. When he learned of what had transpired at Lambeth, he must have realized that his bishops could do nothing but live with the compromise agreed to by the royal council. He himself was free to do otherwise or at least attempt to do so. Some time in 1383 it appears that he (Urban VI) did issue a direct summons to Wyclif to come to Rome, through what channels it is impossible to know. But Wyclif excused himself from complying with the order on the grounds of poor health and a royal order that he ignore the summons.[66] The royal order must have been the duke's.

{5}

EVENTS OF 1378-1382

THE HAULAY-SHAKYL INCIDENT

Although the duke and Courtenay, the two principals in the Wyclif settlement, may have admitted to themselves that the compromise over Wyclif was a reasonable one under the circumstances, that realization did not make them friends. The Haulay-Shakyl incident, which must have broken just a month or so after the controversy over Wyclif had been settled, found them as bitter opponents as ever.

Two English squires, by name Robert Haulay and Richard Chamberlain, had helped the Black Prince win a great victory at Nájera in Castile in the spring of 1367. In an age when the taking of booty was almost the only motive the ordinary soldier had for fighting and when few spoils were more eagerly sought after than enemy knights and noblemen, the two Englishmen had brought back with them from Spain a great prize indeed, a Spanish magnate, the count of Denia. The Black Prince, as commander of the expedition, retained principal claim to the ransom. As time passed, however, and the probability grew ever more remote of collecting even a sizable fraction of what had started out as a royal ransom, Haulay and a John Shakyl who had assumed Chamberlain's equity, were left sole claimants—and custodians, at the same time—of the count of Denia's eldest son Alphonso whom they held as hostage.

Then in August 1377 the count of Denia's agent appeared with part of the ransom and, of a sudden, London was filled with people having claims, among them London capitalists who had advanced Alphonso money. The government, more particularly John of Gaunt, was taking new interest in the hostage, perhaps to use Alphonso to gain friends in Spain for a projected attack on Castile. At any rate, this great interest in Alphonso worried Haulay and Shakyl who feared they were about to lose all the time, money, and hopes they had invested in their hostage. When parliament in October ordered them to turn over their hostage, they accordingly refused to give him up and were sent to the Tower. There they lay for nearly a year, when they effected their escape in August 1378 and fled to Westminster Abbey for sanctuary.[1]

   This did not stop the crown. Despite the violation of West-minster Abbey its action would entail, it promptly directed Sir Alan Buxhill, the constable of the Tower, to enter the church and seize the two men. Buxhill took a company of fifty soldiers with him to the abbey where he managed to capture Shakyl by means of a ruse. With Haulay it was not so easy. He was hearing mass when the soldiers entered the abbey, but they approached him, nevertheless, and sought to persuade him to give himself up. After a heated argument over their right to take refuge in the abbey, he broke away from the group and twice led the fifty men in a merry chase around the choir. The soldiers finally cornered him near the main altar where high mass was being celebrated, and one of Buxhill's men split his skull while another ran him through with his sword. They also slew a sacristan who had attempted to interfere. The sacristan's body they left lying where it fell, but Haulay's they took by the legs and after "horribly dragging it through the most sacred part of the choir and the church, bespattering everything with his blood and brains," they threw it out in the street.[2]

   Three days later Archbishop Sudbury issued a general decree excommunicating all persons who had had any part in the desecration of Westminster Abbey. The deliberate, ruthless manner in which the crown and its officials had handled the matter must have frightened, as much as it shocked, the fearful archbishop, and he may have waited the three days before denouncing the act until an aroused populace had shored up his courage. Even then he shrank from issuing anything but a general excommunica-tion on the plea that the actual perpetrators of the outrage were not known.[3] Courtenay, on the other hand, did not mince words. Once authorized to proceed, he published the excommunication with all solemnity at St. Paul's and continued to repeat the con-demnation three times each week, on Sundays, Wednesdays, and Fridays. And instead of the general terms of Sudbury's proclama-tion, Courtenay specifically excommunicated Buxhill and Ralph Ferrers, a former councillor who had accompanied Buxhill, to-gether with the soldiers who had invaded the abbey. Just as

pointedly did he exclude from the terms of the sentence of excommunication the boy-king Richard, his mother Joan, and the
duke of Lancaster.[4]

Courtenay's exemption of Gaunt did not please the duke
who may have questioned the bishop's motives in the first place.
For while few Londoners would have linked either the boy Richard or his mother with the sanguinary deed, it was something
they in their dislike of the duke would have liked to pin on
him—and this is what they did.[5] So Courtenay's every mention
of the duke in the excommunication decree had the effect of
reminding the people of the possibility of his guilt. Even if only
a few Londoners might have known that the duke was away
when the outrage had taken place, all did know he was back
in London a few days later "in military disgrace" after the failure
of his expedition at Saint-Malo in Brittany.[6] Furthermore, it was
Gaunt's following that had committed the sacrilege, so it was
not surprising that ordinary folk held the duke responsible. Courtenay must have known better, however, and it is difficult to
rationalize his behavior unless the bishop saw this as his opportunity to break Gaunt's hold on the government. When he continued to publish the excommunication despite appeals from the
crown that he cease altogether or at least modify the nature
of the condemnation, and when he further "contemptuously"
ignored a summons to appear before the council at Windsor,
Gaunt announced that "if the king so directed, he was willing
to hurry to London and bring back that obstinate bishop to the
council by force in spite of the Londoners whom he called
'ribald.' "[7]

Gaunt did not drag Courtenay to Windsor as he had
offered to do, but he did get busy preparing an apologia to defend
the crown for its part in the desecration of Westminster Abbey.
He badly needed this apologia, for parliament was to convene
in barely two months and the ecclesiastical lords would likely
refuse to support the government's request for a subsidy unless
satisfaction was given for the violation of the abbey. Not only
was Courtenay intransigent in the matter but Abbot Litlington
of Westminster as well, who had refused to reconsecrate the
abbey even though the "king sente meny tymes be his
writtes . . . forto appere befor him, and forto cece his cursyng,
and that he sholde halowe agayn his chirche. . . ."[8]

When parliament convened at Gloucester in October—
meeting there probably to protect itself from a London mob[9]—

and Archbishop Sudbury rose to present a formal protest against the violation of Westminster Abbey, the crown was ready with its defense. This had been prepared by a group of "doctors of theology, canon and civil law, and other clerks,"[10] and Wyclif himself had had a hand. In fact, with an unnamed doctor of laws he presented the crown's defense.[11] Wyclif had a double task: first, to clear the duke of any personal onus in the outrage; second, to exculpate the crown on the argument that in the Haulay-Shakyl affair the welfare of the realm was involved and that the crown was, accordingly, justified in violating sanctuary. Neither bishops nor crown could have assumed an unbending position under the circumstances. The bishops were told that Buxhill and his group had intended no bloodshed and that Haulay had been the first to draw a sword.[12] The bishops must also have realized that so frequently had the right of sanctuary been abused, that to insist upon the privilege for all criminals was hardly realistic. The crown had, on the other hand, no real desire to destroy a convention so much a part of medieval life. The duke's position, and the crown's too for that matter, was to uphold the right of sanctuary as a principle, although reserving for the king the prerogative of violating sanctuary when the welfare of the realm demanded.[13]

The issue of sanctuary was not settled at Gloucester, nor for many years to come. Parliament did make another attempt in 1379 to improve an impossible practice, however, by accepting sanctuary for persons guilty of felony but denying it to fraudulent debtors.[14]

The Gloucester parliament accomplished little, but it has this significance. It was the last occasion when Wyclif appeared in the service of the crown, and it was also the last occasion when Courtenay and the duke were pitted against one another. Were these two "lasts" related?

THE TRANSLATION OF COURTENAY TO CANTERBURY

The year 1381 proved epochal for England, for Wyclif, and for Courtenay. The most serious peasant uprising in English history took place during the summer, and although the revolt affected only a few counties and had almost spent itself within two months, it might easily have toppled the throne, so difficult was it for a medieval crown to marshal up troops within short notice. The uprising of 1381 also shook Wyclif. Though he had no sympathy for the rebels and had done nothing directly to inspire their revolt, contemporary opinion, among the lay and ecclesiastical aristocracy at least, held his theories on dominion and his general attack on the church a major contributing factor in the unrest.[15] More serious for Wyclif, however, than the uprising itself was an indirect consequence of the revolt. In slaying Archbishop Sudbury, the chancellor, the rebels opened the way to Canterbury for Courtenay, Wyclif's most implacable enemy among the hierarchy. Courtenay's first undertaking as archbishop was the condemnation of Lollardy and the quashing of Wycliffitism at the university of Oxford. The year 1381 that brought Courtenay to the fore also announced the final eclipse of Wyclif.

Even though Courtenay was only the third bishop of London to rise to Canterbury,[16] that fact was not due to London's deficiencies as a spring board to the archiepiscopal office. For London was the largest and most influential city in the country and was growing more important all the time. Even in ecclesiastical affairs, its prelate could hardly help but reflect a measure of that importance. As bishop of London, Courtenay served as transmitter of the archbishop's instructions to the other suffragan bishops of the province of Canterbury. As bishop of London, he normally presided at convocation when the archbishop was unable to be present. When some matter of urgency called for consultation with another bishop or bishops, the archbishop had the bishop of London at hand, only a few miles away. That Pope Gregory addressed his bulls relating to Wyclif to both Sudbury and Courtenay suggests the growing association between the two prelates in the conduct of the church's business. And the quiescence of Sudbury enabled the vigorous Courtenay to play a more independent role than was ordinarily permitted the bishop of London.[17]

If Courtenay's presence in London enhanced his influence in ecclesiastical affairs, it proved of even greater value to his aspirations in the realm of politics. His position as bishop of London kept him in the thick of political developments, and as long as the crown had most to say in the selection of a new archbishop, this would advance what ambitions he might have had to Canterbury, at least so long as he did not make many enemies. From the spring of 1376, when the commons in the Good Parliament had selected Courtenay to serve with an advisory group of twelve to guide them in their discussions, until his translation to Canterbury in 1381, there was probably no bishop in England who wielded greater political influence. He was one of the three bishops appointed by Edward in the early summer of 1376, upon the advice of this same commons, to serve on a council of nine to pass upon all important business contemplated by the crown. The rise of Gaunt during the late summer of 1376 to a position of virtual dictator in political matters temporarily sidelined Courtenay,[18] but he was not forced out of politics. In February 1377 it was he who was principally responsible for convocation's taking the stand that it would not consider the crown's request for a subsidy unless Wykeham, the banished bishop of Winchester, was recalled. That same February saw Courtenay more openly defying the duke in St. Paul's when Gaunt appeared as Wyclif's champion.

Edward's death in June 1377 effected a reduction in Gaunt's influence, and soon Courtenay was back in the thick of political affairs again. During the first days of emotional goodwill engendered by Edward's death, a reconciliation was arranged between Gaunt and the civic leaders of London and between Gaunt and Wykeham. An interest in harmony also brought Peter de la Mare out of his easy confinement in Nottingham Castle and saw him compensated for his "unjust inconvenience." More important was the move of the great council on July 17 in setting up a "continual council" consisting of twelve peers, a kind of regency, which was to advise the chancellor and treasurer on all important matters. An effort was made to establish a balance in this council among the different factions. Of the two bishops appointed to this powerful committee, Gaunt's chancellor, Erghum, the bishop of Salisbury, was paired off against Courtenay who represented generally the aristocratic element opposed to the duke.[19]

This first "continual council" had a short history. In the fall of 1377 parliament followed the duke's urging and established another "continual council," this one to consist of nine peers, with responsibilities similar to those of the first, and with its members limited to one-year terms and eligible for another term only after an interval of two years. Of the six carry-overs from the first "continual council" one was Courtenay.[20] In the early summer of 1379, some months after his year of tenure had lapsed, Courtenay received an important assignment as member of a special committee of magnates which was given the responsibility

of inspecting the accounts of the treasurer and of the royal household in the hope that some explanation or remedy might be discovered for the financial bankruptcy of the crown.[21] The following spring parliament appointed Courtenay to a committee of
sixteen which was composed of both lords and commoners. The
broader representation given the council was the product of the
hope that a different approach to the financial problem might
succeed where the earlier committee had failed.[22] It was fortunate
that Courtenay was no longer a member of the "continual council" after October 1378, for as economic conditions steadily
worsened that group came in for increasing criticism for its failure to reverse the situation. Courtenay's highest office, that of
chancellor, he held as archbishop-elect. This will be considered
later.[23]

Over and above Courtenay's powerful position as bishop
of London and his appointment to the most important councils
in the government during the years immediately preceding his
translation to Canterbury, the circumstance which recommended
his eligibility before that of all other bishops for promotion to
Canterbury was his courageous fight against Wyclif. Such opposition would have done little to enhance his candidacy had Canterbury become vacant in 1377. At that time there were still
a good many people, even theologians, who sympathized with
Wyclif's attack on the wealth of unworthy churchmen and on
the political power of others. But this sympathy began to ebb
late in 1378 and more quickly thereafter, when Wyclif's attacks
on the institution of the papacy, on monastic orders, and on transubstantiation revealed his revolutionary bent. Most of his earlier
friends could no longer support him. Then when the revolt broke
in 1381 there were many who remembered, or were reminded
of, 1377 and 1378 when Courtenay and other churchmen had
warned against the peril to society inherent in Wyclif's theses.
The Peasants' Revolt of 1381 assured Courtenay's rise to Canterbury: it removed Sudbury and it left the bishop, the most outspoken of Wyclif's antagonists, the logical prelate to fill the
vacancy.

Wyclif's responsibility for the Peasants' Revolt was much
more manifest to his unsympathetic contemporaries than to scholars today.[24] There was the case of John Ball, for instance, one
of the insurgent leaders, whose name was frequently linked with
that of Wyclif. John Ball was a vagrant priest who had a long
record of defying ecclesiastical and civil authority. He was ac-

tually lodged in the archbishop's jail at Maidstone when the first wave of insurgents from Kent sprang him loose. For some twenty years he had been roaming England, preaching a doctrine almost as distasteful to the crown and aristocracy as to the church. All lords, clerical and lay, he would have abolished, and unworthy lords were no more entitled to their rents than were unworthy priests to their tithes. Some of this message could be found in Wyclif's writings, and Walsingham among others believed that Ball taught the "perverse dogmas of the perfidious John Wiclyf, and the opinions which he held. . . ."[25]

Like the other insurgent leaders, Ball was eventually hunted down and ordered executed, although he secured a reprieve of two days upon Courtenay's request. The bishop hoped the respite would provide Ball an opportunity to bethink himself of his crimes and repent. The chronicler continues his narrative:

> [Ball] realizing that he was doomed, asked that William, bishop of London, late of Canterbury, Walter Lee, a guard, and John Profete, a notary, be brought to him. In their presence he confessed that for two years past he had been a follower of Wycclyff and that it was from him that he had learned the heresies he had preached; that he preached the heresy of the eucharist that [Wyclif] had introduced and other of his doctrines as well. He further confessed that a group of Wyclif's followers had organized a sort of confederation and had planned to travel all over England and disseminate the doctrines Wyclif had taught, in the hope that all England would in time accept his perverse views. Then [Ball] told them that Wycclyff was the principal leader, and next came Nicholas Herford, John Aston, and Laurence Bedeman, master of arts. And he declared that had these men not encountered any resistance, they would have destroyed the entire kingdom within two years.[26]

There were others who linked Wyclif's name with the uprising, notably the clergy—bishops, priests, and monks—who had long denounced his doctrines. Whether heretical or not, they found Wyclif's attack most offensive since it combined an implied charge of their unworthiness with the suggestion to the laity that they do something about it. Walsingham must only have been stating the conviction of many when he laid responsibility for the disturbances at the door of the hierarchy for its negligence in suppressing Wyclif and his followers.[27] Surely, therefore, the name of one bishop who could not be charged with negligence in this matter, that is, Courtenay, must have been on many lips in 1381 as the logical man to help lead the English church and people back to normalcy.[28]

Of the pope's responsiveness to the question of Courtenay's ecclesiastical advancement there could be no question. If Urban VI did not recall Courtenay's impetuous haste in carrying out the mandate his predecessor Gregory XI had issued against the Florentines back in 1375, he must have learned since what a doughty warrior Courtenay had proved himself, first against Wyclif, then against the crown when Westminster Abbey had been violated. The pope only gave up his intention of creating Courtenay a cardinal upon the objections of the Londoners.[29]

Still it was not Urban VI's prerogative to fill Canterbury, although he might have been consulted. It was the crown's, but who or what was the crown in 1381? Richard had, indeed, asserted his competency in most dramatic fashion during the critical days of June 1381 when he had assumed the responsibility for negotiating with the rebels just as everyone else seemed either to have lost his head figuratively or actually.[30] He must have had a voice in the selection of Courtenay, although probably only a weak one. Whatever it was, it supported Courtenay's candidacy. His mother Joan might have reminded him that Courtenay owed his rise to the Black Prince and that the bishop had since been linked with the party of his father as opposed to that of the duke. Above all was Richard's appreciation of the fact that the man who stood between him and a greater role in the government was Gaunt, Courtenay's ancient opponent.

How about the duke? He was away in the north negotiating a truce with the Scots. His absence, incidentally, may have saved his life, for there was no one the rebels wanted more to kill.[31] Courtenay's selection was probably already a fact when the duke returned to London, although his followers in the council could have blocked this during his absence. Yet after the terrifying events of June 1381 and the heavy losses sustained by several members of this group—and no one of them lost more than the duke—neither he nor his party could have felt quite the same about Courtenay. Under the circumstances they would have been willing to approve of the elevation of their former adversary to Canterbury. True, he had attempted to discipline Wyclif, but Wyclif was now safe and silent at Lutterworth. On second thought, the way Wyclif's name was being linked with the rebellion, the bishop may have been right about Wyclif all the time. Such reasoning might have given the duke's followers pause, for they did not share his personal interest in Wyclif. Even the duke had other matters on his mind, such as the legitimization of his children by Catherine Swynford. With Courtenay beholden to him and in Canterbury, this would not be difficult to accomplish. That Courtenay was acceptable to the crown or to those who spoke in its name is revealed most clearly by the fact that he was appointed chancellor in August 1381, the same month Richard gave his approval for his translation to Canterbury.

First to act to fill the vacancy at Canterbury left by the death of Sudbury was, properly enough, the chapter of the cathedral. On June 17, just three days after Sudbury's murder, the chapter through the prior requested permission of the king to proceed with the election of a successor. His *congé d'élire* Richard issued from Barnet in an order dated July 12, with instructions that the monks elect that person for archbishop who was a "devout man of God, necessary to your church, and useful and loyal to us and our realm." On July 31, slightly more than two weeks later, the prior notified the king that the monks had "unanimously" elected Courtenay and asked his approval of their action. This the prior must have assumed would be forthcoming—Richard had probably indicated with his *congé d'élire* whom they would be expected to elect—for on the very day that he asked the king's approval of Courtenay's election, he notified Courtenay himself of the action of the chapter and requested his acceptance. A week later, on August 6, the day after Richard had formally given his consent, the prior wrote to Pope Urban to notify him of the election of Courtenay and to ask his approval.[32]

It is probable that Urban did not wait until he heard from the prior before making his own "independent" appointment of Courtenay to fill the Canterbury vacancy. While he claimed sole right to fill the vacancy, as he declared in his bull, it would have been prudent for him to postpone action until he had learned whom the crown wanted. This information he must have received before acting. At any rate, Courtenay's clerk made a point of the fact that the pope had not known of the chapter's unanimous choice of Courtenay prior to his own appointment of Courtenay. That the pope's bull of appointment is dated less than six weeks after the chapter had notified the crown of Courtenay's election serves to confirm the truth of the clerk's statement.[33]

Pope Urban in his letter from Rome to Courtenay dated September 9 affirmed his exclusive right to appoint a successor to the deceased Sudbury. He had, in fact, specifically reserved the right to provide to that see during the very time Sudbury was holding the post of archbishop, and, therefore, any appointment made knowingly, or in ignorance of his decree, was null and void. He had just learned of the death of Sudbury, and he was making an early appointment in order to save the see certain inconveniences and because no one else had the right to do this in view of his express reservation of the see. After deliberating with his cardinals, he had decided upon Courtenay who had distinguished himself by his great virtues and his excellent administration of the diocese of London. So he was translating him from London to Canterbury and handing over to him full control of both the see's spiritualities and temporalities. Courtenay was to make his oath of obedience, according to the form enclosed, to the bishops of London and Rochester.[34]

Ten days later, on September 19, Pope Urban sent a mandate to the bishops of London and Rochester with instructions that either or both serve as his proxy and that of the Roman church and receive Courtenay's oath of obedience. The pope wished to spare the elect the labor and expense which a personal trip to Rome would entail. The oath the pope wanted Courtenay to take was enclosed with his letter. The bishops were to instruct Courtenay to put this oath in writing, which they were to forward by proper messenger to Rome.[35] The pope's bull of translation which was dated September 9 only reached Croydon (ten miles south of London) three months later on December 10.[36] Whether it was because of the season of advent and the Christmas holidays immediately following or because the arrival of the pallium was momentarily expected, it was not until January 5 that Courtenay took his oath, according to the form directed in the bull, to the bishop of Rochester in the archiepiscopal chapel at Lambeth.[37] The following day he took the same oath in the presence of Braybroke, the newly consecrated bishop of London. On January 9 the bulls of translation were published in Christ Church, Canterbury, and on the following day the prior sent Courtenay the archiepiscopal cross.

But where was the pallium, the symbol of the metropolitan's authority? This stole-like band of white wool the pope issued as a mark of his approval for the consecration of the arch-bishop-elect. In the ceremony of consecration, the presiding bishop ordinarily placed this pallium over the shoulders of the new archbishop after accepting his profession of obedience. This was at least the normal procedure, since only after the arch-bishop-elect had given his oath of obedience would the pope au-thorize him to begin the exercise of his new powers.[38] In Cour-tenay's case, either caution on Urban's part, confusion, or mishap, occasioned a long delay in the arrival of the pallium. The arch-bishop-elect may have expected the pallium to reach Canterbury shortly after Urban's bull of translation which arrived in England on December 10. When the pallium had not arrived by January 5, he waited no longer as we have seen, but made his profession of obedience to the bishop of Rochester. What caused this delay?

Pope Urban may not have been entirely certain that the crown had agreed upon Courtenay. Would not his hesitation to move without absolute certainty account for the interval of four months between September 9 when he issued the bull of translation and January 10 when he informed Courtenay that he was sending the pallium?[39] Or might some confusion have arisen as to what the proper procedure was in procuring the pallium? Was Urban perhaps waiting for the appearance of Cour-tenay's proctors, and when these had not arrived after four months, notified Courtenay by letter that he was sending the pallium? But then why did not the pallium arrive with this letter as the language of the pope's missive appears to indicate it would? Was the pallium lost or had it never been sent? Courtenay for his part must have become increasingly anxious about the matter, and finally on January 3 appointed proctors to go to Rome for the pallium. They were authorized to do what was necessary, including making the profession of obedience in his name.[40]

Although the absence of the pallium occasioned some awkwardness, even annoyance, things could have been worse. For the king had not waited for receipt of papal confirmation of Courtenay's election before doing his part, which was to re-lease the temporalities of Canterbury on October 23, after Cour-tenay had "renounced voluntarily, openly, and expressly all words therein [in the oath to be taken to the pope] prejudicial to the king or his crown."[41] Yet there remained the question whether Courtenay could act like an archbishop since he was only a *de facto* archbishop. On January 5 when Robert Braybroke and John Fordham were consecrated bishops of London and Durham respectively, Courtenay was present "sed minime consecrante eo quod protunc pallium non recepit."[42]

And what about the archiepiscopal cross? Could Courtenay have this borne before him prior to the arrival of the pallium? On January 12 Walter Causton, a monk of Christ Church, Canterbury, had made formal presentation of it to Courtenay in Lambeth palace chapel with the words:

> Reverend father: I am the messenger of the Highest King who asks, instructs, and orders you to accept the responsibility of directing His church and of cherishing and protecting it with genuine faith. In token of this appointment I present you this cross. Receive it willingly and bear it faithfully, so that you may be happy in eternity with your holy predecessors and patrons of the church of Canterbury.[43]

Courtenay accepted the cross "humbly and devoutly" and handed it over to the cross-bearer. But "he refused to have it carried in public until first ascertaining whether this was permissible before arrival of the pallium." This the canonists he questioned assured him he could do, for such was the custom of Canterbury. Whereupon, on January 20, in the presence of the five bishops of Ely, Salisbury, Exeter, Rochester, and Bangor, and many other persons, he announced that he would order his cross to be borne before him. He protested, however, that he meant no offense thereby to the pope or to the Roman church, and that he was only doing this in order to preserve the laws and customs of Canterbury.[44]

Courtenay then asked the bishops and canon lawyers present whether it would be proper for him to preside at the coronation of Anne of Bohemia who was soon to become the wife of Richard. They agreed that it would be proper, in fact, for the sake of the rights and prerogatives of Canterbury, he should do so.[45] If we are to believe the chronicler, Courtenay remained unconvinced, however, and for that reason announced that he would not perform the marriage ceremony uniting Anne and Richard. When Richard refused to postpone his marriage until the pallium arrived and had the bishop of London perform the ceremony, the archbishop was "provoked, although unjustly so." In order to avoid the establishment of yet another precedent prejudicial to the rights of Canterbury, Courtenay managed to overcome his scruples sufficiently to preside at the coronation of Anne even though, as the chronicler observed, the "pallium had not yet been obtained from the pope."[46] The summoning of convocation, however, could wait, and it did, not meeting until November although Richard had asked Courtenay in January to call it as soon as possible.[47]

Finally on May 4, 1382, Thomas Cheyne, one of the archbishop's proctors who had been sent off to Rome four months before (January 3), reached the archiepiscopal manor at Croydon and delivered the long awaited pallium. Two days later, Braybroke, the bishop of London, invested Courtenay with the pallium after again receiving from him his profession of obedience. The formula used by Braybroke in conferring the pallium read:

> To the honor of Almighty God, the Blessed Virgin Mary, the Holy Apostles Peter and Paul, of Pope Urban VI and the holy Roman church, as well as the church of Canterbury which is entrusted to your care, we do transfer to you the pallium which is taken from the body of St. Peter and which represents the fullness of the pontifical office, which you will use within your church on those days indicated in the privileges granted by the apostolic see.[48]

⑥

COURTENAY: LOLLARDY
AND OXFORD

Just two weeks after the arrival of the pallium, Courtenay set out upon what was to prove his greatest work—the condemnation of Lollard doctrines and suppression of Wycliffitism at Oxford. For this endeavor he received wide support. Crown, aristocracy, and hierarchy gave him active encouragement, while that of the gentry may be generally assumed. How the lower classes viewed the archbishop's efforts, if their position could be ascertained, is a matter of little consequence since they were without influence. Because it was popular for many years to magnify evidences of popular discontent with the late medieval church, the tendency in the past has been to exaggerate the number of Lollards and to take at face value extravagant observations by occasional chroniclers which helped establish that view. Knighton, for example, warned his readers that "scarcely would there be two men on the road but one of them was a disciple of Wyclif."[1] Modern opinion is much more reserved regarding the number of Lollards and reduces fourteenth-century Lollardy to hardly more than a small minority.[2]

To men of influence in 1382, however, Lollards were numerous and dangerous. Had it not been principally these Lollards who had come within a whisper of toppling the throne in 1381? Was not their prophet the heresiarch Wyclif, their more immediate leaders insurgents like John Ball who had taken a prominent part in the uprising? Before the general horror and revulsion of the aristocracy and gentry to the excesses committed during the Peasants' Revolt, there were none to protest the easy identification of rebels with Lollards and the temptation to dismiss the just grievances of the peasantry as the unreasonable demands of heretical revolutionaries. Walsingham voiced a popular view when he condemned the deaths and destruction of 1381 as the work of heretical elements.[3] Parliament early in 1382 expressed apprehension at the activities of unauthorized preachers who were stirring the embers of this revolt by sowing discontent.[4] Courtenay's reply was to summon a council of bishops and theologians to meet at the chapter house of the Blackfriars in London on May 17 following, for the purpose of examining the orthodoxy of views generally attributed to Lollards and officially condemning those judged heretical.

Wyclif was not on trial, only Lollard doctrines, even though it was generally assumed that he was the author of most of these. Wyclif was no longer an issue, not at least so long as Gaunt retained a position of influence in the government. The duke had agreed that Wyclif be silenced, with the understanding, however, that he was not to be molested, and Courtenay, as archbishop, had not forgotten the settlement he had been partner to as bishop.[5] So in summoning the council to meet at the Blackfriars in London, the archbishop made no mention of Wyclif, only of "certain doctrines, heretical and erroneous, and opposed to the teaching of the church," which threatened "to subvert the position of the entire church and of our province of Canterbury and the peace of the realm."[6]

The group Courtenay summoned to London included seven bishops (Winchester, Durham, Exeter, Hereford, Salisbury, Rochester, Nantes),[7] sixteen masters of theology, all friars (three Dominicans, four Franciscans, four Augustinians, four Carmelites), six bachelors of theology (three Dominicans, one Franciscan, two Carmelites), fourteen doctors of canon and civil law, and the warden of Merton Hall who is listed as a licentiate in theology. Of the theologians, not counting the bishop of Nantes who is identified as a master of theology, all were friars with the exception of John Blexham, the warden of Merton Hall, and John Welles, a monk of Ramsey abbey. The lawyers, on the other hand, were secular priests and included members of the archbishop's household. The preponderance of friars among the theologians prompted Wyclif to dismiss the group as a "council of friars,"[8] a classification the friars could have accepted as recognition of their eminence in the study of theology at that time.

When the council convened on May 17, the doctrines under suspicion were read "distinctly and clearly," whereupon the archbishop charged the group to study the propositions carefully and to return in a few days prepared to pass formal judgment on their orthodoxy.[9] This they did on May 21, but before they could announce any decisions, a severe earthquake which struck London that afternoon threw the meeting into panic. Several of the bishops urged immediate adjournment, but Courtenay would have nothing of this. They were not to permit the earthquake to frighten them from performing their duty to the church he warned them; the earthquake was a good omen in fact, for it symbolized the cleansing of the realm of heresy. "For as air and the spirit of infection are held in the bowels of the earth and escape by means of an earthquake, which thus purifies the earth, although not without great violence, in like manner there were many heresies buried in the hearts of the reprobate in the past, of which the kingdom has been cleansed after their condemnation, but not without travail and great effort."[10]

The council either accepted Courtenay's explanation or respected his authority, for, as indicated above, they continued their deliberations. After several hours of discussion, they agreed unanimously on the condemnation of twenty-four propositions, ten as heretical, fourteen as erroneous. The narrative leaves the impression that the council considered only these twenty-four propositions. This is possible, although not probable, unless care had been taken to present the council only with doctrines generally considered heretical. For one might otherwise assume that among the propositions deliberated upon would be several of those belonging to Wyclif that the group of theologians at Oxford a year or so before had judged ill-sounding, not unorthodox.[11] The occasion called for unanimity; anything less would encourage the spread of heterodoxy. Courtenay at least must have insisted upon unanimity. Unlike his predecessor Sudbury, when the occasion demanded, he acted with firmness and despatch, and he never moved until success was assured. It is therefore probable, that where unanimity upon a particular proposition was not possible, that proposition was never formally recognized as having been debated.

The ten propositions condemned as heretical were the following:

> 1. That the substance of the material bread and wine remains in the sacrament of the altar after consecration.
> 2. That after consecration the accidents do not remain without the subject in the same sacrament.

3. That Christ is not present in the sacrament of the altar identically, truly, and really in his own corporal presence.

4. That if a bishop or priest be in mortal sin, he may not ordain, consecrate, or baptize.

5. That if a man be truly contrite, all exterior confession is superfluous for him or unprofitable.

6. To declare stubbornly that it is not established in the gospel that Christ ordained the mass.

7. That God must obey the devil.

8. That if the pope be foreknown[12] and a wicked man and, as a consequence, belongs to the devil, he has received no authority over Christ's faithful from anyone save perhaps from the emperor.

9. That after Urban VI, no one is to be recognized as pope, but every one should live after the manner of the Greeks, under his own laws.

10. To say it is contrary to sacred scripture for the clergy to have temporal possessions.

The fourteen propositions judged erroneous were the following:

11. That no prelate may excommunicate anyone unless he knows beforehand that that person has been excommunicated by God.

12. That he who excommunicates in that manner is for that reason himself either a heretic or excommunicate.

13. That a prelate who excommunicates a clerk who has appealed to the king and to the royal council, becomes by that act a traitor to God, king, and country.

14. That those who leave off preaching or hearing the word of God or his gospel preached because of the excommunication of men, are excommunicated and will be condemned as traitors of God on the day of judgment.

15. To declare that it is lawful for anyone, even a deacon or priest, to preach the word of God without authorization of the apostolic see or a catholic bishop or of any other established authority.

16. To say that no one can act as civil magistrate, bishop, or prelate, while he is in mortal sin.

17. That temporal lords may at their discretion deprive those members of the clergy who are habitually delinquent

of their possessions, or that the people may discipline delinquent lords at their discretion.

18. That tithes are pure alms and parishioners may withhold these because of the wickedness of their curates and may bestow them on others at their discretion.

19. That under similar circumstances, special prayers applied to a particular person by prelates or religious are no more profitable to him than general prayers.

20. That any person who enters a religious order is thereby rendered the less capable and fit to observe the commands of God.

21. That those holy men who founded religious orders, whether for possessioners or mendicants, sinned in so doing.

22. That members of the clergy who belong to religious orders are not members of the Christian religion.[13]

23. That friars must earn their living by the labor of their hands and not by begging.

24. That whoever bestows alms on friars[14] or a preaching friar is excommunicated, and so is the person who accepts the alms."[15]

Even a quick glance at these propositions will reveal how much more revolutionary they were than the nineteen theses of Wyclif's which had drawn Pope Gregory's fire in 1377. Among the twenty-four propositions now coming under attack for the first time were such fundamental doctrines as transubstantiation, the divine institution of the mass, the sacrament of penance, the papacy, the inherent sacramental powers of the priesthood, and religious orders.

This raises the question whether the twenty-four theses condemned by the Blackfriars council were actually Wyclif's and not those of the more radical Lollards. Courtenay never said they were Wyclif's. Perhaps for fear of antagonizing Gaunt, the archbishop appears to have carefully avoided linking Wyclif's name with the propositions he had his council deliberate upon at the Blackfriars house.[16] As for Wyclif, he declared that of the propositions condemned by that council, "some are catholic and some are plainly heretical."[17] One regrets Wyclif was not more specific, since a study of his works suggests he would have endorsed in substance all propositions save number ten. This tenth proposition condemned the holding of property by priests as contrary to scripture, a position Wyclif could scarcely have supported inasmuch as he himself possessed material goods. And it is also probable that he would not have pressed the force of propositions sixteen and seventeen as they affected civil lords with the same enthusiasm as some of his leveling supporters.[18]

That it was the complaints of parliament against unauthorized preachers and their revolutionary doctrines that prompted Courtenay to convene the council at Blackfriars is revealed by the alacrity with which that body responded to the condemnation of the twenty-four propositions. Less than a week after the action of the council, parliament enacted on May 26 a statute which would provide the hierarchy the assistance of the government in suppressing such unauthorized preaching. In the statute, parliament referred to "wicked men . . . in certain habits and under pretense of great sanctity,"[19] who had been going about the country preaching doctrines that threatened not only the destruction of the church and the ruination of men's souls, but aroused "discord and dissension among the different estates of the realm . . . to the disturbance of the people and the serious peril of the entire kingdom." That these preachers taught heresy had been established, so the statute affirmed, by the archbishop of Canterbury and his council of bishops and theologians. Because the efforts of the hierarchy to curb such practices had proved fruitless in the past, since such vagrant preachers "do not obey their summonses and decrees . . . but expressly despise them," parliament was directing the chancellor to order the sheriff and other authorized officials to arrest any such preachers and their abettors whose seizure a bishop might recommend, and "to hold them arrested and in strong prison until they are willing to clear themselves according to reason and the law of holy church."[20]

On May 30, four days after the enactment of the statute against unauthorized preaching, Courtenay moved against these preachers directly. He sent a mandate to Braybroke, the bishop of London, with instructions that copies of it be forwarded with all possible speed to the other bishops of the province of Canterbury. The mandate directed the bishops to publish the condemnation of the twenty-four propositions in all the churches of their dioceses and to prohibit under pain of excommunication anyone from accepting, preaching, or listening to the preaching of the propositions or showing favor to those who did. Each bishop was to direct the search for persons who might be guilty of maintaining such propositions and to take immediate action against them.[21]

Braybroke proceeded to carry out the archbishop's mandate the day it was issued. Some weeks earlier Courtenay had ordered the bishops of the province to hold processions on that very day, May 30, for the purpose of begging God's help in an outbreak of the plague.[22] This would provide an admirable opportunity for publishing the archbishop's mandate, Braybroke decided, so after he had headed a procession through the streets of London and back to St. Paul's, he directed John Cunningham, a Carmelite friar, to publicly read the archbishop's mandate with its condemnation of the twenty-four propositions.[23]

Courtenay issued this mandate on May 30. A few weeks later the inadequacy of parliament's statute and his own orders in curbing the activities of unauthorized preachers must have been revealed, for he appealed to the crown for further assistance. While the statute had committed the government, through its sheriffs, to help the bishops in apprehending such preachers, the machinery the bishop had to employ to secure the cooperation of the sheriff was so time-consuming as to make the procedure unworkable. For whenever a bishop wished a particular preacher who had ignored his summons apprehended, he was obliged to request the chancellor in Westminster to issue a writ to the sheriff of the particular county involved, with instructions that he make the arrest. Such action might require weeks, more than time enough for a preacher to escape into another county, whose sheriff could not act until he too had received instructions from the chancellor.

The crown responded to the archbishop's request with a patent dated June 26. This extended "authority and permission . . . to the archbishop and his suffragans to arrest and commit to their prisons or others, as they choose, all and every person who shall preach or maintain, privately or publicly, the condemned propositions, whenever they can be seized, and to keep them there until they have recovered their senses from the pravities of these errors and heresies, or until it will have been provided otherwise concerning the arrested by us or our council." The patent further warned all officials and subjects of the realm not to show such preachers any favor under pain of forfeiture; rather directed them to cooperate with the hierarchy in apprehending the preachers.[24]

Meantime trouble had broken out in Oxford over the publication of Courtenay's mandate against unauthorized preaching and the twenty-four propositions. The archbishop had sent this mandate on May 28 directly to Peter Stokes, a Carmelite friar and professor of scripture, with instructions that he read it before the assembled university community. The mandate was similar to the one that the archbishop had sent Braybroke with this exception, namely, that it specifically forbade anyone to "hold, teach, preach, or defend in the future in the university of Oxford, the aforesaid heresies or errors or any of them, either in the schools or outside them, publicly or in secret, or to listen to anyone preaching any of them, or to show favor or adhere to them, publicly or in secret. . . ." And Courtenay gave explicit instructions that Stokes read the mandate on the feast of Corpus Christi "before the sermon of Philip."[25]

That Courtenay sent his mandate to Stokes rather than to Robert Rigg, the chancellor of the university, suggested that not all was well at Oxford—and it was not. Several days before, information had come to Courtenay from Oxford about Philip Repingdon—how he had been given the honor of preaching the sermon on the feast of Corpus Christi. That was a great honor at any time, and an unusual one in this case, for Repingdon, as the chronicler complains, was still not a doctor.[26] That Repingdon was to preach on Corpus Christi was doubly significant. Corpus Christi was the great feast of the eucharist, and Repingdon was one of Wyclif's disciples. It could be generally assumed, therefore, that Repingdon would take this occasion to endorse his mentor's views on transubstantiation. That is what the "catholics" feared, as the chronicler calls them, and it was for that reason that they had appealed to Courtenay and had asked him to give orders that the condemnation of the twenty-four propositions be announced prior to Repingdon's sermon. If this would not force Repingdon to modify the nature of his sermon, it might at least neutralize its effect.

Courtenay had sent his instructions concerning the publication of the condemnation of the propositions to Stokes rather than Rigg because he had reservations about the chancellor's orthodoxy. Stokes on the other hand had been among those carrying the fight against Wycliffitism at the university.[27] It may have been Stokes who notified Courtenay of Repingdon's appointment to preach on Corpus Christi, and he may also have told him of the even greater honor given to Nicholas Hereford just a few weeks earlier of preaching the sermon on Ascension Day.

Now Hereford, like Repingdon, was a disciple of Wyclif, and ordinarily no one but the chancellor himself preached the sermon on Ascension Day since that occasion was considered the most eminent of the year. According to the chronicler, Stokes had been sparring with the Wycliffites at Oxford during the past year and had assigned notaries to make official records of all of Hereford's public statements. Hereford's Ascension Day sermon must have proved most unpalatable to Stokes, for he "preached much that was abominable and detestable . . . exciting the people to insurrection and excusing and defending Wycclyff."[28]

Although Courtenay had learned of Repingdon's appointment to preach the sermon on Corpus Christi early enough to countermand it, he chose not to interfere. He had been a student at Oxford himself, even a chancellor, and he knew how sensitive the university was about "foreign" interference.[29] He may also have hoped to accomplish what he wished without risking the danger of antagonizing the entire university, including the group that opposed Wycliffitism. Furthermore, if he showed his forbearance in this matter and left the university to handle the problem he could hope that moderation might prevail at the university and that Repingdon be cautioned against preaching anything the archbishop might find offensive.

Courtenay did write to Rigg, however, and warn him to cooperate with Stokes. He chided him for having appointed Hereford, about whose possible heterodoxy he had earlier notified him, to preach the sermon on Ascension Day "without any hesitation whatsoever." Rigg should take care not to repeat such action lest he be counted among the suspect, in which event he would be removed, for the king and his council had assured the archbishop of their assistance in quashing Wycliffitism. To clear himself of suspicion he must cooperate with Stokes in the publication of the condemnation of the propositions, and he was also to arrange to have this condemnation "published in the theological schools of the university by the beadle of the faculty in the next lecture to be delivered there, without the slightest alteration. . . ."[30]

Courtenay's admonition made little impression upon Rigg and his friends, so long had Wycliffite ideas been permitted free expression at the university. So Rigg ignored both Courtenay's personal instructions to cooperate with Stokes and also the archbishop's warning that the crown had promised its assistance.

Instead "he began to upbraid Stokes and to turn the university against him, accusing him of seeking to destroy the liberties and privileges of the university of Oxford. . . . And he affirmed that neither bishop nor archbishop had any authority over the university, even in a question of heresy."[31]

More prudent counsel moved the proctors of the university, however, and the other secular regents whom Rigg consulted about the matter. It was decided, therefore, that at least a gesture of cooperation be made the archbishop. Whereupon Rigg announced publicly that he would assist Stokes in carrying out Courtenay's instructions, although in fact "he did what he could to obstruct him and assembled against him many armed men, about a hundred in number, with hauberks and swords, either to kill or to restrain Peter [Stokes], should he attempt anything. Indeed, he won the mayor to his side by telling him to have a hundred armed men ready for Peter the Carmelite."[32]

So Repingdon delivered his sermon as scheduled, without any prior condemnation of the twenty-four propositions. Neither did Repingdon apparently modify the thrust of his sermon in keeping with the intent of Courtenay's instructions, but presented a vigorous endorsement of Wyclif's views. Wyclif he called a "doctor eminently catholic," who had "never lectured or taught other concerning the subject of the sacrament of the altar than what the entire church of God maintained, and that his position on the sacrament of the altar was most true. . . ."[33] "And he defended Master John Wycclyff and supported him in all matters, as when he preached among other things that temporal lords should be recommended in sermons before pope or bishops, and that whoever does not recommend in that order violates sacred scripture. Many other opprobrious things did he say concerning the estates and different persons. And among other things he said the duke of Lancaster was very sympathetic, and that he was ready to protect all Lollards, whom he in fact referred to as holy priests."[34]

After Repingdon had finished his sermon, he left the hall and entered St. Frideswide's in the company of twenty men who carried weapons under their gowns. Later he waited at the door of the church for Rigg and "walked away with him smiling. And great was the rejoicing among the Lollards at that sermon." Stokes for his part was so shaken by what he had heard and witnessed that he did not risk leaving the church.

The following morning found Rigg in more subdued

spirits. At a meeting of the full congregation of the university he explained his failure to cooperate with Stokes: he had simply not received any officially sealed instructions from the archbishop to do so. This was perhaps technically true, for Courtenay had sent his sealed mandate to Stokes, while sending Rigg only his personal letter with instructions that he cooperate with Stokes in carrying out the orders contained in the mandate. Still Stokes had given Rigg a copy of this mandate, the original of which, under Courtenay's own seal, he now produced before the assembly. Whereupon Rigg protested his willingness to assist him in publishing the condemnation of the twenty-four propositions, although he must first consult the university about the matter and follow its advice. What he actually did, however, was to hurry off to Lambeth to explain his position to the archbishop.

Rigg's words did not reassure Stokes, and he sent a full account of what had happened to the archbishop. He told Courtenay that he did not know what more might be done under the circumstances, but one thing he did know, namely, "that in this matter I dare do nothing further for fear of death." He begged the archbishop to attend to this matter immediately lest either he or his associates suffer injury or death. Additional information would the bearer of his letter convey to the archbishop.[35]

Except for another provocative address by Repingdon, nothing untoward took place during the next few days. By Tuesday (June 10) Stokes had screwed up his courage sufficiently to dispute publicly Repingdon's statement about the proper order of recommending ecclesiastical and civil authorities. He maintained, contrary to Repingdon, that spiritual lords, such as the pope and bishops, should be recommended before temporal lords, and he proved this was not contrary to sacred scripture.[36] But Stokes' newborn courage died abruptly when he caught sight of some men, twelve of them, who had weapons half-hidden beneath their gowns. In fact he feared he would be murdered before he left his chair.[37] Nothing could he have welcomed with greater relief than a letter, dated June 9, that reached him that day from Courtenay, with instructions that he come to Lambeth immediately to report on matters touching the condemnation of the propositions and other developments at the university.

Early next morning (June 11) Stokes set out for London and arrived there that same night. The following morning he presented himself to the archbishop at Lambeth and explained that it was "fear of death" that had prevented him from carrying out his orders. "And he related other things that he had witnessed."[38] Meantime some days earlier Rigg and Thomas Brightwell, professor of sacred scripture, had presented themselves to the archbishop, but Courtenay had refused to hear their explanations. He directed them to come back on June 12 when the Blackfriars council would reconvene.

This second session of the council convened on June 12, as the archbishop had indicated, with roughly the same membership as at the first meeting.[39] The principal matter of business was Rigg and Wycliffitism at Oxford. Because of what Stokes had reported to the archbishop, Rigg and the university's proctors, Walter Dasch and John Hunteman, were charged with favoring heretical views, in particular the views of Repingdon, Hereford, and Wyclif. The specific charges brought against them were: that they had failed to silence or discipline Hereford and his disciples in their disputes with the orthodox theologians over his views and those of Wyclif; that they had not censured, had even defended, Hereford for affirming in a sermon he had given during Lent, that any member of a religious order could not take a degree at the university without apostatizing, even though such a statement was contrary to the customs and statutes of the university—this fact had been brought to their attention by Peter Stokes and John Wellys, doctors of theology; that Rigg had appointed Hereford to preach the English sermon on Ascension Day, even though Hereford had earlier declared in sermons "that he could find no error in the doctrines of Master John Wycclyff" and had expelled those doctors who had objected to this; that he had assigned the honor of preaching the sermon on the feast of Corpus Christi to Repingdon whose orthodoxy was equally suspect; that although Repingdon had stated openly in the schools that he would defend all doctrines of Wyclif and that he wanted to keep his finger in his mouth on the material bread of the sacrament of the altar until God would illuminate the hearts of the clergy—which statements had led Stokes to appeal to the archbishop to have Repingdon's appointment to speak cancelled—Rigg had blocked the condemnation of the propositions and had even organized students and laymen to prevent Stokes from doing so; that although Repingdon in his sermon on the feast of Corpus Christi had commended Wyclif most extravagantly and had defended his heretical views on the eucharist as "most true," he "had neither punished nor corrected him, but after the sermon applauded him with a smiling countenance"; that instead of punishing William James, a regent in the arts, who had stated "that there is no idolatry except in the sacrament of the altar," had merely observed, "Now you speak like a philosopher"; that Rigg and the proctors, as well as the greater number of the regents in the arts, were hostile to those scholars who opposed Hereford and Repingdon, although they had once been friends.[40]

After the reading of the charges against Rigg and the two proctors, Courtenay questioned Rigg about his position on the twenty-four condemned propositions. Without hesitation the chancellor agreed with the council's judgment that some of them were heretical, others erroneous. Then Courtenay turned to Thomas Brightwell, Rigg's companion, who had accompanied the chancellor to Lambeth, probably in order to provide him theological advice. Brightwell showed some reluctance to accept the condemnation of the propositions, but under Courtenay's prodding finally gave unqualified endorsement of the council's action. A third Oxford scholar, referred to only as a bachelor, also hesitated at first, but then accepted their condemnation.[41]

Then Courtenay turned back to Rigg and asked him to explain his refusal to carry out his instructions and cooperate with Stokes. All Rigg could do by way of reply was to fall on his knees and humbly ask the archbishop's pardon for his negligence. This Courtenay granted him upon the request of Bishop Wykeham. Courtenay then ordered a mandate read which Rigg was to carry back to Oxford. He was to publish the condemnation of the twenty-four propositions clearly, plainly, and without equivocation or sophistry, in both English and Latin; to prohibit the teaching or defending of the propositions and to bar from preaching Wyclif, Hereford, Repingdon, John Aston, and Lawrence Bedeman, whom Courtenay was suspending, until they had cleared themselves of suspicion of heresy before the archbishop; that he was to announce the suspension of these men; that he have diligent search made in the university for persons who might sympathize with these men and punish them with excommunication should they refuse to abjure their errors; finally, that in the future he was to devote himself to preventing the rise of heresy and error at the university.[42]

After this mandate had been read, the archbishop handed it to Rigg and with it a monitory letter that warned him that his record and attitude were such as to leave him under suspicion of heresy. The archbishop sternly warned him under threat of excommunication "not to annoy, obstruct, or molest, judicially or extra-judicially, publicly or secretly, those clerks, secular or regular, or those who supported them in any way"; not to permit anyone in the university "to hold, teach, preach, or defend the condemned heresies or errors"; to bar Wyclif, Hereford, Repingdon, Aston, and Bedeman from preaching, and all other persons under suspicion of heresy, until they had established their orthodoxy before the archbishop.[43]

Rigg had no choice but to accept the two mandates. He warned Courtenay, however, that "he did not dare publish them for fear of death." To which the archbishop replied: "Then is the university a patron of heresies, if she does not permit catholic truthes to be published." Rigg's observation, nevertheless, disturbed the archbishop, for it raised new doubts concerning his willingness to carry out the provisions of the mandate. So the next day (June 13) Courtenay had Rigg appear before the privy council, where the royal chancellor, Richard le Scrope, gave him explicit instructions to carry out the archbishop's orders.

Rigg returned to Oxford on June 14 a much sobered individual, yet with still some fight in him. As instructed by Courtenay and Scrope, he did publish the archbishop's mandate the next day, which was Sunday, and proclaimed the condemnation of the twenty-four propositions and the suspension of Wyclif and his disciples. But in making these announcements, he interpolated remarks of his own which were not consistent with the point of the condemnations. These remarks "so incited the seculars against the regulars at this time, that many [regulars] feared for their lives because they [the seculars] were accusing them of wanting to destroy the university. . . ."[44]

Among the seculars most concerned over the condemnation of the propositions and the curbs placed upon Wycliffitism at the university were Wyclif's leading disciples there, Hereford and Repingdon. On Monday, the day following publication of Courtenay's mandate, they took themselves "complaining" to the duke of Lancaster who was in London. In their predicament he was the logical man to turn to, that is, if he was as sympathetic toward the Lollards as Repingdon had affirmed in his Corpus Christi sermon.[45] They found the duke at Totenhale and told him that the "condemnation of the propositions by the council of the clergy threatened the destruction and weakening of secular rule and secular kings."[46]

They must have persuaded the duke of the justice of their

cause, for they spent the night at his house. Next morning (June 17), another group came to see the duke, this one consisting of several doctors of sacred theology. Their mission was the reverse of Repingdon's and Hereford's: they wanted him to use his influence to suppress Wycliffitism, specifically to silence men like Repingdon and Hereford. For some moments Gaunt's receiving room was bedlam. The chronicler says that "Master Nicholas and Master Philip stormed among them immediately as Satans." And the duke sympathized with them, for "at first the duke showed the catholic masters countenance and words tolerably harsh. . . ." This was only at first, however, for once he had listened to their explanations, "the lord duke called Philip and Nicholas laymen or devils,"[47] and after learning what their views on the eucharist actually were, "he judged them detestable." Then, rather than permit the theologians present to do so, the duke personally discussed the eucharist with Repingdon and Hereford, and did this so persuasively "that they had nothing more to say." He next had the twenty-four propositions read to him, which convinced him "that they had told him falsehoods, and he ordered them to accept the instructions of the lord archbishop."[48]

Repingdon and Hereford left the duke in a "disturbed" state of mind, so the chronicler writes. They took themselves to Lambeth, where the archbishop instructed them to return the following morning (June 18) when the Blackfriars council would be back in session. They appeared the next morning as instructed and brought with them another Oxford suspect, John Aston, a bachelor of theology. All three took oaths to state truthfully their opinions concerning the twenty-four propositions. When Courtenay questioned Repingdon and Hereford individually on the propositions, he found them unwilling to commit themselves. Instead they asked for a day of grace in which to prepare a written critique of the propositions, a respite the archbishop readily extended them.

The archbishop next turned to Aston but made no better progress here, for his answers were devious and sophistical. A warning to answer *plene et plane* brought no improvement. So Courtenay offered him a day's grace as he had the other two, in which to think the matter over. But Aston replied that he was ready to give his reply immediately, which was to remain silent on the propositions. This did not satisfy the archbishop, and he forbade Aston ever to preach again in the province of

Canterbury without his permission. When further questioning brought out the fact that Aston had been fully aware of the mandate against unauthorized preaching but had simply ignored it, he was directed to present himself on June 20 to show cause why he should not be excommunicated as a heretic. Repingdon and Hereford received similar instructions, and all three were warned that complete and unequivocal answers would be demanded of them on the twentieth.[49]

When the Blackfriars council reconvened with Courtenay on June 20, the three "Lollards" Repingdon, Hereford, and Aston, presented themselves as instructed.[50] A fourth suspect from Oxford, Thomas Hilman, bachelor of divinity, accompanied them. Repingdon and Hereford produced a written critique of their views on the twenty-four propositions. It was evident that they had made good use of the days of grace in studying the propositions, for they presented no simple acceptance or rejection as the archbishop wanted, but carefully qualified answers in the case of several propositions. Their position on proposition number one, for example—that the substance of the material bread and wine remains in the eucharist after consecration—was this, that "in a sense contrary to the decretal *Firmiter credimus*, we concede this to be a heresy." Altogether they accepted without reservation the condemnation of ten propositions. They gave qualified acceptances of the condemnation of the other fourteen, although in only seven instances were their reservations considered sufficiently serious to warrant examination. What this means is that they were willing to endorse the action taken by the Blackfriars council in condemning seventeen of the twenty-four propositions. What is even more significant is that they either lacked the courage or the conviction to accept the orthodoxy of even one of the condemned propositions. In this they parted company with their master Wyclif.[51]

This fact must have pleased the archbishop and he must, too, have taken comfort in the statement with which Repingdon and Hereford concluded their apologia. If, they declared, in the "meagerness" of their talents they had affirmed something to which the archbishop would object, they were willing to accept his correction as based upon sacred scripture, the teaching of the church, or the statements of the holy doctors. They finally assured the archbishop that they had never accepted the propositions as true and that they had never affirmed them in the schools nor preached them in their sermons.[52]

Courtenay was, however, less concerned for the moment with the propositions Repingdon and Hereford were willing to accept as heretical or erroneous than those whose condemnation they had elected to question. He and his assessors took them to task, accordingly, on those seven propositions they were only willing to condemn with reservations. Concerning proposition one whose condemnation they were willing to accept, as indicated, if understood in a sense contrary to the decretal *Firmiter credimus*, they were asked in what sense they meant this. But they refused to explain. Pressed further whether the material bread and wine remained in the eucharist in precisely the same condition as prior to consecration, they replied that they would make no answer beyond that contained in their apologia.

The archbishop and his advisers then questioned them on proposition two. The condemnation of this proposition—that after consecration the accidents do not remain without the substance in the same sacrament—they were willing to accept "in a sense contrary to the decretal *Cum Marthae.*" When asked what particular sense they had in mind, they refused as before to explain but referred their questioners to what they had written. They similarly refused to elaborate on their qualified acceptance of the condemnation of proposition three—that Christ is not present in the sacrament of the altar identically, truly, and really in his own corporal presence—if in a sense contrary to the decretal *Clement Si Dominum.* Proposition four—that if a bishop or priest be in mortal sin, he may not ordain, consecrate, or baptize—was next considered, even though Repingdon and Hereford had accepted the council's condemnation. Their questioners must have suspected that they might be taking refuge behind some mental reservation. So they asked them whether anyone in mortal sin could be a bishop or priest, and they conceded that he could in so far as his episcopal or priestly authority was concerned.

Of the condemnation of proposition seven[53]—that God must obey the devil—Repingdon and Hereford had also given only qualified approval. They were accordingly asked whether God ever owes the devil any kind of obedience. They replied that he did "because God owes the devil the obedience of charity with which he loves and punishes him. And to prove this Master Nicholas [Hereford] offered himself voluntarily under penalty of fire." Next came proposition eleven—that no prelate may excommunicate anyone unless he knows beforehand that that person has been excommunicated by God. Initially Repingdon and Hereford had offered some reservation to accepting its condemnation. Now when questioned whether a prelate could excommunicate anyone in the state of grace, they agreed that he could.

Repingdon and Hereford had accepted the condemnation of proposition nineteen—that under similar circumstances, special prayers applied to a particular person by prelates or religious are no more profitable to him than general prayers—only in the sense of special prayers being motivated from special charity and general prayers from general charity. When asked whether special prayers were more efficacious than general prayers, they were not willing to say more than what they had already stated in their critique. They were next queried about their position regarding proposition twenty-three—that friars must earn their living by the labor of their hands and not by begging. They had been willing to accept its condemnation if taken universally. Upon being questioned whether a friar was obliged to live off the labor of his hands, in fact, was not allowed to beg or live by begging, they again refused to answer anything further.

At the conclusion of the interrogation, Courtenay asked the assembled theologians and canon lawyers how each of them judged the answers given by Repingdon and Hereford. They all agreed that they considered their responses to propositions one, two, three, and six as "insufficient, heretical, and deceitful," and that several other responses they had made, particularly those concerning propositions nineteen and twenty-three were "insufficient, erroneous, and perverse." Thereupon Courtenay ordered the two men to give answer concerning the propositions, "fully and intelligibly, without use of subtle, sophistical, or dialectical terms." Upon their refusal to do this, Courtenay dismissed them with orders to present themselves eight days later, on June 27, to hear his decision.[54]

Now it came John Aston's turn, and what an extraordinary person he turned out to be! Knighton provides a colorful description of the man, perhaps as fine a picture of the vagrant priest of the late fourteenth century as contemporary literature has to offer. According to Knighton, Aston gave "no thought to the comfort of his body, nor did he require a horse-drawn carriage, but was quite ready to go on foot. With his staff in his hand, he visited churches all over the realm wherever he could find them, and ran about unweariedly with his flask of poison,[55] never waiting for horse or meal lest such delay his journey or weaken his intention. Like a dog springing up from its bed and ready to bark at the slightest sound, without impediment of any kind he took to the road like an argumentative bee ready to preach dogma."[56]

Like other unauthorized preachers, Aston not only disseminated the views of "his master Wyclyf . . . but was not ashamed to add very many others of his own subtle invention . . . and everywhere in his sermons in the churches of the kingdom, he sowed cockle with the grain." The sermon he delivered at Leicester on Palm Sunday must have been one of his most "notorious," for Knighton singles it out for especial condemnation. Among other "heresies" Aston preached on that occasion, so Knighton states, was that bishops purchased their benefices and that the kingdom would not enjoy peace and plenty until they were deprived of their wealth; "and he did indeed implore the people with outstretched hands that each of them do what he could in this matter"; that if the king confiscated the wealth of the church, taxes would no longer be necessary; that members of religious orders should live by the labor of their hands as did St. Paul and his disciples; that the bread remains after consecration and that theologians were in disagreement about this doctrine.[57]

During their interrogation by the archbishop, Repingdon and Hereford had been respectful even though unyielding. Aston was impertinent, if not insolent, and he answered Courtenay's questions with a combination of flippancy and impudence. Unlike Repingdon and Hereford, he brought no written apologia, but then as he had told Courtenay several days before, he had no need for time in which to prepare his defense. Aston's experience and popularity as an itinerant preacher gave him confidence, and he probably hoped to arouse so much sympathy among the lay people present that the archbishop would not dare to censure him. At any rate, he insisted on answering the archbishop in English even though repeatedly requested to do so in Latin "because of the lay people present." These people had broken into the hall where the questioning was underway and were attempting to obstruct the proceedings.[58] Their sympathies were with the defendant, and this knowledge helps explain Aston's abusive attitude.

Courtenay warned Aston at the beginning of his questioning to give his answers on each proposition plainly and without dissimulation. But all the archbishop got as he proceeded to ask him about each proposition were words in English, "frivolous, opprobrious, and extremely abusive," with which he hoped, so the scribe says, to incite the crowd against his inquisitor. He refused to state his position on any of the propositions "frequently saying that since he was a layman[59] it was only necessary for him to believe as the church believed." To the archbishop's question concerning proposition one and his belief concerning the substance of the material bread in the eucharist, he replied that the term *materia* (substance) transcended his intellect, and that as for the term *materialis*, "he said by way of deriding the lord of Canterbury, 'you can put that word *materialis* in your pocket if you have one.'"

Courtenay thereupon condemned his answers as insolent, as did the doctors present, "since he was a clerk and graduated from the schools." Inasmuch as he had "contemptuously refused" to give answer concerning the condemned propositions, he was judged to have accepted them. For this reason he was officially declared a heretic and turned over to the civil authorities.[60]

One last matter remained for Courtenay and the council before adjourning. This concerned Thomas Hilman, bachelor of theology, who had advised Aston concerning his views on the condemned propositions. Upon Hilman's request for a day's grace for further thought, Courtenay dismissed him with orders to present himself a week later, on June 27, prepared to state his opinion concerning the propositions *plene et plane*.

Repingdon, Hereford, and Hilman presented themselves as instructed on June 27 in the chapel of Courtenay's manor at Otford, but for some unexplained reason no members of the Blackfriars council were on hand. One hesitates to say their absence was a deliberate maneuver to inconvenience the three men, although it is strange they were not notified of this fact, particularly since Otford was some twenty miles from London. Whatever the explanation, Courtenay directed the three men to present themselves again the following Tuesday (July 1) in Christ Church at Canterbury.[61] Now it came turn for Repingdon, Hereford, and Hilman not to show when the Blackfriars council reconvened. It may have been the news about the newly issued royal ordinance authorizing the arrest of Wycliffites that led Hereford and Repingdon to flee, since, as their subsequent behavior indicated, they were not at all ready to make their submissions. The archbishop held up proceedings until "the second hour after dinner" when Hilman put in his belated appearance and after some hesitation, made his submission. His abjuration read as follows:

Each and everyone of those conclusions that have been recently condemned by my lord of Canterbury, with the counsel of his clergy, as heretical and erroneous, I judge in the same manner as my lord of Canterbury and the other doctors of theology and of canon and civil law have judged by their common counsel, and I condemn them as damnable heresies and errors, as above said, as far as I am able, protesting that I want to hold and affirm the contrary of those propositions and to live and die in that faith.[62]

Then after waiting for Repingdon and Hereford a good while longer (*diutius*), Courtenay finally denounced the two as contumacious and formally excommunicated them. Their sentence read:

We William, by divine permission archbishop of Canterbury, primate of all England, legate of the apostolic see and inquisitor of heretical pravity through the whole of our province of Canterbury, do pronounce Masters Nicholas Hereford and Philip Repyngdon, professors of sacred scripture, contumacious inasmuch as they in no way put in their appearance on this day and this place appointed them by us to hear our decree in the matter of heretical pravity, although summoned and awaited for a very long time, and in punishment of their contumaciousness, we by these presents do excommunicate them and each of them.[63]

Hereford and Repingdon had decided to lay their case before the pope and to this end drew up an appeal against "some grievances" they claimed to have suffered at the hands of the archbishop. Copies of this appeal they attached to the doors of St. Paul's and the church of St. Mary of the Arches in London. To their request for the usual *apostoli*,[64] Courtenay countered on July 12 with a dismissal of their appeal as "frivolous and based maliciously on frivolous and false and falsely fabricated and contrived premises." The following day he issued orders that their excommunication be solemnly proclaimed at Paul's Cross.[65]

Courtenay also sent a letter to Rigg at Oxford with instructions that he publish the excommunication of Hereford and Repingdon in the church of St. Mary and in the halls of the university. He was also to cite them to appear before the archbishop within fifteen days of the publication of their summons. Rigg published the excommunication of the two men "publicly and solemnly" as directed, so he assured the archbishop in his letter of July 25, but cite them he could not, since despite diligent efforts on his part, he could not locate them.[66] Courtenay therefore sent directions to Braybroke on July 30 to arrange to have the excommunication of the two men proclaimed throughout the province of Canterbury.[67]

The fourteenth day of July proved a black day for Rigg. That was the day the mandate from Courtenay reached him with instructions to publish the excommunication of his friends Hereford and Repingdon. That was also the day he had presented himself as instructed, before the privy council, when he was handed two royal patents concerned with the suppression of Wycliffitism at the university.[68] His summons to Westminster had come because of his treatment of one Henry Crump. This in turn had aroused suspicion concerning the sincerity of his submission and the degree of cooperation he would give Courtenay in suppressing Wycliffitism at the university.

Crump, a Cistercian monk and regent in sacred theology at Oxford, had been one of Stokes's most ardent assistants in combating the spread of Lollardy at the university. The year previous to the events of 1382 he had served on a committee of twelve which William Berton, the chancellor at that time, had appointed to pass judgment on two of Wyclif's theses concerning transubstantiation. On that occasion he had joined the others in unanimously condemning the theses as heretical.[69] He was also a member of the Blackfriars council and had not only voted condemnation of the twenty-four propositions but had also been witness to Rigg's humiliation before the archbishop. All this had not endeared Crump to Rigg, and the growing bitterness between the two had finally erupted into an open break. The immediate provocation was the epithet "Lollards" that Crump was supposed to have employed in his last lecture in theology when referring to the Wycliffites at Oxford. The term had stirred much resentment, and Rigg, in violation of the archbishop's strict warning not to molest the "catholic" doctors at the university, promptly charged Crump with disturbing the peace and summoned him to appear for questioning. When Crump did not appear—he had as yet not returned from the Blackfriars session in London—Rigg suspended him forthwith. Then when Crump did return and learned of his suspension, he wasted no time but hurried back to London to lay his case before the archbishop and privy council. It was then that Rigg had received his summons to appear before the privy council at Westminster and to bring the university's proctors with him.[70]

There they received oral instructions concerning their responsibilities in the eradication of Wycliffite sentiment at Oxford and were handed royal patents to corroborate these. The first patent, dated July 13, was addressed to Rigg and the proctors of the university. It instructed them to make diligent search throughout the university, with the assistance of all regents in theology, for persons who might favor any heresy or error, particularly any condemned by the archbishop of Canterbury, or who were known to associate with Wyclif, Hereford, or Aston. Such persons they were to expel from the university and from Oxford within a week, nor were those expelled to be permitted to return until they had established their orthodoxy before the archbishop. They were further enjoined to search out any book or tract of Wyclif or Hereford and turn these over within the month to the archbishop "without correction, corruption, or alteration of any kind as to its meaning or words." These instructions they were to carry out with zeal and dispatch, and to "obey the archbishop and the lawful and honest commands he will direct to you in this matter," under threat of forfeiture of the university's privileges. The patent concluded with an order to the civil officials of Oxford, the sheriff and mayor in particular, to cooperate in the execution of these instructions.[71]

The second patent, dated July 14 and also addressed to Rigg and the university's proctors, concerned principally Rigg's past actions and what future actions he was to undertake at Oxford to undo these. It reviewed the nature of Crump's complaint against Rigg, noted that the controversy had been discussed among the principals to the dispute and the members of the privy council, and finally announced the decision of the latter following their consideration of the incident. This was to declare Rigg's action against Crump "null, invalid, vain, and of no effect," and to order his scholastic privileges restored. It next inhibited the chancellor, proctors, and all officials and scholars of the university from ever annoying or discriminating against Crump, Stokes, or Stephen Patrington in the future, or, for that matter, any member of the community who might support these men in their opposition to Wyclif, Hereford, and Repingdon. The patent concluded with a warning to Rigg and his proctors to promote the "peace, unity, and tranquility of the university, especially between the regulars and seculars." Failure to carry out these instructions would entail loss of privileges for the university.[72]

These two royal patents sealed the fate of open Wycliffitism at Oxford; they also forced Hereford and Repingdon into hiding. What the two had been doing since July 1 when they failed to appear as instructed and were excommunicated by the archbishop is not evident from the sources. Their friends at Oxford surely kept them informed of developments there, and when word reached them that Rigg had orders to expel them from the university, they must have fled. They were no longer at the university when Rigg notified the archbishop that he could not locate them. To the alternative of accepting the condemnation of the twenty-four propositions and making their peace with Courtenay, they elected for the time being to lead the hunted existence of wanted men. This was a hard life and few men had the courage and convictions of a John Ball to put up with its inconveniences and dangers very long.[73] Repingdon and Bedeman were not among these. Bedeman was the first to submit. In September his name suddenly reappeared, the occasion a summons from Bishop Brantingham of Exeter that he appear for questioning.[74] Nothing more is heard of this summons; he must have ignored it. Then in a letter to the chancellor of Oxford dated October 18, Courtenay notified him that Bedeman had submitted and that he should be restored to his former privileges at the university.[75] He made his formal submission to Bishop Wykeham four days later.[76]

On October 23, the day after Bedeman had abjured his errors, Repingdon appeared before Courtenay and the Blackfriars council in London to do the same.[77] Though this was accepted, Courtenay ordered Repingdon to present himself again at Oxford in November to make a public recantation before a general convocation of the clergy of the province. This move was prompted by the king's request to Courtenay that he summon convocation "at St. Paul's or wherever else it might appear best," in order to consider the grant of a subsidy.[78] Courtenay had decided that Oxford would make a splendid place for convocation to meet, for he would combine its meeting with a formal session of the Blackfriars council, and before that august gathering he would have not only Repingdon make his formal submission but Aston as well.[79] Nothing would provide Oxford more convincing proof that Wycliffitism was a thing of the past than to have all the bishops of the province gather there in solemn convocation and witness in that setting the formal retractions of two of its stalwarts. So on October 15, he instructed Braybroke to notify the clergy of the Oxford meeting with all possible speed.[80]

Convocation opened on November 18 with solemn high mass by the archbishop in St. Frideswide with the bishops of Winchester and Ely serving as deacon and subdeacon. Rigg, now duly repentant and restored, preached the sermon, using for his text the words: "They were gathered together in the valley of blessing." After mass all repaired to the chapter house where the certification of the bishop of London was read covering his actions in carrying out the archbishop's instructions concerning convocation. Then the royal treasurer addressed the assembled clergy and set forth the grave need of the king for financial aid. Next Courtenay rose and explained the purpose of the gathering: to eradicate the heresies that were menacing the church; to correct abuses; to redress the injuries the church was suffering; to provide the crown a fitting subsidy with which to ward off perils that threatened church, king, and kingdom.[81] Then because several late-comers had not put in their appearance, he adjourned the meeting until the following day.

Convocation reconvened next morning but could do little since certain "ex-Lollards" had not yet appeared. That the time might not be entirely lost, Courtenay took the opportunity to appoint a committee consisting of the bishops of Salisbury, Hereford, and Rochester, together with Rigg, Berton, and John Middleton, doctors of theology, to make a search in the community for any persons still remaining there who might be tainted with Wycliffitism.[82] Then convocation sat down to wait for Repingdon and Aston. It is possible, in fact probable, that the two men were already at Oxford but that their willingness to make complete retractions had ebbed somewhat and that time would be required to reconvince them of their errors. For Courtenay would scarcely have kept convocation waiting several days, actually until November 24, when Repingdon and Aston finally appeared, unless he had good reason to believe they would eventually make formal submissions. So finally on November 24 Repingdon did appear and formally retract his errors.[83]

Next it came time for John Aston to make his formal submission. He had not come to this point of surrender without a struggle. It will be recalled how defiant he had been back on June 20 during his hearing before the archbishop and how he had been condemned as a heretic and turned over to the civil authorities. Jail did not break nor silence Aston, at least not immediately. While in prison he drew up a defense of his views, written in both Latin and English, and had his friends scatter copies of this about London. In this *Confessio* he insisted that he had always believed that the bread became Christ at the words of the priest, that he had never preached that the material bread remained in the sacrament of the altar after consecration, and that he professed what the church taught in this matter since it transcended his intellect. He concluded his confession with an appeal to those who heard of his misfortunes to pray for him, "a poor prisoner, who laments his sins and the blindness of the people."[84]

Aston's *Confessio* aroused considerable controversy among the people of London, so much indeed that the ecclesiastical authorities deemed it prudent to draw up a rebuttal. Their apologia they also had distributed "in the churches and streets" of the city. It read:

> Let all christians know that Master John Astone was condemned as a heretic, not because he confessed, as he says, that the bread the priest holds in his hands becomes or is made, by virtue of the sacramental words, truly and really the body of Christ, but because he refused to confess, as holy church teaches, that the body of Christ is present in the sacrament of the altar identically, truly, and really, in its proper corporal presence, and that the substance of the material bread and wine do [not][85] remain after consecration in that same venerable sacrament.
>
> Indeed, although canonically directed and publicly charged to state his opinion concerning the twenty-four heresies and errors which had been condemned by the church and by the inquisitor of heretical pravity, he expressly spurned to do so.[86]

As weeks passed into months the convictions of the prisoner Aston underwent a change. It was probably in October that he drew up a second *Confessio*, this one addressed to Courtenay, in which he acknowledged his errors and begged for pardon. While this confession opened on a dubious note in that he attributed his arraignment on the charge of heresy to "envious persons," the tone of the appeal itself was one of sorrow and humility. He admitted that he had answered the archbishop's questions "very imprudently" and with words both offensive and foolish. In recognition of his crime, he was asking the archbishop to forgive him, even as Christ had recommended forgiveness for sinners who sinned as often as seven times a day. His return to orthodoxy he credited especially to the abbot of St. Albans and to a Nicholas Radclif, professor of sacred literature, who had convinced him from a study of Augustine, Ambrose, Bede, and Chrysostom that the substance of the material bread and wine did not remain after consecration. As a result of their learned efforts, he was now thoroughly enlightened on this subject and was quite ready to make a public statement concerning the condemned propositions.[87]

In the case of Aston, there is no record of any absolution being granted by Courtenay preliminary to the meeting in November at Oxford. It appears probable, therefore, that upon receipt of Aston's appeal, Courtenay ordered him to come directly to Oxford, still unabsolved, and make not only a formal but an actual submission at that time. So now that Repingdon had made his formal submission, Courtenay was ready for Aston. He asked him what his opinion was concerning the condemnation of the twenty-four propositions. To his astonishment, Aston refused to give a forthright endorsement of that condemnation. Instead he chose to procrastinate, even at this late a date. He told Courtenay that "he was too simple and witless, and for that reason he did not wish [to give answer], neither did he know, as he said, how to answer clearly and distinctly to all of the propositions."

Courtenay must have been a man of patience, for "in his kindness" he gave Aston over into the care of Rigg and other theologians "whom said John would have wished to select," with instructions that they clarify his thinking on the propositions and report back after dinner when Aston was to give a final and unequivocal answer. After dinner, because of the large crowd that had gathered about the chapter house, Courtenay and the bishops reassembled in the refectory instead, and there it was that Aston finally made his submission. Courtenay promptly absolved him of his sentence of excommunication inasmuch as he had returned "to his senses" and restored to him his former academic privileges at the university. And lest he later suffer ill will because of his past errancy, the archbishop gave him a "testimonial letter, confirmed by the protection of our seal, to stop up the mouths of those who would speak malicious words."[88]

Aston and Repingdon made their formal submissions on November 24. The following morning Courtenay and his bishops and clergy gathered in the chapter house of St. Frideswide to continue the business of convocation. The archbishop must have been in an excellent mood. Except for a few anxious moments over Aston, his plans had proceeded smoothly and he had accomplished what he had set out to do. This was the suppression of Wycliffitism at the university. With the exception of Hereford who was in hiding, Wyclif's disciples at the university had recanted.[89] And the combination of firmness and moderation with which he had attacked the problem augured well for the endurance of his work. He had not humiliated Repingdon and the others, neither had he demanded of them any penance that might have embittered them. He had treated them as scholars who had momentarily erred, who once they had acknowledged their errors, he had restored to full academic privileges. As he warned in the closing sentence of his *Restitutio* of Aston, they were not to suffer discrimination. The repentant Rigg continued as chancellor, in fact was asked by Courtenay to advise the misguided Aston and even serve on a committee to ferret out the last vestiges of Wycliffitism at the university. It is a tribute to Courtenay that he had handled this delicate problem in such a way as to permit the Wycliffites to continue at Oxford but in the orthodox fold. They did not become islands of resentment outside the university community around which Lollard sentiment could re-form.[90]

Ill feeling at the university between seculars and regulars, however, proved a more difficult problem. This friction had always existed and had actually taken on a new dimension with the rise of Wycliffitism. For Wyclif's views had found greatest acceptance among the seculars at the university, almost none among the regulars. That this animosity still continued was brought home to Courtenay when convocation met on November 24. Rigg appeared before the group and boldly accused Stokes and Crump, together with an unnamed Franciscan friar, of maintaining heretical views. It must have been in his capacity as member of the committee noted above that Rigg had brought the charge. In view of the past bitterness between himself and Stokes and Crump, however, it is just as likely that his action stemmed from personal malice.

Stokes and Crump promptly protested the allegation and insisted that what questionable theses they may have voiced had been proposed only for the sake of stimulating discussion and clarifying doctrine (*causa exercii et doctrine*). The thesis Rigg had charged Crump with maintaining the latter pointed out had been condemned by Pope Urban V, a fact he had made clear to his audience at the time he had discussed the subject. He did not then nor now maintain its orthodoxy and he was quite willing to take an oath on his statement. Courtenay attached no significance to Rigg's charges, but it disturbed him that "serious discord [existed] between the university and the regulars." Before the meeting adjourned, however, he was able, "although with difficulty, to force a reconciliation, and he dismissed them [Rigg, Stokes, and Crump] in peace."[91]

One real regret Courtenay must have had when he left Oxford with the other bishops to finish the work of convocation in London.[92] That was the continued intransigence of Hereford. Nothing had been heard of the man since he had appeared before the archbishop on June 24 and his excommunication three days later. On July 15 Rigg reported to Courtenay that he had not been able to find him at Oxford and that he did not know where he was keeping himself. According to Knighton, Hereford had slipped out of the country and had gone to Rome to lay his case before the pope. Remaining in England was dangerous, since it was only because of his wits and the protection of the duke of Lancaster that he had managed thus far to escape the clutches of the archbishop and his bishops. Rome proved no more sympathetic toward his views than had the Blackfriars council. He did receive an opportunity to present his views to the pope in a meeting of the consistory, but a council of cardinals and clergy which the pope delegated to examine his beliefs judged them heretical. Hereford might have been executed but for the existence of the schism, for the pope commuted his death sentence to life imprisonment lest friendly relations with England be jeopardized. He had a second stroke of fortune when rioters broke open his jail and he escaped back to England. Courtenay learned of his return when reports came in about his preaching. The archbishop wrote to Braybroke in June 1386 to report that Hereford had escaped from the pope's jail "without the permission of our lord the pope" and that his excommunication should again be published lest he lead "simple" souls astray.[93] Later that year the archbishop summoned Hereford to appear for questioning, and when the latter ignored the order, he asked the king for assistance in apprehending him.[94] The king issued the necessary writs,[95] and it is probable that Hereford was seized and spent some time in prison before recanting in 1390. Like Repingdon and Aston, he was permitted to resume his academic career at Oxford, where he shortly became a vigorous opponent of Lollardy.[96]

⁊{7}⸱

VISITATION OF THE
PROVINCE
OF CANTERBURY

Now that Courtenay had disposed of his most pressing problem, the condemnation of Lollard doctrines and the re-establishment of orthodoxy at Oxford, he was ready to undertake a visitation of his province of Canterbury. He must have entered upon this task with some diffidence. For in undertaking a visitation of the dioceses of his suffragan bishops he would be exercising one of the more important, surely the most provocative, powers claimed by his predecessors at Canterbury. That the archbishop should have determined to do this is what one would expect of a prelate like Courtenay who was so eager to assume the full responsibilities of his office and, at the same time, so insistent that his subordinates accept his right to discharge those responsibilities. As befitted a man trained in law, he fought throughout his career for the preservation of rights and prerogatives, and it may have been as much his wish to safeguard the established right of the archbishop of Canterbury to visit as it was to correct possible abuses and irregularities that prompted him to undertake the visitation of his province.

Among motives generally imputed to archbishops in leading them to visit their provinces was an interest in the procuration fees they as metropolitans had a right to collect from the places and persons visited. Churchill suggests, in speaking of the visitation of Archbishop Boniface in 1250, that "the receipt of these [procurations] if not, in all probability, the main motive of the Archbishop in visiting, was nevertheless an important factor."[1] That this consideration did interest metropolitans cannot be denied, but it was surely a minor one with prelates as responsible as Pecham, Winchelsey, and Courtenay. It is true that procuration fees could constitute a significant source of revenue for bishops, as opposed to archbishops, since many bishops did visit their clergy with some regularity. But this was a duty canon law imposed upon them: there was nothing questionable about such visitations, and the collection of the procuration fee was accepted as a reasonable charge. Quite different was the visit of the metropolitan. His right to visit had never been so firmly established as ever to be viewed as anything but extraordinary. Everywhere the archbishop who ventured to visit his province encountered opposition, so much so that many archbishops did not visit at all, and the few that did almost never completed a visitation. Under the circumstances, therefore, it would have been a fatuous prelate who would embark upon a visitation of his province principally for the procuration fees he expected to collect.[2]

Few ecclesiastical traditions had so distracted a history in the Middle Ages as the right of the metropolitan to visit the dioceses of his province. As a right it may date from the fourth century, although it was hardly recognized as an accepted prerogative of the archbishop before the thirteenth.[3] Then Pope Innocent III and his immediate successors encouraged its use as a means of reforming and revitalizing the church. No reform measure that Innocent espoused reaped fewer returns than this right of visitation or occasioned more grief and bitterness among members of the hierarchy. Even bishops as dedicated as Grosseteste fought its use as derogatory to their honor and as unwarranted and mischievous interference in the administration of their dioceses.

Episcopal resistance was entirely understandable, since during the course of a metropolitan visitation the bishop's own authority and the regular administrative machinery of his diocese were inhibited and were replaced by the authority and officials of an alien. Such an extinction of his authority, even for a few weeks, would distress a worthy bishop and embarrass a negligent one. Any bishop might consider such interference demeaning, for he held himself a successor of the apostles, a lord and vassal of the king, and, in civil and ecclesiastical matters, almost sovereign in his diocese. The archbishop was these, too, but only in his own diocese and strictly by virtue of his own episcopal character. Outside his diocese, the archbishop's superiority, so his bishops insisted, was one of ecclesiastical precedence, nothing more. Nevertheless, when the archbishop visited a suffragan, the latter found himself and his administration subjected to scrutiny as though they were suspect, while the archbishop and his officials instituted to parishes, authorized the exchange of benefices, handed down judicial decisions, probated wills, granted dispensations, and, perhaps worst of all, collected the fees which would otherwise have gone to the support of diocesan administration.

For if the collection of procuration fees was not the archbishop's principal motive in undertaking a visitation of his province, it was a primary source of episcopal objection to the exercise of that right.[4] In a period of bullion scarcity such as the Middle Ages, money fees were always onerous and procuration fees to metropolitans doubly so since they were resented as unnecessary. Some procuration fees were, indeed, excessive. The chronicler writes in indignation that Archbishop Boniface visited the cathedral of Rochester and "extorted from that poor church more than 30 marks."[5] The Third Lateran Council of 1179 sought to correct this evil and restricted the size of the archbishop's visiting party to 50 horsemen,[6] while Innocent IV stipulated in 1252 that the amount charged for procurations was not to exceed 4 marks for food and lodging. He exempted entirely parish churches on the ground that they were visited by their bishops.[7] The council of Lyons in 1274 forbade the payment of procurations in money and outlawed the assessment of fees against any church that had not actually been visited.[8]

Perhaps more expensive in the end than the procuration fees paid by the clergy of the diocese was the cost of appeals to Rome with which the bishop frequently resisted the attempt of the archbishop to visit. Such appeals involved both the direct cost of sending proctors to Rome and the much heavier expense of raising the costly fees and gifts expected by members of the papal judiciary. In 1251, for example, seven bishops of the province of Canterbury were prepared to spend as much as 4,000 marks in Rome in order to block Archbishop Boniface's visitation.[9]

Equally regrettable, if not more so since this was the root cause why those appeals kept coming, was the ambivalence of Rome in handing down its belated decisions. A particularly flagrant instance of such ambivalence contributed to Courtenay's difficulties in his coming visitation. The bishop of Salisbury, as we shall find, appealed to Pope Boniface IX against what he denounced as unlawful acts committed by Courtenay in his earlier visitation of other dioceses: viz., the probation of wills, the conferring of minor and major orders, and the institution to vacant benefices.[10] The bishop also pointed out that by virtue of a special indult of Pope Urban, Courtenay had been authorized to visit any diocese in his province he might choose to visit, whether his own diocese of Canterbury had been first visited or not. This was contrary to common law, and it was for this reason among others that Courtenay had requested the indult. Therefore, upon receiving the bishop of Salisbury's request that he be protected from the exercise by Courtenay of usurped powers, Pope Boniface abrogated the privileges extended by Urban. But he warned the bishop that he would have to submit to Courtenay's visitation if the archbishop conducted this according to common law. This meant that the archbishop would have to visit his own diocese before proceeding to Salisbury. But the pope carefully avoided committing himself in his letter to the bishop of Salisbury on the really crucial issues in all these contests, that is, whether the visiting archbishop had the right to exercise such powers as the conferring of orders, the proving of wills, and the institution to benefices.

The medieval papacy never gave a decisive judgment in favor of the bishop or metropolitan which would have eliminated future disputes. It is difficult to dismiss the charge, accordingly, that the papal curia deliberately followed a course that would bring in a large harvest of appeals. Over and beyond the business and fees these appeals would produce, they served yet another purpose. They encouraged the dependence of proud, independent-minded bishops and archbishops in an age when papal supremacy was still a plant to be nurtured. There is, of course, this other explanation for the ambivalence of the curia in such appeals and its reluctance to issue a definitive judgment which would have removed the need for such appeals. That was the papacy's hope as in the famous problem of the divorce of Henry VIII, that time and circumstance would solve a problem which it considered beyond its competency or courage.[11]

Several of Courtenay's thirteenth–century predecessors assumed the role of metropolitan visitor. Archbishops Rich and Boniface undertook visitations in the first half of the century. That of Boniface covered some seven dioceses in the face of severe obstruction. Archbishop Pecham (1279–1294) conducted what was probably the most extensive visitation prior to that undertaken by Courtenay, although his register provides only scattered references to his activities.[12] Pecham's ambitious efforts aroused much opposition from monasteries and churches which claimed complete exemption and from his bishops who raised a number of the customary objections: that he adjudicated causes which were hidden and not notorious (from point of view of the bishop, only those causes which were sources of scandal or manifestly reflected episcopal negligence fell within the archbishop's jurisdiction); that certain causes which the archbishop had undertaken but had not terminated during his visitation he took with him when he left; that he sent his clerks into a diocese after he had completed its visitation to carry out matters which were properly those of the ordinary; that he appointed agents to visit entire dioceses in his stead.[13]

Archbishop Winchelsey (1294–1313) undertook a limited visitation of his province, his successor Reynolds (1313–1328) an extensive one, principally by means of commissaries which a papal indult permitted him to employ. There is passing reference to the successful resistance of Bishop Grandisson to Archbishop Mepeham's attempt to visit his diocese of Exeter a few years later[14] but no information beyond this to suggest a general metropolitan visitation. Archbishop Islip (1349–1362) visited only two dioceses in addition to his own, while his successors, Langham, Witlesey, and Sudbury, probably did even less visiting for little record of such survives.[15] Quite unusual in its extensiveness, therefore, was to be the visitation Courtenay announced to Brantingham in January 1384 which he would initiate in that bishop's diocese of Exeter in March.

Courtenay was now forty years of age and for a dozen of those years he had been a bishop. Time, responsibilities, and difficulties had matured the young prelate. He was no longer apt to act so imprudently as he had done in the Florentine crisis. So in 1382 when he first gave serious thought to the visitation of his province, he decided to move cautiously. In view of the hostility with which bishops normally reacted toward visitations by their metropolitans, they could be expected to oppose even more vigorously any visitation he might attempt, now that a generation had elapsed since the last major one undertaken. Courtenay decided, therefore, to secure papal confirmation of his right to visit, and he asked the pope to grant him wide latitude in the manner he might wish to visit his province: to exempt him, for instance, from the canonical necessity of first visiting his own diocese of Canterbury before entering those of his suffragans. Pope Urban proved receptive to Courtenay's request and extended him sweeping privileges to bolster those he enjoyed as metropolitan in the visitation of his province. He must, however, limit his visiting in this "irregular" manner to two years, for after two years these special privileges would lapse.[16]

VISITATION OF THE DIOCESE OF EXETER

Courtenay began his visitations with the diocese of Exeter. He may have had a number of reasons for beginning there. Exeter lay in the southwestern corner of the province; and if he started there, he would be moving closer to London and Canterbury as he progressed. The archbishop knew something of the situation in Exeter both personally and from his relatives who lived there, and he may have felt that reform was in order. (Brantingham must have spent the bulk of his time in Westminster.) Then there is the possibility that he was concerned about initiating his visitations on a happy note. Brantingham was his friend and would likely cooperate with him. A happy beginning would set a valuable precedent and discourage other suffragans who might be minded to object. Finally, the archbishop's mother lived near Exeter.

Though Urban's bull was issued November 22, 1382, it was a full fourteen months (January 8, 1384) before Courtenay issued his own mandate to Brantingham.[17] He instructed the bishop of Exeter to notify all persons holding benefices in the diocese of Exeter to be prepared to prove their titles before the archbishop. Courtenay expected to be at the chapter house in Exeter the morning of March 7, when he would visit the dean, members of the chapter, and other persons associated with the cathedral. He concluded his announcement with a warning against persons who might attempt to obstruct his visitation.[18]

If Courtenay anticipated any difficulty, none materialized, at least not for the moment. Brantingham instructed his chapter and archdeacon to carry out the archbishop's orders and to be ready to receive Courtenay when he arrived. The precentor, Hugh de Hyckelynge, informed Brantingham on February 23 that all matters had been attended to preparatory to Courtenay's arrival, and he enclosed with his letter a list of the canons, vicars, and other clerks attached to the cathedral church of Exeter whom he had personally cited. As Courtenay had directed, Brantingham forwarded him a full report of these actions with the assurance that all would be in readiness for him when he reached Exeter.[19]

Courtenay reached Exeter several days before March 7 and spent the intervening time with his mother, the countess of Devon, who made her home at Exminster, four miles away. What was planned to be a short visit grew into more than a week, however, when word came that Brantingham would be away for several days. On the morning of March 7, the day the archbishop had appointed for beginning the visitation at the cathedral, his chancellor, Adam Mottrum, appeared instead at the chapter house and announced that the archbishop would postpone his appearance for one week. Before Mottrum left the chapter house, a representative of the bishop presented the bishop's certification, dated March 3, in which Brantingham, Courtenay's "humble and faithful suffragan," reported that he had carried out the archbishop's instructions in every detail, "saving always and in all matters our episcopal dignity, rights, and customs, as well as those of our person, our church, city, and diocese. . . ."[20]

On the morning of March 14, Courtenay rode in to Exeter with his clerks and attendants. About a mile or so from the city he was met by many burghers of Exeter who came to do the archbishop honor. As he crossed the bridge into the city, the clergy of the city, religious and secular, met him in procession, garbed in surplices and bearing crosses. Courtenay dismounted to do reverence to the crosses they carried, then remounted and, to the sound of all the church bells in the city, proceeded on the main road to the churchyard of the cathedral. There he again dismounted and received Brantingham. The bishop was clothed in full pontificals and was attended by his canons, vicars, and other priests of the church. They conducted the archbishop to the cathedral and inside to the main altar where Brantingham recited a prayer over Courtenay as he knelt before him. Then Brantingham took Courtenay to his palace near the cathedral, where the archbishop changed his riding attire for something more suitable.

Courtenay and Brantingham next made their way to the chapter house with the canons, vicars, and other clergy of the cathedral, to begin the visitation. The archbishop opened the proceedings with a sermon in Latin. For his text he chose the words of Ezekiel, "*Visitabo sicut pastor.*" At the conclusion of the sermon, Courtenay ordered his mandate read, together with the papal bull and the certification of the bishop. After this all the clergy with the exception of a few of the clerks were asked

to leave, whereupon Courtenay "diligently examined and personally visited" the bishop. He also inquired about the condition
of the church of Exeter and other matters touching the bishop,
canons, vicars, and other ministers of the cathedral. When the
visitation was finished, Courtenay and his clerks had dinner with
the bishop. He spent the night with his mother in a house she
owned in Exeter.

The following morning, Tuesday, Courtenay repaired as
scheduled to the chapter house to visit the dean and the members
of the chapter. First, the roll containing the names of the canons,
vicars, "annuellary" chaplains,[21] and other ministers of the church
of Exeter, as listed in Brantingham's schedule, was formally
called. At the completion of the roll, Courtenay ordered the
following monition to be read:

> In the name of God, Amen. We William, by divine per-
> mission archbishop of Canterbury, primate of all England
> and legate of the apostolic see, now by metropolitan right
> visiting in head and members the cathedral church of
> Exeter, do admonish once, twice, and a third time, each
> and every person we are to visit here, not to conceal,
> hide, or arrange to conceal by any means whatsoever,
> those matters which should be revealed during our visita-
> tion and which should or can be corrected by us; rather
> that you reveal and report those matters you know should
> be revealed and reformed, under pain of the greater ex-
> communication which we by these presents do pronounce
> against those persons who do not obey our monition, as-
> suming their negligence and fault; and we reserve the
> absolution of those incurring such sentence specifically
> to ourselves. And because it customarily happens that a
> visitation is impeded by means of pacts and conspiracies,
> we do declare void, do invalidate and annul all such pacts
> and conspiracies, whether fortified by oath or by whatever
> other means, and pronounce them to be and always to
> have been without validity.[22]

Following the reading of the monition, Courtenay visited
the precentor, treasurer, and chancellor of the church of Exeter,
the archdeacons of Totnes, Barnstaple, and Cornwall, and the
canons resident in the cathedral church. While he was thus occupied, he had his clerks inspect the titles and deeds presented
by the different persons present, which confirmed their rights
to benefices, tithes, dispensations (*viz.*, that of holding more than
one benefice), and letters of ordination. At the conclusion of

the day's business, he and his clerks rode to Exminster where they ate and spent the night. The following morning (Wednesday), after "hearing masses" in the chapel of his mother's manor, he rode back to the chapter house at Exeter to continue his visitations. He interrupted his day's work with lunch at the hospice of the Brothers Minor in the company of his mother. Then because several clerks for whom he had been waiting had still not put in their appearance by late afternoon, Courtenay announced the extension of the visitation for another day. But another day was not enough. After visiting the remaining members of the lower clergy associated with the cathedral "individually and secretly" and examining two papal bulls which one of the canons, a John Cheyne, brought with him, together with a legal document to confirm the legitimization of his birth, Courtenay felt constrained to prorogue his visitation for a week, until Friday, March 25, since there still remained some priests who had not yet appeared.[23]

While the delay probably annoyed Courtenay, he did not spend the week in idle fretting. From his mother's house in Exminster where he stayed during the interval, he commissioned three of his clerks, Adam Mottrum, Nicholas Haddeley, and John Prophet, to act as his agents in different parts of the diocese. He delegated them full authority to inquire into conditions, to correct abuses, adjudicate disputes, and to probate wills and appoint executors.[24] He also conferred upon several priests of the diocese faculties to administer the sacrament of penance and to absolve persons charged with perjury and murder. For himself he reserved absolution for acts of physical violence against members of the clergy.[25] The nature of these last powers and those he authorized his commissioners to employ represented a sharp departure from the role of visitor he had filled up to this time. He was now assuming the exercise of powers traditionally reserved to the ordinary of the diocese, at least in the judgment of the bishop.

On the morning of March 25, the day appointed for the resumption of the visitation proceedings at the chapter house in Exeter, the archbishop directed his clerk Nicholas Haddeley to announce a postponement of the visitation until March 28. No explanation is given for the delay. The archbishop may have been physically indisposed;[26] more likely it was noncooperation at Exeter that occasioned the delay. For on March 28 when Courtenay appeared at the chapter house, he first questioned several ministers there over abuses, whether they knew of any that required correction, and then declared the dean of the chapter and three canons contumacious for failure to appear.[27]

The dean may have had a double reason for absenting himself. He may have learned, in the first place, of Brantingham's decision to resist the archbishop and to block his visitation. Another explanation for his nonappearance can perhaps be found in his own deficiencies. For in the detailed sequestration order Courtenay issued that day against the dean, the archbishop charged the dean not only with failing to appear for the visitation but also for having absented himself for long periods from his duties at the chapter house; for having appropriated the income of the deanery for his own use; for having permitted the principal building of the deanery to fall into a state of serious disrepair, together with the chantries, books, ornaments, houses, walls, hedges, and fences belonging to the deanery.[28]

Courtenay remained with his mother in Exminster until April 18. If the 150 miles to London did not rule out a quick visit to Lambeth, it may have been his health or mounting difficulties over his visitation that kept him in Exeter. He did attend to a number of minor problems during the interim. Because the Franciscans at Plympton had erected several structures without first receiving his authorization and had also ignored his summons, he issued an order forbidding the faithful of the diocese to donate anything to their needs. It appears that the friars were exempt from archiepiscopal authority, and Courtenay had nothing but this indirect means of forcing their submission.[29]

Then there was the case of the people of Sherford who brought a complaint against the priest at nearby Stokenham who should have provided them divine services. This he had neglected to do, even though the income of the chapel at Sherford was adequate. Courtenay ordered an investigation and, on the basis of the report given him, ordered the negligent priest to have a mass read at Sherford on all Sundays and double feastdays of the year. On great feasts such as Christmas, Epiphany, Palm Sunday, and the feast of St. John the Baptist, however, the people of Sherford would have to go to Stokenham for services.[30]

A similar situation at Kocton led to a clash between Courtenay and Brantingham. Here again it was the case of failing to provide divine services. The priest at Donlysche was neglecting his obligations to the people at Kocton, or so at least was the charge. To demonstrate their resentment at this negligence,

several of the more impatient parishioners at Kocton had aggravated the situation by seizing the offerings left in their chapel
which were intended for the priest at Donlysche. Courtenay's
first move was to order the priest to appeal to the disgruntled
faithful of Kocton to turn over the money they had seized. The
priest declared he had already attempted this, but without success, even though he had warned them in the confessional and
had appealed to them in his "best sermons." Brantingham must
have been aware of the situation at Kocton, for he chose this
moment to appoint a chaplain for the community. Courtenay
denounced this appointment as prejudicial to his rights as metropolitan. He promptly nullifed the appointment and cited the
unfortunate chaplain to appear for questioning.[31]

When April 18 rolled around, Courtenay found himself
unable to continue the work of visitation. He excused himself
on the grounds of illness and *alias causas legitimas* and commissioned his chancellor, Adam Mottrum, to take his place in the
chapter house at Exeter. What remained to be done there was
principally the correction of *comperta et detecta*[32] that had come
to light during the preceding weeks of visitation. Since it would
be difficult to question or correct certain practices until it was
clear what customs and regulations were supposed to be observed
at Exeter, Adam Mottrum inquired first what these might be.
For answer he was told that Stapleton and Grandisson, earlier
bishops of Exeter, had issued a number of statutes for observance
by the chapter, but that these statutes were not actually observed
so much as ancient custom and practice. Whereupon Mottrum
instructed the chapter to prepare a list of the statutes they considered binding and have the list ready for the archbishop when
he appeared. Mottrum then directed individual members of the
chapter to come forward and produce credentials in support of
their titles to benefices. Here he made no more progress. Several
priests told him they had already confirmed their titles, others
asked for more time, while still others made it clear that they
would produce credentials neither then nor later. All Mottrum
could do was to warn all to have confirmation of their titles
in hand when the archbishop returned. Courtenay's metropolitan
visitation was clearly grinding to a halt, and not so much because
of the archbishop's illness as the *alias causas legitimas*, specifically the defiance of Brantingham.[33]

Brantingham had actually expressed misgivings concerning
Courtenay's visitation a month before the archbishop appeared

in Exeter. On February 6, that is some time after he had received
Courtenay's mandate but before the archbishop's arrival, he had
formally announced that he was sending an appeal to Rome and
to the Court of Canterbury against the actions of some person
not specified, whose actions he feared would prejudice his episcopal prerogatives. He had this appeal or *provocacio* attached
to the doors of the cathedral at Exeter.[34]

There appears to have been nothing beyond the issuance
of the *provocacio* during this early period that might have
aroused doubt over the success of Courtenay's projected visitation. Perhaps because Brantingham's *provocacio* had not been
addressed to him personally, Courtenay had ignored it. As we
have seen, Brantingham did direct his chapter and archdeacons
to carry out the archbishop's mandate. Still some uneasiness might
have been occasioned over the saving clause Brantingham had
attached to his certification, namely, that he had carried out
the archbishop's instructions, saving his episcopal dignity and
rights. And then there was the further disturbing fact that he
had not been on hand the morning of March 7, when Courtenay
said he would expect to see him at Exeter for the formal opening
of the visitation.

If these were hints Brantingham had thrown out in the
hope of warning Courtenay away from his episcopal prerogatives,
they passed the archbishop by unnoticed. Hardly a week after
the archbishop's visitation had gotten under way, Brantingham
felt compelled to clarify and reaffirm his position. From his manor
at Clyst he issued an inhibitory mandate dated March 23 and
addressed to his clergy, which forbade them to obey Courtenay
in all matters touching benefices, the adjudication of disputes,
and the correction of ordinary abuses. Only notorious crimes
that came to light during the visitation, the bishop affirmed, fell
within the province of the metropolitan. The clergy was also
to disregard the archbishop's instructions and actions in matters
concerned with the conferring of orders, the probation of wills,
and the administration of intestate properties. These matters had
always been properly the sole prerogative of the bishop, and
in denying the archbishop any jurisdiction in these areas, he
was not prejudicing Courtenay's rights as metropolitan since
neither common law, custom, privilege, nor special right conferred upon him the right to exercise those powers.[35]

The claims made by Brantingham in this inhibitory mandate of March 23 were then compressed into a series of articles

that the bishop ordered published throughout the diocese. These articles restated the position Brantingham had claimed in his mandate, namely, that what powers he could legitimately exercise as bishop, even including the right to visit, he could continue to exercise when the archbishop was himself visiting his diocese.[36]

When it became evident by April 4 that the bishop's inhibitory mandate and the articles would have no effect, Brantingham issued his first formal appeal (*appellacio*). In this lengthy document he reaffirmed the rights he had enumerated in the articles, referred to the appeal he had made to Rome, and assailed the archbishop for having usurped several of his episcopal powers: *viz.*, the conferring of orders, the probating of wills, the appointment of executors to administer the estates of deceased persons, and the collection of the income of vacant benefices. Because of these usurpations, Brantingham was sending a second appeal to the pope and was demanding that the bishop grant him *apostoli*.[37]

Two days later, on April 6, Brantingham issued his second *provocacio*.[38] This repeated in substance the argument of the first. A second *appellacio* dated April 8 followed similarly the argument of the first appeal. A third *appellacio* dated three days later contained a new charge against the archbishop, namely, that he had made an appointment to a vacant parish.[39] All these documents were attached to the doors of the cathedral at Exeter.

Up to this time Courtenay had remained silent. He issued no statement in defense of his position, nor did he attack that assumed by Brantingham. Finally, on April 18, the day he had been scheduled to reappear at the chapter house in Exeter to discuss the correction of the *comperta et detecta*,[40] he issued a detailed statement setting forth at length the rights and prerogatives he enjoyed as metropolitan visitor. These rights corresponded with those claimed by Brantingham as announced in the bishop's inhibitory mandate and the articles. Courtenay insisted, however, that only he could exercise such powers during the duration of a visitation, for which reason he was declaring null and void the bishop's prohibition to his clergy against cooperating with the archbishop. The archbishop concluded his denunication of the bishop with the peremptory order that he and his officials undo immediately, under threat of excommunication, what they might have done to prejudice and obstruct his visitation.[41]

The archbishop issued his inhibitory mandate against

Brantingham from Exminster on April 18 and probably saw to it that it was attached to the doors of the cathedral that very day. It is possible that his agent while doing this tampered with Brantingham's appeals and articles which were already on the doors, for on April 19 Brantingham published a stern warning against anyone daring to remove his documents from those doors.[42] That same day William Hornby, one of Courtenay's clerks, came to the cathedral and asked for copies of Branting-ham's appeals. He explained to the clerk there that he did not quite have the courage, after the bishop's threats, to remove them from the cathedral doors. But Roger Hunt, Brantingham's proc-tor, turned him away emptyhanded, possibly because the only copies of the bishop's appeals were those nailed to the doors. The failure to get the copies did not delay the archbishop, how-ever, and his agent Hornby was back at the cathedral again on April 22. This time he brought with him *apostoli*, although not the kind the bishop had demanded. Instead of a reasoned reply to the bishop's appeal which *apostoli* were normally ex-pected to provide, these were *apostoli refutatorii* which summar-ily dismissed the bishop's appeals as without foundation and void.[43]

On April 23 Brantingham countered Courtenay's *apostoli* with a fourth appeal. This repeated substantially the arguments of the earlier appeals but at greater length, since to the *gravimina* he had earlier charged Courtenay with, he could now add several new grievances. The bishop accused Courtenay of ordering the sequestration of an estate whose owner, a priest, had held prop-erty only within the limits of the diocese of Exeter; that he had instituted to a benefice a person who had been fraudulently presented; and that he had condemned the bishop's exercise of his legitimate episcopal powers as invalid and had threatened him with excommunication without first citing and admonishing him.[44] Brantingham and his clerks might have spared themselves this labor, for this lengthy appeal evoked only further terse *apos-toli refutatorii*.[45]

At this point the controversy between Courtenay and Brantingham moved from the level of words to action. On April 21, the day Courtenay issued his first *apostoli*, he drew up a far more formidable document, an order, in fact, citing Branting-ham to appear before him at the chapter house on June 6. The bishop was to come prepared to explain the existence of certain irregularities uncovered at the cathedral, to accept proper correction regarding these, and to discuss measures of reform with the archbishop.

That Courtenay was able to recruit one of Brantingham's archdeacons and two of his canons to carry the summons to the bishop, instead of employing his own clerks, suggests the possibility of friction between that prelate and his subordinates. The existence of some unfriendliness between the bishop and his clergy would, of course, not be unusual. According to the chronicler, the bishop's canons had reported the acts of negligence for which the bishop was being cited.[46] Be this as it may, the three emissaries found their assignment to deliver the summons a more exciting mission than they had anticipated. As they neared Clyst where the bishop's manor was located, on the evening of April 25, they found a large and hostile crowd waiting for them. Among the clerks and laymen making up the group were members of the bishop's household, some of them with weapons. These not only prevented the emissaries from reaching the manor, but they threatened to cut off the arm of the one who would dare unroll the archbishop's mandate. All the terrified messengers could do was to turn their horses around and ride away as fast as possible. As they neared the village of Topsham[47] in their flight, relieved for the moment that they had not been slain or thrown over the bridge into the river, they were suddenly confronted by three squires of the bishop's household. These men ordered the archbishop's emissaries to stop, directed the one bearing the summons to produce it, tear it up, and "with terrible insults cruelly compelled the unwilling emissary to eat the wax with which the mandate had been sealed."[48]

When Courtenay learned of the outrage, he excommunicated everyone who had had any part in the affair, even if among the guilty persons there was one who "reflects pontifical dignity."[49] Then on June 6, the day Brantingham was to have appeared for questioning, Courtenay presided at a formal meeting in the chapter house at which the precentor, treasurer, the archdeacons of Barnstaple and Totnes, and several canons were present. Courtenay first explained the long time his visitation was taking. He attributed the difficulty to the fact that he had been ill for a good part of the time; that he had been attending a meeting of parliament at Salisbury;[50] that the cathedral clergy had failed to cooperate with him. Next a report was made describing the fruitless effort of the three emissaries to summon Brantingham. Because it appeared dangerous, if not impossible, to cite the bishop personally, Courtenay now ordered him summoned *viis et modis*,[51] with instructions that he appear the first juridical day following the feast of St. John the Baptist (June 24).[52]

Next Courtenay turned his attention to the correction of irregular practices among the clergy of the cathedral. It was reported that four or five vicars of canons who happened to be away from the cathedral, were not taking their meals in the homes of these canons, but "to the scandal of the church" were eating in the taverns of the town. The archbishop questioned each of the canons in secret about this matter, and all but two of them admitted that, for the honor of the church, the ancient custom should be observed, namely, that vicars should eat at the homes of the canons even when these were absent. The two canons who disagreed were Henry Whitefeld and William Pile. They maintained that it was not proper to oblige the vicars to do this since there were canons who required this of their vicars as an obligation. A third canon, Nicholas Braybroke, agreed with the two, declaring further that such action on the part of the vicars in no way contributed to the denigration of divine worship. Then the archbishop instructed the canons to acquaint him, both as a chapter and individually, with what statutes and customs they were required to observe. He also ordered them to present credentials to establish their right to the benefices they held and to bring along letters of ordination as well. Finally, he set Lammas Day (August 1) as the deadline for having the chantries of their churches repaired, "otherwise he would most assuredly sequester the revenues of those benefices until they had been adequately repaired."[53]

Meantime the messenger who had been entrusted with the task of summoning the bishop *viis et modis* failed to locate either Brantingham or his proctor in or about the chapter house, so he took himself immediately to the bishop's palace nearby. There he read the summons in the hearing of a notary public and several ministers of the church. After this he attached a copy of the summons to the doors of the cathedral.[54]

The archbishop's register is silent concerning the developments of the next two weeks. A good deal must have been accomplished, however, toward affecting a reconcilation between the archbishop and bishop, for on June 25 the register resumes its account with a description of the meeting of Courtenay and Brantingham in the chapter house at Exeter. What had transpired to bring the two together is not explained. Was it mutual friends? Had Brantingham decided that continued defiance would be profitless? The position he had taken on the question of respective rights during a metropolitan visitation was an extreme one. Against a timid metropolitan it might have prevailed; against a man like Courtenay a more moderate tack would have provided him a stronger case. The incident at Topsham involving members of his own household did his cause no good, and approximately seven miles from Exeter was Powderham Castle, the home of Courtenay's nephew, the earl of Devon. What encouragement Brantingham received from the bishops with whom he discussed his problem at the Salisbury meeting of parliament is not clear. The chronicler says they gave him only sympathy,[55] although Courtenay's register speaks of other bishops having appealed to Rome against him at this time.[56] The continued support of Brantingham's own clergy may have been doubtful, for his archdeacons had either obeyed Courtenay from the beginning of the visitation or had since capitulated. Then there is also the probability that the clash between the two prelates was much sharper on the official level than on the personal. They may even have remained friends through it all, for Brantingham visited Courtenay the day before Easter when the archbishop was confined to his bed and kept himself informed of his health during the weeks following.[57]

The archbishop opened the meeting on June 25 on a conciliatory note. He apologized for the long time his visitation was taking and this time attributed the delay solely to his illness.[58] From April 10 until April 25 "he had suffered such and so great infirmity of body, that he could not ride, travel, work, or scarcely move himself in bed without the assistance of others, nor could he in any way go to said church of Exeter to conduct the visitation. To verify this he then called upon Masters Henry Whitefeld, Robert Broke, and William Trevelles, canons of said church who were learned in the physician's art, who had examined him when he lay ill. He also called upon the venerable father, lord bishop of Exeter, who had visited him the day before Easter and had sent messengers and servants to him during that time that he might keep informed of his convalescence; whose infirmity the same bishop of Exeter thereupon testified had lasted for the periods indicated."[59]

After this aside about his health which Courtenay must have emphasized lest he be later criticized for spending so much time on a visitation of a single diocese, he got down to business. He ordered William Byde, one of Brantingham's counsellors and an "alleged" advocate of the Court of Canterbury, to take the oath he handed him to read. But Byde, after studying the oath, announced that he would not do so. Whereupon Courtenay suspended him "totally" from his office as advocate. The oath Byde refused to take read as follows:

> In the name of God, Amen. I . . . swear by these holy gospels of God that I shall never attempt to oppose, diminish, or injure the right, liberty, or privilege of the church of Canterbury, nor in any way oppose or arrange to have opposed the right, liberty, or privilege of said church, nor give counsel, aid, or favor to one who so opposes or who secures such opposition; on the contrary, I shall always support to the best of my ability all the rights, privileges, and liberties of that church. So help me God and these the holy gospels of God.

Then Courtenay demanded of Radulph Tregesiou, dean of the church of Exeter and also advocate of the Court of Canterbury that he read and take this oath, which he did after some "deliberation." Then the certification of the precentor was presented. This recounted the story of the outrage at Topsham and ended with a description of the futile effort to cite the bishop personally *viis et modis* and of the precentor's attaching the summons to the door of the cathedral. After reading of the certification, Courtenay turned to Brantingham and demanded (*instanter requisivit*) that he swear an oath of obedience to the church of Canterbury. Whereupon the bishop swore the following oath:

> In the name of God, Amen. I Thomas, bishop of Exeter, profess and promise that in all matters I shall pay to you William, by the grace of God archbishop of Canterbury, primate of all England and legate of the apostolic see, and to your successors who will be canonically instituted in that church as archbishops of Canterbury, and to the holy metropolitan church of Canterbury, the proper canonical obedience, reverence, and submission, according to the decrees of the Roman pontiffs; and I shall be ready to defend, maintain, and preserve, saving my order, your rights as archbishop of Canterbury and those of your successors and of said holy church of Canterbury. So help me God and these His holy gospels. And all these promises I confirm in writing by my own hand.

As the bishop read his oath, he kept his hand on the bible and, in confirmation of his oath, wrote the word *Volo* upon the document.[60]

After Brantingham had taken the oath, Courtenay again took up the question of what decrees were binding upon the members of the chapter. One of these presumably required all canons enjoying rents in the church to have paid for them within the time stipulated under pain of deprivation and other punishment assigned at the discretion of their superior. To the archbishop's question whether this statute was being observed, the dean and chapter confessed that it was not. Then there was another statute, this one requiring all clerks who held dignities in the church and all resident canons to be *in missa et in mensa* for forty-six days each quarter, for each benefice they held in the church of Exeter. This statute they also admitted was not being observed.

The archbishop than asked, first the bishop of Exeter as the superior and next the others who held dignities and prebends in the church, whether they felt the observance of the first statute would be beneficial to the church of Exeter. All allowed that it would with the exception of three canons, Hugo Bridham, John Cheyne, and Robert Braybroke.[61] These three maintained that the statute had not been observed for the past sixty years and that, in any event, they were not bound by oath to observe it. As for the second statute, that requiring them to be *in missa et in mensa*, the great majority of the canons again admitted that its observance would benefit the church of Exeter. Two or three canons disagreed, however, and pointed out that the resident canons had any two days they wished each week for recreation, yet they received just as much as had they been continually *in missa et in mensa*.

Next Courtenay called attention to the generally ruinous condition of the chantries of churches appropriated to Exeter and how the laity suffered an inevitable loss in divine services as a consequence. To this criticism, the dean and chapter answered that the vicars of those churches were obliged to keep the chantries in a state of repair and that the archbishop should prod them about their negligence. But Courtenay rejoined that the portions of the vicars were so small they could ill afford to do this. To which the canons replied that had the vicars complained, they would have been ready to do what was just in the matter. At the end of this exchange the archbishop appointed the dean and chapter the following Saturday, July 2, when they were to reassemble in the chapter house to consider with him what statutes they would be expected to observe.

Courtenay now dismissed the dean and canons since "he wished, as he said, to discuss matters with the lord bishop concerning his person and what had been brought up against him in the course of his metropolitan visitation." These matters, obviously claims made by the bishop regarding his rights during a visitation, proved too difficult to resolve at one meeting, so the archbishop and bishop agreed to turn the problem over to their assessors. Courtenay warned Brantingham, however, that should their clerks fail to reach a satisfactory solution to their dispute, he was to be back in the chapter house on Tuesday, July 5, to hear the archbishop's decision.[62]

Courtenay must have been pleased over the bishop's appearance here at the chapter house on June 25, and the fact that their dispute had moved from the barren level of charge and counter charge to the more constructive one of discussion. Nevertheless, a tremendous gap still yawned between the positions each claimed regarding respective rights during a metropolitan visitation. The archbishop could not afford to assume an easy and early resolution of the dispute.[63] He accordingly had his clerks prepare two appeals, the one dated June 30 to be sent to the pope, the other, dated July 1, to be sent to a cardinal.[64] A third appeal which Courtenay presumably asked the king to prepare and send to the pope is dated May 31. According to the rubrics introducing these three appeals, none of them left England because of the early settlement of the dispute. Courtenay begged the pontiff in his letter not to give credence to the appeals several of his suffragans were forwarding him in an effort to have his right to visit revoked.[65] In the letter to the cardinal Courtenay asked that prelate to present his side of the dispute to the pope and to support other matters he had pending at the curia. As an earnest of his appreciation, he was sending the cardinal the sum of 200 florins.[66] Richard's letter urged the pope to intervene in the dispute between the archbishop and the bishop of Exeter (and several other of Courtenay's suffragans), lest irreparable injury be done the English church. Prudence deterred the crown from expressing more than general sympathy for the archbishop's plight.[67]

Meantime Brantingham's clerks had been busy gathering what evidence the registers of earlier bishops of Exeter and archbishops of Canterbury yielded on the question of a metropolitan's rights during the visitation of his province. Their findings must have proved damaging to the claims Brantingham had advanced, for the bishop presented himself on July 2 at the chapter house before Courtenay ready to make his submission.[68] In the prepared statement he had his clerk read, he admitted that he had never realized what extensive rights former archbishops of Canterbury had exercised during the course of a metropolitan visitation or that they possessed any prerogatives beyond those based upon common law. He had not known that they had the right to investigate and correct abuses; to hear and determine causes; to confer minor and major orders; to admit, institute, and induct persons; to confer benefices and prebends and to authorize the exchange, and accept the resignation, of benefices declared vacant on the archbishop's authority; to confirm the election of abbots, abbesses, and priors, and to bless those confirmed; to remove priors and to appoint others in their place; to probate the testaments of beneficed and noble persons and to appoint administrators even when these died intestate; to receive the revenue of vacant benefices and to dispose of this. An examination of the muniments and registers of past archbishops of Canterbury had substantiated all these claims with the exception of the rights to authorize the exchange of benefices and to collect the income of vacant benefices.

An examination of the registers of former bishops of Exeter had revealed, on the other hand, that they had exercised all these same powers during the course of a metropolitan visitation. In the interest of peace, Brantingham was agreeable to the archbishop's proceeding with his visitation in the manner suggested, that is, that both archbishop and bishop exercise all powers concurrently with the exception of the following which were exclusively the prerogative of the archbishop: namely, the correction of abuses, the probation of wills of persons who left property in different dioceses of the province, the institution to benefices of clerks presented to the archbishop, and the appointment of priors to offices declared vacant by the archbishop. Should further investigation reveal that the right to authorize exchanges of benefices and the collection of the fruits of vacant benefices had also been exercised by Courtenay's predecessors, the bishop expressed his willingness to grant Courtenay those same privileges. He confessed he had erred in his original contention that a metropolitan visitor was limited to the correction of notorious abuses brought to the archbishop's notice during the course of a visitation, and he begged Courtenay, in concluding his submission, to put out of his mind any base suspicions he might have entertained concerning him. When the clerk had completed the reading of the document, Brantingham handed it to Courtenay who accepted it and its contents, "saving the rights of the church of Canterbury."[69]

It will be seen that Brantingham, at least officially, made less than an unqualified capitulation. His principal mistake, so he insisted, was that he had reduced the metropolitan's prerogative, when visiting the diocese of a suffragan, to the correction of serious transgressions and abuses. He was now prepared to recognize Courtenay's right to exercise all the powers the archbishop had claimed, save only the right to authorize the exchange of benefices and the collection of the income of vacant benefices. These two powers he would deny the archbishop at least pending further investigation. He was also denying Courtenay's claim—and this was far more important—that once an archbishop moved into a diocese to visit, the bishop's right to exercise his ordinary episcopal powers immediately lapsed and remained suspended as long as the archbishop remained as an inquisitor in that diocese. In the mandate announcing his coming visitation, Courtenay had not mentioned this point, probably because he feared a formal statement to that effect would needlessly irritate episcopal sensibilities. Courtenay's action did demonstrate that to be his position, however, as when he invalidated Brantingham's order sequestrating the fruits of the church of Sutton on the ground that the bishop had no authority to issue such an order during the course of a metropolitan visitation.[70]

The realities of the situation may have convinced Courtenay to accept something less than the full neutralization of episcopal authority he had initially assumed. Except for authorizing the exchange of benefices and the collection of the fruits of vacant benefices. Brantingham had conceded him the right to proceed with his visitation as he chose. The archbishop and his clerks might even have been able to convince Brantingham that past archbishops had exercised both those rights, in which event Brantingham had promised he would withdraw his objections there. Courtenay might have reasoned, too, that he had already spent too much time in Exeter and to insist upon total capitulation on the part of Brantingham might hold him up indefinitely. Still he may not have conceded the bishop the right to exercise his episcopal rights concurrently with himself, for the day following their *concordia*, Brantingham asked Courtenay for permission to resume the exercise of his episcopal authority, which Courtenay agreed to grant him.[71] The promise of this permission subsequent to Brantingham's submission might have been part of the "settlement." There is no way of knowing. We, do know, however, that Courtenay was quite elated over the termination of the dispute, and he sent his effusive thanks to the chapter at Canterbury in acknowledgment of their assistance in bringing the dispute to a happy conclusion.[72]

Courtenay probably completed his visitation of the deanery of Exeter shortly after reaching his agreement with Brantingham in early July. On August 2 he transferred his investigations to the western part of the diocese of Exeter, to Cornwall, where his commissaries had already been engaged. Although little is recorded of his inquiries, his register provides elaborate itineraries he and his commissaries planned to follow in their visitation of that wild and sparsely settled country.[73]

The dispute between Courtenay and Brantingham over their respective rights during a metropolitan visitation extended on occasion beyond the screen of inhibitory mandates and *apostoli* and precipitated actual clashes over specific matters. When the pastor of St. Lawrence died, for example, Courtenay ordered the property of the deceased sequestrated and instituted one John Avery to the vacancy.[74] Brantingham protested the action of the archbishop as illegal and sought to invalidate it but without success,[75] although he covered his vexation by himself instituting Avery.[76] In the case of William de Wolastone, victory went to the bishop. When William died both archbishop and bishop issued orders of sequestration, although Brantingham succeeded in probating his will and appointing a successor.[77] Brantingham also prevailed when both he and Courtenay instituted presentees to the rectory of Camborne. Here the issue devolved ultimately over the question of who had the right to present. Since the crown made good its right, it was the crown's presentee whom Brantingham instituted and his appointment stood.[78]

What devious circumstances could attend the exercise of the right of presentation was demonstrated in the case of the benefice of St. Nectan in distant Cornwall. A certain William Fitz-Water presumed upon Courtenay's ignorance of the area, claimed the right to present to St. Nectan which he did not possess, and asked the archbishop to institute one Robert Baby.

Courtenay instructed his chancellor, Adam Mottrum, to make the necessary investigation, which Mottrum must have done in a cursory fashion, for he failed to discover the fraudulent nature of Fitz-Water's claim to present. When the archbishop, upon Mottrum's certification, ordered the archdeacon of Cornwall to induct Baby, that official refused for fear of incurring the sentence of excommunication threatened by Brantingham.[79] Whereupon Courtenay sent the archdeacon a second order, sharper than the first, with the assurance that Brantingham's censures were invalid and should be ignored. Although there is no further word in the register concerning this matter, Fitz-Water's deceit must eventually have become clear and Baby must have been removed.[80]

The register records several instances during Courtenay's visitation of Exeter of his having issued orders to correct questionable practices or halt cases of negligence. He directed the pastor of the church at Wydecombe, for instance, to cease demanding a half-mark for performing marriages. The pastor sought to justify the fee on the plea that it had been established by ancient custom. But Courtenay denounced the fee as exorbitant and as responsible for the practice of poorer members of the parish to cohabit without benefit of the sacrament of matrimony. He ordered the parishioners of Wydecombe, on the other hand, to make the offerings their rector had demanded on the four principal feasts of the year, that is, on Christmas, Easter, patron feast, and All Saints. They had been neglecting to do this.[81]

A general directive to the clergy of the diocese of Exeter excoriated ecclesiastical justices for demanding fees from litigants who had settled their differences outside of court. The recourse to ecclesiastical censure to compel such litigants to pay, the archbishop denounced as particularly reprehensible.[82]

A fairly general criticism Courtenay had occasion to level at almost every turn during his visitation of the diocese was the neglect of church buildings, walls, and chantries. In the instance of negligence on the part of the Cistercian monastery with respect to the vicarage at Luppit for which it was responsible, he personally took a hand. When the monks ignored his summons to discuss the inadequacy of the support they provided, he alienated a portion of their monastic lands and turned these over to the church. He also ordered the monastery to bear the cost of repairing the chantry of the church, of providing new prayer books, and of meeting the taxes assessed the church.[83]

During his visitation of the priory of St. Augustine at Plympton, he learned of the bitterness which existed between the priory and its dependent chapel of St. Mary. He left instructions, later implemented by formal mandate, that divine services in the chapel follow the Salisbury or secular rite rather than that of the Augustinian order; that the faithful of the chapel assume the expense of providing prayer books; that on the major feastdays of the year the faithful make their customary offerings of a penny, half-penny, or farthing, depending upon the income of the individual parishioners; that the faithful also attend services at the convent on the anniversary of its dedication as a demonstration of their loyalty and that they also go there to take part in the procession on Palm Sunday.[84]

Courtenay concluded his visitation of the diocese of Exeter about the end of August.[85] One bit of unfinished business concerning Exeter remained for him to attend to several months later when he was visiting the diocese of Worcester. This concerned the punishment of the three squires who had perpetrated the outrage against the archbishop's emissaries at Topsham. The register provides this description of their submission and of the severe penance the archbishop imposed upon them.

> On November 2, that is the day of the Commemoration of Souls, in the choir of the abbey or monastery of Gloucester in the diocese of Worcester, there presented themselves before the archbishop of Canterbury William Hughlot, John Usflet, and John Maundeware[86] who genuflected and humbly begged absolution, so it appeared, from the same reverend father for the offense they had recently committed against God and the church. With their hands upon the holy gospels, they swore to observe the laws of the church and to faithfully execute the penance imposed upon them. Whereupon the said lord of Canterbury absolved them according to the form of the law from the sentence of excommunication by which they were bound, but reserved their penance for the octave of St. Martin, which day the lord [archbishop] assigned them for receiving their penance, wherever the lord might then happen to be in his province of Canterbury. . . . Let it be noted that on November 18, that is the octave of the feast of St. Martin, the year of our Lord 1384, in the private chapel of the manor at Lambeth, there appeared before the lord archbishop of Canterbury William Hughlot, John Usflet, and John Maundeware; upon whom

the same lord of Canterbury imposed the following penance: namely, that each of them, on some double feastday before next Easter, take part in a procession in each of the cathedral churches of Exeter, London, and Canterbury, with their heads uncovered, and each carrying in his hand a wax taper weighing three pounds, which they will offer to God and to the church during the solemnities of the mass, after the gospel; and the same William, John, and John will provide the necessary funds to have a suitable chaplain celebrate mass for an entire year before the tomb of the earl of Devon, recently deceased and buried in the said cathedral of Exeter, for his soul, those of his parents, and for the souls of all the faithful departed; and each of them shall pay 20 shillings toward the repair of the walls of the city of Canterbury and shall bring to the lord of Canterbury free testimonials attesting to their having fully carried out their penance, signed with the seals of the prior and convent of Canterbury and of the deans of the cathedral churches of Exeter and London.[87]

VISITATION OF THE DIOCESE OF BATH AND WELLS

Next on Courtenay's itinerary after Exeter in his progress about the province as metropolitan visitor was the adjoining diocese of Bath and Wells. He had originally planned to begin its visitation on July 11, but "because of certain difficult matters experienced in our yet uncompleted metropolitan visitation of the diocese of Exeter," as he explained to John Harewell, the bishop of Bath and Wells, he would not be able to do so before September 15.[88]

Bishop Harewell was advanced in years and may have been in declining health for he died two years later. Whether it was because of his age, the archbishop's eminence which perhaps impressed him more than it had Brantingham, or the futility of resistance as demonstrated in neighboring Exeter, the bishop offered no opposition and the visitation of his diocese proved accordingly short and uneventful.

Courtenay spent a week, September 15 to 22, visiting the cathedral, and the following two weeks visiting the religious houses of Bath, Bruton, Michelney, Athelney, Taunton, the Hospital of St. John the Baptist at Bridgwater, and the abbey of

Glastonbury. At the parish church of Yeovil (Yeuele), which he visited on September 24, he conferred minor and major orders. The register records his cross-examination of a Peter Gardiner in the chapter house of the priory of Taunton over Gardiner's title to the parish church of Meriet (Meriott). To prove the genuineness of his title, Peter presented two letters, one of his institution under the seal of the bishop of Bath, the other a certification of his induction as rector of the church under the seal of the official of the archdeacon of Taunton. Courtenay in his examination learned that although Gardiner had been properly inducted as pastor of the church, he had agreed before his collation to resign the benefice into the hands of the abbot of Muchelney, with the understanding that should the abbot manage to secure possession of it for his abbey, Gardiner could expect to be compensated with either another benefice or a pension.[89]

Despite the straightforwardness of Gardiner's answers, Courtenay felt obliged to order the fruits of Meriet sequestrated in view of the understanding between Gardiner and the abbot. He thereupon dismissed Gardiner with instructions to return on the eighth juridical day following the feast of All Saints to learn his decision in the matter. Gardiner must have decided to accept the inevitable and resign his benefice without further ado, for he presented himself on October 22, several weeks earlier than the day appointed, when the archbishop was busy visiting the college at Stratford-on-Avon. Courtenay accepted Gardiner's resignation of Meriet but then promptly reinstated him upon the request of Bishop Harewell and because, too, of the man's "honesty."[90] Courtenay left the rest of the visitation of the diocese to his commissaries.[91]

VISITATION OF THE DIOCESE OF WORCESTER

From Bath and Wells Courtenay moved into the diocese of Worcester early in October and began his investigations on the eighth of the month in the monastery of St. Augustine at Bristol. He would ordinarily have had to begin his visitation with the cathedral at Worcester, but Pope Urban's indult had exempted him from that requirement. While at St. Augustine's Courtenay was told of the great difficulty the canons had in keeping their white habits and the vestments used for divine service tidy because of the high, black boots that they wore. He therefore issued the following mandate:

> William . . . to the abbot and canons of the monastery of St. Augustine. . . . Although it is proper that in the house of God holy religion should possess that beauty of character which pleases God internally while being pleasant to those looking at its externals, nevertheless, it was reported to us during our recent metropolitan visitation of your monastery, that the canons of said monastery, whose habit is white, wear high boots of black leather for footwear, whose lack of cleanliness, together with the fullness of their habits, cause the vestments of the altar to become soiled, unseemly, and filthy, so that visitors are scandalized and the cost of new habits and sacred vestments grows extremely heavy.
>
> We, therefore, wishing to enhance your honor as is proper and your service as is necessary, by these presents do extend you permission to use shoes of black or brown cloth instead of boots within the walls of the monastery, so long as the price of cloth does not exceed twenty pence a yard. And lest our indulgence provide you the occasion of levity and sensuality, we ordain that when it becomes necessary to go outside the monastery, not shoes as we have permitted, except for reasonable cause and with permission of the abbot, but boots shall be used.[92]

Courtenay also discovered at St. Augustine's that the properties belonging to the monastery were being poorly administered and that the buildings and walls were becoming dilapidated. He accordingly left instructions that the treasurer introduce certain reform measures in order to correct that situation. This the treasurer failed to do, and in an undated order issued some time later, Courtenay denounced the treasurer for his "manifest contempt of our orders" and suspended him and his six assistants. The treasurer was to be permanently barred from ever again administering the properties belonging to the monastery.[93]

The archbishop visited without incident the cathedral and its chapter on October 13 and 14 and during the three weeks following the abbeys at Pershore, Alencestre, Tewkesbury, Gloucester (St. Peter, by commissaries), Wynchcombe, and Cirencester; the churches at Fladbury, Tredyngton, Kempsey, and Cleeve; the collegiate churches at Stratford-on-Avon and Warwick; and, with the assistance of commissaries, the priories at Warwick, Studley, Great Malvern, Lanthony, Gloucester (St.

Bartholomew), and Lechlade. When he found the prior at Lechlade lacked a title to his office, he provided him one.[94]

Three weeks after leaving the cathedral, Courtenay sent the bishop a mandate from Gloucester with instructions that he permit a clerk of the diocese to clear himself by means of compurgation. The clerk was languishing in prison, in a civil prison at that, on the charge of stealing a black horse. Despite the fact that the clerk had steadfastly insisted upon his innocence and that the testimony brought against him was false, he had been denied the opportunity to clear himself.[95]

While Courtenay was visiting the diocese of Worcester, the cause of a certain Agnes Ayet, a resident of the town of Walton, was brought to his attention. Agnes had married William Straunge, son of John Straunge, and the two had lived together as man and wife and had been referred to as Mr. and Mrs. by their neighbors. Some time after the marriage, William, "unmindful of his salvation," had abandoned Agnes without apparent cause or permission. Courtenay cited both William and John to appear for questioning, the father presumably because he must have had something to do with his son's delinquency. The register reports nothing further concerning Agnes' problem.[96]

Approximately ten miles from the cathedral city of Worcester lay the great Benedictine abbey of Evesham. Since the archiepiscopal register is silent about the monastery and there is no echo anywhere of a contest between the monastery and the archbishop over the latter's right to visit, one may assume Courtenay never had that institution on his itinerary. The chronicler does describe, however, the anxiety occasioned in the monastery by the archbishop's proximity while visiting Worcester. He says that the abbot, Roger Zatton, hurried over to Worcester when he learned of Courtenay's arrival, and invited the archbishop to stop at his manor at Offensham on his way to Alcester, an invitation the archbishop gladly accepted. When the abbot had gone, however, certain persons who were envious of Evesham's proud independence suggested to Courtenay that the only reason the abbot had proffered the invitation was to make sure the archbishop would not take the road past Evesham to Alcester. They charged the abbot further with having instructed his monks at Evesham to bar the archbishop entrance should he put in an appearance. The gossipy chronicler tells us that the archbishop's back went up at this information and he swore he would visit Evesham, exemption or no exemption. When the abbot learned of this unfortunate turn, he hurried back to Worcester but failed to convince the indignant archbishop of the sincerity of his invitation.

After dining with the rector of Fladbury, the archbishop rode up to the monastery on the afternoon of October 18 where the abbot, monks, and many of the townspeople were on hand to greet him. The abbot received him humbly and in the hearing of all invited him to enter the abbey, but only if he came as an ordinary prelate, not in the role of metropolitan inquisitor. Courtenay reassured the abbot that he had never intended to violate the privileged position of the monastery by the exercise of his archiepiscopal authority. He then dismounted, entered the abbey church, and knelt in prayer before the high altar for some time before taking his leave.[97]

VISITATION OF THE DIOCESE OF CHICHESTER

Courtenay completed his visitation of the diocese of Worcester on November 10, after which he returned to Lambeth.[98] It may have been only a coincidence, but the special privileges Pope Urban had extended him in 1382 lapsed that same November. Apart from some investigations conducted in his own diocese of Canterbury,[99] Courtenay now interrupted his visiting until the summer of 1388 when he sent a mandate to the president of the cathedral chapter at Chichester informing him of his early arrival.[100]

That Courtenay may not have interrupted his progress through his province in November 1384 simply by accident is suggested by his appeal to Pope Urban late in 1385 or early 1386[101] for an extension of the privileges he had granted him in 1382. Caution had recommended the first appeal to Rome for special privileges; after his experience with Brantingham, Courtenay would have been the first to admit the foolhardiness of attempting a visitation without such special privileges.

Pope Urban proved receptive to Courtenay's request and in a bull dated April 23, 1386, extended the same sweeping privileges he had granted in his first bull and even more. For in response to Courtenay's complaint that by the time the bull of 1382 had reached England, more than a year had elapsed of the two-year period the bull was to run, and that the archbishop had only visited three of the eighteen dioceses of his province and had not even visited all the institutions in those three dioceses, the pope placed no time restriction on this second indult. And he swept aside "contrary apostolic constitutions and statutes and customs of any kind."[102]

The visitation of Chichester began with the cathedral on July 22. Since the bishop, Thomas Rushook, was in exile,[103] the president of the chapter had made the necessary preparations, and it was he who presented Courtenay the certification. After part of this lengthy document had been read, Courtenay ordered a halt and had his own monition read which warned all members of the clergy to cooperate with him and his commissaries in this visitation. Of the visitation itself, the register has little to record. There may have been little to record. A year later, after Rushook's exile had been decided and the pope had officially translated him to the Irish see of Kilmore, Courtenay appointed Philip Galeys vicar general of the diocese and gave him instructions to visit monasteries, hospitals, churches, and holy places of the diocese.[104] Since a second visitation within a period of two years would scarcely have been necessary, one may assume the archbishop's own visitation in July of 1388 did not extend beyond the cathedral itself. For so brief a visitation the short note in the register would suffice, namely, that "the said lord archbishop discovered some abuses in this visitation which required correction."[105]

VISITATION OF THE DIOCESE OF ROCHESTER

Courtenay's register notes next after Chichester the visitation of the diocese of Rochester a year later in the summer of 1389. The death of Thomas Brunton, its ordinary, earlier that year, may have prompted the archbishop to undertake the visitation of the diocese at this particular time. His letter, dated June 16, 1389, notified the prior of the cathedral chapter to expect him at the cathedral on July 5 but was followed by a second letter postponing his arrival to July 26. Then because of "difficult business elsewhere," he appointed his chancellor, Adam Mottrum, to take his place. The register provides but a brief notice of Mottrum's visitation of the cathedral clergy and nothing further.[106] Courtenay must have assigned the major burden of visiting to Robert Bradegar, whom he appointed vicar general of the diocese in June 1389.[107]

VISITATION OF THE DIOCESE OF LINCOLN

Less than two months after Courtenay announced his intention to visit Rochester, he sent a letter to John Buckingham, bishop of Lincoln, dated August 5, 1389, with notice of his expected arrival at Lincoln cathedral on October 7. Because of the great size of the diocese, the archbishop explained to the bishop that, in the interest of time and convenience, he would begin his visitation in the southern part which reached within twenty miles of London.[108] Somewhat puzzling was Courtenay's observation in this letter to the bishop that, in accordance with Pope Urban's wish, he was continuing his visitation where he left off, which, he said, was with the visitation of Worcester. The archbishop may not have classified the visitations of the dioceses of Chichester and Rochester that intervened as formal visitations inasmuch as he had turned the bulk of the work over to his commissaries.

Courtenay began his visitation on September 16 with the church at Hatfield in the archdeaconry of Huntington. Because the rector failed to appear, the archbishop ordered the church's income sequestrated.[109] He also took time to correct certain abuses which had come to his attention before moving to the deanery of Baldock. On September 18 he conferred minor and major orders on some fifty candidates at Biggleswade. The church at Biggleswade was exempt from episcopal jurisdiction, which might account for its receiving direct announcement of the visitation from Courtenay to supplement notice it received from the bishop. The vicar announced to Courtenay that he had carried out his instructions pertaining to the visitation and, as ordered, had cited all the priests living within the confines of the parish, together with "parishioners of said church, that is, of the village of Bykeleswade four, and from each vill of the parish two of the more responsible. . . ."[110]

Courtenay visited the priory of St. Neot on September 19, that of Huntington on September 20. During the solemnities of the mass said by the archbishop at Huntington, a certain woman of the aristocracy, Dame Matilda Wake by name, "upon her urgent insistence," made a public vow of chastity. Her vow, spoken in French, is recorded in the register with Matilda's sign, a cross, inscribed at the end.[111]

The archbishop visited Ramsey abbey on September 23 and celebrated mass upon the request of the abbot. The scribe notes that Courtenay said mass all the more willingly after learning that his predecessor, Archbishop Walter Reynolds, had read mass there exactly 69 years before.[112]

On September 23 Courtenay visited Peterborough Abbey and preached on the text, "*Religio munda est se immaculatum custodire.*" Among other matters that required his attention at Peterborough was the orthodoxy of William Broughton, one of the monks of the community, who was

> erring in his Catholic faith and had become infected by several of the conclusions, heresies, and errors of Master John Wycklyff which the church had condemned. The full official account concerning these conclusions, heresies, and errors is given above in this register. With paternal sollicitude, the [archbishop] brought the same Brother William back to the way of truth and had him say mass in his presence, although, because of his defection, he had refused to say mass or receive communion for a long time. The lord archbishop also ordered and instructed the abbot and members of the community to notify him as quickly as possible should Brother William not celebrate mass two or three times a week as he was required, assuming no legitimate impediment. Whereupon the abbot and several monks of the monastery spoke commendably of the life and speech of said Brother William.[113]

Courtenay next visited the abbey at Croyland on September 28 and addressed the community in a talk *utilem et solempnem* on the text, "*Alligatus spiritu vade in Jerusalem.*" Before he left the abbey he confirmed the abbey in its claims to its appropriated churches, to the chaplaincy of Croyland, to the pensions and demesne tithes owed by different parishes, and to its archidiaconal jurisdiction in Croyland.[114]

On September 30 he visited Spalding priory where one of the monks, Thomas Chyllenden, a "man of extraordinary distinction," preached *excellenter* on the text, "*Videamus si floruerit vinea.*"[115] Among the instructions Courtenay issued orally and in writing for the correction of certain irregularities and abuses that had come to light at Spalding were a series of rules relating to the practice of "seynys." The English term "seynys" or Latin *minutio* referred to a regimen of bloodletting; a *minutus* was a person undergoing such a regimen. Medieval medical thought credited significant health benefits to bloodletting, and it was considered a practice particularly beneficial to people who led a sedentary life. For this reason the *minutio* became popular in certain monastic orders, and monks might be permitted to go on what amounted to a furlough from monastic life and regulations as frequently as five times a year.[116]

Courtenay visited the rector of the church of St. Botulph on October 3 and the priests who said mass there, together with the clergy and people of Boston (Boteston) and several of the neighboring parishes. Two days later he visited the abbey at Bardney, issued orders looking to the correction of various abuses, and composed the bitterness which existed there between the abbot and the monks over the condition and administration of the monastery.[117]

Then on October 7, true to his advance schedule, the archbishop reached the cathedral at Lincoln. John Buckingham, the bishop, was there to greet him, together with the dean, canons, vicars, and other ministers of the church. After the archbishop had addressed the group on the text "*Quem diligit corripit pater,*" the dean, John Shepey, presented another discourse, his on a similarly apt text, "*Benedictus qui venit in nomine Domini.*" The bearing of the bishop and the dean must have been unusually respectful, for the scribe in describing this formal opening twice refers to the extreme reverence (*cum maxima* and *cum omni reverencia*) that the two men showed the archbishop. After the formal opening of the visitation in the cathedral followed by dinner, the actual investigations got under way when the bishop, "humbly rising, reported a number of irregularities in his church of Lincoln and begged [the archbishop] to provide a remedy for them."

The following three days Courtenay was busy visiting the dean and chapter and other ministers of the church. Not only must the "very many" abuses he discovered there have disturbed him, but also the negligence of the bishop in failing to cite the canons that were not in residence as he had been directed to do. The bishop humbly begged the archbishop's indulgence for his negligence, whereupon Courtenay issued a new mandate and adjourned the visitation for another month. He left the task of visiting these latecomers to his commissaries.

After leaving Lincoln the archbishop visited the monastery at Wellowe by Grimsby on October 13, Thornton on October 15 and 16, the vicar of St. Peter's at Barton-on-Humber on October 17, together with the twelve chaplains who celebrated mass there and the clergy and people of the parish. He also granted a certain John Bayly permission to have mass celebrated in the oratory of his hospice for the convenience of members of his household and for travelers for as long as he lived, provided the rights of the neighboring parish were not violated.

On October 18 the archbishop visited the Augustinian priory at Thornholm, the priory at Torkesey on October 20, the monastery at Ulveston on October 24, the priory at Landa on the following day, that at Kirkeby-Bellers on October 28, and the new college of Saint Mary at Leicester on October 29.[118] On October 30 he rode over to the monastery of St. Mary de Pré at Leicester and spent the night there before beginning his visitation of the community the following morning. The discord between the abbot and the monks he "benevolently" resolved, and he confirmed the settlement to which the two parties agreed, namely, that the community would select four of the more prudent monks annually to assist the abbot in the administration of the monastery.[119]

Next there came forward several of the "more responsible" men of the village, lay and clerical, with information that Lollardy had appeared in the area. They identified eight Lollards by name, one of them a chaplain;[120] "very many" others they could not identify. Courtenay ordered the eight men accused of Lollardy to be summoned by "dependable couriers" to appear before him the following morning (November 1). But they, "preferring to walk in darkness than in light," hid themselves so they could not be cited. "Thereupon, on the first day of November, that is, the feast of All Saints, after celebrating high mass at the main altar of the monastery, the lord archbishop, garbed in his pontificals and his attending clergy in stoles, holding a cross erect in his hands, with bells ringing, candles burning, then being extinguished and thrown to the ground, publicly and solemnly denounced as excommunicate and excommunicated each and all in general who openly taught, maintained, favored, and affirmed the said condemned heresies, errors, and conclusions, along with those who gave such persons aid, counsel, or sympathy."[121]

On November 2 Courtenay presided at a meeting to which several priests and "trustworthy" laymen of the community were invited for the purpose of discussing the problem of Lollardy there in Leicester. He questioned the members of the group individually—there were five priests, three of them pastors of the three churches in Leicester, and three burghers—who testified against the eight Lollards. These Lollards Courtenay then excommunicated by name, and in order to hurry them into submitting, interdicted divine services in the churches of Leicester as long as they tarried in the area. Several days later he issued two mandates on the issue of heresy. The first he addressed to the clergy of Leicester with instructions that they solemnly excommunicate the eight Lollards and continue their denunciations until word from him; furthermore, that they cite these Lollards to appear before him on the tenth juridical day following their citation. If possible, the eight were to be issued individual summonses. Should this be impossible, their friends and relatives should be notified and the summons posted in places where they might be expected to be hiding.[122] Courtenay addressed his second mandate to the mayor and bailiffs of Leicester. He instructed them to arrest the eight Lollards on authority of the king and to hold them for himself (the archbishop).[123]

Among the people of Leicester who were tainted by Lollard doctrines was an anchoritess, Matilda by name, who made her home in a cell in the churchyard of St. Peter's. Courtenay examined her "diligently" regarding Lollard tenets and because "she answered not fully to the questions but rather sophistically," he directed her to appear before him on November 6 in the monastery of St. James at Northampton for further questioning. She was expected to use the three days of grace to think better of her spiritual aberrations. As instructed, she presented herself at Northampton on November 6, confessed and abjured her errors, and declared her willingness to carry out the penance the archbishop might impose. Her humble bearing and sincerity must have touched the archbishop, for he dismissed her without demanding any penance, permitted her to return to her cell, and even granted an indulgence of forty days to anyone who might contribute to her support.[124]

Daventry presented the archbishop a bizarre situation when he visited that town on November 4. Relations between the townspeople and the Benedictine monastery had reached an impasse. It appears the townspeople wanted a right of way across the churchyard of the monastery which the monastery refused to yield them. Either to show their resentment or to bring pressure on the monastic community, the people in retaliation had conspired to steal tithes and other offerings made to the monastery and had hung a bell opposite the monks' dormitory and

were ringing this at "unusual hours." Courtenay prohibited further use of the bell and with the assistance of mutual friends
successfully resolved the controversy.[125] Exactly how he did this,
the scribe does not say.

On November 5 and 6 Courtenay visited St. James monastery at Northampton, Burcester on November 8, and Eynesham
on November 10. His visitation of the abbess and nuns at
Godstow which was scheduled to take no more than November
11, he extended an additional day because of "certain reasons."
On November 13 he visited the monastery at Oseney, St.
Frideswide's priory and Canterbury Hall at Oxford on November
14, and Merton College where he corrected certain abuses on
the two days following.[126]

The archbishop's register simply notes without elaboration
Courtenay's visitation of St. Frideswide's priory. The details are
left to the chronicler who, as in the case of Evesham, delights
in describing instances when a monastic establishment was able
to thwart a proud archbishop's ambition. He says the Benedictine
monks were in consternation when the archbishop's letter reached
them notifying them of his coming "for they had never seen
nor heard of a similar mandate of visitation." They busied themselves with devising stratagems to block the archbishop, but in
the end they decided against any deception. The soundest counsel
appeared that of seeking the advice of the abbot of St. Albans,
a man "universally revered,"[127] who was also a good friend of
the archbishop and, at the same time, the superior of some of
the monks studying at Oxford. Upon the prior's request, the
abbot wrote to Courtenay, accordingly, and asked him not to
visit the monks at Frideswide for it would prove as vexing an
experience for him as it would be for the students. The abbot's
letter must have mingled seriousness with humor, for the chronicler notes that the archbishop read it with a "merry countenance
and happy heart and invited the monk of St. Albans, the bearer
of the letter, *humanissime* to dinner."

After dinner, however, the archbishop was all business.
He explained to the monk that while he would very much like
to please the abbot of St. Albans, "his special friend," yet for
the sake of the rights of Canterbury he would not drop his plan
to visit the college of Black Monks, not even if "the king of
England threatened him with his edicts." Since it was a college
and had a prior, he must visit its monks.

"To this the monk of St. Albans replied that it was not a college since those living there possessed no common seal, nor was the place endowed with temporalities and spiritualities; and many other things were missing to make it a college. The archbishop answered: 'We wish,' he said, 'to come and see and inquire how things are with you.' The monk replied: 'Lord,' he said, 'if you should come to that place you will have no authority to inquire about such matters, except from the non-exempt monks, and you have already visited them in their own monasteries. They should not be visited a second time by you.' The archbishop answered: 'It is certain,' he said, 'that they have not been visited by me in their monasteries; indeed, their abbots excused them on the plea that they were in school. Wherefore in their schools we plan to visit them.' "

Here one of Courtenay's clerks interposed, a doctor of laws, and declared that the archbishop could even visit the monks from exempt monasteries since, as long as they were in school, they were under the jurisdiction of the chancellor. This statement the monk of St. Albans denied, but insisted rather that exempt monks enjoyed such privileges that only the pope himself or his legate *a latere* could exercise any authority over them when they were outside the monastery.

Although the chronicler says the archbishop appeared to be giving way to the persuasiveness of the monk, when the prior returned from St. Albans and spoke to Courtenay, the archbishop told him quite firmly that he would visit St. Frideswide. The following Sunday evening the prior and all the monks of the college, exempt and nonexempt, presented themselves before Courtenay in the church of St. Frideswide. When the archbishop asked "whether they had come to submit, the prior answered, no, rather to gain his good will. And the lord archbishop answered kindly: 'And I hold you excused; nor do I ever intend to disturb you.' And that was the end of said business."[128]

Several considerations could have deterred Courtenay from visiting the college of Black Monks at Frideswide had he been so minded. There was, first, the probability that the presence of exempt monks in the community could have made the task impractical or embarrassing. Then his good friend, the abbot of St. Albans, had personally intervened, and if their friendship was not sufficiently powerful to discourage Courtenay from visiting, prudence should have. For the abbot had great influence both at Rome and Westminster, and the archbishop might have hesitated over antagonizing so distinguished a churchman.[129]

The abbot may have appreciated Courtenay's good will in not visiting St. Frideswide, for when the archbishop was visiting Dunstable he sent his prior to him with an invitation to come to St. Albans "to refresh himself and stay overnight." Courtenay was most happy to accept the invitation, and he ate and slept at the monastery "at the expense of the abbot." This fact the chronicler is careful to note, and also the fact that the archbishop "did not ask to visit nor did he attempt anything that might threaten our privileges, nor were the bells of the monastery or the churches of the village rung at his coming or leaving." Courtenay did advise the monastery to draw up a list of the exempt Benedictine houses and churches in the province which his successors might use as a guide in their visiting. "But in our dilatoriness," the chronicler laments, "we failed to do this, nor did we obey his salutary advice, so that we had nothing from this archbishop to show to later ones."[130]

To return to the archbishop in his progress southward from Lincoln—he visited the abbey at Dorchester on November 17 where three of the Lollards he had excommunicated at Leicester, together with the wife of one of them, presented themselves and made their submission. One of the three was Richard Waystathe, apparently the only priest tainted with Lollardy at this time in the area of Leicester. What penance the archbishop gave Waystathe is not revealed. The penance he imposed upon the two men, William Smyth and Roger Dexter, and upon the latter's wife, Alice, is recorded in the register. The document reads as follows:

> On the Sunday following their return to their homes, each of them shall walk in front of the procession in the collegiate church of St. Mary's in Newark, William and Roger in their undershirts and drawers, Alice in her shift, with feet and heads bare; said William with an image of St. Catherine,[131] Roger and Alice with crucifixes in their right hands, and each of them carrying in their left hands candles of one-half pound weight. They will genuflect and devoutly kiss those images three times, once at the beginning of the procession, again when it is half completed, and again at the end, in reverence to the crucifix, in memory of His passion, and in honor of the Virgin. They will enter said church with the procession and will stand before the image of the crucifix while high mass

is being sung, with their images and candles in their hands as indicated. At the conclusion of the mass of the day, said William, Roger, and Alice will offer these [candles] to the celebrant of the mass.

Then on the Saturday following, in the open public square or marketplace of said village of Leicester, the same William, Roger, and Alice, wearing as before nothing beyond their underwear, and with said images in their right hands, will kiss these three times while genuflecting, once at one end of the marketplace, again at the middle, and finally at the farther end. William, because he has had some education, will recite with devotion an antiphon and the collect of the feast of St. Catherine, said Roger and Alice, being illiterate, will recite the Lord's prayer and Ave Maria. On the Sunday immediately following they will stand in the parish church of said village and do in all respects as they did the preceding Sunday in the collegiate church. The candles they will be carrying, they will humbly and devoutly offer to the vicar or chaplain who celebrated the mass.

Because the said penitents may suffer bodily injury from standing so long uncovered during the present cold weather, we are willing to so moderate the severity of this penance, that after they have entered said churches, while they are hearing mass, they may put on what additional clothes they may need, providing, however, that their feet and heads remain uncovered.[132]

One can appreciate Knighton's observation on this penance: "and so in great measure was the public arrogance of the profane doctrines of the Lollards or Wycliffites suppressed more from fear of the archbishop than from love of God. . . ."[133]

The running account of the visitation of the diocese of Lincoln as provided by the Lambeth register concludes with the description of the penance imposed upon the three Lollards. From scattered references it appears that the archbishop visited Nutley abbey on November 20, Whitchurch on November 21, and Ashridge on November 25.[134] Some time earlier that month he visited the abbey at Nuncoton where he instituted a young clerk as vicar of one of the abbey's dependent parishes after first examining him and receiving his oath to remain always in residence. He also left orders with the abbey to increase the revenues allotted this parish since he considered them inadequate.[135]

The most impressive list of instructions the archbishop gave any of the institutions he visited in his circuit about his province was the one he left the Benedictine abbess and nuns of Elstow. He had learned from actual investigation during his visitation, from conversation with responsible persons, and from documents sent him, so he explained in the preface to his decree, that although the convent had prospered and was then realizing an income of more than 600 marks annually, nevertheless, the nuns had not benefited from this prosperity even though "laboring in the vineyard of the Lord and carrying the burden of the day and the heat. . . ." To correct this situation he left these among other instructions: that the daily fare of the nuns be increased; that no difference be made between the bread served the abbess and that given the other members of the community; that no money or gift be demanded of girls seeking to become nuns; that two mature nuns be entrusted with the finances of the community and that the chest in which the valuables were kept should be locked with three keys, the abbess and two treasurers each having one; that all officials of the convent, including the abbess, provide an accounting of the funds passing through their hands; that particular care be taken in the selection of such officials as the sacristan and custodian of the gate; that the sick in the infirmary be properly attended to; that lay women no longer be permitted to occupy rooms within the cloister; that no men, religious or lay, be allowed within the precincts of the monastery when the gates were to be closed; that all nuns take part in the recitation of the divine office unless prevented by illness or other reasonable cause.[136]

The archbishop also left the monks of Caldwell priory a formidable list of instructions for the purpose of correcting irregularities he had learned of during his visitation of the community. All monks were expected to be prompt and regular in attendance at the recitation of the divine office. Because occasional monks delegated with the task of collecting rents had apparently succumbed to temptation and absconded, rents were now to be paid directly to the monastery's agent who lived in the neighboring town. The sick were not to be neglected, nor were members of the laity to have access to the cloister at any time. These and other regulations, notably those of Archbishop Kilwardby, were to be read two or three times each year in the hearing of all in the chapter house, with any monk guilty of nonobservance being strictly "disciplined each time with fasts and other severe punishment, according to the nature of his transgression. . . ."[137]

Perhaps the religious community where Courtenay found most awry was the chapter of the cathedral of Lincoln.[138] It will be recalled that he had spent a full three days visiting the priests associated with the cathedral and that he had discovered "very many" abuses. Among the injunctions the archbishop issued for the priests of the cathedral—which did not necessarily reflect any negligence on their part—was one concerned with the chantries attached to the church. He had learned that in many of these chantries only Requiem masses were being said in accordance with the wishes of their patrons, but the result was that a "lack of devotion grows stronger in both celebrant and those hearing mass, while the will to do good grows weak." He accordingly gave orders that chantry priests say the mass of the day on all feasts of the Blessed Virgin and of St. Hugo, on nine simple feastdays of their choice during the year, and during Lent when they said mass for the convenience of travelers, artisans, and servants. Courtenay warned those priests who received prebends to which were appropriated houses and hospices owing gratuities to the poor that they assume such responsibilities under pain of sequestration.[139] The archbishop finally authorized the dean to combine chantries which were too poor to provide for a priest and which had become a serious financial burden for the cathedral, with the stipulation, however, that all deceased patrons be remembered in the masses read in the chantries that remained.[140]

Of quite a different character was a second series of injunctions Courtenay left the cathedral chapter at Lincoln. The nature of these injunctions suggests, in fact, the presence of positive corruption in the community, the result probably of a long period of negligence in the observance of monastic regulations and carelessness in the recruitment of new members. Nowhere in his visitations did the archbishop encounter such great need for reform as at Lincoln. His mandate, issued at Croydon on May 12, 1390, condemned by implication the monastery for bending to influence and appointing men as vicars who were unworthy either for lack of learning or virtue or both. The archbishop also reminded the community that levity and idle conversation were entirely out of order during divine services or the recitation of the office, and he ordered immediate suppression of the boisterous and frivolous antics that were permitted annually to disgrace the feast of Circumcision.[141]

VISITATION OF THE DIOCESE OF SALISBURY

It was probably some time in November 1389 when Courtenay completed his visitation of the diocese of Lincoln. He had been on the road since July when he began his investigations at Chichester, and a weary road he must have found it, traveling the long distances around the diocese of Lincoln on horseback and eating and sleeping at some different place almost every day during those months. Nevertheless, in the spring of 1390 he was ready to resume his travels. He decided to begin with the diocese of Salisbury which lay west of London, its easternmost point hardly twenty miles from the city. How early he notified John Waltham, the bishop, of his intention to visit Salisbury is not known—incidentally no reference to Courtenay's visitation is recorded in Waltham's register—but it must have been some time before May 14. For it was on that day that Waltham presented himself to Courtenay in the latter's manor at Croydon and, with the air of the proverbial cat that had swallowed the canary, handed the archbishop a letter he had received from Pope Boniface IX.

What Pope Boniface had given Waltham was a brief nullifying the special privileges Pope Urban had extended Courtenay in 1382 and renewed in 1386 for the visitation of his province. Bishop Waltham probably welcomed Pope Urban's death in October 1389 as providing him an opportunity to block Courtenay's visitation, and he promptly appealed to the new pope Boniface IX, for an exemption.[142] Boniface apparently sympathized with Waltham's plea that he needed protection against arbitrary acts he had reason to believe Courtenay would attempt under cover of Urban's indult. He accordingly issued a bull in his behalf freeing him from the effect of the extraordinary privileges his predecessor had granted Courtenay. But he did remind Waltham that he must submit to Courtenay's visitation should this be conducted "in accordance with his [the archbishop's] rights under common law. . . ."[143]

Bishop Waltham would have preferred a complete revocation of Courtenay's right to visit, although that would have been expecting too much. What Boniface had conceded him would, nevertheless, serve his purpose and would hold up the archbishop indefinitely in his plan to visit Salisbury. For if Courtenay might only visit the diocese of Salisbury by virtue of his metropolitan authority and according to the canonical form, he would first be obliged to visit his own cathedral and diocese of Canterbury which Waltham was convinced he had not done; furthermore, he would also have to visit every diocese of the province which had not been visited since the last visitation of Salisbury.

Courtenay must have been expecting Waltham's visit on May 14, for the register describes how he received the bishop "sitting judicially" in his manor at Croydon. It is probable that Courtenay had learned of Waltham's appeal to Rome and even possible that he had decided to visit Salisbury rather than some other diocese in order to punish Waltham for his audacity in seeking to challenge his authority.[144] The archbishop was, at any rate, not taken aback when Waltham showed him the bull nullifying his extraordinary powers, but bluntly informed the bishop that he was about to visit him and his diocese. He had, so he declared, "fully visited" his own diocese of Canterbury and other dioceses of the province as well and was now preparing to initiate a visitation of the diocese of Salisbury. And he warned the bishop not to offer any opposition.[145]

A few days later, probably on May 18,[146] Courtenay notified the bishop of the day and place he should expect him, namely July 11 at the cathedral, for which occasion he was to make the necessary preparations and summon the clergy Courtenay planned to visit there. In this mandate to Waltham, Courtenay made no reference to the papal indult Pope Urban had given him. He announced rather his intention to visit simply by virtue of "our metropolitan authority." And as if to warn Waltham again that he lacked any valid grounds for opposing his visitation, he prefaced his instructions to him with the reminder that he had already visited "fully our church of Canterbury, its chapter, the city and diocese of Canterbury, and its clergy and people." To make certain that his visitation would get under way as scheduled, whether the bishop honored his instructions or not, he had his mandate announcing the visitation sent to the dean of the chapter.[147]

Courtenay's suspicions concerning Waltham's lack of cooperation proved correct. Instead of summoning the clergy to the cathedral to meet there with the archbishop, the bishop instructed them to meet rather with himself or his delegated representatives in order to take counsel how best they might thwart the plan of the archbishop to visit. When Courtenay learned of the bishop's action, he issued an *inhibicio* dated June 15, addressed to the rectors, vicars, chaplains, curates, notaries public, and other clergy of the diocese, instructing them to warn the bishop, the dean, chapter, all those holding benefices in the diocese, and all other priests and ministers, to halt any obstructionism within ten days of receiving this notice and to honor his instructions under pain of the greater excommunication. The chapter was warned to do so under threat of an interdict.[148] Five days later he issued a similar *inhibicio* from Oxford.[149] Then as canons, vicars, and other members of the clergy, including several abbots, began gathering at Salisbury during the week following June 21 in answer to the bishop's summons, Courtenay issued yet another *inhibicio* for their special attention, with the warning "not to attempt anything to prejudice the visitation of the lord [archbishop] or in any way have anything attempted."[150]

True to his announcement, Courtenay rode up to Salisbury the evening of July 10, the day before he was to begin his visitation. Here is the scribe's description of the archbishop's arrival. "First to meet him on the road, some distance from the city near the old fort of Salisbury, were the mendicant friars in procession. The dean and chapter and other ministers of the church of Salisbury, in their copes and with cross and lighted candles, met him in procession at the entrance to the churchyard, whence they escorted him with honor to the high altar of the church of Salisbury. After the customary prayers had been recited and sung, the lord archbishop withdrew to the hospice which had been prepared for him." It was evident that the archbishop would have more cooperation here than perhaps the bishop would have liked.

Early next morning, "about the first hour," the archbishop entered the chapter house and formally opened his visitation. In the presence of a large number of the clergy, including the dean and his chapter, and "very many knights and noblemen," he delivered an address on what sounded like a particularly appropriate text under the circumstances, namely, "*Habete pacem et Deus pacis et dileccionis erit vobiscum.*" At the end of his sermon, Courtenay ordered the bishop to come forward to certify the execution of the mandate of visitation. But no bishop appeared, whereupon Courtenay prepared to excommunicate Waltham. Montagu, the Earl of Salisbury, and other noblemen "interceded," however, for the bishop and prevailed upon Courtenay to hold up action until after dinner.[151] Meantime, in order to expedite matters, the archbishop had the dean read his certification. This document listed the names of all clerks who held benefices or dignities in the cathedral whom the dean had either cited personally or, failing this, had posted notice thereof in their choir stalls.[152]

After these names had been called out and the few absent clerks declared contumacious, Henry Corbrygg, the bishop's proctor, stepped forward and presented his *procuratorium*.[153] When this had been read, he handed Courtenay the bishop's *provocacio* and informed him of its contents. This followed in substance the argument of Brantingham's *provocaciones*. It began with Waltham's assertion of his legitimacy as bishop of Salisbury and his consequent prerogative to exercise powers which prescribed right and long hallowed custom had established for "10, 20, 30, 40, 50, 60, 100 years and more, in fact, since the memory of man runs not the contrary. . . ." Included in these powers were all those Brantingham had enumerated and more still, for Bishop Waltham also claimed the right to prove the wills of persons who died leaving property in different dioceses of the province. The bishop insisted that during the progress of a metropolitan visitation, only he could exercise these powers, a fact he insisted was as well known to all of Courtenay's predecessors in Canterbury as it was to the present incumbent. But in order to bolster his position, he had secured an indult from Pope Boniface which exempted him from the force of the special privileges that Pope Urban had granted Courtenay, although it left him under obligation to submit to a visitation should the archbishop conduct this under common law. Under present circumstances he was, therefore, under no obligation to permit Courtenay to visit his diocese since Courtenay must first have visited his own diocese and all other dioceses not visited since the last visitation of Salisbury. This the archbishop had not done. Therefore, he was appealing to the apostolic see against Courtenay's manifest defiance of the law, and he was willing to include with his appeal those of his subordinates who might be interested. And he was asking for *apostoli*.[154]

Upon completion of the reading of this very long *provocacio* Courtenay handed Corbrygg *incontinenti* his *apostoli refutatorii* which dismissed the bishop's claims as wholly false. Whereupon Corbrygg produced an *appelacio*, similar in character

to the *provocacio* that had just been read, which he refused
to hand over to the archbishop, but insisted on reading it. "And
perceiving what the nature of the appeal was, the lord [arch-
bishop] handed said proctor *apostoli refutatorii* according to this
form of words: We judge said appeal to be introduced for false,
fictitious, and fabricated reasons, to be frivolous, vain, unjust,
invalid, and null, and for that reason we shall not honor it, but
repudiate it absolutely and in place of *apostoli* we give this our
answer and we present it in these writings."

The archbishop then adjourned proceedings until three
that afternoon and retired to a room in the cloister. At three
he returned to the chapter house, only to adjourn the meeting
again upon the request of the earl and other noblemen, this time
until the following morning at eight. That morning (July 12),
"in the hope of expediting his visitation, he diligently examined
the titles to the benefices of the dean and chapter to dignities,
minor dignities (*personatus*), administrations, or offices they held
in said church, as well as the letters of ordination of vicars, priests,
and other ministers of the church, together with the foundation
and endowment of chantries." He and his commissaries next questioned the assembled clerks "individually and in a group" on
certain matters relating to the visitation and made a record of
the information they gathered.

Upon completion of the visitation of the chapter, Courtenay ordered the bishop "publicly and solemnly'" summoned,
and when Waltham did not appear, waited for him until nine
o'clock.[155] Then upon the appeal of the earl, he agreed to adjourn
the meeting until three that afternoon, when he again returned
to the chapter house and ordered the bishop formally cited. Here-
upon Corbrygg came forward and presented yet another appeal
on the bishop's behalf. This reiterated the charge that the archbishop was conducting an illegal visitation inasmuch as he had
not yet visited his own diocese nor the other dioceses not visited
since the last visitation of Salisbury. It also accused Courtenay
of unlawful procedure in that he had prevented Corbrygg from
reading the bishop's first appeal, that to the request for *apostoli*
he had issued only *apostoli refutatorii*, and that he planned to
ignore the bishop's appeal to the apostolic see and excommunicate
him.[156]

Courtenay dismissed this appeal as quite as frivolous as
the first. Then after having carefully confirmed the fact that
Waltham had actually received a personal summons, he directed

him to be formally cited "frequently," and after waiting a "very long time" for him to put in his appearance, finally declared him contumacious and excommunicated him in these words:

> In the name of God, Amen. We William, by divine permission archbishop of Canterbury, primate of all England and legate of the apostolic see, do declare our venerable brother John, bishop of Salisbury, our suffragan and suffragan of our church of Canterbury, prebendary of the prebend of Potterne in the church of Salisbury, contumacious inasmuch as he has been lawfully cited and summoned to come here this day and to submit to our metropolitan visitation; and after waiting for him a very long time and he in no way appearing, we excommunicate him in these writings.[157]

Corbrygg now produced an *adhesio* which was a formal announcement containing the names of those persons who had declared their support of the bishop in his dispute with the archbishop and were joining their appeal to the apostolic see with his. The document listed the names of four archdeacons, several abbots, and a number of priests. This *adhesio* Courtenay also dismissed as a vain and frivolous appeal. Whereupon those members of the clergy who supported the archbishop in this controversy came forward with their own counter *adhesio*, this one including significantly the names of the dean and chapter, together with those of many priests associated with the cathedral, two abbots, and an abbess.

Courtenay adjourned his visitation of the cathedral at this point, but the following day ordered two of his clerks to go to Waltham's palace in Salisbury where the bishop "is well known to be staying. . . ." They were to summon him to appear at the cathedral on Thursday (July 14) to answer to charges of contempt, perjury, and disobedience.[158]

Although the controversy between Courtenay and Waltham had now deteriorated to the same nadir as the earlier one between the archbishop and Brantingham, several circumstances promised an easier settlement in the case of Salisbury. One was the presence of influential people like the earl of Salisbury who had watched the developments of the past few days with anxiety, had striven to prevent the excommunication of the bishop, and were now working hard for a reconciliation. Another was the fact that the bishop had not left the neighborhood, an implicit admission on his part that he did not plan to wage an extended campaign. Perhaps a third circumstance favoring an early termination of the dispute was the intervention of the crown. It issued instructions to the earls of Kent and Salisbury to keep themselves and their retainers on hand in order to maintain law and order, while warning the archbishop and bishop against doing anything that might endanger the peace of the land.[159]

The result was a quick settlement of the dispute and the submission of the bishop. The register credits the earl of Salisbury and "very many other knights" with persuading Waltham to revoke his appeals and to submit to Courtenay's visitation. Courtenay withdrew his censures accordingly and commissioned Stephen Percy, a vicar of the cathedral, to absolve the bishop of his sentence of excommunication and all the others who had been similarly censured. "And afterwards the bishop immediately revoked each and all his appeals and those made in his name against the lord [archbishop] and his metropolitan visitation. And the bishop humbly and publicly submitted himself in the chapter house to the visitation and, after their clerks had withdrawn to a distance, was diligently examined and actually visited by the lord [archbishop]. . . ."[160]

The submission of the bishop took place on Wednesday, July 13. On the following day Courtenay commissioned two of his clerks to continue the work of visitation at the cathedral, while he rode over to Wilton abbey where he visited the abbess and the older nuns on July 15, leaving the younger nuns to be visited by his commissary.[161] On July 17 he visited the monastery at Shafton and the monastery at Shirborne on July 20. The abbot of Shirborne, whose name had appeared in the bishop's *adhesio*, assured the archbishop that this had been done without his knowledge and wish.

From Shirborne the archbishop rode over to Exminster and spent more than a week with his mother. On July 31 he resumed his visitation with the parish church of Symondysbury, where he and his deputies visited the clergy and people of the deanery of Bridport. On August 1 he visited the monastery at Abbotsbury, the monastery at Cerne on August 2, that at Middleton on August 3, the parish church at Newton Castle on August 4, and had dinner there with the abbot of Glaston abbey. On August 5 he visited Maiden Bradley, the day following the college at Edyndon, on August 7 the church at Bedewynd, and the monastery at Abingdon on August 8. On August 9 he visited the church at Sutton Courtenay and spent the night at the priory of Wallingford. His visitation of the monastery at Reading covered August 10 and 11, while he visited the priory of Bisham on August 12. "And there the lord archbishop made an end to his progress in the diocese."[162]

While Courtenay's clerk recorded a detailed description of the archbishop's itinerary about the diocese of Salisbury, he appears to have overlooked the visitation of an occasional monastery. One such monastery was that of Shaftesbury which we must assume the archbishop visited on the basis of a mandate he issued more than two years after leaving the diocese. This was the grant of a dispensation to the aged abbess of the monastery permitting her to eat meat on days of abstinence. Courtenay probably dispensed her orally the day he visited the monastery, his mandate simply confirming the dispensation and making it official. The dispensation may be of interest.

> William . . . to Johanna Formage, abbess of the monastery of the nuns at Shaftesbury in the diocese of Salisbury. . . . While recently visiting by metropolitan right your monastery in head and members, we found you advanced in great and extreme old age. For that reason we are moved to mercifully grant you, by legitimate authority, a dispensation from the requirement to abstain, whether a voluntary denial and the result of a vow on your part or that generally required by the church or specifically by the diocesan, and to permit you to eat and use not only the products of animals such as milk, cheese, and eggs, but also to take, on days of extreme infirmity, not for pleasure sake but as a comfort to old age and debility, the flesh of animals.[163]

VISITATION OF THE DIOCESE OF CANTERBURY

In July 1393 Courtenay visited his own diocese of Canterbury. Was this for the first time as Bishop Waltham of Salisbury would have insisted, or had he already visited it in 1386 and 1387? Courtenay undoubtedly classified this earlier visitation as an official visitation. He had clearly made plans to visit his diocese in person in 1386, for he instructed the official of the archdeacon of Canterbury to summon all the clergy who were required to submit to his questioning. Something upset his plans, however, and prevented his doing any visiting in person, so he delegated the task to three commissaries.[164] Their commission he extended on January 6 when he instructed them to visit specifically the deaneries of Sutton and Dover, the parish church of Wingham, and other places in the diocese that were "not yet visited."[165]

One is inclined to accept the essential accuracy of the archbishop's contention that his visitation of 1386–1387 constituted a formal visitation, and that some time during 1387 Courtenay's commissaries completed the visitation of those places "not yet visited."[166] That no details of this visitation have been entered in the archepiscopal register need not arouse suspicion. Although the register provides a full account of the archbishop's own progress about the province, there is scarcely a word concerning the very considerable visiting his commissaries must have done in such dioceses as Exeter, Chichester, and Rochester. It would, furthermore, appear most inconsistent for Courtenay to have accepted all the inconveniences and annoyances of provincial visitation while ignoring the visitation of his own diocese, particularly since he could delegate this task so readily to deputies and have no fear their investigations would be blocked by clergy subject to other bishops. The deanery of Sutton was visited in 1386, and it was in that jurisdiction that Courtenay initiated his visitation in 1393.[167]

The visitation of the diocese began with the parish church of Lenham in the deanery of Sutton on July 8, 1393, with mass, followed by a sermon by Adam Mottrum, the archbishop's chancellor, and the reading of the articles of visitation. Next the dean of the deanery of Sutton read his certification concerning orders he had received from Courtenay's representative Robert Bradegar, the commissary general of Canterbury. Among these instructions, which were quite as detailed as those Courtenay had sent his different bishops preparatory to his appearing to visit their dioceses, was an order to collect the customary procuration fees "in victuals and beverages" from all persons who would be visited. After the reading of the dean's certification, Courtenay and his agents visited those members of the clergy who were present and spent the night there at Lenham.

The following day, July 9, Courtenay visited the clergy of Charing deanery at Ashford and had dinner and supper there. On July 10 he visited the priory of Bilsington and the clergy of the deanery of Lympne in the church of St. Nicholas at Romney on July 11. The day following he removed a sentence of interdict from the church of St. Martin at Romney.[168] Since his castle at Saltwood stood nearby, he rested there on July 13. On July 14 he visited the clergy of the deanery of Elham, on July 15 and 16 the priory of Dover, the Domus Dei, and the clergy of the deanery with the help of commissaries. "And the lord [archbishop] was there for two days at dinner and supper and was honorably received."

On July 17[169] Courtenay visited the clergy of the deanery of Sandwich and the clergy of the deanery of Bridge on the day following. For the three days, July 19 through July 21, he and his commissaries were busy visiting the priory and chapter at Canterbury. The task of visiting the clergy of the deanery he assigned his agents. He himself visited the monastery of St. Gregory at Canterbury on July 21, while his commissaries were visiting the clergy of the deanery of Westbere in the cathedral.[170]

Here at Canterbury, presumably on the occasion of this visitation, Courtenay found himself involved in a dispute with the bailiff and citizenry of the city. What had happened was that several officials of the city had carried their maces with them when they entered the precincts of the priory. The bailiff of the city, these officials, and members of the citizenry appeared before the archbishop in answer to his summons and received a sharp reminder from him that "from a time and through a time whereof the memory of man ran not to the contrary," no official of the city had presumed to carry his mace within the precincts of the priory for any cause whatsoever. Fortunately for the peace of the community, the bailiff and officials confessed their error and promised to respect in the future the traditional immunity of the priory.[171]

Courtenay continued his visitation on July 22 in the parish church of Ospringe where he visited the clergy of the deanery. The day following he visited the monastery of Faversham and the prioress and nuns of Davington. On July 24 he visited the clergy of the deanery of Sittingbourne in the parish church of that town. The next day, July 25, he visited the monastery of the nuns of Sheppey, where he received the solemn profession of the abbess and of individual nuns. Sheppey proved the last stop on his progress about his diocese, for on July 26 he notified the official of the archdeacon from his manor at Maidstone that since he had completed his visitation of Canterbury, he could resume his office of proving wills and administering the goods of the deceased.[172]

VISITATION OF THE DIOCESE OF HEREFORD

On April 15, 1396, three years after the visitation of the diocese of Canterbury, Courtenay addressed a mandate to John Trefnant, the bishop of Hereford, notifying him of his intention to visit his diocese. The bishop was to make the usual preparations, principally that of summoning all members of the clergy who held benefices. He was to expect him at the cathedral on June 5. To lend his order added authority, the archbishop cited the bull he had received from Pope Urban in 1386 which had extended him special privileges in the visitation of his province.[173]

Was there any particular reason why Courtenay should have decided to visit Hereford rather than any one of a half-dozen other dioceses he had still to visit? There may have been. In 1393 he had become involved in a dispute with Trefnant which had lasted two years and had ended in the archbishop's yielding.[174] Then even before this controversy had ended, Trefnant had raised vigorous objection to a tax that the province was to pay to the archbishop and had announced that he would not pay it.[175] And in April 1396 he had still made no move to do so. Would not Courtenay have welcomed the opportunity to visit Hereford in order to bring this fiery, recalcitrant young bishop to heel?[176]

Trefnant responded to the archbishop's mandate as Courtenay probably expected. He issued a *provocacio* or protest, more defiant than any of Brantingham's or Waltham's, against the attempt of anyone, even of one clothed with episcopal dignity, who might seek to prejudice his rights, liberties, and privileges, and those of his church, by "citing, suspending, interdicting, excommunicating, or oppressing in anyway," and he was appealing to the apostolic see against any such attempt.[177] His formal appeal followed on April 30. He protested first against the instructions the archbishop had given him. He was "above charge and service"; the duty of summoning his clergy which the archbishop had assigned him was "base and counted among low services, not suitable or worthy of a bishop; that it was contrary to justice to require him to summon clerks who had received their benefices from him; that he was taking his appeal to the apostolic see, and that he was asking for *apostoli*.[178]

How Courtenay reacted to the bishop's protest and request for *apostoli* we shall never know. The Lambeth scribe makes no mention of the visitation mandate Courtenay sent to Trefnant, probably because the matter never proceeded beyond that point. What probably happened is that Courtenay grew ill shortly after issuing this mandate and was never again in a position to follow it up. His death in July therefore terminated a dispute which promised to exceed in bitterness those in which he had become involved with Brantingham and Waltham. Would Trefnant have prevailed against the archbishop? He had long service in Rome behind him; in fact, he probably owed his appointment as bishop of Hereford to Pope Boniface, since he stepped directly from the papal curia to the diocese; and he was an expert in canon law, at least in his own opinion.[179] Still this was the same Pope Boniface who had warned Waltham that he would have to accept Courtenay's right to visit if this were carried out according to canonical form. The pope could hardly have done an about-face and have excused Trefnant from this same obligation, although he could have directed the curia to hold up a decision indefinitely. In all probability, however, Courtenay would have forced the issue long before Rome could have interfered. He had done this when Waltham had defied his order. Had the archbishop been in good health, he would undoubtedly have appeared at the cathedral on June 5 as he had announced and, with the indirect assistance of the crown, he would have forced Trefnant to submit.[180]

⸭{8}⸭

COURTENAY AND
THE STATE

A significant phase of Courtenay's career was his relations with
the crown and his achievement in the realm of political affairs.
It was inevitable, in view of his strong personality, his courage,
and his deep concern for the rights of the church, that he would
exercise considerable influence upon the course of religio-political
developments. He was "primate of all England"[1] and Henry
VIII's Act of Supremacy was still almost a hundred and fifty
years in the future. Until the sixteenth century the archbishop
of Canterbury would continue to serve as the pope's spokesman
in that peculiarly medieval atmosphere which accepted as God's
design a society resting on the twin pillars of church and state,
both pillars distinct and independent, yet, because of the order
in God's plan, complementary and necessarily cooperative. The
competition and rivalry between these two institutions over their
proper share of rights in God's plan for the universe was balanced
to a degree and restrained by a mutual respect for the indispens-
ability of the other.

It was the responsibility of the archbishop of Canterbury
to preserve a *modus vivendi* between the demands or ambitions
of the papacy on the one hand and those of the crown on the
other. As high ecclesiastic and Englishman, this was not an impossible task during the Middle Ages, even under a vigorous pope
like Boniface VIII or an absolutist king like Richard II. For
though it might be impossible to persuade pope and king to agree
to an official delineation of their mutual rights, both were willing
to grant the other independence and supremacy in his proper
sphere as each saw this. Until the beginning of the fourteenth
century, the contest over rights and jurisdiction had been in

the main evenly matched, and increasing efficiency on the part of one institution was countered by that of the other. Since 1300, whatever the efficiency of the papal curia, it could no longer match the growing might of the crown, and in the late fourteenth century when Courtenay was archbishop, the church was clearly on the defensive. A rectifying of the balance between the two institutions in favor of the church Courtenay could not have achieved even had he contemplated this. But he did accomplish all any archbishop could have done under the circumstances. He slowed the victory of the crown.

Courtenay exercised influence in public life principally by virtue of his position as archbishop of Canterbury. He did occupy the highest office in the state, but that for only two months, when as archbishop-elect he was given custody of the great seal. It will be recalled that Sudbury had been murdered during the uprising in June 1381. His chancellorship which had made him the target of the rebels' wrath, he had actually surrendered two days before his death. The great seal was then given to Richard, earl of Arundel, to hold "for a set time," and then to Hugh Segrave, steward of the king's household to keep "until the lord king could more conveniently provide himself with another chancellor." Then on August 10 Courtenay was invested with the office in the presence of the duke of Lancaster and other high nobles of the realm.[2]

Courtenay served as chancellor for slightly more than two months, not sufficient time either to distinguish or to disgrace himself. Why he resigned so soon is not revealed. His appointment, like Arundel's and Segrave's, may have been in the nature of a stopgap, although Courtenay was not the kind of person who would ordinarily take a position for a short time pending the selection of a permanent or more suitable appointee. The few weeks in the chancellor's office may have convinced the archbishop that he could not handle the duties of both chancery and archdiocese properly since grave problems in both areas required close attention. Lollardy, for example, appeared to pose a real threat to the established church, and he may have surrendered the great seal voluntarily in order to devote his full attention to its suppression. It may be significant that he made this his first order of business once the pallium had arrived.

If Courtenay did not resign the office of chancellor entirely of his own volition, it may have been that he sensed the hostility of commons and stepped out in anticipation of the plea they would make in parliament in November. Commons requested the crown at that time to select for chancellor a "wise, prudent, and the most competent person that could be found in the realm, be he either clerk or layman. . . ." That Courtenay's replacement may have been in their minds is suggested from their criticism. They complained that the great majority of those who had been holding the office were too fat in body and purse and too well furred.[3] Courtenay's tomb and effigy do suggest the probability that the archbishop was a big man physically, and his critics must surely have classified him among those who were fat in purse and well furred.

In view of the long history of hostility between Gaunt and Courtenay, however, it is most likely that the wishes of the duke of Lancaster had something to do with the archbishop's resignation. Gaunt had been away in Scotland during the uprising where he had concluded a much desired truce with the Scots. His success in the north, together with his indignation to discover on his return how severely his property and reputation had suffered during his absence, prompted him to seek to re-establish himself as the dominant power in the government.[4] That he had suffered more than any other man earned him the sympathy of lords who had shared his losses and who perhaps shared his views for the future. With their cooperation he had no difficulty regaining the political eminence he had enjoyed during the final months of Edward's reign. Gaunt would accept Courtenay as archbishop of Canterbury, but to permit his adversary to hold the highest office in the state at the same time was asking too much. So on October 20 Courtenay resigned that office to Sir Richard Scrope, whose "appointment," Tout says, "was substantially the work of John Gaunt. . . ."[5]

If the episode wounded Courtenay's pride, he gained a measure of balm from the privilege of addressing parliament when it convened on November 9.[6] The rolls note that he spoke in English and that he presented "a fine discourse." He selected the text, "Rex convenire fecit consilium," as his introduction for an attack on bad government, "to redress which this parliament was called," so he declared, "since the laws now in being are not able to do so."[7] Then he sat down with the other ecclesiastical lords and heard Sir Hugh Segrave, the treasurer, introduce the issues the crown wanted parliament to consider.[8]

CONVOCATION AND THE CROWN

Courtenay's principal association with the crown as archbishop of Canterbury derived from his responsibility for convening convocation and directing its deliberations.[9] While such deliberations might cover a host of problems, all related somehow to the state of the English church. The fact that convocation rarely met except when parliament was in session reveals what had become its primary function by the latter quarter of the fourteenth century. It was a tax-granting assembly even though it had started out as a provincial synod entrusted with responsibility over purely ecclesiastical matters. As such archbishops were under obligation to call it regularly. Canon 6 of the Fourth Lateran Council required metropolitans to summon councils annually for the correction of abuses, but within fifty years few archbishops were still observing this decree. What did compel them to summon their clergy with increasing regularity, however, was the crown's demand for money. Until the close of the thirteenth century, whenever the king needed a clerical subsidy he normally appealed to the pope to impose an aid. Then because of the crown's increasing need for revenue and Pope Boniface VIII's inability to block its direct access to clerical wealth, it became normal for the king in the fourteenth century to summon hierarchy and clergy when he called parliament, although permitting them to meet by themselves and to vote their own taxes. Like parliament they might discuss the demands of the government and discuss their legitimacy. In the end they would normally vote an amount substantially equal to that granted by parliament.[10]

To induce convocation to cooperate with parliament in making financial grants had become the principal responsibility of the archbishop of Canterbury in the eyes of the crown during the last centuries of the Middle Ages.[11] There had been a time when the hostility of an archbishop might have endangered even the throne of an English monarch, but that time was far in the past. Nevertheless, the loyalty of the archbishop and his ability to influence the clergy remained matters of the utmost concern to the crown, since it could not hope to function without the funds voted by convocation. It was the archbishop's responsibility to persuade the assembled bishops of the validity of the crown's demands and to secure an affirmative vote on a subsidy. This explains the crown's continued insistence upon having a man of its liking in Canterbury even after the church could no longer threaten its existence. This fact also explains why the archbishop, as a consequence of his sharing with the chancellor and treasurer the duty of keeping the government solvent, acquired progressively during the fourteenth century the character of a servant of the government.[12]

Courtenay aspired to be a churchman, not an agent of the crown. The danger that the two roles were incompatible may have prompted him to give up the great seal. Yet while he could resign the office of chancellor, he still remained the crown's representative in making financial demands upon the English church. He did have some choice in the role he would fill. He could use his office as had Archbishop Stratford (1333–1349) and serve the crown with zeal, or he might retain as much independence of action as possible in order to preserve what remained of the church's dwindling prerogatives. He chose the latter role. He would cooperate with the crown to a degree he considered consistent with his character as a churchman. He would not press royal demands he considered unnecessary, nor would he permit crown or parliament to whittle away at the few privileges convocation still retained in the matter of considering royal subsidies. His efforts, in the main successful, slowed perceptibly the drift toward a state-controlled church.[13]

Already as bishop of London Courtenay had joined his colleagues in blocking an attempt by commons to force the clergy to commit itself on a grant prior to formal action in convocation. The chronicler's words speak for themselves.

> At which tyme ther was great debate betwene the duke and the bishops for the said grante. For the bishops of London [Courtenay], Norwich, Rochester, and Bangor, wist not for what cause they shold give tenthes and graunt subsidies; and at the same tyme the commons were examined of theyr purpose, and how they would doe to help the kinge; and they said that they ought not to promise any thing before the bishops and clergye had delivered their mindes of the graunt, what they would grante. Afterward the bishops and clergie entending to their businesse and speech took counsaile, and aunswered that the clergie is of such auctority and so free that the lay people ought not to iudge them neither to medle with them, and that therfore they would not be at their appointment, but would if they list neither promise nor give anything, doe what they would.[14]

Small comfort to be sure, but still a privilege for the clergy to consider and vote its grant in convocation and not have it determined beforehand by others.

The first clash between the new archbishop and parliament over the rights of convocation was caused by substantially the same issue, that is, an attempt by parliament to force the clergy's vote. Parliament attempted to do this in the fall of 1384 when it voted the crown two fifteenths, the first fifteenth conditioned upon the king's taking the field in person against the French, the second made contingent on the clergy's matching the grant.[15] Why Courtenay took sharp issue with parliament over this proviso in 1384 after having ignored similar action by parliament the year previous is hard to explain.[16] The poverty of the clergy may have increased and their objection to the consideration of a subsidy may have been appreciably greater in 1384. Or Courtenay may have feared what would be the fate of the little liberty still left convocation should such conditional grants become the rule. In any event, he rose in parliament on December 17, 1384, and declared "that he would never again discuss with his clergy the grant of any subsidy to the king or summon convocation for that purpose until said condition be rejected and deleted."[17]

If Courtenay expected his stout protest in defense of the rights of convocation would cause parliament to disavow with apologies the condition it had placed upon its grant, he was in for a shock. His protest provoked instead of apologies a short but bitter attack on the privileges and wealth of the church. Several lords joined commons in denouncing the wealth which they claimed had destroyed both the piety of the church and its sense of responsibility to the poor. It had become their duty to deprive the church of this wealth and in doing so to reform it. They even drew up proposals to this end and presented them to the king, while they discussed among themselves how much each would realize from the different monasteries in which they were interested. "And I heard in truth," wrote the horrified chronicler, "one of these knights swear a violent oath that he wanted to receive a thousand marks a year from the properties of St. Albans."[18]

The vehemence of the attack of commons on the church did not please the king. Their outburst may have outraged his Christian piety and it was on that basis that he quashed the proposal to expropriate the wealth of the clergy. But Richard was shrewd and ambitious, however devoted to the church he may

have been. He must have realized that anything like expropria-
tion would shake his already troubled realm. Even more immediate was the danger that in permitting parliament to gain control
over convocation, he would be helping weld laity and clergy
into a common block against himself. Better to bargain with
two diverse groups separately than to persuade one large one.
Furthermore, as long as convocation remained "free," especially
if he felt it owed him any gratitude, he could wring "free gifts"
from it, even when parliament had not anticipated such action
with grants of its own. In effect then, if parliament should gain
control of convocation, he could never hope to do so.

After listening to the "inordinate clamoring" of the one
side and the "reasonable rejoinders" of the other, Richard accordingly ordered the proposals destroyed and an end made to such
petitions, and he "declared that during his reign he would preserve the English church in that same condition in which she
was when he became king, or even better." Convocation
applauded the king's action in its behalf and by unanimous action
voted him a tenth. This act in turn so pleased the king, so the
chronicler writes, that he "publicly announced he was more
satisfied with this grant freely voted to him by convocation than
if they had voted him one four times that amount under duress."[19]

If Richard made that statement, and there is no reason
to suppose he did not since both Walsingham and the Lambeth
scribe report his words, one can sympathize with Courtenay's
exasperation when hardly a month later he received instructions
from the king to convene convocation again and vote him a
new grant. The crown was in critical need of funds, so the
king affirmed. He had learned "with certainty" that the French
and their allies were planning an imminent invasion aimed at
destroying the kingdom, church, and the "English language."
Upon the advice of prelates and magnates of the realm, he had
decided that the best way of preventing this invasion was for
him to lead an army in person across the channel "as quickly
as possible this very summer." To cover the "inestimable
expenses" such an operation would involve, he needed immediate
assistance from convocation. The archbishop was to summon that
body before the fourth Sunday of Lent (March 12) and explain
the great need of the king.[20]

There is a special significance attaching to this request
of Richard's to convocation for funds beyond the fact that it
came directly on the heels of the grant made in December. It

is this: since convocation had voted its last subsidy parliament had not met. There is no question that Richard needed the money, and just having dismissed parliament the day before Christmas, it would be impolitic if not impossible to call that body back so soon. Convocation was another matter. This was a smaller body of men and, at the same time, a group of men more apt to sympathize with the royal demands than the lay lords and commons in view of the king's recent action in coming to their defense. This was his opportunity, therefore, of establishing the precedent that convocation could make grants to the crown quite independently of parliament. Thus having saved convocation from becoming a tool of parliament, he would be making it his own.

Courtenay may not have appreciated all the implications in Richard's action. The unreasonable features of the king's demand were sufficient to justify a vigorous protest. He wrote to the king early in February from Exminster[21] to say that the clergy could "reasonably marvel" at the nature of the royal request. It came so soon after their grant in December, on which occasion they had given just as much as they could possibly afford. Their poverty was so great, indeed, that they could not even make the pope the gift of a "small subsidy" even though he had so earnestly begged them to do this.[22] Should the archbishop carry out the king's wishes and summon convocation, great injury might come to the church, to its rights and liberties, something that had never happened during the reigns of his predecessors. The archbishop asked the king to consider the poverty of the clergy and hold them excused; to be content with what they had just granted him, together with their prayers. A final reason for not summoning the clergy in convocation by mid-Lent was the fact that the expiration date for the grant made in December was only June 24. Convocation should not meet before that time.[23]

The archbishop did not rest with his letter to the king. He also appealed to the chancellor and treasurer to urge the king to withdraw his request, and he wrote to the three most influential bishops in the province—Braybroke of London, Wykeham of Winchester, and Brantingham of Exeter—to enlist their assistance. He wrote even to the king's confessor, the bishop of Llandaff, and asked him to put in a good word for the clergy and church should the subject of the subsidy come up for discussion. The archbishop was enclosing a copy of the letter he had sent the king, and he would be beholden to the confessor for any counsel he might give as to how the clergy could be spared this demand, even if in the process he, the archbishop, might "incur the royal indignation and suffer the confiscation of our temporal goods." In fact, if he did not summon convocation, "the clergy would continue in peace and only myself would suffer distress, to which danger we gladly expose ourselves."[24]

Courtenay's appeals and those of his intermediaries had no effect on Richard. He issued another brief dated February 24 with orders that Courtenay summon convocation to meet in London on the Monday before the feast of St. George (April 17).[25] Here again the king was breaking with tradition and perhaps attempting to set a precedent. In the past the crown had confined itself, when asking the archbishop to summon convocation, to suggesting a possible meeting place and a day, usually several months in the future, before which date the group should meet. Now Richard had stipulated both the place and the time of meeting. How precious was the privilege of choosing within limits of two or three weeks the specific place and time convocation was to meet one might wonder. It was, nevertheless, a courtesy that helped preserve the tradition that convocation was a free and voluntary meeting of the clergy.

This time Courtenay did not waste effort on another appeal, although he dared not ignore Richard's order. He issued directions for the clergy to gather, not on April 17 as Richard had specified, however, but on May 4.[26] And to demonstrate further his displeasure to the king and to provide convocation a cue should they have need of one, he pointedly[27] absented himself and delegated the bishops of London and Winchester to preside in his stead. As expected, the clergy had no difficulty finding "sufficient and reasonable causes" for not voting the king the subsidy he had asked, whereupon Courtenay ordered convocation to rise.[28]

That round was Courtenay's; Richard won the next. The king did not renew his request for a meeting of the clergy, but on June 12 he notified Courtenay to proceed with the payment to the exchequer of the second half-tenth the clergy had voted the previous December.[29] At that time, convocation—and parliament too for that matter—had made half of their total grant contingent upon the king's leading an army in person against the French. In the event the king did take command, convocation had agreed that the second half-tenth be collected no later than fifteen days following the feast of St. John the Baptist (June 24). Now in the king's letter of June 12, Courtenay was instructed that "as the king, with the assent and deliberate council of the nobles and magnates of the realm, intends to set forth with all possible speed in person toward the parts of Scotland to meet the attacks of his enemies," he should proceed immediately with the collection of the subsidy and have the amount certified on July 22.[30]

Courtenay again protested, this time questioning not the propriety but the validity of the king's order. In a letter to Bishop Braybroke of London he explained that when convocation had voted the grant the previous December (1384), it had specified that should the king lead an army in person and thus qualify for the second half-tenth, then the money should be collected within fifteen days of the feast of St. John the Baptist. Inasmuch as Richard's order of June 12 was issued too late to permit the collection of the grant by that date, the grant must be assumed to have lapsed. The archbishop wrote:

> It is not strange we wonder that without a new grant being made by us, such a royal brief should be forthcoming, as though, which one would conclude from the king's letter . . . the terminal date might be moved back or extended to some future date at the whim of the person requesting the grant. Such we firmly believe was not the intention of those making the grant.[31]

Whether Courtenay believed it would make any difference in the end or not, he did direct Braybroke to inquire with all speed of the suffragan bishops of the province as to what their intention had been when they had voted the grant. There is no way of ascertaining what number sustained Courtenay in his interpretation of the grant. One suspects that whatever they may have told Braybroke in answer to his query, they must have felt the archbishop's argument was too technical to press. The fact remains the clergy paid the grant.[32]

A further royal encroachment upon the prerogatives of the archbishop and convocation came in the fall of 1386. Courtenay formally opened convocation at St. Paul's with an address on the text, "Videte, vigilitate, et orate." His selection of this particular text may have reflected the high tension at court. Richard was seeking to secure a larger voice in the administration of the government, a move with which neither Courtenay nor the clergy had much sympathy. The purpose of this meeting of convocation was, as usual, the king's request for a subsidy, and as usual the clergy was raising objections. But the objections on this occasion were more personal than those convocation normally raised. They wondered whether the king's need was genuine since he repeatedly asked for funds with which to defend the realm from its enemies, but had never seemed to use the money for that purpose. They also wondered why it was that Richard stood in such constant need of funds, whereas his predecessors, for all their "fierce wars" had but "very rarely" come to them for assistance. Richard's demands had been so persistent that he had reduced the clergy to the point of ruin.[33]

All this proved empty talk in the end, however, and convocation voted a subsidy, this one to consist of two half-tenths. The first half-tenth was to be paid within fifteen days of Easter, the second on November 1. The second half-tenth was also made contingent upon the king's promise to defend the rights of the church in the manner his predecessors had done in times past, and provided, furthermore, that he consult with the spiritual and temporal lords who had been appointed to advise him.[34]

Because of the regularity with which Richard brushed aside such conditions, one may ask whether convocation ever attached them with anything more than a forlorn hope of somehow influencing his actions. They probably never expected him to lead an army in person, for instance, when they attached that kind of rider to a grant, intending their qualification to serve nothing more than an expression of their wishes. In the case of this last grant, however, Richard went much further than ever before when he brushed aside the conditions set by convocation. Until now the king had always respected the right of convocation to set the dates when a subsidy was to be paid. Now Richard notified Courtenay that the full grant was to be paid within fifteen days of Easter, and that included the half-tenth they had stipulated would be paid only on November 1. Richard would have his money when he wanted it, however many ifs and buts convocation might propose. Still the fact that convocation had had the temerity to make the second part of its grant contingent upon his consulting this newly appointed council may have aroused his anger and have prompted his demand. In his judgment convocation's proviso was as much an infringement upon his prerogative as was his demand for full payment within two weeks of Easter upon theirs.

RICHARD'S FIRST "TYRANNY"

Courtenay found himself dragged on several occasions during the fifteen years of his archiepiscopacy into the political turmoil of Richard's reign. Such involvement he strenuously resisted, for he considered it only proper that as primate of England he maintain a position of neutrality, if not aloofness, toward public affairs. That his relations with Gaunt grew almost friendly during the years after 1381, and that he died the king's friend although on one occasion a victim of his violent temper, suggest that he was successful in holding himself above politics. Walsingham does not list him among the leaders of the two groups in the early eighties who supported or opposed Richard,[35] while during the years that followed there is no evidence that he ever permitted himself to become identified with one faction or the other.

The first development to involve the archbishop, following a return to normalcy after 1381, was the crusade of Henry Despenser, bishop of Norwich. As a member of the committee of nine lords that commons had selected to confer with them in the spring parliament of 1383, Courtenay probably joined the majority in endorsing Norwich's plan to invade Flanders in preference to supporting Gaunt's ambitions in Castile. Norwich's expedition aroused wide enthusiasm. The clergy saw it as a crusade against the Clementines,[36] mercantile interests feared a complete rupture of the wool trade unless the French were promptly expelled from newly-won Bruges, and the crown shuddered at the thought of losing the revenues this wool trade produced. Two of Courtenay's nephews, Philip and Peter Courtenay, participated in the Norwich venture,[37] and William, as archbishop, ordered prayers for its success.[38] These prayers did no good. After a promising beginning, the element of luck, so constant a factor in medieval warfare, turned against the English. All they could be grateful for was that the end came quickly. Courtenay suffered no opprobrium for his part in the disaster. He deserves some credit, in fact, for not turning against the bishop of Norwich in his disgrace as so many did. In 1384 he joined his prayers with those of convocation that the king restore the fallen prelate to favor.[39]

Meanwhile Richard had attained his seventeenth year (January 6, 1384) and was feeling considerably older. As he grew older, his own ambitions and the prodding of certain friends who kept reminding him how Gaunt was still his guardian, caused a coolness to spring up between uncle and nephew. In the spring of 1384 this almost erupted into tragic violence. The proximate cause was a Carmelite friar, one John Latimer, who came to the king with the accusation that Gaunt was plotting his death. The story roused Richard to fury, although the duke and other lords managed, seemingly without great difficulty, to convince the king of the ridiculousness of the charge.[40] Then early in 1385 an attempt was made on the duke's life and it was generally believed that the king had been partner to the plot. The duke, at any rate, was so convinced, and he rode to Richard's palace at Sheen with several hundred men and charged the king to his face with attempted murder. He also upbraided him for the evil councillors he had chosen to gather about himself and of following their advice in misgoverning the kingdom. The chronicler says the king accepted the duke's remonstrances with surprising calmness and even promised to give earnest thought to what he had said.[41]

It was almost a year later, during the meeting of the council at Westminster in March 1385, that Courtenay decided to take a hand in the dispute. Along with many others, he had followed the events of the past three years with growing apprehension over what might happen unless the king put a bridle to his temper and to his ambitions and rid himself of his "evil" advisers. He told Richard as much on this occasion and chided him for having countenanced the attack on the duke's life. Such behavior he told Richard was doubly heinous in a king because of the scandal it created. Unless the king mended his ways, the archbishop warned him, and expelled his wicked councillors, the realm would shortly come to ruin.[42]

Because of the presence of courtiers and attendants, Richard could do nothing but swallow his anger over Courtenay's vituperation. But that afternoon, after dinner, his barge and that of the archbishop chanced to meet on the Thames somewhere between the royal palace and Lambeth. The chronicler does not say which boat hailed the other, although the fact that Courtenay first secured a safe conduct from the earl of Buckingham before boarding the king's barge suggests that it was the king who directed him to approach. If Richard expected to find Courtenay in an apologetic mood, he was mistaken. For the archbishop reopened the subject of the king's evil councillors and his own reprehensible conduct. Whereupon Richard fell into a rage, drew his sword, and "would have run the archbishop through had not the earl of Buckingham, John Devereux, and Thomas Trivet stoutly resisted him. . . ."[43] Courtenay fled back to his barge and with his cross hidden beneath his robes "secretly withdrew and sought out a hiding place,"[44] all the way to Devon, according to Adam of Usk.[45]

Seven months later, through the good offices of the bishop of London, Courtenay and Richard were reconciled. To the sorrow of the chronicler, it was the archbishop who acknowledged his fault and begged pardon rather than the king. "For the king in his desire for glory and in order that he might be honored by all men as befit a king, permitted the archbishop to beg forgiveness as he knelt before him. Had that same strong constancy and strength of mind shone as brightly in the archbishop on that occasion as we know it did in the holy martyr Thomas [Becket], for the sake of the faith and the course of right justice he would never have bent head or knee in that manner to anyone, since in keeping with sacred canons it is rather kings and princes who should incline and bow heads before the feet of bishops."[46]

It was shortly after this reconciliation, perhaps before the emotion of re-established friendship had worn off, that Richard granted "for life, to the king's kinsman, William, archbishop of Canterbury, that no purveyor, buyer or other minister of the king take wheat, oats, beans or other corn, oxen, cows, calves, sheep, hogs, porkers, geese, capons, fowls, pullets or other poultry or victual, or horses, hay, straw, carts or other carriage belonging to him or any of his tenants or within his demesne for the term aforesaid."[47] Six months later Richard ordered the privilege revoked "as prejudicial to the king. . . ."[48]

Richard meanwhile retained his same councillors despite the flare-up with Gaunt and Courtenay and the growing opposition of the majority of the lords. Equally disturbing to the latter was the manner in which he kept heaping powers and wealth upon these councillors, notably upon Robert de Vere, the earl of Oxford, whom he elevated to the rank of marquis of Dublin and duke of Ireland. Even commons became concerned over such actions as the king's continued refusal to appoint new ministers or to permit a review of his household. To the petition that he replace his ministers, he gave the curt answer that "the king has officers sufficient at present, and will change them at his pleasure."[49]

Another crisis broke when parliament met in October 1386. Michael de la Pole, Richard's chancellor, presented the crown's request for a subsidy. When parliament responded with a demand that he dismiss Pole and his treasurer, Richard retorted that at their bidding he would not dismiss the meanest scullion in his kitchen.[50] He then withdrew to Eltham, approximately seven miles from the city, and let it be known that he would be ready to receive a delegation of the commons at that place. Parliament refused to humor him, however, and announced that they would do nothing until he returned to Westminster. The lords did finally delegate Thomas of Woodstock, the duke of Gloucester who was the king's uncle, and Thomas Arundel, bishop of Ely, to go to Eltham to remonstrate with Richard.[51] Their meeting proved a painful and, for the king, a sobering experience. What probably brought him around in the end was the warning that his behavior, so much like that of his unfortunate predecessor, Edward II, might end on the same tragic note. Richard thereupon dismissed Pole and his treasurer and accepted the appointment of an executive commission of fourteen lords. This council was to have authority to supervise the affairs of state and the actions of the king's household and servants. The tacit purpose of the commission was to eliminate the influence of Richard's "evil" councillors and to reform the administration.

Courtenay's name headed the list of the commission's membership. When he learned that each of the fourteen members would be required to swear to the crown that he would carry out his duties faithfully, the archbishop demurred. He declared that as archbishop of Canterbury it was not proper for him to take an oath to anyone beneath the dignity of the pope. He did comply with the requirement, however, although under protest that his action was not to serve as a precedent.[52]

As it proved, the king's spirit was not broken. His concluding statement as recorded in the rolls was to the effect "that nothing done in that parliament was to prejudice either him or his crown, and that his prerogative and liberties must remain safe and undiminished."[53] Not long afterwards he had Pole back in his counsel again, together with Robert de Vere, Alexander, the archbishop of York, Robert Tresilian, the chief justice of the king's bench, and Nicholas Brembre, the mayor of London. The executive commission whose authority he had found confining, he dismissed after a court of five justices in August (1387) at Nottingham had declared its appointment illegal. These judges ruled that not only was the commission prejudicial to the king's prerogative but also that any person who had interfered with the king in the exercise of that prerogative was guilty of treason.[54]

On November 11 Richard summoned the duke of Gloucester and the earl of Arundel to answer to charges of conspiracy. Instead of heeding the summons, the two men and their friends began to gather troops. Their defiance frightened Richard and he directed several members of the late executive commission, one of them Courtenay, to inquire the meaning of their action. Courtenay and the other commissioners reported back to the king that the hostile moves were aimed at his councillors whom they demanded be arrested. Further negotiations between the king and his enemies led to what appeared capitulation on the part of Richard. He agreed to the arrest of his five councillors and promised to hold them over for trial before the parliament he would summon for February.

February was eleven weeks off and Richard needed time, time for his friends to gather arms, time for his councillors to escape. But his friends failed to gather in sufficient numbers, and the escape of his councillors only made parliament more bitter when it convened. Because of the king's manifest bad faith—he had even attempted to recruit troops among the Londoners[55]—parliament proceeded to deal with the king's friends with a vindictiveness that has earned it the name, the "Merciless Parliament."

Courtenay who sensed the temper of parliament, that it would be satisfied with nothing short of blood, issued a formal protest in the name of the clergy. While the clergy had equal right with the lay nobility to advise, counsel, and consult, inasmuch as the present session would deal with matters "in which our holy canons do not permit us to interest ourselves in any way," they would withdraw. Their absenting themselves was, however, not to serve as a precedent.[56] Since Courtenay and his fellow bishops were, therefore, not present, they bear no direct responsibility for the excesses of this parliament. It is possible that had they remained and pressed for moderation, parliament might have meted out less harsh sentences. Still canon law was on the side of Courtenay and the hierarchy, although they found in time that their nonattendance when the lords considered judgments of blood would cost them their right of peerage.[57]

The "Merciless Parliament" marked the end of Courtenay's personal association with the government. He may have felt his responsibilities to the church should preempt his time; more likely he abandoned whatever place he had elected to fill in political affairs now that they had become so bitterly partisan. There was no longer any neutral ground left, even to an archbishop, only involvement or disassociation, and Courtenay chose the latter. Even in the seventies when he had received appointment to various councils and committees as a representative of the anti-Gaunt faction, he had never been so "political" a bishop as had Wykeham in the sixties or as Arundel would be in the nineties.[58] Upon his election to Canterbury Courtenay had assumed the role of moderator, of one standing above politics and of intervening only when peace or justice required. In 1388 he even surrendered that role and divorced himself completely from public affairs, leaving to prelates like Arundel whatever political leadership members of the hierarchy might still wish to exercise.

STATUTES OF PROVISORS AND PRAEMUNIRE

Though Courtenay divorced himself from political affairs, when these involved the church he re-entered the arena without hesitation. The issue that brought him back to the thick of things was the problem of papal provisions. The reappearance of this issue in the late eighties was not unexpected, for this had been the principal irritant in church-state relations since the beginning of the century. The practice had grown in spite of repressive legislation, so much so that by the middle of the fourteenth century papal provision had become the ordinary means of attaining a benefice.

A large but confusing literature has grown up on the subject of papal provisions.[59] Undoubtedly the source of most confusion is the modern mistake of viewing the benefice as a congregation of souls. To the pope in the fourteenth century, to the king, to the patron whether an individual or an ecclesiastical corporation, even to the presentee oftentimes,[60] the benefice was property or an endowment that produced revenue.[61] By means of benefices the king could shift the cost of royal administration to the English church; by means of canonries and prebends the pope could hope to maintain his large staff of curial officials. Those who suffered principally from the practice of papal provisions were cathedrals and lay patrons.

The failure of legislation, notably the law enacted by the Carlisle parliament in 1307, the statute of provisors in 1351, and the statute of praemunire of 1353, to reduce the practice to tolerable proportions was due to the refusal of the king to enforce this legislation. Parliament could only secure the enactment of repressive measures; it was the king's responsibility to carry them out. Since foreign affairs were the king's prerogative and since parliament had neither inducements nor threats to offer Rome, it left the crown to negotiate with the papacy. Crown and papacy did negotiate, frequently and at length, but without great success. The pope steadfastly refused to surrender his claim to provide when he chose, the king on his part hesitated to cut off a practice from which he reaped so many benefices and concessions for himself. The statute of provisors, for example, empowered the king to assume the right of provision in case an ecclesiastical patron protested the pope's provision to a benefice, which he was most happy to do. The threat, furthermore, of prohibiting papal provisions entirely provided the king a wonderfully potent lever to force concessions from Rome, among these concessions that of sharing benefices at the expense of ecclesiastical patrons.

Had parliament possessed a clearer notion of the king's part in the practice of papal provisions, they might have brought him to heel by withholding subsidies. And had the king stood alone in condoning the practice, effective curbs could have been interposed. But even members of the aristocracy on occasion sought favors from the Roman curia, where nothing could better assure sympathy than the gift of a benefice to a cardinal. The universities defended the practice of papal provisions since they depended upon it for scholarships and prebends for their scholars. Even parliament did not follow a consistent policy. In 1389 when the pope set aside the chapter's election of a bishop to the see of St. Asaph in order to please the king, parliament permitted the aggrieved candidate to go to Rome to seek some other benefice from the pope.[62]

The practice of papal provisions fluctuated with pope and circumstance. The Avignonese popes, in an effort to meet the cost of an expanding curia and to replace revenues no longer collectible in Rome, exploited this source of revenue on an unprecedented scale. Though the statute of provisors brought some relief after 1351, this was offset by an increasing awareness of the practice as revenues grew scarce. So the clamor for an end to the practice continued. After 1378 the schism urged a more moderate policy upon Urban VI, but even though he appreciated this fact, the issue would not down. It reappeared in the Cambridge parliament of 1388 on the heels of Urban's request for a clerical subsidy. Parliament countered the pope's action by reaffirming the provisions of the statute of provisors and coupling with this a prohibition against the shipment of gold and silver out of the country.[63] Since the pope had received tacit assurance that he could have his subsidy if he cooperated in translating a number of bishops, which he had done, he denounced the action of parliament and ordered Courtenay to proceed with the collection of the subsidy, "the pope being in greater need thereof than usual."[64] He also reserved provision to all vacant sees to himself and, to demonstrate further his loss of patience with the crown, announced a number of episcopal appointments.

Richard hesitated to interfere with Urban's episcopal appointments. To have done so would have been most unusual; furthermore, they generally met his approval. But he did prohibit the collection of the papal subsidy under pain of forfeiture.[65] Before news of the king's action reached Rome, Urban was dead, whereupon Richard hastened to mend his fences with the new pope Boniface IX. He succeeded in doing this so successfully that parliament became incensed. They did not object that Boniface appointed the king's confessor to St. Asaph and approved the consecration of the king's secretary as bishop of Chichester. What they did object to, however, was Boniface's *quid*, which was a green light on collecting the subsidy the pope had ordered and easy permission for clerks to go to the continent.[66] When parliament convened in January 1390, that body proceeded to reaffirm in substance the statute of 1351 and to attach to the law several clauses for the purpose of remedying the weaknesses that had appeared.

The second statute of provisors declared void any provision made after January 20 (1390) unless made in conformity with the statute of 1351. Any member of the upper clergy who accepted a benefice in violation of this statute was to be banished; if a member of the lower clergy, he was to be executed. Harsh penalties were imposed upon persons who assisted in the procurement of a provision contrary to the act. Equally severe penalties were provided for persons who brought papal summonses or instruments into the country for the purpose of penalizing individuals who had conformed with the provisions of the statute.[67]

The crown was willing to accept these proposals although

it refused the petition of commons that the papal collector be expelled within forty hours. But the statute evoked formal protests from both Archbishops Courtenay and Arundel. They condemned the statute as prejudicial to the rights and prerogatives of the church, and they requested that their protest be entered on the parliamentary roll.[68]

The very month parliament enacted this statute of provisors Pope Boniface sent an appeal to Courtenay and Arundel that they lay the desperate financial need of the papacy before their bishops and prevail upon them to vote a subsidy.[69] When the crown learned of this, the great council promptly condemned the pope's action with the king's approval. Pope Boniface in turn formally invalidated the statutes of provisors and threatened to excommunicate anyone who dared execute them. Richard retaliated with an order to Courtenay to cease collection of a subsidy the clergy had voted the pope contingent upon the crown's approval, and he also announced that all English subjects who were in Rome in defiance of the statutes must return to England by November 1 under pain of forfeiture and death.[70]

The first move to break the resulting impasse in Anglo-papal relations was made by the papal emissary, Nicholas, abbot of Nonantola, who approached Archbishop Courtenay about the crisis. Courtenay must have been of significant assistance in easing the situation, for he claims a share in bringing about the reopening of negotiations.[71] The papal emissary urged Richard to revoke the statutes, to step up the war against France, and to permit the levying of a tax upon the English church. All Richard offered to do was to lay the pope's request for the revocation of the statutes before parliament since only that body had the authority to repeal them. As for the subsidy, the king professed ignorance how this could be permitted if the pope expected England to prosecute the war against France with greater vigor. Should peace come, there might be no objection to a clerical subsidy.[72]

When parliament reconvened in November 1390, the crown proposed the repeal or the relaxation of the statutes of provisors. As expected, parliament refused even to consider the proposal. The king had probably made the request simply as a gesture of good will. Yet "lest they appear to have respect for neither pope nor king," parliament authorized the crown to continue negotiations for a concordat. This they would ratify if they found it acceptable.[73]

Before the papal emissary and council had completed work on a concordat, news reached England that Boniface had granted a prebend in the church of Wells to Cardinal Brancacio. This was most imprudent. What made the pope's action doubly provocative was the fact, first, that the benefice was the king's to fill; second, that the king had already presented the benefice to a William Langbroke. What made the pope's action doubly foolish was the fact that he not only stiffened parliamentary hostility by this act but also antagonized the king, the one person in England who might have been able to help him. When the court ruled against the cardinal in the suit he brought against William Langbroke, rumor had it that the pope planned to excommunicate any bishop who dared execute the court's order and to translate him out of the country, even though he were a member of the king's council.[74]

Early in 1393 parliament took steps to prevent this eventuality. This answer took the form of the second statute of praemunire, a statutory block to reprisals Pope Boniface might undertake against English bishops and other persons who respected and carried out the provisions of the statute of provisors. The petition as offered by the commons read:

> If anyone sues . . . in the court of Rome or elsewhere any such translations, processes, and sentences of excommunication, bulls, instruments, or anything else whatsoever which touches the king . . . against him, his crown and regality, or his realm, or receives, notifies, or executes them, he shall be put out of the king's protection, incur forfeiture of lands and goods, and be brought before the king and his council to make answer, or process shall be made against him by writ of *praemunire facias.*[75]

The temporal lords accepted the formula proposed by the lower house without demur. When asked what the mind of the ecclesiastical lords might be on the proposal, Courtenay rose and presented their position: that although they did not question the pope's right to excommunicate and translate, the pope in this instance would be exercising that right in an unreasonable fashion and to the injury of the crown. For this reason the clergy would adhere to the crown and "support His Highness in this and all other instances in which the rights of his crown are concerned." This statement Courtenay asked the scribe to enter upon the roll.[76]

Scholars in the past have generally given broad application

to the provisions of this, the second statute of praemunire. Under
the circumstances it is not surprising that they have judged it
the most antipapal expression of English sentiment to appear in
the Middle Ages. Recent scholars find the act appreciably less
hostile in tone and intent. They place strict limits to the application of the statute. The aim of the bill, in their judgment, was
not to bar papal bulls in general, but only those that were punitive
in character and, more specifically, those that infringed upon
the king's right to present to such benefices as the prebend of
Wells. That contemporary chroniclers ignore the action of parliament confirms the view that the statute was relatively unimpor-
tant. That the statute lacks great significance reduces, of course,
the significance of the words spoken by Courtenay when expressing the position of the English Church. Had the act carried the
broad implications some later historians have given it, it is doubtful whether parliament would have enacted it in the first place,
and in the second place, quite certain that the English bishops
of the fourteenth century would never have accepted it.[77]

CANTERBURY AND CROWN

Richard and Courtenay might disagree in their official capacities
as king and archbishop when subsidies or the traditional rights
of church and state were at issue. More routine business usually
found them willing to cooperate. This was true, for example, on
the many occasions when Courtenay was compelled to appeal
to Richard for the assistance of the civil arm in compelling
obstinate excommunicates to make their peace with the church.
So in the case of one Alice Grenes who had been excommunicated but had ignored her summons, Courtenay asked the king
for help. As he complained, "since . . . holy mother church
has nothing further it can do in this matter, we humbly appeal
to your majesty to issue orders concerning the apprehension of
this excommunicate in accordance with the customs of the
kingdom, so that those who are not deterred from evil by the
fear of God may be restrained by the power of the secular
arm."[78]

Characteristic of the support the king ordinarily gave
Courtenay in such instances was the case of a Lollard whom
the abbot of Oxney had imprisoned upon his refusal to pay tithes
to the abbey. The king's chancellor, Michael de la Pole, had

ordered the release of the defendant, whereupon Courtenay had brought the matter to the attention of the king. Richard upheld the abbot and authorized the archbishop to act in this and in all ecclesiastical matters according to his rights. "We do not wish now," he assured the archbishop, "nor do we intend to diminish in any way the rights of the church."[79] Where religion was clearly involved, Richard was on occasion even more cooperative than the bishops might desire. So in 1391 the hierarchy asked him to revoke the permission he had extended to archdeacons to invoke the secular arm against excommunicates. That was to remain an episcopal prerogative.[80]

There were occasions when the king interposed his authority in behalf of persons who had appealed to him against disciplinary measures taken by the archbishop. In most such instances, Richard confessed his mistake in the end and rescinded his restraining orders. That is what happened in the case of several men whom Courtenay had excommunicated for cutting down trees on property belonging to the parish church of Leneston. The men had appealed to the king, whereupon the king directed Courtenay to drop his action against them. When further inquiries established their guilt, however, he withdrew his prohibition and authorized the archbishop to proceed as before.[81] Somewhat similar was the case of a John Rayscheleghe whom Courtenay had excommunicated, together with other persons, for his part in the murder of a chaplain. The king ordered Courtenay to revoke the sentence of excommunication he had issued inasmuch as the royal court had found Rayscheleghe innocent and the law of the land forbade anyone being arraigned twice for the same charge. Not long after, however, Courtenay received notice from the king that he might resume action against John since there was grave doubt that the royal justices had considered all the evidence.[82]

Somewhat the reverse was the case of a Nicholas Ames whom the king's sheriff had imprisoned upon request of the bishop of Worcester. Nicholas had been excommunicated but had ignored the bishop's summons. The Court of Canterbury, to which Nicholas appealed, found him innocent of the charge for which he had been excommunicated. Courtenay asked the king, accordingly, to order his release from prison.[83]

The dispute between Courtenay and the village of Romney, in which controversy the king eventually became involved, had to do with the leading citizens of the community over their action in usurping the authority of the archbishop's bailiff. (Romney lay within the liberty of the diocese of Canterbury.) Apparently with the consent of the majority of the villagers, they had not only taken over the administration of the affairs of the village but had also imposed heavy fines on the bailiff and stopped payment of manorial dues to the archbishop. Courtenay gave orders that the principals in the usurpation appear before him at his manor in Slyndon, which two of these, William Holyngborn and William Chyld, did on June 25, 1388.

There the following charges were preferred: that they had prevented the bailiff from taking action in instances of escheat; that they had prevented him from conducting investigations concerning such matters as the chattels of felons, waifs, strays, the goods of fugitives, even thefts, murders, and other crimes, because of which interference the archbishop had suffered a loss of forty pounds; that they had prevented the tenants of the village of Romney, all of whose inhabitants were the archbishop's mediate and immediate tenants, from paying their dues, which action cost the archbishop ten marks; that they had prevented the bailiff from arresting malefactors and had usurped that authority themselves; that they had prevented the bailiff from summoning the assize to consider the punishment of persons guilty of crime; that the brewers of the town, with their co-operation and that of the village, had prevented the bailiff from fining those persons, to the injury of the archbishop of forty marks; that they had prevented tenants whom the bailiff had summoned from appearing at court, maintaining that the bailiff could not hold court without the presence of jurors, and these had deliberately absented themselves; that they had held their own court instead and had fined the bailiff ten pounds when he refused to carry out the judgment of that court; that they had assessed the bailiff ten pounds and seized his property because his absence from court had resulted in the quashing of a debt of twenty-two pounds (the bailiff had been seriously ill, although he had actually appointed a competent substitute); that they had levied a tax on the village and had seized the property of the bailiff and of others who had refused to pay this tax. The two Williams were examined on these and other charges, found guilty, and excommunicated.

The charges that the archbishop's clerks preferred against the community of Romney were equally serious. They were accused of having a regulation which forbade any villager to

leave the community to answer a summons, even from an ecclesiastical judge; of fining any person ten pounds who defied
that order; of fining the archbishop's bailiff for having cited a
William Pope to appear before the archbishop; of preventing
the archbishop's apparitor from citing members of the community
to appear before the archbishop; of decreeing that the tithe
of fish be paid only at certain times; of holding their meetings
and courts on Sunday and holy days in the church of St. Nicholas
where they had interfered with the divine service with their
wrangling and disputes.

Because of the large number of villagers who were partner
to these violations, Courtenay placed the entire village of Romney
and its churches under an interdict. He directed that the villagers
be called together by the ringing of the village bell, when the
sentence was to be proclaimed.[84]

William Holyngborn and William Chyld took their cause
and that of the village to the king and persuaded him to issue
an order inhibiting the archbishop from carrying out the sentence
of excommunication. But when they learned that Courtenay had
also gone to the king and was discussing the matter with him,
they submitted without further ado, "for they knew that in their
revolt and usurpation against the lord archbishop they could in
no way prevail. . . ." So the interdict was placed on Romney
and remained in effect until October 14 when Courtenay lifted
it and absolved those persons who had suffered excommunication.
There is no mention of a punishment or fine.[85]

Richard was a reasonably pious Christian and revealed
no reluctance to cooperate with Courtenay in forcing excommunicates to submit to ecclesiastical authority. When presentation
to benefices was involved, however, he showed himself as sensitive
over patronage rights as any English patron, lay or ecclesiastical.
In his disputes with the archbishop over the right to present
it must be said to his credit, however, that not his will but the
courts usually decided the issue. In several instances when Courtenay was moving to present to a benefice, he ordered him to
hold up action until the "question of right of advowson had been
decided."[86]

In the case of the rectory of Camborne in the diocese
of Exeter where Courtenay and the king collided over the right
to present, there was no need for a court to resolve the difficulty.
The archbishop was clearly in the wrong. During his visitation
of Exeter he had occasion to order the induction of a Robert

Nevylle to the parish. William Nevylle, Robert's kinsman, had made the presentation, and Courtenay only issued his induction order after the official of the archdeacon of Cornwall had confirmed William's right of patronage.[87] A few days before Courtenay had issued his order, however, Brantingham, the bishop of Exeter, had instituted a John Kirkeby upon his presentation by the king. The king claimed this right as heir of the deceased William Basset, although there was some suggestion that the latter had delegated his rights to William Nevylle. The king's presentee remained in possession of Camborne.[88]

Richard showed commendable forbearance and understanding when he discovered on another occasion how both he and the archbishop had appointed clerks to the one and same church of Tunstall. The man Courtenay collated was Thomas Symond, pastor of the church of Freshwater. As the king charged, the archbishop had done this "in the belief that it was in his collation, which it was not. . . ." The king had meantime presented his clerk, Thomas Butiller, to Tunstall and another of his clerks to Freshwater, "thus leaving the said Symond destitute of a benefice." So in order to permit Symond to go back to his former parish of Freshwater, Richard rescinded the appointment of this unnamed clerk. No doubt he took care of the disappointed clerk elsewhere.[89]

In the case of the vicarage of Sydlesham, the king first ordered Courtenay to stay his institution. He had heard that three clerks were being considered for the benefice to which he actually held the right of presentation. When he later learned that it was not the right of advowson but rather the qualifications of the men being considered for the appointment that Courtenay's court was investigating, he instructed the archbishop to ignore his prohibition and proceed with his inquiries.[90]

⁋{9}⁋

COURTENAY AS METROPOLITAN AND BISHOP

COURTENAY AND THE POPE

Courtenay's visitation of his province constituted his most pretentious work as archbishop. His greatest work, both in volume and importance, he did in the quiet of Lambeth. There he served as bishop of his own diocese of Canterbury; from there he sent out instructions to the bishops and monasteries of the province; from there he handled correspondence with the pope in Rome; and from there, too, ideally located for this phase of his work, he directed business with the crown. This last was sufficiently significant to warrant a separate chapter. Least demanding in time and concern was Courtenay's business with the pope. Not that nothing of note was afoot that could have disturbed church-state relations and have involved Courtenay as primate. There was Lollardy; there was the perennial problem of papal provisions; there was the equally perennial need of the pope for financial assistance. But the Lollards were equally detested by crown and Rome, and the pope could count on the crown's cooperation without enlisting the asssitance of Courtenay. The problem of papal provisions parliament would solve, or attempt to solve, without benefit of either pope or Courtenay.[1] And the schism, together with the long history of English irresponsiveness to papal demands for subsidies, precluded much trouble from Rome on that score. Official correspondence between Lambeth and Rome during the period of Courtenay's archiepiscopacy was, accordingly, small and of little moment.

The fact of the schism accounts in large measure for the

relative insignificance of this correspondence. England was on
Pope Urban's side and for this the pope was profoundly grateful.
What demands he and his successors might wish to make on
the English church and the English crown, they would never
press with an insistence that could endanger that allegiance. The
English were more than friends. They were active allies in the
papal war against the French Clementines. Under the circumstances, therefore, the pope would not demand of Courtenay
action that might precipitate a break in England's loyalty. English
sensitivity over papal intervention in English affairs also discouraged the raising of controversial issues. Even the crown's solution
of Wyclif's problem, the papacy had accepted without official
protest.[2] What communications may have passed between Rome
and Lambeth via papal legates on subjects such as provisions,
Wyclif, and subsidies, might have been noteworthy. But what
remains in the chronicles and in official documents is small.[3]

Of England's adherence to Urban rather than Clement
VII there had never been any doubt.[4] Parliament had settled
that question in 1378 at Gloucester where the crown had summoned it rather than London lest the infinitely more explosive
issue over the breach of sanctuary at Westminster Abbey cause
a riot in the capital.[5] This issue and the crown's demand for
money preempted the attention of the chroniclers, not the question who was the rightful pope. England had already made up
its mind. Archbishop Sudbury with the assistance of Courtenay
and other prelatical and theological advisers interrogated the two
delegations from Rome and Avignon and, as expected, ruled in
favor of the first. Parliament thereupon officially proclaimed
Urban pope, refused to discuss the matter with the Clementine
delegation, and declared all persons who favored Clement traitors
of the crown. Courtenay promptly published the condemnation
of Clement and the excommunication of all persons who might
accept honors from him.[6]

The schism may have indirectly precipitated a crisis in
Courtenay's own career. Among the Clementine cardinals whom
Urban deprived of their dignities was the cardinal of Albano
who appears to have enjoyed some influence in England. In order
not to jeopardize English loyalty, Urban offered the red hat to
Courtenay, then bishop of London.[7] Had Courtenay proved receptive and the crown not objected, Courtenay might have spent
the balance of his career in the relative obscurity of the papal
curia rather than at Lambeth, since it was then customary for

cardinals to make their home in Rome. The civic leaders of London were concerned over the possibility of losing their popular and powerful prelate, and made three successive appeals to Urban in late 1378 and early 1379 to induce him to change his mind.[8] These appeals may have influenced Urban, or it may have been Courtenay's lack of interest, for he bestowed the dignity instead upon Adam Easton, a Benedictine monk of Norwich.

Clement VII, although repudiated by the English crown and church, made a number of attempts to send bulls and legates to England in the hope of gaining sympathy. Most of his emissaries, like William Buxton, a Dominican friar, ended up in prison. Buxton who had been consecrated titular bishop of Maragha in Persia, reached England during the summer of 1384, when he was promptly arrested on the charge of treason. The dignity of the court that examined him on November 19 at Westminster reflects the importance of the man. The king was present, as were also the duke of Lancaster and other magnates, while Courtenay presided. Buxton proved himself a courageous and slippery defendant. In his replies to his questioners, he interpolated on occasion the exhortation from the Epistle of St. Peter: "Fear God, honor the king, love the brotherhood." To the charge that he had been preaching in England, he answered that he had just arrived, although he admitted that he had come to that country in the hope of convincing the English of the legitimacy of Clement's claims. When he countered "many plausible reasons and strong arguments" offered by Courtenay, Richard, and the duke of Lancaster, with reasoning his interrogators considered deceitful, the archbishop charged him to speak "freely and openly without sophistry and subterfuge."

Whereupon Buxton explained that among other evidence that had convinced him of the validity of Clement's claim were the statements and writings of the cardinals who had taken part in the election, particularly the testimony of the cardinal of Albano. If legal experts could convince him that their statements were untrue, he would be willing to accept Urban. Courtenay explained how these same cardinals had left Rome following their election of Urban and had returned again to ask and accept favors from him for themselves and their friends. This information impressed Buxton and he declared "quite firmly, so it appeared," that if he could be convinced the cardinals had done this after they were "beyond the territory of the Romans," he would believe as his questioners did. Upon his request not to be given over for questioning to certain Urbanist prelates and clerks, the court appointed a committee consisting of the bishops of Ely, Salisbury, and Rochester, to examine him inasmuch as Courtenay "flatly" refused. Though these bishops were able to persuade Buxton to confess his error and accept Urban, upon the recommendation of Courtenay the king ordered him sent to Blackfriars to be held there until word had been received from Rome.[9]

One way Courtenay as archbishop early demonstrated his loyalty to Urban was by strongly urging upon the English clergy and people the worthiness of the crusade undertaken by Henry Despenser against the Clementine count of Flanders. Despenser, bishop of Norwich, who was probably more warrior than prelate, had convinced crown and parliament early in 1383 of the wisdom of such a campaign. Pope Urban enthusiastically endorsed the plan and promised those who participated or cooperated in the enterprise such rich spiritual rewards that "none of either sex thought they should end the year happily, nor have any chance of entering paradise, if they did not give handsomely to it" (expedition).[10] Courtenay published the pope's appeals on behalf of the crusade to the faithful throughout the province and added several of his own.[11] After a brilliant beginning the expedition ended a debacle, and the bishop returned in disgrace. Courtenay was among the few who had the courage to befriend the fallen prelate and help secure him the return of his confiscated temporalities.[12]

Courtenay received on occasion special assignments from the pope such as that concerning the irregular marriage of Reginald of Cobham to Elinor, widow of Sir John Arundel. Reginald and the widow had married in full knowledge that their relationship within the forbidden third degree made their union invalid. Their consciences, the status of their children, or some other consideration prompted them after four years to have their marriage validated, and they appealed to Pope Urban for a dispensation. In his letter to Courtenay, Urban left instructions that the archbishop attend to the matter, and he proposed that for the sake of the spiritual well-being of the couple and the avoidance of scandal, a dispensation be granted. The archbishop was to legitimize the children and impose a suitable penance.

Since Courtenay was busily engaged at the time with the visitation of his province, he asked the bishop of Rochester to undertake the assignment.[13] Some weeks later the bishop informed

Courtenay that he had absolved the couple of the sentence of excommunication they had automatically incurred through their illegal marriage and had directed them to apply to the archbishop for a formal dispensation to marry.

Ordinarily Reginald and his wife would have been obliged to make the trip to Canterbury or Lambeth to receive penance and dispensation from the archbishop in person, but Courtenay dispensed them. He had learned that the wife was pregnant, and because of "the great inconvenience and expense" such a trip would entail, he directed the bishop of Rochester to notify the couple himself of the nature of their penance. This was to be a harsh penance, the archbishop explained, since the nobility of the guilty parties, their awareness of their crime when they committed it, and the existence of other circumstances which are implied but not described, left the archbishop no choice but to be severe. The penance he imposed required them to do the following: as long as they lived or one of them, they were to bear the cost of a chaplain who would say mass daily in their behalf in a chapel to be designated by the prior of Christ Church, Canterbury; because they had lived together for four years in illicit union, for four years they would abstain every fourth day from meat and wine, every sixth day from wine and from one of the better kinds of fish they were particularly fond of; during those four years they were to feed four poor people each day and serve them with their own hands, should they be at home, in the hall a little before their own dinner, each of the four to receive one loaf, a dish of meat or fish according to the season, and a half-gallon of wine; during that same period they were to fit out four poor people each year with tunic and hood; they were, finally, to contribute 200 marks for the repair of the walls of the city of Canterbury and 100 marks for the construction of a bridge at Rochester, both amounts to be paid by March 25 following.[14]

The now properly married couple must have had difficulty raising the 300 marks or they may have convinced themselves that their penance was unreasonably heavy. For Courtenay wrote them in early December that unless they paid the specified amounts by Christmas—until then they had offered only "frivolous excuses"—they would incur the sentence of greater excommunication.[15] There is nothing more in the register about Reginald and Elinor, so one may safely assume the couple managed to scrape up the money by Christmas.

Several months after disposing of this marriage problem, Courtenay received another assignment from Urban, this one appreciably easier. A priest of Bristol, by the name of Solomon Russel, had appealed to the pope for a parish. Urban ordered Courtenay to make diligent inquiry concerning the qualifications of Russel: whether he was "able to read well and to think well and to sing well and to read Latin words satisfactorily, and whether he was suitable in other respects." Should he be satisfied about the competency of the applicant, he was to collate him to the parish church of Essheteford.[16]

Courtenay showed the papacy the greatest deference throughout his career. Unswerving loyalty marked his attitude from the time he held his first public office as chancellor of Oxford through his years as bishop of Hereford and London and as archbishop of Canterbury. As Courtenay grew older, the exigencies of responsible leadership tempered the enthusiasm with which he had responded to Pope Gregory's instructions in 1377 to excommunicate the Florentines in London. Just a few years before his death, in the controversy over praemunire, he even assumed a position the pope might have found treasonable.[17] This the pope probably did not do. After so many years of loyal cooperation from Courtenay, he could have had no reason to doubt his sincerity. Courtenay had refused to exercise the powers of archbishop until the arrival of the pallium, despite considerable pressure and inconvenience. He had been careful to secure papal authorization to use certain liberties before proceeding with the visitation of his province. He had forced the citation of Wyclif in 1377 despite Gaunt's known objections and a year later, upon Pope Gregory's request, had questioned him at Lambeth. Courtenay's failure to insist that Wyclif make a formal retraction of his heretical views and his failure to denounce the reaffirmation of the statute of praemunire may have grieved the pope. Still the pope should and may have realized that, in light of Courtenay's courage and his respect for Rome, the archbishop had only done what reason and prudence recommended. Since dogma was not an issue, no good would have been served had the archbishop assumed an unrealistic position.[18]

The papacy repaid Courtenay's cooperation with good will and privileges. The first privilege the pope granted Courtenay was the permission he extended him in November 1382 of visiting the dioceses of his province in any manner he chose, whether, as canon law required, he had first visited his own cathedral and diocese or not. Although Pope Boniface later rescinded these privileges, he did warn the bishop of Salisbury he would have to submit to Courtenay's right to visit his diocese should he do so in accordance with common law. In December 1382 Pope Urban extended Courtenay, upon the archbishop's request, the privilege of instituting, "for this time only," to a canonry in each of the cathedral and collegiate churches of the province. He might institute to these canonries almost any clerk he chose, even should the person already hold one or two benefices elsewhere and have pastoral duties.[19] On another occasion Pope Urban granted the archbishop permission to present to all benefices whose provision had devolved upon the papacy for having remained vacant for six months.[20] Because the schism had severed the link between the Cluniac houses in England and the motherhouse in France, the pope delegated Courtenay to act as their vicar general.[21] Pope Boniface gave him permission to release twenty holders of permanent vicarates so that they might attend some *studium generale* or for some other worthy purpose.[22] The same pope authorized the clergy attached to the household of Courtenay's mother, the countess of Devon, to keep the revenues of any benefice they held or might acquire over a period of three years.[23] In 1395, the year before he died, Courtenay received permission from Pope Boniface to levy a tax on the clergy of the province of Canterbury to be used for his own needs.[24]

COURTENAY AND HIS BISHOPS

The tranquillity of Courtenay's relations with the papacy did not always attend his relations with his suffragans. A thousand miles, hostile France, and a crown at home sensitive to papal interference separated the archbishop from Rome. Just a few miles divided him from his suffragans, and in his differences with them the king seldom intervened and then only in the interest of peace. Fortunately, the paths of archbishop and suffragans crossed rarely. They might meet with some regularity in parliament and convocation and when bishops and abbots were consecrated or buried. But then they met as equals and, as in their discussions in parliament and convocation, usually in harmony. Where archbishop and bishop clashed most frequently was when both attempted to appoint to the same benefice or when both claimed the right to probate the wills of persons leaving property in several dioceses. Had such contacts been multiplied, given Courtenay's determination to preserve what he considered the prerogatives of Canterbury, he might have expended the fifteen years of his archiepiscopacy in acrimonious and fruitless controversy.

Courtenay's sharpest clashes with his suffragans came over the question of his right to visit their dioceses. This is not surprising. Less assertive metropolitans who attempted to visit usually experienced their most painful moments in their progress, or attempted progress, about their provinces. Should friction arise, and it regularly did, the metropolitan usually found himself very much alone and faced with the general disapproval of his suffragans. Word that Courtenay had appealed to Pope Urban in 1382 for sweeping privileges to bolster his right to visit must have sent shivers up the spines of all his bishops. Of their general hostility in this matter Courtenay complained in his letter to the pope in the summer of 1384 on the occasion of his controversy with Bishop Brantingham. Not only did he find the conduct of Brantingham reprehensible but that of

> other of my and the church's suffragans, who, although bound firmly by personal oaths to guard and preserve, to the best of their ability, the liberties, privileges, and rights of the church, have as ungrateful sons and unmindful of their oaths, opposed rather than supported me, and have striven with vigor to attack the church their mother, indeed to destroy wholly and to emasculate her privileges, liberties, and rights.[25]

On several occasions Courtenay became involved in disputes with his suffragans over testamentary matters, such as the proving of wills, the appointment of executors, and the hearing of their final accounts in the case of persons dying testate or intestate with goods in more than one diocese of the province. Jurisdiction in such instances was claimed by the archbishop by prerogative of the church of Canterbury. This claim paralleled that of the bishop over the property of deceased persons where this was located in several archdeaconries or jurisdictions of the diocese. Reason recommended that a superior authority assume the responsibility in such cases in order to obviate the need of separate letters of administration being issued in each jurisdiction, together with the inevitable conflict and confusion that might arise. The right of the archbishop of Canterbury to probate such wills or to appoint administrators in case of intestacy dates from the reign of Henry III, but even by Courtenay's time it had not become so firmly established as to pass unchallenged by suffragan bishops. That some archbishops neglected to press their prerogative in all such instances contributed to the continuance of controversy. No doubt many wills passed by unnoticed, especially when the amount of property in a second diocese was inconsequential and reason suggested that the diocesan court retain jurisdiction.[26]

Courtenay, who was not one to permit any prerogative of his church of Canterbury to remain unused, contributed significantly to the evolution of a separate court, known as the Prerogative Court, which eventually assumed full and final responsibility over the disposition of the property of persons dying with possessions in more than one diocese of the province. When in the thirteenth century the archbishop first began to assert his claim to jurisdiction in such matters, he had the testaments proved before himself or his vicar general. Then as the number of such wills increased, he began to delegate specific cases to his clerks, reserving always final approval of their actions to himself. In 1361 Archbishop Islip appointed a commissioner to handle all testamentary matters concerned with persons leaving property in two or more dioceses, although he too reserved the final dismissal of the cases to himself. The use of a regular commissioner lapsed with Islip's death but was revived by Courtenay who empowered Thomas Baketon, dean of the church of St. Mary of the Arches, and John Lynton, registrar of the Court of Canterbury, to prove the wills of persons dying with goods in different dioceses and to grant power of administration in the case of intestates. They were authorized to handle all phases involved in the settlement of such properties, including their final dismissal. Only in the case of the wills of magnates or of magnates dying intestate did the archbishop reserve the final accounts and dismissal from the official to himself.[27]

Courtenay may also have contributed to the establishment of the principle that the archbishop would assume jurisdiction in testamentary cases only when the deceased had possessed *bona notabilia* outside the diocese in which he had lived. The qualifying term *notabilia* appears perhaps first in 1376 when Archbishop Sudbury claimed jurisdiction on that basis.[28] But this was exceptional. Courtenay was the first archbishop to employ the phrase *bona notabilia* consistently. It appears significantly in the preamble which introduces the probates and commissions handled during the years of his archiepiscopacy. This speaks "of administrations of goods of testators and intestates of the province of Canterbury having at the time of their death many and diverse notable goods within several dioceses of the province. . . ."[29] The exact value of *bona notabilia* was not above dispute. It appears that a minimum value of five pounds was expected before archiepiscopal jurisdiction should interpose itself.[30] In his claim to the right of proving the will of Thomas Walkot, rector of the parish church of Cavendisch, as opposed to that of the bishop of Norwich, Courtenay emphasized the fact that the deceased had left "goods mobile and immobile, notable and of considerable quantity and variety . . . in different dioceses of our province of Canterbury at the time of his death."[31]

The *cause célèbre* among controversies over testamentary jurisdiction in which Courtenay became involved was one that concerned the will of one Richard Mydelton who had died in the diocese of Hereford. Some time before his death Richard had loaned his brother who lived in the diocese of Lincoln, two books that had not been returned when he died. Courtenay's official promptly declared that the proving of the will lay within the prerogative of the Court of Canterbury inasmuch as the testator had left property in two different dioceses of the province. There is no way of knowing whether the value of the books exceeded five pounds. Even had their value been appreciably more, the litigiously minded bishop of Hereford, John Trefnant, would undoubtedly have protested the claim of the archbishop's official to prove. And long before the case had run its course Courtenay must have had second thoughts about the wisdom of having pressed his prerogative against as persistent and legalistically minded an opponent as Trefnant, whatever the values involved.

Trefnant drew up an appeal to the apostolic see in August 1393 in which he charged Courtenay not only with usurping his rights in the case of the will of Richard Mydelton but with other usurpations as well.[32] Courtenay held up this appeal for nearly two years, possibly in the hope that Trefnant would drop the matter. Then when he finally did forward it to Rome, he accompanied it with his denunciation of the bishop's charges as false.[33] Trefnant did not wait to learn what decision the papal tribunal might make. He forwarded another appeal some months later in which he charged the archbishop with personal animosity toward himself, and he argued learnedly and at length—ten pages in his printed register—citing an impressive catalog of canons, decretals, and precedents in support of his claim.[34] Whether Courtenay found these arguments convincing or whether he feared the decision of the curia would be in Trefnant's favor in view of his long service in Rome, he dropped the matter and conceded the victory to his suffragan.[35]

Courtenay also became involved in a controversy over the execution of the will of Michael Northburgh, once bishop of London who had died in 1362. When Archbishop Islip proved the bishop's will, he noted that among the property of the deceased was a box in St. Paul's church containing "large and notable sums" which were set aside for the care of the poor. Archbishop Courtenay learned that Henry Welewes who had charge of administering the will had expended some of the money for purposes other than those stipulated by the deceased. For this action Courtenay ordered him cited. He was directed to produce a full report of the manner in which he had executed the will of the deceased.[36]

Less than a year before his death Courtenay's rapport with his suffragans reached its nadir. What cost him their good will was the permission he received from Pope Boniface to collect a tax of four pence on the pound of the taxed value of all ecclesiastical wealth in the province. The register makes no mention of the levy, so there is no way of ascertaining Courtenay's motive in seeking the funds. Walsingham declares he did it "for no true or legitimate reason."[37] The entry in Capgrave's chronicle is brief but to the point: "In this year, William, bishop of Canterbury, having no consideration what cost the cherchies in his province had bore, paying of subsidies to the king eviry year, yet got he bulles from the Court to have IIII d. of the pount, both of exempt and not exempt. Many that loved pes payed. And summe made apeel in this matere. But the end of all this strif was, the death of William whech followed sone."[38]

Among those who "made apeel" was our contentious bishop of Hereford, John Trefnant. He learned of the tax from a letter the archbishop of York sent him in October 1395. He was directed to arrange for the collection of the tax and its transferal to the archbishop of Canterbury's commissioners in London before February 2, 1396.[39] Again Trefnant made appeal to the pope. He condemned the tax as unjust and illegal, that laying down the deadline of Februrary 2 was itself an imposition, that to require a bishop to collect such a tax was denigrating to the episcopal dignity. He even suggested the possibility that the bull authorizing the archbishop to levy the tax was fraudulent. These and other objections to the tax, coupled with additional grievances he had against Courtenay, he forwarded to Rome. He did conclude his appeal with the announcement, however, that he was both able and willing to raise the tax, but that he would only pay it over to the person "having the power of requesting it of us and of receiving it."[40] Courtenay's death followed a few months later and nothing more is heard of the matter.

Would Pope Boniface have supported Courtenay against the troublesome Trefnant? This was the third appeal in approximately three years that Trefnant had filed against the archbishop.[41] Maybe Trefant himself was beginning to wonder whether he was not "protesting" too much. His acknowledgment that he was willing to pay the tax once he was certain Courtenay was entitled to it, may have been inserted to meet just that criticism. He could not afford to stamp himself at the curia as a constitutionally uncooperative and obstinate suffragan.

Because of the impersonal character of most medieval sources, it is not easy to penetrate beyond the office of the man and his role in public life to the individual himself. In this account of Courtenay's clashes with his suffragans, a little light appears to slip behind the hard exterior of the man and bring the person of the archbishop out of the shadow of time. For these rare moments when the thoughts and feelings of men and women long dead are revealed, the reader of medieval history is grateful—but he must be wary. Courtenay was not involved in any more controversies with his suffragans than the usual archbishop who occupied Canterbury for so long a time, and his disputes with them were probably no more bitter. These controversies were, furthermore, probably more legal than personal. The dispute with Trefnant over the two books, for instance, may not have reached the archbishop's desk at all. Law and convention required an aggressive, if not vituperative, front, even in differences among friends. It will be recalled in this connection that Brantingham paid a personal visit to the ailing Courtenay just at the height of their clash over the archbishop's rights to visit the diocese of Exeter. Official documents reveal only one face of history and this may frequently be a badly distorted face.[42]

Frequent communication of a personal nature must have

passed between Courtenay and his suffragans, but what remains recorded in the archbishop's register are for the most part official announcements and notices: summonses to convocation; instructions concerning the collection of subsidies voted the crown; authorization of prayers for matters of national interest, such as the success of Earl Arundel, the admiral of the fleet, that of the bishop of Norwich and his crusade, even of Gaunt and his expedition to Castile. In 1394 Courtenay announced through his suffragans the granting of an indulgence to those persons who prayed for the success of Richard's invasion of Ireland. On several occasions, either on his own initiative or that of the king, he issued instructions through his intermediary, the bishop of London, for general prayers throughout the province for the mitigation of natural misfortunes such as pestilence and storms.[43]

COURTENAY AND CHRIST CHURCH MONASTERY

With no group did Courtenay have closer and more frequent contact than with the prior and monks of Christ Church cathedral in Canterbury. Though he spent much time at Lambeth and in and about his diocese and province in the exercise of his episcopal and archiepiscopal authority, and at his different manors to eat up his farm, Canterbury always remained his home. He had been officially elected by its chapter. He in turn presided at the election of the prior and made appointments to other offices in the monastery from names presented him by the community. Already in September 1382, because of "certain and reasonable causes," he removed the subprior, cellarer, chamberlain, and cantor. Shortly after he announced the appointment of new incumbents to those offices and to the offices of precentor and sacristan as well, from nominees recommended to him by the chapter.[44] From entries in the register, it is clear that he kept close watch on the monastery, although it is not stated whether the initiative to remove from office originated with him or with the prior or chapter.

 The register contains a description of the election of Thomas Chillenden (Chylynden) to the office of prior on February 15, 1390. Upon receiving notice of the death of Prior John Ffynche, Courtenay immediately instructed the subprior to assemble the monks as speedily as possible for the election of a successor.[45] These gathered with the archbishop and his clerks

on February 13 at the priory. The first business was that of
burying the deceased prior, which was done the following day
with the archbishop presiding at the solemn exequies. Then on
Wednesday when all had assembled in the chapter house, principally eighty monks of the community, Courtenay formally in-
augurated proceedings with a sermon on the text "They select
a head for themselves." Next a certificate was read which contained the names of all the monks who were eligible to cast a
vote. Then the archbishop's clerks withdrew, leaving the archbishop alone with the monks. Each monk now came forward
in turn and voted, using pen and ink with which to write the
name of his choice. After all the monks had voted, Courtenay
counted the ballots and that night deliberated "diligently" in
his palace over the returns.[46] The following morning (February
16), he returned to the chapter house with his clerks and
preached another sermon, this one on the appropriate text
"Wood, strong and incorruptible, has the wise man selected."

"And at the close of his sermon, he spoke these words:
'Thomas Chillenden, elect, rise and come forward.' And immediately the same brother Thomas, stunned as he later said by
this word, rose and prostrated himself on his face before the
feet of the lord archbishop. The lord archbishop summoned him
a second time and placed a gold ring on his right hand, appointed
him prior of that church, and ordered the *Te Deum Laudamus*
sung loud and clear. Then the lord archbishop with joy led
Thomas with the monks and people to the high altar of the
church and, after having recited the traditional prayer, he installed him."[47]

The mutual good will that attended this meeting of monastery and archbishop did not always extend to their relationship
in the administraton of Canterbury College at Oxford which
they shared. Archbishop Islip had established this college in 1361
in the hope of encouraging the clergy of the diocese of Canterbury to attend the university in greater numbers. In order to
provide financial support for the institution, he appropriated the
revenues of the living of Pagham, a parish belonging to Christ
Church. To conciliate the monks, Islip promised the monastery
that the warden of the college would always be a monk and that
he would select the college's warden from three candidates the
community would have the right to nominate.[48]

In 1367 Archbishop Langham removed John de Radyngate
and appointed Henry Wodhull to the office of prior.[49] The man-

date announcing Wodhull's appointment does not reveal whether the initiative in removing Radyngate had originated with the chapter or with the archbishop. It states only that Islip was removing him "for good and legitimate reasons." That the prior and chapter recommended three names to him from whom he selected Wodhull may suggest their approval of the change. During the archiepiscopacy of Simon Sudbury, the prior and chapter attempted to circumvent the archbishop's authority in the selection of a warden, but failed. On March 19, 1380, Sudbury accused them of prejudicing his rights in "appointing a warden without his wish or approval." Not only was he patron, so he reminded them, but his right to appoint was explicitly confirmed by college statute. The prior and chapter confessed their fault and begged the archbishop's pardon, whereupon the regular procedure was reaffirmed. Three names were given Sudbury and from these he selected William Dovor to be warden.[50]

With Sudbury it had been the prior and chapter who had attempted to exclude the archbishop in the selection of the warden. With Courtenay it was the reverse: he sought to eliminate the voice of the monastery. In September 1382, shortly after his translation to Canterbury, Courtenay notified the prior and chapter that for "just and legitimate reasons" he was removing John Aleyn from his office as warden and was also dismissing other obedientiaries whom Sudbury had appointed.[51] The action of the prior and chapter in nominating Aleyn again some time later for the post makes it reasonably certain that the archbishop's removal of Aleyn had not met with their approval. For the moment, however, they demonstrated their displeasure over the archbishop's action by simply refusing to bring forward any new names for the office. Consequently on October 18 Courtenay announced that, lest the property of the college become dilapidated and be improperly administered because of the vacancy in the office of the warden, he was appointing William Dovor as temporary administrator "until provision is made by us of a warden for the college."[52]

Although Courtenay announced the appointment of Dovor in October as only a temporary adminstrator, the months kept slipping by without any move on his part to regularize the situation. If the monastery had refused to propose three candidates when he informed them of his dismissal of Aleyn in September, as it did, he was not one to renew the request. Finally on July 19, 1383, the prior and chapter forced the issue by laying before the archbishop a series of regulations which would govern the appointment of the warden, fellows, and "poor scholars" of the college. They proposed that the office of the warden be filled as in the past, that is, that they would suggest three names from whom Courtenay would select the one he preferred for warden. Of the two fellows to be appointed, one of these the prior and chapter would select independently of the archbishop, while the other fellow the archbishop would choose from three names given him by the chapter. Of the five "poor scholars" privileged to live in the college, the chapter would select two and the archbishop three, although one of these three must be from the parish of Pagham.[53]

The chapter's plan, which was largely a reaffirmation of what had been normal procedure in the past, did not please Courtenay. He demanded nothing less than unrestricted choice in the appointment of the warden. That this was his position we can deduce from a letter the prior sent to the archbishop on August 5 in which he announced the monastery's acceptance of the "compromise" they had agreed upon. The compromise consisted of this: the archbishop would select a warden from the names of three candidates they would present him, but "for this time only" one of these three candidates would be a man Courtenay had himself directed them to nominate. They also agreed to make a concession in the selection of the fellows. In the past, of the two fellows appointed, they had selected one, while the archbishop appointed a second from three nominees they proposed. Now they agreed to surrender their right to make any independent selection. The archbishop would appoint each fellow, although he would choose them in each instance from among three candidates nominated by the chapter. Even in the matter of the "poor scholars" it is likely some concession was made to Courtenay. According to the new arrangement, he would be permitted to appoint any three persons and would not be obliged to select at least one from the parish of Pagham.

This new plan constituted a complete capitulation on the part of the priory over the issue of the selection of the warden, although the use of three names might conceal this fact from the outside world. The phrase, "for this time only," did not mean that Courtenay would nominate one of the three candidates for the post of warden but once. That was to be the procedure for as long as he was archbishop. This the prior admitted in his letter, although he also warned the archbishop that no man lives forever, and once a new prelate occupied the see of Canterbury, the old plan would go back into effect. The prior's letter read:

> After you will have left the archiepiscopal dignity by some means or another, we, the prior and chapter, shall freely nominate to your successors who will then be archbishops of Canterbury, however often and by whatever manner the office of warden of the college happens to be vacant, three monks of the Canterbury church for that office, from whom so nominated the lord archbishop will appoint one to the office of warden of said college.[54]

The use of three names was a concession to the monastery—they could still pretend they had a voice in the choice of a warden. Courtenay was willing to concede them this privilege since he had gained his point. But the controversy must have evoked some ill feeling, and the prior was careful to preface his letter with an appeal to Courtenay that, out of respect for the sainted Becket, he put aside any rancor he might feel toward the monastery for proposing this solution of their disagreement.

The prior's letter is dated August 5, 1383. Ten days later, on August 15, the prior and chapter sent Courtenay their nominations for the office of warden and for the two fellowships. The three names proposed for warden were those of John Aleyn, Thomas Chillenden, and William Dovor. The choice of nominees is interesting. John Aleyn was the monk Courtenay had demoted from the office of warden the previous fall. Thomas Chillenden's name appeared above as a future prior of Christ Church.[55] William Dovor was the temporary administrator of the college Courtenay had appointed when he removed Aleyn. Some significance may attach to the sequence in which the three names appear. Aleyn was undoubtedly the monastery's first choice, Dovor, the third name listed, was the nominee Courtenay had forced them to include with the two others. And Dovor was the one whom Courtenay appointed warden.[56]

These differences with Christ Church over Canterbury College proved painful and disturbing to both monks and archbishop. For the monks and Courtenay were more than neighbors in Canterbury; in a sense, they were members of the same household. Friction, even hostility, between medieval bishops and cathedral chapters was not uncommon, but such a situation usually meant an impairment of the efficiency of the archbishop's administration. For a new archbishop like Courtenay, such open conflict was especially bad since it would serve to mark him in the eyes of the majority of the clergy as an ambitious autocrat. The burden of such a reputation would reduce his effectiveness in his own diocese and province among his bishops and clergy and might well reduce his influence in political circles. Of these dangers Courtenay must have been aware. Prudence recommended the re-establishment of amiable relations with the monks of Christ Church, and this he set out to accomplish.

It was probably some time during the fall of 1383, after his appointment of Dovor as warden, that Courtenay sat down with the prior and chapter of Christ Church to discuss their differences over Canterbury College and to examine the statutes earlier archbishops had made for the guidance of the community. Their study took them back to 1361 when Archbishop Islip had issued his first statutes in the establishment of the college. Little survives of these foundation statutes except as reissued by Courtenay.[57] Several years later, probably in 1365, Islip issued a series of secular statutes that were clearly designed for a community of seculars which Canterbury College had become for a time when Wyclif was warden late in 1365. Whether these secular statutes had ever been accepted and enforced is doubtful, since Archbishop Langham expelled Wyclif and the seculars the following year.[58] It was not these secular statutes but the earlier ones Islip had issued in 1361 that Courtenay revised in consultation with the prior and chapter late in 1383. The initiative to do so had come from the warden and fellows of Canterbury College, so Courtenay declared, who had complained about all the confusion and controversy they had occasioned. The archbishop declared he was quite ready to revise these, since the church was always willing to alter rules and regulations which time and experience had proved unwise. After a careful inspection of the statutes and "serious and diligent" deliberation with the prior and chapter, Courtenay issued a new series of statutes, some Islip's, others that they had agreed to revise, and still others that were entirely new, all intended to serve the "peace and utility" of the college.

Concerning the office of warden, Archbishop Islip had provided that the prior and chapter would nominate three of their members, one of whom the archbishop would appoint as warden; that only the archbishop might remove the warden from office without formal trial, should he prove unsatisfactory, and appoint another in his place, following the above procedure; that should any future archbishop wish to make a particular warden's appointment permanent because of the man's superior talents, he might do so with the unanimous consent of the chapter. The statute did not specify what was to be the warden's tenure of office.

This statute of Islip's governing the selection of the warden was retained. The archbishop also agreed to accept Islip's ruling that the prior and chapter have free choice in the selection of the fellows who would attend Canterbury College.[59] Other statutes issued by Islip were also permitted to stand, such as those concerning the course of studies and degrees, the common seal of the college, and the financial administration of the college. All the fellows and scholars were to continue to eat together in the refectory except those who were ill. They would be cared for in their rooms. Should the illness of a scholar prove extended and be considered incurable, he was to be removed to the priory. Silence was to be observed at all meals. During these meals one of the "poor scholars" would read sacred scripture to the community.

Any student wishing to go out for a walk should not take his servant with him or a stranger, but a "proper person" of the community, so that he would derive some benefit from their conversation. No one was to absent himself from the college except for good cause, as perhaps upon invitation to attend the inception of another student. Fellows and scholars could secure permission to spend a month on vacation in the fall, although should the young man remain away beyond a month, he was to forfeit six pence each day from his pension. Again, should any scholar be sent by the prior to give a sermon or on some other assignment, he might absent himself for no more than three weeks, after which time he would also be fined six pence a day.

Latin was to be spoken at all times except with lay people. Visitors and relatives were not permitted into the college lest their coming disturb the tranquillity of the community. Hunting dogs and hunting itself were prohibited to all members of the community including the warden, neither were any members of the college to visit taverns or private homes in Oxford or the vicinity unless in the company of an older and more discreet monk. The warden was to have a special place at table and was also to occupy the principal room. All other rooms were to be assigned in such a manner as to leave younger scholars occupying rooms next to older ones, in order to "curb altercations and horseplay." Rooms for visiting clergy were to be provided, that is, for those who were "respectable, virtuous, peaceful, quiet, humble, and given to study," and especially for those who wished to advance in logic, canon law, and theology. Exception could be made in case the visitor were a graduate or a noble person, whose learning and manners would serve as a source of edification to the community.

Should the warden neglect for a third time to keep peace among the scholars or if he himself were the cause of disturbance, or should he be negligent or unjust in disciplining the members of the community, or should he give bad example by perjury, adultery, a failing of the flesh, failure to keep up the property, or have injured another person with a club, sword, or knife, or be under grave suspicion for some other crime, an older monk of the college, with the consent of the others or the majority of them, should approach him with charity and reserve within fifteen days and instruct him to mend his ways. Should the warden refuse to do this, he was to be reported to the archbishop. The warden in his turn should keep a watchful eye on the conduct of those under his supervision and remonstrate with and discipline them. If following a third reminder the guilty party should fail to correct his ways, he was to be reported to the prior and chapter. Should the prior neglect the matter, the warden should notify the archbishop.

Courtenay and the chapter found these statutes "reasonable and useful," whereupon the archbishop declared them officially accepted. All other statutes that Islip had issued, together with those made by his successors in Canterbury, Courtenay declared null and void. Then he added a number of his own, either as revised statutes of earlier ones Islip had made or entirely new and intended to cover matters that required attention for the first time. The first of these concerned "poor scholars." These scholars were to be young men, free, legitimate, of upright character, and talented, who were planning to go on to holy orders, of whom the archbishop would appoint three, the prior and chapter two. Each of these scholars would receive a room in the hall and be given ten pence each week for his expenses within the university. They were to assist in the chapel on feast days and at the discretion of the warden read the lessons and sing at the services. They were also to wait upon the warden and the fellows when they were at table and at other times when they were drinking, provided this was at a proper time. They were to be diligent in their studies, taking up first the study of grammar, then, upon the advice of their master and fellows, proceeding to logic. No more than two of them should be permitted to major in civil law should that appear expedient to the warden and fellows, so that with this foundation in logic and civil law they could progress more rapidly in the study of sacred theology and canon law. These "poor scholars" should be permitted to remain at the college no more than seven years, and during those seven years the warden and fellows were strictly enjoined from assigning them responsibilities that might impede their studies. Should any of these scholars become negligent in his studies or give scandal by his conduct and fail to amend after receiving proper warning, he was to be expelled by the warden with the consent of the fellows or the majority of them.

The college should hold disputations twice a week, from the feast of St. Michael (September 29) until the Annunciation (March 25) by candlelight, during the rest of the year by sunlight. They were to hold these disputations in the hall after supper if a sufficiently large group was on hand. On such evenings, time spent at supper should be curtailed. At the conclusion of such disputations, an antiphon to the Blessed Virgin or St. Thomas should be recited and a prayer said by the warden or by some older member present. Then after taking a drink, if this was necessary, each fellow and scholar was to return to his studies without delay, "so that small talk and frivolities that could contribute to discord be wholly avoided." Two observers should be on hand at these disputations to regulate the amount of time taken by each student, lest the older ones appropriate so much time as to leave the younger ones insufficient opportunity to gain experience.

The number of scholars in the college should not be permitted to grow to a point where the upkeep of the institution be jeopardized. At least one sixth of the annual revenues of the college should be available for expenditure on new buildings and on the repair of old ones, and this included chapels and granges at both Oxford and Pagham. No books or plate belonging to the college were to be pawned without special permission of the prior and chapter. Infraction of this rule would be punished with excommunication. The warden should receive a record of what books each student was given when he arrived at the college, and he should check these once or twice a year. Three of the older fellows should check those used by the warden.

Each day mass was to be said in the chapel of the college for the king and queen and for the souls of their ancestors, also for the souls of Islip, Langham, and Sudbury, Courtenay's immediate predecessors, as well as for Courtenay, the souls of his ancestors, and for the deceased and living benefactors of the college. The fellows and warden were to take turns saying mass, although each fellow who was a priest was to say mass at least three times each week. Each of the poor scholars was to recite certain prayers and psalms for the souls of the above and, with the fellows, to attend mass and vespers on the principal feasts of the year. Solemn vespers, matins, and mass were ordered for great feast days such as Christmas, Easter, Ascension, Pentecost, and the Assumption of the Blessed Virgin. Each Saturday a mass was to be said for the souls of the above. Finally, a fellow was to have the care of the vestments, books, and furnishings of the chapel, while a monk was to serve as precentor and supervise the divine services and have the care of the sacristy.[60]

These statutes, that is, those of Islip's that Courtenay had confirmed and those he had added, the prior and chapter of Christ Church monastery promptly ratified, as did the warden and fellows of the college.[61] On January 29, 1384, two weeks after the formal announcement of these statutes and their ratification, Courtenay notified William Dovor, the warden of the college, that his appointment would be permanent. He also forwarded a letter to this effect to the prior.[62] Since this announcement followed so closely on the heels of the agreement between monastery and archbishop regarding the new set of statutes for the college, it is safe to assume that Courtenay and the monks had discussed the matter and had agreed to making Dovor's wardenship permanent. Courtenay's action, in any event, was fully authorized under provision of the new constitution, that is, if he had the unanimous approval of the monastery. No hint of what might have been the monastery's reaction to this development is revealed in the prior's letter to Courtenay in which he acknowledged receipt of this information. He simply stated that "after diligent and solemn discussion in common," the chapter had agreed to ratify the archbishop's action.[63]

This settlement represented a victory for moderation and compromise. Both monastery and archbishop had made some concessions, although there is no point in denying that Courtenay emerged the victor. Yet it appears that his victory in making Dovor permanent warden of Canterbury College did not leave the monastery in a hostile frame of mind. There is no record of any further differences between him and the community. Early in his career Courtenay had been instrumental in securing from the king for the monastery the right to hold four annual fairs, each of nine days' duration.[64] During the course of his fifteen years as their neighbor, he extended them evidence of his good will on many different occasions, favors which the monks gratefully acknowledged on the occasion of the archbishop's death.[65]

COURTENAY AND THE ABBEY OF ST. AUGUSTINE

Courtenay's contacts with the other great monastic establishment at Canterbury, the abbey of St. Augustine, were minimal. This monastery which lay just outside the walls of the city enjoyed an exempt position. It was one of that small but proud group of monastic houses in the province that continued to defy the ambitions of many archbishops of Canterbury to exercise unrestricted spiritual jurisdiction over every person and community in that province. Because of the proximity of the archbishop, greater vigilance was perhaps required of the abbot and chapter to preserve that exempt character than was the case with distant St. Albans, for instance. For the physical presence of the abbey served as a constant reminder to the archbishop that whatever his grand title and pretensions might be, to the abbey he was no better than a foreign prelate. Fear of the archbishop undoubtedly produced an undue sensitivity at St. Augustine's. Its chronicler, at any rate, was forever smelling encroachment, surely on most occasions where none was intended. He has only hostile words for Courtenay.

There is no record of any archbishop ever actually attempting an inquisitorial visitation of the abbey, although a number did make an effort to breach its proud independence to the extent of visiting the chapel with the archiepiscopal cross carried before them. Pecham did so in 1279, but he announced on that occasion, possibly in order not to offend the king who happened to be visiting the abbey at the time, that he did not intend with his visit any prejudice to the exempt position of the community.[66] Even such a visit, made for reasons of piety, the abbey was loath to tolerate. When Sudbury attempted to enter the abbey with his cross carried before him, they barred his way with armed

guards. Sudbury appealed the matter to the pope, who directed
the bishop of Winchester to investigate the dispute. The archbishop gained his point in the end and visited the abbey, a privilege he actually had a right to according to canon law. But the
abbot warned Sudbury that God would intervene to protect the
rights of St. Augustine's, and the chronicler sees the working of
God's justice in the murder of the archbishop in 1381.[67]

From the moment of Courtenay's translation to Canterbury, St. Augustine's chronicler was suspicious. When Courtenay
appealed to the pope for special privileges in order to facilitate
the visitation of his province, the chronicler charged him with
having sought permission to visit even the exempt monasteries
of the province. This request, according to the chronicler, "the
prudent high priest of God" refused to grant because he recognized the archbishop's cunning. Although the archbishop was
disappointed, he consoled himself with the hope of finding the
pope in a more generous mood on some later occasion. In the
meantime, however, he made the abbey feel his ill will and "he
began to show hatred to our church and those living therein,
and to enslave it in various ways." He was no longer content,
for example, in being addressed in letters from the abbey as
all archbishops from time out of mind had been addressed. The
ancient usage—"To the venerable father in Christ and lord N,
by the grace of God archbishop of Canterbury, primate of all
England, N, by the same permission, abbot, *etc.*, greeting for
ever in the Lord"—he demanded be replaced by the following:
"To the most reverend father and lord in Christ, the Lord
William, by the grace of God archbishop of Canterbury, primate
of all England and legate of the apostolic see, N, by the same
permission abbot, *etc.*, due reverence and honor owed to so
mighty a father." Whenever the abbot made a presentation to
the archbishop according to the earlier address, the archbishop
simply refused to admit the presentee.[68]

Shortly after this incident, Courtenay, "not favoring our
exemption, as if our abbot were subject to his rule," appointed
him collector of the half-tenth voted by convocation to be raised
in the city and diocese of Canterbury. When Courtenay's appointment reached the abbey, the abbot and older heads took
counsel and agreed to send the order back whence it came. But
the support the abbot hurried off to Westminster to secure from
the king's council and the duke of Lancaster in confirmation

of his action he failed to secure, so Courtenay's appointment stood. The council did humor the abbot, however, to the extent of issuing its own order appointing him collector of the subsidy for the diocese of Canterbury. And it was the council's order, not Courtenay's, that the abbot referred to in his letters to the different deans of the diocese concerning the payment of the subsidy.[69]

This is a chronicle of small beer compared to the archbishop's final act of maliciousness toward the abbey. The chronicler leaves no doubt concerning Courtenay's malevolence. "In those days," he wrote, "the archbishop here in his own church was puffed up with arrogance over his secular power and the preeminence of his ecclesiastical dignity and decided to arrogate rights over exempt houses now that he had the pope on his right hand and the king was there to support his arm. . . . Thinking the time opportune since our newly appointed abbot had just arrived at the abbey and was worn out by his labors and excessive expenses, something the archbishop knew but gave no thought to, but eager rather to add affliction to the afflicted, he did not delay any longer but on the day of his installation notified him that he would be coming to see him within a few days."[70]

Courtenay's message threw the abbey into consternation, for the archbishop had indicated that he was coming with his cross carried before him. The abbot hastened immediatly to the archiepiscopal palace at Canterbury and reminded Courtenay that "the monastery was fortified with such privileges and immunities, that no archbishop of Canterbury, for whatever cause, could legitimately enter it with cross carried before him." This reminder only angered the archbishop and when the abbot begged him to change his plans, Courtenay replied brusquely that "whether he liked it or whether he did not like it, he wished and planned to visit the monastery for the sake of devotion and that he would pray as frequently as he chose before the tombs of the saints there."[71]

The account in the register says the abbot returned to his monastery in anger. By the following morning, however, his indignation must have abated, for he and many of his monks went out to meet Courtenay as he was returning from a pilgrimage to Hakyngton. When they reached the archbishop, they all genuflected three times before him, bowed their heads, and "humbly begged him to please to come to their monastery in the manner he had planned, even with his cross borne erect and publicly, and that in his charity he pardon the abbot his offense."

Later that day, Courtenay did ride over to the abbey and was met at the gate by the abbot and chapter. He visited the tombs of the saints buried in the church[72] and, after completing his devotions, returned to his palace. Then in order to convince the people that such a visit was not to be viewed as anything extraordinary, he visited the abbey three additional times that same week, each time with his cross borne before him and each time being received with due reverence by the abbot and monks. But he assured the abbot that he had no wish to prejudice the abbey's immunities by his visits, and he issued a public announcement to that effect.

Whether abbot and chapter were finally persuaded that such was actually Courtenay's intention or whether they felt they had no other choice left them, they agreed after consultation with the archbishop that in the future any archbishop of Canterbury might visit the abbey whenever he chose and with his cross carried before him.[73] Their own secret feelings may have been those of the unconvinced scribe who wrote of Courtenay: "under pretence of devotion he approached the tombs of his predecessors, and having washed his feet in the abbot's chamber, returned with the curse of God to his own place, with his boots on."[74]

COURTENAY AND THE CLERGY OF HIS PROVINCE

A significant phase of Courtenay's work as archbishop was the attention he gave to the correction of clerical irregularities. His interest in clerical reform may actually have been his principal motive for undertaking the visitation of his province, that is, to learn of the existence of clerical abuses and to correct them. That he issued his most extensive correctives in the early nineties after he had completed the bulk of his visiting suggests that it was the extent of clerical abuses he discovered on his travels that prompted him to legislate against them. Monastic abuses in the dioceses of his suffragans were not his direct concern. Once he had visited their houses and issued the necessary injunctions, such as in the case of Caldwell priory in the diocese of Lincoln,[75] his responsibilities there were over. For monastic establishments in his own diocese, however, that were not exempt from his jurisdiction, he had a continuing responsibility. The responsibility extended, of course, to all the secular clergy of the province of Canterbury.

One instance when he concerned himself about conditions in a monastery in his own diocese appeared in 1387 with his appointment of the prior of Leeds and two of his own clerks to visit Combwell priory. Disturbing reports had been brought him from that house. When his emissaries reached the monastery they found these reports only too true. The prior had absconded with a good bit of the moveable wealth of the priory that he had not already squandered, including four horses, much gold and silver, and the best bed in the house, and to cap off his crimes was presently living with a married woman. A summons was delivered to the erring prior, which he apparently heeded without delay. As expected, the archbishop removed him from his office. So greatly did the sinner's sorrow and humility impress the archbishop, however, that he directed the new prior to accord the penitent first place in the community after the subprior.[76]

Such evidences of conspicuous crime were fortunately rare, although the presence of less serious practices was quite universal. Two common abuses of the time that reformers had been attacking long before Courtenay's day and would continue to deplore until the sixteenth century were the related practices of pluralities and nonresidence. These two practices were closely linked although not necessarily present at one and the same time. A priest could be a nonresident pastor and still hold but one benefice. This kind of nonresidence was bad but not common, for a priest with the income of but one benefice to draw upon could not afford to be absent from his cure very long. It was the priest who had been instituted to several parishes that aroused the indignation of reformers, for so often he failed to provide vicars for the parish or parishes he could not personally serve. That the reformer Wyclif had drawn fire for his negligence in this matter reveals how common the practice was.[77] In Wyclif's case the motive of avarice was not present. In the case of many other priests it was, for the temptation was great to increase one's income by acquiring additional benefices. If the motive to secure several benefices was purely mercenary in the first place, it was not difficult for the priest to take the further step of neglecting to appoint a vicar to any additional benefice he might acquire. This quest for benefices developed into something approaching a business, and it was not uncommon for priests to exchange parishes with the very same motivation that impelled merchants to exchange goods. Attendant practices might be even more vicious. A priest might offer money or other inducement in order to receive a particular benefice, or he might even stoop to fraud in order to gain his object. And if a priest did accumulate a number of benefices and realize a good income from them, what better place to spend his ill-gotten gains than London.

Many bishops did not view the practice of pluralities as itself an abuse, nor even nonresidence, provided the pastor appointed a vicar to serve the people within his cures. This was Courtenay's approach. He could not well have had any other position on pluralities. The practice was general and presumably necessary, and he himself had benefited from it as a young man and was most probably continuing to do so as archbishop. As noted above, on one occasion in 1392 he had asked and received permission from the pope to extend leaves to twenty priests so that they might attend some *studium generale* or absent themselves from their charges for some other worthy purpose.[78] Yet if he did not wish to abolish the practice, he did make an earnest effort to suppress related abuses. He frequently granted individuals permission to attend Oxford, although such privileges were for the purpose of study and nothing else, as he warned one priest.[79] He permitted the vicar of Gonthust to absent himself "for the purpose of making a pilgrimage," on condition that his brother-priest take his place.[80] Whenever the archbishop instituted a priest to a parish, he made the presentee swear to remain in residence. Thus he admitted William Lyngee to the church at Wormenhale, "after having received from William his corporal oath that he would remain continually and personally in residence in said vicarage in accordance with the constitutions of Otho and Othobon."[81] Another pastor, the vicar of Aldington, he cited "for being so little in residence."[82]

Courtenay issued his most ambitious statute on the subject of pluralities and nonresidence in March 1391, just a month before confirming an earlier decree of Archbishop Winchelsey on the same general problem.[83] His target was "choppechurches," the term popularly applied to priests who trafficked in benefices, priests who "deal in the gifts of the Holy Spirit and who acquire, by purchase or secret simoniacal contract, churches and ecclesiastical benefices." The activities of such "choppechurches" were

various. Some in their greed misrepresented the value of their
own benefices in negotiating exchanges for others. Some were
so hardened as to swindle less worldly priests entirely out of
their benefices. Some "choppechurches" derived a steady income
from priests from whom they had secured benefices upon promise
of a percentage of the fruits.[84] Because of detestable practices
of this kind, priests who had been the victims of fraudulent exchanges might find themselves destitute, learned and distinguished
men would seek in vain for benefices to provide themselves the
means of livelihood, divine services and the cure of souls were
neglected, and priests who were incapable of handling even one
small benefice would acquire a number, none of which they
would serve properly. Well might such merchants in the goods
of the Holy Spirit ponder what happened to the money-changers
Christ found in the temple: he had not just upbraided them as
he did other sinners; no, he had made himself a scourge and
had driven them physically from the temple of God. Nothing
less should these *"non rectores, sed raptores"* expect, who neglected their cures and spent their sordid gains in luxurious living
in London.

Such practices must cease, Courtenay declared in his letter
to the bishop of London, and he instructed him to take certain
preventive measures in his diocese and to send these instructions
on to all the suffragan bishops of the province. He and they
were to insist that every priest, upon being instituted to a
benefice, swear that he had not entered in any agreement with
the presentee or other person concerning the benefice; that when
benefices were exchanged, the principals to the exchange, not
just their agents, be present, and that an accurate evaluation
of the benefices be presented; that all nonresidents be compelled
to return to their cures immediately unless they had good cause
not to; that priests who had acquired benefices by means of
simoniacal agreements be deprived of these benefices; that all
simoniacal contracts be nullified, and should the partners to such
agreements find this impossible, the matter should be reported
to the diocesan so that he could impose fitting penances; finally,
that they "strike with ecclesiastical censure especially those who
are in orders, those detestable merchants of the Lord's inheritance
who have fraudulently obtained possession of several churches
or dignities, and, in particular, those sons of perdition, the
'choppechurches.' "[85]

A month later Courtenay followed up this statute with

a confirmation of Archbishop Winchelsey's decree against stipendiary priests. Again the subject was clerical avarice, in this case the activities of priests who lived off stipends or incomes given them by the faithful in return for saying mass. A priest in such circumstances found himself relatively free to come and go, with no responsibility for providing spiritual services to any parish. His need to say mass, however, did oblige him to secure the use of some church, and this usually in the area in which the donor of his stipends lived. He might remain here so long as to become identified as one of the resident priests attached to the church. Friction between himself and the rector would be almost inevitable. It might develop for a number of reasons, such as the failure of the stipendiary priest to assist in the divine services. The most common source of ill will was, however, the practice of such priests in accepting gifts and casual offerings from the parishioners that might otherwise have gone to the rector. Such priests, Courtenay warned in his preface to Winchelsey's statutes, who without the consent of the rector appropriated gifts and offerings, were guilty not only of theft but of sacrilege as well, since the goods they appropriated were ecclesiastical.

He then proceeded to confirm the statutes his predecessor had issued approximately twenty years earlier in an effort to suppress the irregularities of stipendiary priests.[86] These priests were not to accept offerings of any kind from the parishioners of the churches in which they said mass without the permission of the rector or vicar there resident. Some time during the divine services on Sunday or similar feastday they were to take a public oath that they would not accept such offerings or gifts which should be properly made to the rector, and that they would not sow or encourage difficulties between the resident clergy and their parishioners, but would rather work for the preservation of harmony and peace. Should the rector or vicar so require, they were to take this oath before saying mass in the church, and in case it be proved later that they had violated that oath, they were to be barred from celebrating mass in any of the churches of the province.

Such stipendiary priest should not hear confessions except with permission, although they should take part in the recitation of the divine office and the regular liturgical services, always using a surplice of their own. And at such times they should surely not be roaming about the nave of the church or outside in the churchyard. Should the rector have occasion to correct them for some irregularity, they should accept his censure with humility. They should not begin their own mass on Sunday, feastdays, or funerals, until after the gospel had been read at the high altar. They were not to say anything disparaging of the rector or vicar, but learn with the psalmist to place a guard upon their mouth. Finally, they should avoid taverns and similar places of amusement and shun unseemly and forbidden plays, and always conduct themselves in a manner befitting a priest.

Provident and useful though these statutes of Winchelsey's were, they had come to be forgotten and ignored as quite antiquated. But the abuses committed by stipendiary priests persisted, and it was with the consent of the bishops and clergy recently gathered in convocation at London that Courtenay was now reissuing these statutes. And "lest anyone be able to plead ignorance of these matters, we wish the said statutes to be published in each diocese of our province of Canterbury . . . at least once a year."[87]

In his journey about the province, Courtenay often had occasion to deplore the ruinous condition of church buildings and the walls about church property. If this condition was due to negligence, that fact would support the picture of a general decline of the church in the late Middle Ages. If such dilapidation sprang from the poverty of the church, the conclusion would not be greatly different, since it would suggest clerical inefficiency or growing popular indifference. Whatever the cause, the situation greatly disturbed the archbishop. When he learned of such a situation, he issued stern orders to the negligent priest to correct the condition under threat of sequestration. In the case of deceased rectors, as of Richard Crissenyle, late rector of the church of Konenden, who had neglected the care of "books and ornaments . . . whose repair was his responsibility," he ordered the estate sequestrated until the necessary repairs had been made.[88] It was his invariable practice when imposing penances that involved money, to assign some of the fine for the repair of the walls and buildings belonging to a church.

Not all Courtenay's mandates to his clergy were admonitory or disciplinary. Indicative of the wide responsibilities a medieval bishop might assume was an order he addressed the clergy of his diocese in August 1386 concerning the danger of an invasion from France. His priests were to make provision for this peril with all possible speed and in proportion to the value of their benefices. Priests with an income of 100 marks were to provide equipment for one man and two archers; those with an income of 40 pounds or more, equipment for two archers; those with an income of 20 pounds, equipment for one archer; those with less than 20 pounds, hauberks, light helmets and gear, bows and arrows or other weapons.[89]

COURTENAY AND THE LAITY

How much contact did Courtenay have with the common people who made up the great majority of the faithful under his jurisdiction? One can only speculate. Medieval documents are particularly uncommunicative about the lives of humble folk. Not only did the medieval clerks in the chanceries of bishops and kings generally ignore them, but even the monastic chroniclers. Since Courtenay was a bishop, one may assume he had little association with ordinary laymen and laywomen—even modern bishops who are not lords seldom meet the "people"—and since Courtenay was born of aristocratic parentage, that little was perhaps reduced to nothing. What communication he had with them was indirect, through his clergy and officials. His bishops and clergy kept him informed of their faith, their failings, and what complaints they might have had against their pastors. His bishops and clergy, in turn, conveyed his directives and admonitions to them, publicly from the pulpit if they applied to many, privately if only an individual or a few persons were involved. The only occasion the archbishop spoke to them directly of which there is any record was when he questioned selected laymen in the course of his visitation. He also had direct contact with excommunicates and individuals in similar difficulties who had been cited to appear before him.

Whatever the nature of Courtenay's personal relationship with the common people, there were frequent occasions during the course of his fifteen years at Canterbury when he issued instructions that were concerned with their behavior. A common complaint that the clergy brought to the archbishop's attention against their charges concerned the payment, more often nonpayment of tithes. Though tithing was as old as the law of Moses, no less ancient were the repugnance of those paying the tithe and their efforts to evade that duty. Part of the popular resistance to tithing, at least the argument generally advanced by those

who sought to justify that resistance, was the presence of con-
flicting views on such questions as to what persons actually owed
a tithe; whether this obligation amounted in every instance to
a full tenth; whether certain expenses might be deducted before
the payment of the tithe; to whom the tithe was finally to be
paid; how and when the tithe was to be turned over to the
church. Confusion and lack of uniformity in these matters contributed to losses of revenue for the church, bitterness between
laity and clergy, and, consequently, to hostility toward the
church. In an effort to standardize policies and procedures and
to eliminate irregularities, Courtenay issued a detailed directive
in 1389 that was to serve as a guide for the clergy and laity
of his diocese of Canterbury.

Men who owned timber were required to pay a tithe of
all they cut, whether this was cut from woods, grove, swamp,
or ditch, and whatever the shape into which the wood was cut,
that is, billets, faggots, "tallwood," or simple branches. A farmer
paid a tithe of all his stock. If he had six calves, he paid six
pence as his tithe; if seven, eight, nine, or ten calves, he gave
an animal, although receiving back for the seventh calf three
pence, for the eighth calf two pence, and for the ninth calf
one penny. Should the priest to whom the tithe was owed choose
to wait a second year before collecting his tithe, he was entitled
to at least the third best calf. The same rule applied to sheep
and pigs except that instead of pence as in the case of calves,
half-pence would be paid to equalize the transaction. When
young animals such as calves and sheep were sold with their
dams, the farmer was held to a full tenth of their value. Colts
were in the same category as calves. When calf, colt, sheep,
pig, goose, or other animal was able to fend for itself, it was
considered fully grown as far as the tithe was concerned.

A full tithe was to be paid of the wool sheared from
sheep. In the case of sheep pastured in one place in summer
and another in winter, the tithe was to be divided between the
two parishes in whose limits the sheep had grazed. If there remained a question whence the sheep came, that parish was entitled to the tithe within whose limits the sheep were sheared.

Farmers were to pay a tithe of milk and cheese, although
financial arrangements made between priest and farmer covering
the payment of this tenth were entirely permissible. Custom
recommended the payment of three pence to cover the milk and
cheese tithe for each cow. The farmer must also pay a tithe of his

pasture and the hay that might be cut therefrom, whether this was from the commons or from land of his own. If the animals that grazed on this pasture land were unfertile, such as horses, colts, and steers, then the tithe was to be calculated on the basis of the value of each acre as pasture. If the animals were cows and mares, or even sheep that were not fertile, then a tithe of the offspring, wool, or milk must be paid.

Millers were obligated to a tenth of their income. A tithe was also required of those who owned fisheries, ponds, beehives, and similar kinds of property. Craftsmen paid personal tithes, that is, pelterers, butchers, carpenters, tailors, weavers, brewers, and all hired workers. Those things that the earth or water produced were subject to tithing with no deduction for expenses permitted. In the case of other personal tithes, however, the tither might deduct expenses at the end of the year before computing his charge.

In all instances people who owed a tithe were to pay their dues promptly and at the proper time of the year. Should they neglect this grave obligation, priests were to deny them entrance to the church. Should they continue obdurate, ecclesiastical censures were to be applied, from which only the archbishop could absolve. On the other hand, priests who from fear or for the purpose of gaining good will did not enforce the collection of the tithe, were threatened with suspension. Finally, any person who prevented a priest or his servant from entering his fields in order to investigate the tithe and collect it, was to be excommunicated.[90]

Four years later, in 1393, Courtenay issued a supplementary directive on the same subject of tithes. Indignant rectors had informed him that parishioners were turning over calves that were four or five weeks old, pigs two or three weeks old, and sheep before Lent, as well as geese and goslings at Easter and Pentecost. Since animals so young were not able to take care of themselves, many of them had died before the clergy could make use of them. Other farmers were appropriating tithes of hay, wood, geese, pigs, calves, lambs, flax, hemp, fruit, and other products for their own use, without consulting their rectors and obtaining their permission. Then after using such tithes at their pleasure, they might pay for such appropriations when and what they chose, in fact, at times concealing the very fact of their appropriation. Such practices the archbishop sternly prohibited. No geese, pigs, or lambs were to be paid as tithes so

long as they were not old enough to fend for themselves. Furthermore, to delay in paying one's tithes was as much a sin as refusing
to pay them at all. All persons owing tithes were required to pay
these on time under pain of excommunication.[91]

If one quality stands out in Courtenay's character as archbishop it was his sensitivity to possible encroachments upon the
rights and prerogatives of the church, his own church of Canterbury in particular. As early as August 1382 he had occasion
to issue a protest in defense of the church's rights. He had learned
that the bailiff of Canterbury, Edmund Horum, and his assistants
had presumed to investigate and punish such offenses as adultery
and fornication, even though the prosecution of moral offenses
of this kind lay exclusively within the province of the ecclesiastical authorities. He accordingly instructed the prior of St. Gregory's in Canterbury to warn Horum to desist from such practices
under pain of excommunication and interdict. Perhaps Courtenay
viewed the bailiff's action as an extension of what had recently
taken place in London, where the mayor and his officials had
seized several women charged with adultery and fornication, cut
off their hair, and marched them through the city to the accom-
paniment of trumpet and flute. According to the chronicler, the
followers of Wyclif had persuaded the mayor and his men to
take this action since the bishops had either failed to do anything
about it or had been paid to ignore the matter. The chronicler
had also said that it was because of his fear of the mayor who
was a headstrong and violent man, and of the Londoners too,
that the bishop of London had failed to protest the action of
these laymen as an encroachment on the prerogatives of the
church.[92]

Courtenay did not lack the courage, although, of course,
Canterbury was not London. At any rate, when he learned later
that Horum and his assistants had not heeded the prior's warning
and had arrested Isabella, wife of Nicholas Chappecote, on the
charge of adultery, a "malicious charge" brought by one Robert
Hanten, Courtenay directed his official to cite Horum to appear
for questioning. Both Horum and Hanten appeared in answer
to the summons and asked the archbishop to present them a
written copy of the charges and to permit them a day in which
to study them. What threatened to develop into a serious clash
over a question of jurisdiction cleared quickly upon Horum's
protest that he had never intended anything prejudicial to the
rights of the church and that he had been and would always

continue to be completely faithful in his recognition of those rights.[93]

It was about this same time that the archbishop directed his official to excommunicate the bailiffs who had entered "our house" of Hollingbourne and had taken several monks into custody.[94] On another occasion he ordered the excommunication of several bailiffs who had entered the church of Thibourne and had seized three of his tenants who had come there to hear mass. Not only had the bailiffs no right to enter the church and take these people away, but they had also disturbed the recitation of the divine office with their intrusion.[95]

In December 1382 Courtenay ordered the prior of the church of St. Gregory and the official of the diocese to denounce the men who had entered an estate belonging to Canterbury where they had seized a Robert Someno and had carried him off to prison. By that act they had incurred automatic excommunication inasmuch as no justiciar, sheriff, bailiff, or other official of the king had the right to trespass upon Canterbury property.[96] To the chaplain of the parish church of Godehurst he sent instructions that he warn the people of the village to cease transacting their buying and selling in the church yard. Such conduct was disrespectful of the rights of the church. Should the practice persist, the chaplain was to cite the rebellious ones to appear before the archbishop for disciplining.[97]

A different kind of infringement upon the rights of the church of Canterbury concerned the negligence of the tenants of the archbishop to pay their rents. "Ignorance, the mother of error, had so blinded" several of these tenants, that instead of bringing in the hay and straw they owed, publicly and in wagons, they had brought less than they owed and they had brought this in secretly and in sacks. Upon their appearance before the archbishop in answer to his summons, he imposed upon them the following penance: "on the Sunday following, the penitents, with bared heads and feet, were to lead the procession in the collegiate church of Wengham, walking slowly and with humility and devotion, each with a sack on his shoulder, so full of hay and straw that these protruded from the mouths of the sacks and were visible to all."[98]

As was the case with all executives whose responsibilities covered so broad an area, Courtenay had to rely heavily upon the officials of his household in the administration of his diocese and province. Routine matters seldom received his attention, and such would ordinarily include issues raised over the conduct of laymen. On the other hand, when heresy or the rights of the clergy were involved, Courtenay seems to have taken a strong personal interest. One such instance was the sacrilegious conduct of certain inhabitants of the town of Wye. Several of the towns-people had stolen vestments, books, chalices, and sundry other articles from the church, and "over these, with invocations to the evil spirits, had practised the art of necromancy." Not content with these enormities, they had then accused Thomas Brelwester, the rector, and two of his parishioners, Thomas Kempe and John Lese, with having stolen the sacred articles. According to the information given to the archbishop, the charge against the priest and his two parishioners was preposterous, so he instructed his commissary general to permit the three men to clear themselves by compurgation. They had requested that privilege. He also directed his official to cite six villagers who were believed to have been the ringleaders in the crime, and have them appear before him for questioning.[99]

Two weeks later the commissary general sent the arch-bishop a report of his progress in the case. The two laymen, Kempe and Lese, who had been maliciously accused of the crime, had each produced twelve "good and trustworthy men" who swore to their innocence. For "legitimate reasons" which are explained, the priest, Thomas Brelwester, had not appeared for compurgation. But of the six men he had been instructed to summon, he could locate only one, so he had proclaimed the citation of the others from the pulpit of the church of Wye when a large number of the parishioners were gathered there.[100]

From the nature of a mandate Courtenay issued four days later, it appears that the "legitimate reasons" that had kept the priest from clearing himself had been nothing less than jail. Several men, probably the same ones guilty of the robbery, had seized the priest and had taken him to prison where they kept him for some time in "terrible bonds." While he was in that condition, they had laid hold of him one night and, with a sorcerer presiding, had cut crosses into his face in mockery of Christ and had burned other signs into it by means of a mixture of sulphur and ashes. Courtenay announced the excommunication of all persons implicated in the sacrilege and laid an interdict upon the town since the crime had apparently been committed with the consent or connivance of the community.[101]

In the mandate announcing the interdict, Courtenay explained that one of the purposes of this censure was that of forcing the townspeople to make an early peace with the church. This they indicated they wanted to do after a lapse of two weeks. Whereupon Courtenay met with the men whom he had originally summoned, together with a good number of the townspeople, in the church of Wye. There these men acknowledged their guilt and asked that the interdict be lifted, promising to carry out whatever "salutary penance" the archbishop might wish to impose. The following day procurators for the townspeople presented themselves to Courtenay in the chapel of his manor at Otford, formally confessed in the name of the town to the sacrilege, asked the archbishop to lift the interdict, and promised to do what he might demand for penance. Courtenay then lifted the interdict and announced that he was reserving punishment until a later date.[102] Nothing further is recorded concerning the incident.

A problem Courtenay inherited from his predecessor Archbishop Sudbury concerned a clerk by the name of John Greneley, an inhabitant of Galeys. Greneley's "enemies" had "falsely and maliciously defamed" him, and had accused him of stealing 36 bundles of wool from a Boston merchant by the name of John Hunyngton. In his trial before the mayor, aldermen, and other secular judges, Greneley had been convicted of the crime and had been turned over to Sudbury to be lodged in the archbishop's jail "in accordance with the privileges and customs of the church of England." Sudbury had given instructions to William Grene, the rector of the church of St. Mary at Galeys, to permit the clerk to clear himself by compurgation. But the disturbances attendant upon the Peasants' Revolt of 1381 had prevented this being done, so Courtenay was now assuming responsibility for seeing the matter through.

On May 22, 1382, Courtenay sent William Grene, the priest at Galeys, essentially the same instructions the priest had received from Sudbury more than a year before. He was to have announcement made in the church of St. Mary at Galeys and in any other place where it might appear advisable, to the effect that any person wishing to object to Greneley's being permitted to clear himself by compurgation should present himself before the archbishop or his commissary at St. Mary of the Arches on the twentieth juridical day following the announcement.[103] No one came forward to protest the compurgation, so the dean of St. Mary of the Arches reported to Courtenay, whereupon he had proceeded with the process. Upon the testimony of twelve clerks and laymen, he declared Greneley innocent.[104]

With properties scattered about the province, it happened that the archbishop was obliged on occasion to denounce poachers who fished or hunted on estates belonging to Canterbury. In September 1383 he directed the bishop of Chichester to excommunicate those persons guilty of stealing fish from the fishery near Southmalling. It was "not without bitterness of soul," so the archbishop wrote to the bishop, that he had learned that certain "sons of eternal malediction" whose names were unknown, "impelled by diabolical motive," had caught a large multitude of fish with their nets and "had taken them away and sacrilegiously consumed them in grave offense of God and the privileges of our church." Their excommunication was to be published on Sundays and holydays at Chichester and in all the churches of the diocese, particularly in each of the churches of Lewes.[105] For some reason not stated, the king interposed his will and Courtenay, "out of reverence to our lord the king," was obliged to countermand his order to the bishop of Chichester.[106]

What was the exact offense of one Richard Ismonger of Aylesford is not stated. He had confessed before the archbishop in the episcopal manor at Otford on May 23, 1383, that he had violated the rights of the church of Canterbury, for which violation he had incurred the sentence of excommunication. Courtenay absolved him from the censure after Ismonger had sworn never to repeat his crime, then imposed a harsh penance. Ismonger was to submit to three whippings in the market place of Wesmalling, to the same number at Maidstone, and again to another three at Canterbury, each time clad only in his shirt and drawers. On the occasion of his last whipping at Canterbury, he was to carry a candle, weight five pounds, and offer it to the cathedral for the tomb of Thomas Becket.[107]

The problem that occasioned Courtenay most annoyance during the fifteen years of his archiepiscopacy was probably Lollardy. That this heretical group had continued its existence after its unofficial intellectual headquarters at Oxford had been smashed in 1382 is evident from the complaints of the chroniclers, occasional references to it in the episcopal registers, and from attacks recorded in the rolls of parliament.[108] Yet the number of Lollards was never great. Only in the area about Leicester in the diocese of Lincoln do their views appear to have found anything even approaching general acceptance. Scattered Lollards could, however, be found all over England, and if not actual Lollards, at least persons whom their more timorous neighbors suspected of being heterodox. For to suspicious souls, almost any person critical of the church in the late fourteenth century was apt to pass as a Lollard. That many people attributed the Peasants' Revolt of 1381 to their machinations accounts in large measure for the exaggerated fears expressed during the eighties and nineties over their number and influence. They never constituted more than a small minority, and the influence they enjoyed was even smaller than their numbers would normally suggest since they recruited almost only the poorest commoners. Richard did little to suppress the group, while Courtenay, although he abominated Lollards as heretics, appears to have had no real fear of them. The relative indifference of both king and archbishop is significant. It speaks louder than the statistics that do not exist or the extravagant cry of the alarmist chronicler.

Parliament did question several Lollards in 1388 and so shocked were they by the views they heard expressed, that they appealed to the crown to suppress them without delay. The king accordingly reminded the archbishop and his suffragans of their duty to preserve orthodoxy, to root out heresy, and to examine all suspect writings.[109] Two officials were specifically delegated to ferret out all tracts of Wyclif and Hereford and to bring these writings before the council.[110] But only the bishop of Norwich, according to the critical chronicler, was successful in eradicating all heterodoxy.[111]

The bishop who found Lollardy most troublesome was John Buckingham of the diocese of Lincoln. It will be recalled that only in that diocese did Courtenay encounter Lollards in his visitation of the province. It is possible the archbishop may have decided upon the visitation of that diocese on the basis of reports reaching him concerning the ineffectual measures taken there to suppress the heresy.[112] In 1391 he addressed a mandate to the people of that diocese to warn them against listening to William Swinderby, the most eloquent preacher in the area. According to the archbishop, Swinderby had once abjured his errors before Buckingham and had sworn never to preach again, but he had repudiated his oath and was again active in the diocese. Many people had reported Swinderby's activities to Courtenay during his visitation.[113]

When convocation voted the crown a tenth in 1395, they acknowledged the efforts Richard had made to suppress Lollardy and coupled with this an appeal to the archbishop to secure the adoption of more effective measures in the fight against the heresy.[114] During the absence of Richard to Ireland that same year, the Lollards became so daring as to nail a list of their propositions to the doors of Westminster and St. Paul's. This act must have alarmed the ecclesiastical authorities, for a delegation, including among others the bishop of London and the archbishop of York, was hurried off to Ireland to urge the king to return in order to deal with the heresy in person.[115] Richard did give some attention to the revival of Wycliffitism at Oxford. He ordered all scholars expelled who were tainted with Lollardy and arraigned before his council.[116] To one Oxford scholar who submitted and took an oath to abide by the teaching of the church, the king declared: "And I swere here onto the, if evyr thou breke thin ooth thou schill deye a foul deth."[117]

In 1395 Pope Boniface sent a sharp reminder to Courtenay about the spread of Lollardy. He chided him for his failure to suppress "a certain crafty and bold sect of pseudo-Christians, who call themselves the poor men of the treasure of Christ and His disciples, and whom the vulgar call by the sounder name of Lollards." He was to act with vigor, degrade those members of the clergy tainted with error, and hand the lay Lollards over to the secular authorities. He was to "act without fear or pusillanimity, otherwise the pope will be compelled against his will to provide severely against his negligence."[118] What words to address to the man who had led the fight against Gaunt and Wyclif in the seventies, had defied and quashed Lollardy at Oxford in 1382, and had remonstrated with Richard in 1385 when only lords with retainers at their call dared do so! That the pope addressed this same sharp reminder to the archbishop of York removes most of its sting. Yet what a distorted view must the pope have had of the strength of Lollardy, to say nothing of his view concerning the sense of responsibility of the English hierarchy!

⁊[10]⊦

COURTENAY'S DEATH
AND WILL
AN EVALUATION

Courtenay died in his manor at Maidstone on July 31, 1396, and on August 4, "in the presence of the king, with the great men of the land, was committed to burial near the shrine of St. Thomas."[1] So reads the simple obituary entry of the chronicler. Had the chronicler known what a mass of literature later writers would turn out over the question of the exact location of the archbishop's body, he would have provided additional detail and removed all doubt. Of Courtenay's death about noon on Monday, July 31, at the relatively early age of fifty-five, there is no question, nor that he languished several days at Maidstone before the end came. Nor is there any question that the archbishop had initially planned to be buried "as quickly as possible" in the nave of the cathedral of Exeter by the bishop of Exeter unless the archbishop of York was able to honor an agreement the two prelates had earlier made. But "great lords were not to be invited for the occasion." In fact as the archbishop lay dying on July 28, he had a codicil added to his will in which he acknowledged his unworthiness to be buried in any cathedral or collegiate church and directed that his body be interred rather in the graveyard of the church of Maidstone.[2] King Richard however countermanded Courtenay's instructions. He happened to be passing through Canterbury on his way to France when he learned of Courtenay's death, and he ordered the body brought from Maidstone to Canterbury, where it "was interred in the presence of the King, nobility, clergy, and ten thousand people" near the feet of the Black Prince.[3]

Much thought has been expended on the question of Courtenay's burial place. The principle source of the difficulty is the codicil the archbishop added to his will on his deathbed when he changed his mind about the matter and left instructions that his body be buried at Maidstone. Was his body once actually buried beneath the large altar slab of marble in the floor of the nave just before the rood at the entrance to the chancel, the precise spot where he wished to be interred?[4] When Weever examined the monuments in Maidstone church in 1630 this slab still had resting upon it a bronze effigy of the archbishop with an epitaph in his memory about the verge inlaid with brass.[5] Or was this slab but a cenotaph erected to honor Maidstone's most generous patron and Courtenay's body actually buried in Canterbury cathedral as the chronicler affirms? Yet granting Courtenay to have been a distinguished archbishop, why should he have merited to be buried in so august a place as Canterbury?

It is no longer necessary to consider these and many more arguments scholars have advanced in favor of Maidstone or Canterbury.[6] All question as to Courtenay's final resting place was ended when a scholar happened across several entries in Register G of the Canterbury Chapter Records which established the cathedral of Canterbury as Courtenay's burial place.[7] His remains unquestionably lie inside the tomb of beautiful alabaster upon whose cover rests the recumbent figure of a prelate in full pontificals with miter and crosier, just "east of the marble tomb and golden effigy of the king's father, Edward the Black Prince."[8]

On September 15, 1396, six weeks after Courtenay's burial, the archbishop's will was proved in the chapel of the archiepiscopal manor at Lambeth. It is a long and interesting document.[9] What most impresses the reader of the will is the great wealth the archbishop had to bequeath. In addition to the sizeable outlay to cover the expenses of his obsequies (i.e., torches and money for the clergy who attended), the larger amount required to provide for 15,000 masses and the recitation of 2,000 matins, and the small fortune represented by the vestments, plate, and jewelry he distributed, there were some 200 pounds in money he bequeathed in legacies. An admittedly rough estimate of these 2000 pounds as approximating $350,000 would, with his other property, place Courtenay high among the English aristocracy of wealth of the late fourteenth century.[10] Such affluence would disturb the reformers of the time who were attacking wealth as the principal source of clerical corruption, although modern economists would commend the archbishop for distributing his wealth so widely among so many people. The largest monetary legacy to a single person (not institution), that to his favorite sister Catherine ("Dangayne"), probably did not exceed $35,000, and the next largest gift, the 100 pounds to the king, was half that amount. Reformers would, however, approve Courtenay's remembering the recluses of the province, the legacy of 5 marks he left to each Dominican friar, and the money he gave to the poor of Northgate and Herbaldoune, however trivial these last legacies were.

Courtenay may also be commended for insisting that the expenses of his burial be paid and that his executors make full satisfaction for all his obligations before honoring any of his legacies. That he left four torches to the church of St. Martin in Exminster "where I was born" pleases his biographer since that statement firmly establishes Exminster as the place of his birth. Courtenay's plea to Richard to protect the members of his family should such need arise reflects the uneasiness of the times. That he should have felt constrained to implore the king to assist his executors as well in rebuffing exorbitant claims his successor might advance for dilapidations stirs some uneasiness in the modern reader who may properly wonder why the possibility of such unjust claims by one archbishop upon the estate of another should have existed in fourteenth-century England.

Courtenay's solicitude in remembering those people who had done him kindnesses arouses pleased approval, particularly his charity in leaving legacies to such humble folk as Christina who lived with his sister Catherine, Robert Bradgar who worked so faithfully for the archbishop, John, the companion of one of his household servants, and William, the boy who lived in the almshouse. But one may question his sense of justice in leaving his sister Catherine money and plate in excess of $35,000, while bequeathing his sister Anna no more than $3,500 and a single cup, and to two other sisters apparently nothing. The archbishop may, of course, have had good reason for remembering his sisters in so unequal a fashion.[11]

One notes with interest the bequest to Philip Repingdon, the ex-Lollard, the bequest taking the form of a reduction by one-half of the amount Philip owed the archbishop. In 1367 John Buckingham, the bishop of Lincoln, had protested momentarily Courtenay's appointment as chancellor of Oxford.[12] Twenty-nine years later Courtenay bequeathed John, still bishop of Lincoln, the best jewel in his possession. A gold cross inlaid with precious stones Courtenay willed to John Waltham, the bishop of Salisbury, who had challenged his right to visit his diocese. Had Courtenay and Waltham become friends since their clash in the summer of 1390 or had Waltham's rise in the royal favor recommended him to the archbishop's attention?[13]

The codicil reveals the last recorded thought of the archbishop, and it is a thought that would warm the heart of any God-fearing apologist. For as Courtenay lay languishing on his deathbed, what remained of his pride oozed away with his spirit, and he was left feeling too humble to be buried in Exeter cathedral or any other great church. That his executors would have respected his wish to be buried in the churchyard at Maidstone is improbable, for it would have been most exceptional to have buried any fourteenth-century bishop outside a church. To what extent they honored his other wish, namely, that they void, at their discretion, all legacies to persons outside his household and expend the money instead on the construction of the collegiate church at Maidstone, cannot be determined. During the months since the summer of 1395 when Courtenay drew up his will,[14] he had proceeded with his plans to build the college at Maidstone and had probably begun construction.[15] In view of this committment and the archbishop's strong wish, it is possible that Courtenay's executors managed to allocate sufficient funds to cover the completion of the structure, either from moneys remaining in the estate after payment of the legacies, or, as the archbishop had proposed, by setting aside certain legacies to accomplish this. From the fact that the arms of both Courtenay and Arundel graced the roof of the nave, however, it must be assumed that Arundel finished the nave.[16]

The money expended on Maidstone did not affect Courtenay's legacy to Christ Church, the largest single bequest he made. Beyond his best cope and other vestments, the books his nephew Richard might use during his lifetime, and legacies for the prior, his good friend Thomas Chillenden, and for each member of the community, he bequeathed the church 2000 pounds and "somewhat more according to the discretion of my executors," the money to be used for the construction of the wall of the cloister extending from the door of the archiepiscopal residence to the cathedral. The wall was constructed and for a sum in excess of 300 pounds. These legacies were only the last in a long series of gifts the archbishop had given the monastery. The prior and chapter made grateful acknowledgment of the archbishop's munificence in a formal announcement on November 1, 1396, when they listed the following favors they owed his generosity: the appropriation of the church of Meopham and its repair for the use of sick monks; new kitchens for the infirmary at the cost of 133 pounds, 6 shillings, and 8 pence; 266 pounds, 13 shillings, and 4 pence for the repair of the boundary walls about the precincts of the monastery; 20 pounds for a window in the nave dedicated to St. Elphege; the rebuilding of the section of the cloister noted above at a cost of more than 300 pounds; an expensive image of the Trinity with six apostles of silver costing 340 pounds for the table of the high altar; a sumptuous cope set with rubies and pearls and valued at more than 300 pounds; a thousand pounds which he collected from Richard and other friends for the fabric of the cathedral; a bull of indulgences from Pope Boniface IX amounting to 25 years and 180 days, to be granted on the occasion of certain festivals. In wholly inadequate recognition of these and other favors, the monastery was making perpetual provision of a daily mass for him in the church and commemoration of his name in the daily mass in the infirmary, for which services two priests were to be assigned with a stipend of 40 shillings.[17]

AN EVALUATION

What kind of a man was Courtenay? Was he proud, magisterial, and arrogant, was he humble, kindhearted, and affable, or was he stern and reserved? Medieval sources rarely provide information that permits so careful a delineation of character. The age could boast few memoirs or biographies, and letter-writing of a personal nature was almost unknown. Even the informal chroniclers ordinarily have no time for character analyses. A few hints regarding Courtenay's personality do nevertheless sift through the hard impersonality of contemporary sources. The most personal of these and the longest—nearly a sentence long—is that made by the prior and monks of Christ Church when acknowledging the archbishop's generosity (noted above). They speak of him as the "most reverend and good father who throughout his life had been kind to us and to our church of Canterbury, benevolent, devoted, and forbearing."[18] Because this expression of praise was made after the archbishop's death, one may attach greater significance to it than one can normally give statements by subordinates of ecclesiastical superiors. And the prior and chapter proved the sincerity of their sentiments by founding a daily mass for him.

Courtenay does appear to have had a sympathetic heart. In 1384 he issued a stern order to the prior of Worspring monastery to take back one John Derby who had been encouraged to leave the community and become a secular which "in his simplicity" he had done, only to realize his mistake and seek readmittance. The prior assured the archbishop that his order would be respected.[19] Courtenay sent a similarly sharp warning to the nuns at Godstow to admit a girl whose application they had refused even after he had prodded them about the matter.[20] In order to provide succor for one John Gybbes, a poor clerk of Hereford who had been robbed and severely beaten on his way to Rome, the archbishop granted an indulgence of 40 days to all who gave him alms, for John was in no condition to work.[21] During the visitation of the diocese of Lincoln Courtenay showed real "paternal solicitude" for the spiritual welfare of the erring William Broughton and gave of his time to convince the monk of his errors. A less sympathetic prelate might have ordered him punished forthwith.[22] Again it may have been deep concern over Ball's eternal salvation, as the chronicler affirms, that led the archbishop to secure the rebel a two-day reprieve, when most people were clamoring for his immediate execution and perhaps for his eternal damnation as well.[23] On the other hand, there is no suggestion, except in his will and there only on a modest scale, that Courtenay ever translated his sympathies into the actual giving of his wealth to charity. A critical writer might rule out such a possibility in view of the large fortune he accumulated.

Courtenay's sympathetic nature probably left no room for vindictiveness. To the Oxford Wycliffites, once they had retracted their views, he showed only kindness. While other prelates might have barred them permanently from returning to the university, Courtenay ordered them restored to full academic privileges. To the troublesome Aston he gave a special letter of "good health" to "stop up the mouths of those who would speak malicious words."[24] To Hereford, another Oxford Wycliffite, he advanced some money and forgave him half the loan in his will. Once Brantingham had submitted to his claim to visit Exeter, he extended him the unusual privilege of exercising all his episcopal powers. To Waltham, the other bishop who unsuccessfully challenged his right to visit, he bequeathed a gold cross with precious stones and a handsome missal. One possible instance of vindictiveness, however, might stand revealed in his will, that is, in the unequal treatment of his sisters.

Courtenay was a man of some patience. He demonstrated that quality in his treatment of Aston, although prudence may have had as much to do with dictating the manner he handled that problem as patience. Then at Salisbury he repeatedly postponed excommunicating the absent bishop on the plea of the earl of Salisbury and others that the prelate might still answer his summons and put in an appearance. With Aston and Waltham he proved generous in the end; toward others he could be severe: witness the harsh penances he imposed upon the three Leicester Lollards and upon Reginald of Cobham and his wife for having contracted an invalid marriage.[25] Still he probably punished in these instances with a heavy hand, less to give the penitents material reason for ruing their errors than to provide others a salutary example. So the chronicler observed how Lollardy was suppressed "more from fear of the archbishop than from love of God. . . ."[26] Had Reginald and his wife not been members of the aristocracy, they like the Lollards would have been obliged to march in a procession in order to teach others a lesson. When a salutary lesson could not be taught, as in the case of the towns of Romney and Wye where many if not all the villagers were implicated in the crime, the archbishop apparently imposed no penance.[27]

This was being prudent, one virtue Courtenay possessed to a high degree and one which most accounted for his notable success in dealing with his bishops and with the crown. In his early years he had been imprudent, once when he excommunicated the Florentines and next when he clashed with Gaunt in St. Paul's. Then experience or a native shrewdness or a combination of the two began to assert their influence. He accepted a compromise with the duke over Wyclif and with Christ Church over control of the office of warden of Canterbury Hall. Prudence recommended moderation in suppressing Wycliffitism. Prudence advised him to secure a papal indult to supplement his metropolitan powers before attempting the visitation of his province and to deal generously with the two protesting bishops who had submitted. Prudence convinced him to turn his back on politics in 1388 and to accept praemunire in 1393. In each instance, his choice of prudence proved wise.

If Courtenay was prudent, he was also proud, not proud in the mean way of small men whom fortune had placed in positions of authority, nor haughty like men who consider first the inferiority of others. Courtenay was the son of an earl, a cousin of the king, a graduate of Oxford in law, archbishop of Canterbury, and primate of all England. He came by his pride honestly and he carried it with dignity. He must have delighted in traveling about with a large retinue of clerks and with all the bells of a town sounding out a welcome as he approached or in entering some exempted abbey-church such as St. Augustine's with his archiepiscopal cross carried before him. No doubt he would have stoutly denied that this was pride, only zeal for the protection of the prerogatives of Canterbury, even when he ordered the abbot of St. Augustine's to substitute for the ancient address, one that paid him, the archbishop, greater honor. His pride confirmed his conviction that authority came from above and must be unquestioned. As he practised loyalty to the pope, so he demanded it of his suffragans. As archbishop and primate of England, no suffragan should dare appeal to Rome over his head, and he brushed aside their protests over visitation as entirely out of order. The splendid obsequies he planned for himself bespoke his character, not his dying preference for a humble grave.

On the other hand, his eminence, whether based upon birth or consequent on his office as archbishop, Courtenay never pressed as a personal accomplishment of which others should be reminded. It was a fact one assumed. And since the archbishop made no issue of his superiority, his personal relations with his fellow bishops could have been, and probably were, thoroughly amiable. It seems he could count such influential bishops as Brantingham, Wykeham, and Arundel as his friends, while both the older Buckingham and the youthful Waltham accorded him respectful admiration. The combination of birth, position, and perhaps personality made his assumption of superiority acceptable. Where the monks of St. Augustine's employed force to block the attempt of the common-born Sudbury to visit their abbey with the archiepiscopal cross borne before him, they accepted almost without protest the high-born Courtenay's announcement that he was coming.[28]

Two qualities stand out in Courtenay's character, his love of order and his devotion to the rights of the church. In the practice of these two virtues he accomplished his principal work.

His responsibilities as archbishop as he saw them were two: to direct the work of the church in an effective manner by securing the observance of existing laws and traditions and to preserve the rights of Canterbury and the church. He was no innovator, he had no new theories to preach. Like most of his contemporaries, among the upper classes at least, he accepted as God-ordained the contemporary organization of society and the manner in which the two institutions of church and state were carrying out the divine plan. He was by birth and conviction a conservative. Reforms might be needed, but no fundamental change. Had he conceived the need of any basic alteration in the way men were going about their secular affairs or how under clerical leadership they were doing God's will, he would have been something other than what he was, a product of his age. His age accepted the *status quo* as the way God wanted things. It looked upon change with suspicion. Nothing was awry that the faithful observance of the church's laws and those of the state would not cure.

So he would require his clergy to respect the requirements of canon law and to observe the statutes which earlier bishops and abbots had provided their communities. An interest in ascertaining the measure of this observance prompted him to undertake extensive visiting in his province. What disturbed him on his travels were such visible evidences of clerical negligence as the general disrepair of church property and abuses associated with the practice of pluralities. These he sought to correct. That they may have sprung from a fundamental weakening of the spiritual life he may have suspected, but he issued directives aimed only at eliminating the products of such decline, not their sources. This is no criticism. The decline of the church had not reached a point where specific reform measures could not but be considered adequate. Only a clairvoyant could have predicted what would occur a century and more later. This much can surely be credited Courtenay in the matter of reform, that the level of clerical performance and piety did not deteriorate during the years of his archiepiscopacy.

Corruption might hamper the work of the church from within. From without the principal danger was the state, although during Courtenay's years as archbishop this did not take on any new or threatening dimensions. There was the ambition of parliament and of Richard to secure greater control of convocation which Courtenay successfully blocked. Fortunately for

Courtenay, the confirmation of the statutes of provisors and praemunire in the nineties did not go beyond the intent of those of the fifties, for he could not have prevented their reenactment had they been doubly severe.

Courtenay did more than just hold the line, however, in his efforts to preserve the rights and prerogatives of Canterbury vis-à-vis his suffragans. Though he visited no exempt monasteries, he did enter several sacrosanct abbey churches with his archiepiscopal cross carried before him. One may also credit him with enhancing the right of the metropolitan to visit the dioceses of his province, even though Trefnant, the bishop of Hereford, was still contesting that right when the archbishop died.

What was probably his greatest accomplishment is a matter that cannot be proved, namely, his role in silencing Wyclif. Of this much there can be no question, however, that it was he as bishop of London, not Sudbury the archbishop, who acted as spokesman for the English church in working out the settlement. That he respected this settlement as archbishop confirms his acceptance of it as bishop. More manifest is his success in supressing Wycliffitism at Oxford in the early eighties. Any archbishop would have given the situation there his earnest attention, although it is doubtful whether any other prelate would have achieved Courtenay's success. His firm moderation, the product of his prudence and magnanimity, proved the best approach to the solution of a problem that held real danger for the church. Almost any other policy would have left a disgruntled group of secular intellectuals encouraging the growth of Lollardy from exile. Only Hereford attempted this and he soon gave up. While Wycliffitism did reappear at the university, it was never again so strong and open, and its association with Lollardy all the more distant because of the interval when it had almost ceased to exist.

Courtenay was an able archbishop. He may have been a great one.

⸭{ APPENDIX }⸭

COURTENAY'S OATH OF OBEDIENCE TO
POPE URBAN VI (1382)[1]

I William, elect of Canterbury, do promise and swear that from this hour forward, as long as I live, I shall be loyal and obedient to St. Peter and to the holy, apostolic church of Rome and to my lord Urban VI, by divine providence pope, and to his canonically appointed successors. I shall never by counsel, consent, or deed, do anything which might cause them to lose life or limb or to be captured. Advice which shall be given me by them or their emissaries by letter I shall not knowingly reveal to anyone to their injury. I shall help preserve, defend, and restore the Roman papacy and the *regalia* of St. Peter's, saving my own position, against all men; and as far as I am capable, I shall safeguard their honor and position, and I shall remain loyal to them and show them good will.

Within the limits of my province I shall receive with courtesy legates and emissaries of the apostolic see. I shall guide and defend them and shall provide them a sure escort, and in coming and going I shall deal honorably with them and shall assist them in their needs, nor, so far as I am able, shall I permit any injury to befall them.

I shall oppose and impede, as far as I am able, all who may attempt anything contrary to the above, and shall prevent, as far as possible, any offense or injury to the pope and Roman church. Nor shall I lend counsel, assistance, or confer with those who wish to devise anything evil or prejudicial to him or the Roman church. Should I learn that such things are being planned by any persons or being discussed, I shall oppose these as far as possible, and as quickly as possible I shall properly inform another by whom knowledge of this may be brought to their notice.

Should I be summoned for whatever reason to a synod or to them, I shall comply unless I am prevented by some canonical order, and I shall express and offer to them the obedience and reverence due them. Every three years I shall visit the apostolic limits which lie within the jurisdiction of the Roman curia, whether on this side or that side of the mountains, either personally or by agent, unless excused by apostolic writ. The properties pertaining to my archdiocese I shall neither sell nor give away nor pledge nor enfeoff anew, nor in any way alienate without consulting the Roman pope.

Furthermore, to Robert of Geneva, once priest of the basilica of the Twelve Apostles, now antipope, who calls himself Clement VII, to John of Amiens, once titular priest of St. Marcellus, and to Gerard of Marmoutier, once titular priest of St. Clement, sons of perdition, condemned by the just judgment of God and by apostolic authority, to their followers and to those who give them aid, counsel, or encouragement, whatever their eminence, order, religion, condition, or rank, even if pontifical, kingly, queenly, or any other kind, be they even cardinals of the Roman church, or to any others already designated by the church or to be designated, however long they remain outside the grace and communion of said see, shall I in no way, personally or through another, directly or indirectly, publicly or secretly, give aid, counsel, or encouragement, nor, so far as I am able, shall I permit others to do so, but shall rather oppose them as far as it is just according to my ability, and until in accord with apostolic judgments they will have been converted. So help me God and these His holy gospels.

POPE URBAN'S BULL EXTENDING VISITATION PRIVILEGES TO COURTENAY[2]

Urban bishop, servant of the servants of God, to our venerable brother William, archbishop of Canterbury, greeting and apostolic benediction. The depth of your devotion to ourselves and to the Roman church prompt us to act favorably upon your petitions, in so far as we are able to do this with God's blessing. For this reason we are inclined to grant your petitions and by authority of these presents to permit you—a permission with which we burden your conscience—to visit your province as often as you may choose within a period of two years counting from this day, even though the chapter of your church, city, and your diocese of Canterbury have not been visited; together

with other cities, dioceses, churches, monasteries, and other ecclesiastical places within the province of Canterbury which you
might choose to visit; and that however often you may happen
to leave any city or diocese of said province after having begun
its visitation, whether the work of visitation has been completed
or not, you may freely return to such city and diocese to resume
your visitation, before having visited the other cities and dioceses
of said province and without discussing the matter with your
suffragans or giving them advance notice; that you may similarly
collect the procuration fees properly owing you from churches,
monasteries, places, and persons visited, and that you follow whatever order appears useful and necessary to you regardless of
any opposing constitutions of Pope Innocent IV of happy memory, our predecessor. Let no man violate this our concession and
will nor oppose it by rash effort. Should any one, however, presume to do so, let him know that he will incur the indignation
of Almighty God and of the holy apostles Peter and Paul.

COURTENAY'S MANDATE TO BRANTINGHAM ANNOUNCING VISITATION[3]

William, by divine permission, archbishop of Canterbury, primate
of all England and legate of the apostolic see, to our venerable
brother Thomas, by the grace of God, bishop of Exeter, our
suffragan, greeting and fraternal charity in the Lord.

The most holy father in Christ, our lord Urban VI, pope
by divine providence, in order to expedite our visitation of the
province of Canterbury, has recently granted us his apostolic
letters under the following form: (Pope Urban's bull as given
above.).

Wishing, therefore, as is proper, to execute as efficiently
as possible our duty as metropolitan since justice so obliges, and
supported by those [papal] letters, we notify you by these presents that, inasmuch as we believe it advantageous to begin our
visitation with your church, city, and diocese of Exeter, we plan,
God willing, to visit you, your church of Exeter, its dean and
chapter, and the clergy and people of your diocese, by reason
of our metropolitan authority, either personally or by commissaries should we ourselves be prevented. Wherefore we order
and, by virtue of the obedience you owe the church of Canterbury, do strictly enjoin you that you inform those under your

jurisdiction of this our plan or have them so notified, advise them
yourself or have them advised, to prepare themselves to submit
to our visitation in accordance with canonical decrees.

You will notify, peremptorily and under penalty of the
law, all who hold either churches or portions of churches in
said city or diocese, or who receive pensions or any portions
of tithes from other churches or parishes, or those who claim,
by whatever right, chapels or oratories within the limits of any
parish in which divine services are celebrated; also all rectors
and vicars, and all other persons who possess ecclesiastical benefices of some kind or other, that—since we or our commissaries
will be making a visitation and will meet with them on days
and at places to be later designated by our letters—they reveal,
disclose, and make known to us or to our agents by what right,
should they claim any, they hold said churches, portions of
churches or tithes, also chapels or oratories, and by what canonical dispensation, should they possess any, have rectors, vicars,
and other beneficed persons acquired their titles and through
whose mediation have they secured churches or benefices in case
they have several.

And because we plan to reach your cathedral church of
Exeter on Monday of the second week of Lent, that is, March
7, and to visit during the days following you and our dear sons,
the dean and chapter of your church, and other members of
the same church who by custom or right are subject to our
visitation, we do by these presents peremptorily cite you, and
we wish and order you to peremptorily cite the dean and chapter
together with the other persons, that you appear in person on
said Monday, the dean, chapter, and other persons on the Tuesday following, in the morning as is proper, in your chapter house,
for the visitation we shall there canonically conduct, either in
person or by our commissaries should we be personally impeded,
and to accept, do, and receive, as the law requires, what justice
will advise in accordance with the custom of the visitation.

We also inhibit you, and through you we wish and order
the dean and chapter and the rest of those subject to you to
be inhibited, that you or they attempt nothing or arrange to
have anything attempted to prejudice our projected visitation.
Concerning the day you receive these letters, and what you will
have done concerning the above, and in what manner you will
have executed this our mandate for the morning of the Monday
and place aforementioned, you will arrange to certify to us or

our commissaries by your letters patent, which will contain this information and will also have attached a separate schedule containing the names of those cited. [Dated at Otford, January 8, 1384.]

COURTENAY'S INHIBITORY ORDER DENYING
CLAIMS OF BRANTINGHAM[4]

William . . . to the archdeacon of Exeter and his official.[5] It is known that during the course of our metropolitan visitation of the city and diocese of Exeter in our province of Canterbury now in progress, the following rights are manifestly ours on the basis of law and ancient, praiseworthy, and approved custom and that legitimately prescribed for our province of Canterbury, and also by virtue of the prerogative of our church of Canterbury, *viz.*, to investigate, correct, punish, and canonically reform the crimes and trangressions of any subjects of said city and diocese; to hear any causes and legal matters of any subjects of said city and diocese, whether by mere or promoted office or already introduced or to be introduced to us at the request or instance of any parties of said city and diocese and belonging by whatever manner to an ecclesiastical court, and to decide them; to confer both minor and sacred orders on any subjects of said city and diocese as well as on persons of another diocese who may present us letters dimissory which are acceptable; to admit any persons presented to us during the time of our visitation to ecclesiastical benefices of said city and diocese, whichever and however they are vacant or become vacant and which are subject to presentation by someone, and to institute such persons canonically to same, and to have persons thus admitted and instituted to be inducted upon our authority into corporal possession of these benefices; to confer upon suitable persons other ecclesiastical benefices of said city and diocese of Exeter which have legitimately devolved to our collation because of lapse of time, together with others which happen to be vacant because of deprivation or because those persons have been transferred who occupy or will occupy those benefices, such deprivation or transfer having been ordered or to be ordered upon our metropolitan authority during our visitation; to grant authorization to any in said city and diocese who wish to exchange benefices and, for legitimate cause, to arrange such exchanges;

to confirm those elected abbots or priors in monasteries or priories of said city and diocese which are not exempt, and to bless those confirmed, both exempt and non-exempt, who come to us; to investigate and examine the wills of beneficed and noble persons as well as those of other subjects of said city and diocese, who had mobile or immobile goods at the time of their death in both or either place, concerning which they provided in their wills; to examine these wills and to prove them and to preserve and defend such testaments and final wills, and to entrust the administration of their goods to the executors they may have deputized in said testaments and wills, or, in case they died intestate, to suitable persons; to require and to audit a reckoning or account which those executors or administrators of their goods will present concerning the administration of those goods; to dismiss and finally excuse those executors and administrators from our office as it may appear best to us and for the salvation of their souls; the right, too, of collecting and having the fruits, issues, and incomes of any ecclesiastical benefices in said city and diocese of Exeter which are vacant or will become vacant during our metropolitan visitation.

Our holy precursors and predecessors, archbishops of Canterbury, who lived in their and successive times, were in peaceful possession of the right, as it were, of exercising and procuring all and each of the above powers during the course of a metropolitan visitation, from a time and through a time to which the memory of man runs not to the contrary, and have exercised and done the above during the course of visitations, undisturbedly, peacefully, and quietly.

Nevertheless, our venerable brother Thomas, by the grace of God, bishop of Exeter, our suffragan and suffragan of our church of Canterbury, who is surely aware of the above since being manifest and true they cannot be hidden, asserts and pretends that all and each of the above rights, so far as they concern the aforesaid city and diocese—excepting only notorious crimes and transgressions revealed during the course of our metropolitan visitation—belong to him and to him alone; not to mention his defiance in unjustly opposing us and also said church of Canterbury, his mother, whose privileges, liberties, and rights he pledged himself firmly by corporal oath to preserve to the best of his ability, to defend and protect; and he exerts himself to impede rashly our visitation and metropolitan jurisdiction and to obstruct them as far as possible, and to maliciously deprive us as far as he is able and our church of said privileges, liberties, rights, customs, and prerogatives. Through malicious letters he has warned and ordered to be warned generally those who are subject to him in said city and diocese, that none of them, without his special permission, do request, receive, admit to, or in any way obtain the institution to benefices or their collation, the confirmation of elections, blessings, authorization of exchanges, the celebration of orders by any other than himself, excepting only the authority of the apostolic see; or to request and accept in any way they might presume, the wills of any beneficed or noble persons, deceased in said city and diocese, before any other than himself or his commissaries, or to request and accept from anyone else the administration of the mobile goods of testate or intestate persons, under threat of the greater excommunication which he issued in writing against each and everyone who might defy his orders, instructing certain of his subjects to solemnly publish these matters, each and every part thereof, in his consistory and in other public places of said city and diocese, in prejudice of ourselves and our church and in derogation and to the manifest weakening of our metropolitan visitation and our rights, liberties, privileges, customs, and prerogatives; by which act our venerable brother should justly fear that he has incurred the charge of perjury.

We, therefore, noting that the above have been attempted to our great loss and manifest injury and that of our church, and that more serious injuries could follow unless a halt were quickly made to such presumption, we now revoke each and all of the above and what has followed, which have been presumed and illicitly attempted or in the future will be attempted to the detriment and injury of ourselves and our church and the weakening of said privileges, liberties, rights, customs, and prerogatives, and we make void, annul, and invalidate and pronounce and declare those acts revoked, void, null, and invalid, and we decree them to be without force. Each and every one of you do we order under pain of the greater excommunication, that you solemnly publish our letter and all its contents as quickly as possible and explain even in English or arrange to have the same published and explained in that way by others, in the said church of Exeter and in other public places of said city and archdeanery of Exeter most suitable for this, especially in those places where the letters and monitions of said bishop have been published, of which mention has been made above, inhibiting openly, publicly, and expressly said bishop of Exeter, our suffragan, and his principal official and the president of said consistory in particular, and others in general, whom we inhibit by these presents—and you will warn them, each and everyone, once, twice, a third time and peremptorily, as we admonish in the same manner by these presents, not to attempt or cause to be attempted, directly or indirectly, publicly or secretly, anything to prejudice our said visitation or metropolitan jurisdiction or the privileges, liberties, rights, customs, and prerogatives of same, concerning the above rights or any of them, or give counsel, aid, or consent to this; that if, God forbid, anyone do something in defiance of this, we assign by these presents, to one and all, the six days immediately thereafter, two for the first, two for the second, and the remaining two days for the third monition, in which to repudiate it effectively, and to cease altogether from such obstructionism and disturbances; and whatever unlawful was presumed or attempted in this respect, he will no longer defend in the future under pain of the greater excommunication, which, upon each and all who disobey and ignore our monitions, assuming their fault, deceit, guilt, and negligence and that of each of them—except the case of our suffragan himself—and after the lapse of said six days following notice of this letter and its contents and after our peremptory canonical monition has been issued, for now and for then, we pronounce in this writing the sentence of excommunication.

To our said suffragan we make some concession in view of the reverence due his pontifical dignity. Should he have done anything contrary to the above rights or any of them, either personally or through a subordinate, publicly or secretly, unless he will have effectively repudiated this within the period indicated, our said canonical monition being already issued, we interdict by these writings the right to enter a church. Should he stubbornly tolerate this interdict for another six days, the six immediately following, which God forbid, since it is proper that as the transgression grows the penalty rise and as rebellion mounts the severity of the punishment be increased—against the bishop himself, our suffragan, for now and for then, our canonical monition having been issued, we pronounce the sentence of excommunication in these writings. And lest anyone whom this present process touches might pretend to ignorance in this matter, we will and order and firmly command you to affix this process publicly to the doors of the cathedral church of Exeter. We also inhibit any and all, once, twice, a third time and peremptorily and do warn them by these presents not to tear, remove, or mar such process so attached, under penalty of the sentence of the greater excommunication, which we in these writings, our canonical monition preceding, for now and for then, do pronounce against each person who defies our warning. The absolution of each and all who in any way may have incurred the above sentences or any of them, we specifically reserve to ourselves or to our superior.

You will certify to us before the coming feast of the Ascension of our Lord, by your letters patent which will deal with these matters, concerning the day you have received this and the method and form of its execution.

COURTENAY'S *APOSTOLI* ISSUED IN REPLY TO BRANTINGHAM'S APPEAL[6]

In the name of God, Amen. We William . . . do declare each and every pretended appeal on the part of our venerable brother Thomas, by the grace of God bishop of Exeter, our suffragan and suffragan of our church of Canterbury, against us and certain injuries inflicted by us on the same our venerable brother, as is pretended although falsely, and made as it is said, to the apostolic see and publicly attached on the twentieth day of this present month of April to the doors of the cathedral church of Exeter, to which we refer and which we want to be inserted here—to be frivolous, fraudulent, unjust, null, and invalid, and to have been and to be introduced from frivolous and fraudulent motives in order to delay unjustly and maliciously impede our metropolitan visitation in the city and diocese of Exeter which we have actually begun, and also our jurisdiction which during the same visitation manifestly belongs to us by right and laudably and lawfully prescribed custom and by the prerogative of our said church. And therefore we dismiss each and every one of these appeals nor defer to them in any way, and we give this answer in lieu of the pretended *apostoli* requested in this matter on the part of our said venerable brother, and present it to the same our venerable brother or his lawfully deputized proctor in this matter and to all others who have an interest or can be interested in these writings, signed by our seal and saving always the dignity of said see.

COURTENAY'S ITINERARY IN THE
VISITATION OF CORNWALL[7]

Beginning the day after St. Peter in Chains, that is on Tuesday, the lord [archbishop] will spend the night at Torre with the abbot if he wishes, or at Newton on the Fields.

Next, on Wednesday following, that is August 3, he will visit the priory at Totnes, have dinner there, and spend the night with the prior.

Next, on Thursday following, that is August 4, he will have dinner at Uggeburgh with the rector and will spend the night at Plympton with the prior.

Next, on Friday following, the lord [archbishop] will visit the priory at Plympton, have dinner there and spend the night, and on Saturday following also there for dinner, and there he will preach in Latin.

Next, that same Saturday he will spend the night with the abbot at Tavistock, and on Sunday following he will visit the abbey of Tavistock, and spend the entire day there, and there the lord [archbishop] will preach in the vernacular.

Next, on Monday following he will eat dinner there and spend the night at the priory of St. Germain.

Next, on Tuesday following, that is the vigil of St. Lawrence, he will visit the priory of St. Germain and have dinner there, and will spend the night at Liskeard.

Next, on Wednesday following, that is the feast of St. Lawrence, he will visit the priory of Tywardreath, have dinner and spend the night there; and have dinner there on Thursday and spend the night at Grauntpount [Grampound].

Next, on Friday he will have dinner at the home of the Friars Preachers at Truro and spend the night there.

Next, on Saturday, that is the vigil of the Assumption of Saint Mary, he will visit the priory of Mount St. Michael; he will eat dinner and spend the night there; and on Sunday following he will have dinner there, vespers, and supper, and he will spend the night at Penryn.

Next, he will be at Penryn the entire day of the Assumption of the Blessed Virgin and the following night and Tuesday. He will visit the collegiate church of Penryn and have dinner there and will spend the night at Truro.

Next, on Wednesday he will have dinner at Truro and spend the night at St. Columb.

Next, on Thursday he will have dinner at St. Augustine's and spend the night with Thomas Peverell, and also the entire Friday following.

Next, on Saturday the lord [archbishop] will visit the priory at Bodmin and have dinner there with the prior and spend the night as well as the entire Sunday following, and will spend the night there.

Next, on Monday following, that is before the feast of St. Bartholomew, he will have dinner on the way to Launceston and spend the night with the prior at Launceston.

Next, on Tuesday following the lord [archbishop] will visit the priory at Launceston, have dinner there and spend the night.

Next, on Wednesday following he will have dinner there at Launceston and spend the night with the rector at Kylkhampton.

Next, on Thursday, the day after the feast of St. Bartholomew, the lord [archbishop] will visit the abbey of Hartland, have dinner there and spend the night. And there also at Hartland on Friday for dinner, and he will spend the night at Toryton Magna [Torrington], have dinner with the rector on the Saturday following, and will spend the night at Chulmlegh.

Next, on Sunday following he will have dinner at Chulmlegh and spend the night at Crediton.

Next, on Monday following the feast of St. Bartholomew the lord [archbishop] will visit the collegiate church at Crediton, have dinner there, and will spend the night at Exminster.

COURTENAY'S ORDERS CONCERNING THE PRACTICE OF "SEYNYS"[8]

William . . . to the prior and convent of the priory of Spalding, of the order of St. Benedict. . . . Lest a spirit of weariness grow strong among those laboring in the vineyard of the Lord where the flowers of honor and grace, the fruits of heavenly contemplation ought rather to spring up in abundance and sweetness, we, in our paternal good will and solicitude about the proper character of religion, do consider it our pastoral duty, and especially proper during our metropolitan visitation of your priory, that we favor those occupied with divine services, in view of their daily and nightly labors, with the regular consolation of honest recreation, so that those who work in this vineyard may bring back gloriously to the founder of every household, fruit in the hundredfold on the day of harvest. This is all the more fitting since, as we have been informed, you have realized from those labors only moderate relief because the recreations of your *minuti*, popularly so-called, are burdened with usages from the past that are both severe and irregular.

Wishing, therefore, with paternal generosity to properly increase the occasions and means for your recreations, so that you may render yourselves all the more valiant against the sower of cockle while working in the Lord's field, the more you rest your spirits from continuous labor and become aroused by such recreation to the fervor of contemplation, do we, by these presents, grant you and your successors forever, on our metropolitan authority, to permit your *minuti*, as we use the word in accordance with your customs, to leave for Wikam [Wykeham] when going on such a *minutio*, immediately after the procession on Sunday, for the recreation assigned them, or elsewhere at the discretion of the prior.

During the time of your recreation, we wish, command, and ordain that each monk receive daily two monastic loaves and one gallon and a half of ale, and the same victuals as he would receive were he to take his recreation at the priory; that adequate fuel be given each monk during the time of his *minutio;* that your servants, while you are so recreating, shall also receive each day four gallons of ale of the same quality and victuals, in all things as your mesne servants receive.

We also wish, ordain, and by said authority decree that on one day of each *minutio* two masses be celebrated, one to the Holy Spirit for the soul of Clement, the other for the soul of Thomas, both former priors of this priory, as also for our welfare while living and for our soul when we have died. We further decree and ordain that the *minuti* or those recreating during the period of a *minutio* devoutly sing each day after compline an antiphon to Saint Mary, and after that they will recite the psalm *De Profundis*, with the customary prayers and orations, all for the soul of your foundress and the souls of all your benefactors. And so that we may stimulate your devotion and that of all the faithful the more readily, we grant by these presents an indulgence of forty days to all persons, shriven and contrite, who take part in said antiphon.

We also decree and by our authority ordain that the

minuti return to the priory on the Saturday following, before the reading of the homily. We wish, further, that the above pleasures of the *minutio* be available throughout the year except from the vigil of Christmas through the octave, from Palm Sunday to the octave of Easter, during the weeks of the Rogation Days, Pentecost, and the Assumption of Saint Mary, on the days of Epiphany, the Purification of Saint Mary, Holy Trinity, the feast of Corpus Christi, St. John the Baptist, the birth of Saint Mary, the Exaltation of the Holy Cross, All Saints, and St. Nicholas. During advent they will return home for first vespers on those feastdays, and on the same days, during stormy and wintry weather, because of the shortness of the days, they may return to their recreations as in times past after second vespers and dinner in the priory.

We wish, finally, and ordain that should any monks misbehave during their period of recreation, that they be canonically punished by denying them such recreation or by other means at the discretion of the prior or his representative. We have given orders during our metropolitan visitation that you and your successors strictly observe each and every one of these our ordinances and statutes forever, and we have confirmed these orders with our seal.

COURTENAY'S INJUNCTIONS TO THE MONASTERY OF ELSTOW[9]

. . . in the future each nun of the monastery shall receive on Mondays, Wednesdays, and Saturdays, and have of the goods of the monastery one dish of meat or fish, depending on the time of the year, the value of the meat being no less than one penny, in place of the eggs it has been customary to give them on those days for cooking. On the remaining days of the week each nun shall receive her proper share of food as before. Because in former times every nun of the community received seven measures of ale each week, even when there were more nuns in the convent, that is, four of the better ale and three of the second or weaker brew, yet in these days when there are very many fewer nuns, they receive only four, which, as we learned and were told during our visitation, is hardly sufficient for them, we ordain that in the future each nun shall receive one additional measure beyond the four each week, so that they shall have five measures of the abbess's better wine. And let there be no difference between the bread the abbess eats and that given to the convent, and let the bread be of the accustomed weight, that is, sixty units of weight.

We further ordain and command that in the future only suitable persons be admitted as nuns, for whose acceptance or admittance no money or anything else be exacted, but that free from any unlawful arrangement or agreement, by means of which simoniacal depravity certain sums of money or other things of value were customarily paid, they be admitted in the future to your order purely, simply, and without pact. If they must be clothed at their own expense or that of their friends, let nothing beyond the clothes or a reasonable price for such clothes be accepted or required at any time.

We further ordain that from now on, as was the practice in the past, two prudent and older nuns, who will be selected for this purpose by common counsel, the assent of the abbess, and the more responsible part of the convent, shall administer the office of treasurer, to whom we require that all money from goods, incomes, and proceeds, and of all other kinds of possessions pertaining to the monastery or being realized in any other way, be paid over undiminished and delivered. What they have received they will deposit in the common chest, locked with three keys, of which the abbess shall have one and the treasurers the other two. And they and the abbess shall safeguard, pay out, and dispense this money according to the order of the abbess and the more responsible part of the convent, as necessity and the common good of the house demand and require.

We ordain that the ministers and servants of the monastery who are selected for this purpose will take corporal oaths to levy and collect, to the best of their ability, moneys from incomes and proceeds pertaining to the monastery and will turn over undiminished what they have gathered to the abbess and treasurers. And, of course, let said treasurers and cellarers, sacristans, and other persons holding office and administering temporalities under the abbess, render a full accounting of their administrations once or twice each year before the entire convent or before certain persons deputized for that task by common counsel. If anyone be found guilty of bad administration, deception, squandering, or negligence in matters over which the abbess has given her responsibility, and particularly where the acquisition of property is concerned, she shall be immediately removed from office and be given proper chastisement by the abbess and a suitable person be appointed in her place.

We further ordain that a competent, prudent, and courteous nun be appointed to the office of sacristan, who will receive in the future the offerings and all other things pertaining to and relating to that office. From these incomes she will have proper lights provided for the main altar of the monastery and for other accustomed places, and will assume the cost of other demands made upon her office. As indicated above, she will render a financial statement of her administration.

We expressly forbid that any nun who is accused of incontinency or public scandal be appointed in the future to any office in the monastery and especially not to be custodian of the gate, until she has established her innocence. We also direct that a particularly suitable nun be appointed precentrix of the monastery, and that for that office, as well as for all other offices, older nuns, when these are competent and suitable, be preferred to younger ones.

We further ordain that the infirmarian who will receive without loss all things owing her and belonging to her from times past that are in keeping with her office, will visit the infirmary and the infirm lying there two or three times each day, and will diligently see to it that nothing is lacking them of which they may have need. She will make it known when the provisions she has of the monastery do not suffice, so that she may always be in a position to provide suitable food and drink for the needs of the infirm, according to the ability of the church. A priest should also be appointed who will celebrate mass in the chapel of the infirmary for the infirm there and those languishing in sickness, as has been customary in years past.

We also give orders that the dormitory which threatens to collapse at the present, be properly repaired with all possible speed.

The abbess will not always invite the same nuns to her table, but now these, now those, in particular those whom she knows most need the privilege and the benefit of her conversation. Chapel assistants she shall not fail to change every year, nor will she keep in livery or fee, nor sell any possession, timber, manors, lands, incomes, or possessions of the monastery to any person for any length of time, short or long, without the common consent of the entire convent or of the older and more responsible part thereof, or turn over for rent or in any way alienate. The abbess shall make a report, and an accurate one, at least once or twice a year, to the community concerning the condition of the house.

Lay women shall not occupy rooms or small houses within the cloister, although those who are discreet and of good reputation and have been permitted to live there, may remain and live just outside the cloister. Let the abbess be both wise and prudent in enforcing discipline, lest the secrets of the chapter and of monastic regulation be carried to the laity.

Because it happens, although to the dishonor of the house, that a nun returning to the monastery from a visit to friends is cruelly denied horses and servants to meet her, we direct that each nun so returning, whether during the day for the entire day, whether at night or after the ninth hour for the rest of the day and the following night, shall have at least four horses so provided, according to the ability of the house.

Furthermore, when the bell summons to divine office at the proper and usual time in accordance with regular observances, all the nuns not actually infirm or excused for legitimate cause will assemble in the choir and there devoutly recite, celebrate, and complete the divine office at the proper hours of the day and night. No nun will absent herself before the completion of the office without just cause or permission of the abbess, prioress, or other presiding official, which permission she will have first requested and secured.

We also inhibit under pain of the greater excommunication nuns from holding any secret meetings or conspiring to do anything by which the good will, unity, or reputation of the order might be impaired. Furthermore, because certain nuns of the house observe the custom, although a bad one, of distributing and giving to the servants of the abbess at Christmas for their treasury excessive sums from their own limited savings, and the same servants demand these as owing them, we inhibit in the future such donations and gifts.

We also give orders that the novices and younger nuns be diligently instructed in the observance of the rule, so that they do not violate the law of respect and deem themselves superior to the older nuns; rather that, motivated by proper occupations and the divine office to humility, they will be ready to accept the yoke and burden imposed upon them along with the others. Let the prioress and subprioress frequently tarry and linger in the cloister and supervise those there, so that they conduct themselves properly and so that, with conversation denied them ouside the cloister, they will studiously observe silence within.

In the future let no priest, brother of any order, or other religious be brought in or permitted to enter the monastery during the time the doors are to be closed, unless he is a great or noble person and comes for just cause. No nun may secretly bring priests, brothers, or religious into her room and keep them there very long, but rather by speaking and conferring briefly and in a public place, she will listen with modesty and give answer as is proper. We direct further that the doors be closed at the proper time, and that no nun leave without having requested and obtained the necessary permission from the abbess or other presiding officer. Permission to walk about in the orchard or some other suitable and sheltered place for the purpose of recreation at proper times shall nevertheless not be denied the nuns out of malice, although the younger nuns shall not go about except in company of the older ones.

Furthermore, let the common seal of the monastery and other signs and muniments which help preserve its memory be kept safely stored in a chest and locked with three keys, of which the abbess shall have one, another the prioress, and the third the precentrix.

These injunctions we transmit to you, signed with the impression of our seal, with the blessing of God and with our blessing, for you to observe inviolably in times to come. We strictly inhibit anyone without our authority and consent or that of our successors or superiors from presuming in the future to alter either wholly or in part by arrogant attempt, or contemptuously to violate, under pain of the sentence of the greater excommunication, which we now pronounce against one and all in these writings, who might seek to contravene these, and we reserve specifically to ourselves and to our successors the right to relax these regulations and to add to them in the future and to delete, as well as the power to explain and to change them.

COURTENAY'S INJUNCTIONS TO
CALDWELL PRIORY[10]

. . . in the first place, you will observe in every respect, as though they were our own, the injunctions of Robert de Kylewardeby [Kilwardby] of reverend memory, late archbishop of Canterbury, our predecessor, which he left you on his visitation some time ago.

Since obedience is the greater sacrifice, the canons of the priory will accept devoutly without murmuring the lawful, canonical monitions and orders of the prior and will humbly obey and attend to them; and let the younger monks pay proper respect and honor to the older. As often as any member is found delinquent in this regard, he will fast on bread and water on the Saturday following, and will also receive proper disciplining in addition in the convent.

When the bell rings for matins, all monks not actually sick will immediately rise without sloth and, as it is written, "In the middle of the night I shall rise to confess you," they will strive with dedication to complete them. Because leisure and pleasure are the weapons the ancient enemy uses to ensnare miserable souls, in order that this leisure, which is that stepmother of virtues that ministers warm lotions to other faults, be exiled by you and wisely shunned, we with paternal admonition do direct and command you that, having finished and faithfully completed the divine office in accordance with the instructions and order of your prior and subprior, the solicitude of Martha should not be absent from your activities whatever your inspiration may have been as you rose to the height of contemplation with Mary, following rather the example of Moses who first ascended the mountain in order to behold there with greater freedom the glory of God, then descended to the camp that he might make prudent provision for the needs of the people.

Let canons no longer serve as collectors of the rents which are deposited in the treasury of the convent, lest such occasion provide them the temptation to roam, to the prejudice of the reputation of the house; rather let them pay their rents according to the ordinance of our commissary in the town of Bedeford, which rents together with that of John Marshall amount to fifteen pounds. The prior will, moreover, handle and settle the difficult business of the monastery with the aid of the counsel and consent of the more responsible members of the community.

Let a canon be appointed who will devote himself henceforth to the care of the sick and comfort and help them with the divine office, and let him alleviate their necessities as far as he is able with the facilities of the monastery. Whenever he is negligent in this matter, he shall fast on bread and ale and nothing more.

Lay men and women shall not be given frequent access to cloister, dormitory, or refectory since this may easily disturb those contemplating in the cloister. For this reason, we order the ancient door be reopened so that by means of this lay men and women can make an obscure entrance without any delay.

Lest you be accused at some time in the future of excessive negligence or even of contempt and disobedience, we strictly command that you have our injunctions and ordinances and those of said predecessor publicly read and recited with deliberation two or three times a year in the presence of all in the chapter house, and that you take pains to observe them with care and diligence as far as human frailty permits, under pain of severe canonical censure. Should anyone be remiss concerning any of the above regulations, he shall be strictly disciplined each time with fasts and other severe punishment, according to the nature of his transgression and the zeal of his superior.

COURTENAY'S INJUNCTIONS TO THE CATHEDRAL CHAPTER OF LINCOLN[11]

William . . . to the dean and chapter of the church of Lincoln. . . . We wish first and direct that the guards of the shrine and head of St. Hugo and the masters in charge of the workshop and the day-work of the church, those who are now so employed and those who will be so employed in the future, be required to provide an accurate report and reckoning, at least once a year, of receipts and expenditures to the dean and chapter of said church or to those deputized by them; that these guards and masters do not regard their offices as permanent, but each year, if it appear expedient to the dean and chapter or the more responsible part thereof, they be removed and others substituted, upon the unanimous consent of the dean and the chapter or the more responsible element.

Furthermore, because vicars of said church have been accepted in the past as a result of favor and influence and have very often not been entirely suitable, to the scandal of said church, while others have been accepted because of the requests of friends and their importunate urging, we, in order to bar the way to such injurious favors, do expressly prohibit any person being admitted in the future as vicar of said church without first undergoing a satisfactory examination concerning his conduct and his learning. Let all influence be disregarded since this may be a source of scandal and injury to the church.

We also desire and direct that while the divine service is being celebrated in the church, those ministering at mass round the altar will abstain from idle discourse and conversation, and will instead follow with devotion and attend to the service. Those monks in the choir will also abstain from idle stories and conversation as duty, statute, and custom of the church require, and as they will have to answer to God.

Furthermore, when the anniversary of bishops or kings is being observed in said church, the mass of the day will in no wise be omitted, but will be properly celebrated at the altar of Saint Mary in said church. In the celebration of the feasts of the apostles and the four doctors, let all things be observed and respected concerning the ringing of the bells after the custom of minor double feasts, so that the expense of the wax and other burdens, in case they happen to be more than usual, may be borne not by a single treasury but by the common treasury.

We further command that while the divine office is being chanted, vicars and other ministers of the church will assemble with decorum in the choir and will not leave nor wander outside before the service has been properly completed, without good cause and the special permission of the dean or subdean or of whoever is presiding.

Because domestic cohabitation between clerks and women is prohibited, we strictly forbid women, concerning whom evil suspicion or scandal might very easily arise, to be in any way admitted to the cloister of said church and be allowed to remain or tarry there, or be permitted inside in the future.

We have, moreover, learned during our visitation of the complaint of many, that canons of said church, because they are not permitted to have a light in the choir during the night to say matins, frequently leave the choir and, from necessity and contrary to the reputation of said church, look for a light elsewhere. In our anxiety to stop this practice, we ordain that the canons be permitted to have candles in their stalls so that the divine office may not be impeded in the future.

In obsequies for the dead which are celebrated in said church without the guidance of the choir, let one vicar be assigned who shall sing the final verse after the readings. If the obsequies are recited with the guidance of the choir, let the last verse be sung by the canons or vicars according to the custom observed in the church.

We further direct that the articles of general sentence be solemnly published in said church once every year in accordance with the constitutions of the holy fathers.

Because of information given us on our visitation by certain responsible persons, how vicars and clerks of said church dressed themselves in lay garb on the feast of the Circumcision of our Lord and impeded the divine service repeatedly, according to custom, with the noise of their frivolities—deceits, vileness, jests—their chattering and games which they commonly and appropriately call the feasts of fools, we by these presents inhibit all present and future vicars from presuming to do these things in the future or for these same vicars or any ministers of the church to engage in public drinking bouts and other frivolities in the church, which is a house of prayer.

These injunctions, as far as we have made them our final injunctions and signed with our seal, do we transmit to you after mature deliberation, with the blessing of God and our blessing, to be inviolably observed by you, strictly inhibiting anyone in the future from presuming to violate them in whole or in part by arrogant attempt, under penalty of the sentence of the greater excommunication, which we pronounce in these writings against one and all who may oppose the above or any part thereof.

PRAYERS ORDERED BY COURTENAY FOR THE GENERAL WELFARE[12]

William . . . to Robert, by the grace of God, bishop of London, greeting and fraternal charity in the Lord. Terrible is God above the sons of men, before whose nod all things are subjected by order of his will; whom he loves, he reproves and scolds, and in due time punishes temporally with different kinds of disasters and calamities, in order not to be obliged to condemn them eternally.

This kingdom of England has indeed been many times troubled and afflicted by the perils of war that exhaust and consume the substance of her wealth, and with many other miseries, brought on by the pride and vices of her inhabitants, more grievous now than in the past, and by their innumerable sins, and, it is feared, would be stricken with pestilences and various kinds of calamities which already for a long time have unfortunately raged in other countries, were it not that the merciful God has hearkened to the prayers of the faithful and, mindful of his mercy, has held back his ire. For this reason our most excellent prince and lord, Richard, by the grace of God, illustrious king of England and France, after deep thought concerning the above, has urgently requested us in full parliament, with the peers and commons of the kingdom, that we order devout prayers throughout our whole province for the peace of holy church and his kingdom, for fair weather, and that the omnipotent God in his great mercy save and protect this great kingdom of England from those miseries, pestilences, calamities, and sudden destruction.

We, therefore, charge and order your fraternity that you firmly direct, in our name and on our authority and with all possible speed, each and every one of our colleagues and fellow bishops of our church of Canterbury, the vicars general of those who are absent, if there be any, and their substitutes, also the guardian of the spirituality in the diocese of St. Asaph, the seat now vacant, that each of them exhort and admonish his subjects or arrange to have these exhorted and admonished, that they intercede in devout prayers with the All Highest about these matters; that our suffragans and others in priestly orders celebrate masses in which they will recite the special prayers noted below; that they preach sermons on suitable days and in suitable places, and have processions every fourth and sixth day, or give orders that this be done; that they practice with humility and devotion other services of pious supplication, so that our omnipotent God may be placated by the prayers and save the people of England from those tribulations, and bestow the assistance of his grace, and that in his ineffable goodness he preserve the people from the dangers of calamities and sudden destruction.

And that the hearts of the faithful of our province may be the more readily excited to the above, we mercifully extend to all Christians of this province, who are sorry for their sins, for celebrating these masses, preaching these sermons, holding these processions or being devoutly present and praying with them; also, to those who, being prevented by distance or for some other reason from taking part in those processions on the fourth and sixth days, will devoutly recite the Our Father and Hail Mary five times for the above intentions, an indulgence of forty days from the penances given them.

You will order all the above to be faithfully observed in your city and diocese of London.

The prayers to which we referred above are the following:

Oration: God, you who by your mercy alone saved the people of Nineveh from imminent destruction, to whom you first had granted the grace of penitence so that you could show mercy, look down, we beseech you, on your people prostrate before the image of your mercy, and in your mercy do not permit those whom you have redeemed with the blood of your only-begotten, to suffer the penalty of sudden death. Through the same, *etc.*

Secret: We beseech you, almighty God, to accept the pleasing gift of your church, and let your mercy rather than your anger go before us because, if you choose to consider our iniquities, no creature can stand; but in your admirable goodness with which you made us, do not permit the work of your hands to perish. Through our Lord, *etc.*

Postcommunion: Almighty and merciful God, look down upon your people subject to your majesty, so that the holy reception of your mysteries may help us lest the fury of fierce death overcome us. Through our Lord, *etc.*

COURTENAY'S MANDATE CONDEMNING "CHOPPECHURCHES"[13]

William, by divine permission archbishop of Canterbury, primate of all England and legate of the apostolic see, to our venerable brother Lord Robert, by the grace of God bishop of London, greeting and fraternal charity in the Lord.

We are weighed down by truly great bitterness of soul when one of those in our care provokes the Almighty by his evil deeds and does not hesitate to strike himself with the sentence of damnation by failing to avoid the ruin he has brought upon himself by his arrogance. Indeed, among other practices that should be passionately shunned as displeasing to the Highest Majesty is the crime of vile avarice, which is the worship of idols, and that of damnable, ambitious simony, which is execrated by both human laws and sacred canons. Yet alas! There are men living today whose minds are so obscured by darkness, so corrupted by evil from the outside and ensnared by material consideration, that they do not look inward upon themselves nor give any thought to Him who is invisible, but puffed up with pride and honors in this life and ever seeking what they do not have, despise the ways of God.

Some have no fear to traffic in the gifts of the Holy Spirit, but purchase or by way of secret simoniacal contract secure churches and ecclesiastical benefices which one may not acquire except freely and without payment, not heeding the words of Peter to Simon: "May your money perish with you since with money you thought you could have the gift of God." Others of these sowers of tares, subverters of justice, and inventors of unspeakable abuse, popularly called "choppechurches," driven by their execrable thirst for gain, deceive some by treachery into exchanging benefices and leave them destitute, the consequence being that once wealthy, these men are left indigent and, unable to dig, die of grief and wretchedness or, more often, are driven by extreme need to become miserable beggars, to the scandal of clergy and church.

There are others who, oblivious of the words of the Apostle, "he who serves at the altar deserves to live by the altar, and he who is selected for that office is not to be denied his reward," procure persons to be presented and instituted to churches with cure and ecclesiastical benefices by importunity and money, after first falsely swearing and pledging themselves that so long as they have those benefices, they will claim no profit for themselves nor in any way dispose of them, but leave them always to their direction, benefit, and their pleasure under pretense of an exchange. Wherefore although one church ought to belong to one priest and no one should have several ecclesiastical dignities or parish churches, yet one person who is scarcely capable of filling one office, however small, gains for himself, in violation of the institutes of sacred canons and by treachery, the fruits of many benefices, which, if equitably distributed, would more than suffice for many learned and distinguished men who have real need for them. Divine service is neglected in such benefices and the required hospitality not provided, for which reason the indifference of the people toward church and clergy quite understandably grows and the cure of souls is left unminded.

Such priests, like carnal men, despise spiritual precepts and have no interest in eternal rewards, but demand rather material goods. Would that they, for fear of punishment, gave at least as much thought to their own amendment and had in mind how the redeemer of mankind cast out of the temple those who bought and sold there, overturned the chairs of those selling doves, and poured out the gold of the money-changers, on his authority denouncing them: "Make not the house of my father a house of business." They should also attend to this fact carefully: that nowhere in the entire gospel does the Lord appear to have chastised sinners with such harshness and severe justice, since these he not only upbraided by word but fashioned for himself a whip of ropes and drove them out of the temple. By this he demonstrated clearly that such merchants should not be punished like other sinners but should be driven far from God's church.

Some, moreover, not rectors of churches but robbers unfortunately, not good shepherds who know their flock but rather hirelings who have no concern for the sheep, are piling up for themselves on judgment day, as must truly be feared, the indignation and wrath of Almighty God by neglecting cure and hospitality, to the disgrace of the clergy, not to speak of other excesses of theirs, and who without need or reason impudently spend their time in London, devouring the patrimony of Jesus Christ and, to their own destruction, consuming in villainous ways the goods of the poor, the bread of the hungry, the clothing of the naked, and the ransom of captives.

Who are more unjust than these men or so greedy, men who should provide others a good example and by their virtuous living show them the way, who rather take the food of many, not in moderation for their own use, but in abundance and luxury. These dare not say with the Prophet: "The Lord is the portion of my inheritance"; rather they say: "We desire not the knowledge of Your ways."

Therefore, since the cure of souls is our greatest responsibility and a strict accounting will be required of us in that terrible examination, and not wishing to tolerate and connive further at the above which are a scandal to the clergy of the English church and a danger and pernicious example to very many souls, we, upon the urging of many people, do direct you, our brother, and in virtue of obedience do command you and through you we will and order that our other suffragans and fellow-bishops of our province of Canterbury be enjoined, that you and they require corporal oaths in the future from all persons presented to ecclesiastical benefices in your and their dioceses, that may be or become vacant, to the effect that they have not given or promised anything, directly or indirectly, either personally or through a subordinate to the persons presenting them or to any other person; that they are not obliged nor are their friends, by oath or financial security, to resign or to make exchange of those benefices, that of their will and knowledge they have not made any unlawful agreement, deed, or promise in this matter; and that in the case of exchanges, no proxies, though signed by a notary for public record, be permitted in the future, unless the principals to the transaction be present and an examination be provided of the equality and value of the benefices to be exchanged, with oaths presented by both parties that no public or secret simoniacal pravity or fraud or deceit attended the exchange.

You and they, furthermore, will order back to their residence and duty, for which purpose the benefices were provided nonresident priests in your and their dioceses, unless there is present some evident, useful, and reasonable justification, lest their blood, God forbid, be on your and on their hands. And those whom you will have found to have been installed, more accurately intruded, into ecclesiastical benefices by means of simony or fraud, you and they will eject with the sting of proper censure, since when those intruders, whose root is infected with serious disease, are brought to the place of government, calamity is to be feared in those places rather than the favor of God, since they will have rashly provoked his anger against themselves.

You will also warn those sons of iniquity, publicly and in general, those accursed blasphemers of clergy and church and partners in crime with Gehazi and Simon, commonly called "choppechurches," the greater number of whom, it is said, are in your city of London, that they desist immediately from that diseased contagion and damnable procuring of such exchanges and deceptions by means of conventicles and simoniacal agreements, and that the obligations, agreements, and contracts fraudulently made in this manner in the past, though confirmed by oaths, which by that very fact must be considered wholly invalid, they break as far as they are able, quash and invalidate, and that they do not engage in such activities in the future; that the deceits, frauds, and damnable simoniacal contracts made in the past with their cooperation and consent that are not in their power to break, they discover and reveal to us, to you, or to the ordinaries of the dioceses in which such benefices lie that are involved in such deceptions, without excuse or attempt at concealment of any kind, so that they may humbly receive proper punishment according to the seriousness of their offenses, within fifteen days from the time of the monition, allowing five of the fifteen days for the first monition, another five for the second, and the remaining five for the third and peremptory monition, under pain of the greater excommunication which we, by this writing, pass upon each and every one of them, from this time forward, who does not respect these monitions, after the lapse of the fifteen days and after the fact of their negligence, fault, offense, and notification.

And we strictly enjoin you and through you your fellow bishops and colleagues in like manner, that you and they strike these iniquitous merchants of the Lord's inheritance with the sword of ecclesiastical censure, those men who fraudulently obtained several churches and dignities in your and their dioceses and those sons of perversity commonly known as "choppe-churches," particularly those who are in orders, whose corruption and crime the clergy condemns, the people abominate, and the society of both sexes detest, so that the fear of punishment may set a limit upon their avarice and presumption, and that it restrain other presumptuous souls from doing things that are not permitted, lest, may God forbid, because of your inactivity and that of your fellow bishops, repeated reports concerning this profligacy continue to be brought to our ears, and we, in view of this negligence and indifference, extend our hand to cut off the unfruitful, injurious, and pernicious branches this foolish fig tree produced.

What you have done concerning the above you will certify to us before the coming feast of St. Michael the Archangel by letters patent and enclose a copy of these presents.

ARCHBISHOP COURTENAY'S WILL[14]

In the name and honor of the holy and undivided Trinity, Father, Son, and Holy Spirit, Amen. I William Courtenay, unworthy minister of the holy church of Canterbury, by the grace of God sound in mind and body, considering, nevertheless, the frailty of human fortune and how to every creature both distinguished and humble the end of his present life will appear after the days in his life span have passed, I wish to anticipate, as far as it is permitted me from above, the day of my death and to dispose of my goods by deliberate arrangement. Therefore, concerning myself and the goods that only God in his goodness has given and through no merit of mine, do I with the mind of one writing his will so order, prepare, and draw up my will in this manner.

First I leave my soul to the omnipotent God, my Creator and Redeemer, submitting myself and it to his mercy of which there is no number. My body which will be corrupted and decay I wish to have buried as quickly as possible in a worthy manner in the nave of the cathedral church of Exeter at the place where there now lie three deans in a row before the great cross, for which occasion no great lords should be invited but only the bishop and those in the vicinity. I wish that the bishop of the place bury me unless my venerable brother Lord Thomas, by the grace of God archbishop of York and primate of England, should come in accordance with an earlier agreement between us; in which case I ask my brother, the bishop of Exeter, whoever he is, and all belonging to his church and diocese, that, out of reverence for God, his church, and my poor prayers, they show all reverence, honor, and kindness to it.

I wish that those three deans who will be removed because of my burial be interred at some other honorable place in the same church and wholly at my expense.

Next I wish that there be seven torches at my burial burning around my body, one at the head and another at the feet, and that both of these be 20 pounds in weight. Next I wish that 40 torches be lighted on that day in honor of the Eucharist, and that they burn during the mass of the Blessed Virgin, high mass, and all other masses that may be celebrated on the day of my burial, and also on the day following should a prelate be celebrating.

I also wish that a settlement be made with the present or future treasurer of the church of Exeter for everything owing him by reason of the lights that are to burn on the day of my funeral. In order that this previous arrangement concerning the lights and torches be handled with good will, I wish four torches to remain for use at the high altar of the church of Exeter, four for use in the chapel of the Blessed Virgin in that church, and that a torch remain at every altar in the church where priests customarily celebrate mass. Should there be an altar dedicated to St. Catherine, I wish two torches to remain for use at that altar, two for use at the altar where my most reverend parents are buried, and four torches in the parish church of St. Martin in Exminster where I was born. I wish that one vestment of good silken cloth, one cope, chasuble, tunicle, and three albs with amices and maniples be given to said church in my memory.

Next I want the canons, vicars, assistants, choristers, and other priests who are present at my obsequies on the day of my burial to be remunerated in accordance with their rank and at the discretion of my executors, and in similar manner the priests and other religious of the city.

Next I leave one penny to each poor person coming to my obsequies.

Next I wish that as soon after my death as possible, 15,000 masses be celebrated for my soul, the souls of my father, mother, brothers, and sisters who are deceased, and of all other friends and benefactors, also for the souls of persons from whom I received benefits or with whose goods I may have interfered during my life, and also for all the faithful departed, with collects I will have ordered said to that end.

Next I wish 2,000 matins to be recited of all the saints together with nine lessons, and I wish that they be said in full service just as matins are on those feastdays, and that each person taking part in the full service receive 6 pence for his labor.

The above masses I order to be celebrated in this manner: first, a thousand to be celebrated with proper devotion in honor of the Trinity; in honor of the Holy Spirit a thousand; of the Eucharist a thousand; of the Assumption of the Blessed Virgin a thousand; of her birth a thousand; of the angels a thousand; of the birth of our Lord Jesus Christ a thousand; of the Epiphany a thousand; of the feast of the Purification of the Blessed Virgin a thousand; of the Annunciation a thousand; of the resurrection of our Lord Jesus Christ a thousand; of the Ascension a thousand. I want the *Gloria in excelsis Deo* and the *Credo* said in those masses and the sequences if the time of the year permits; otherwise let the *Credo* and sequences be recited in each of the masses noted above.

Next I leave to my most excellent Lord King Richard my best cross and 100 pounds that he may be my special lord after death as he was my most special lord in life, in whom above all men I have always trusted and do now trust, whom I most devoutly pray and entreat that, of the benignity and goodness born in him, he be lord protector and helper to the members of my poor family and provide them justice with favor as often as they find it necessary to fly to his most excellent dignity for refuge.

I further beg the same most excellent, most dread, and most trustworthy lord, my king, by the love of the Lord Jesus Christ and the most Blessed Virgin Mary his mother, also of St. John the Baptist and Sts. Mary Magdalene and Catherine, and all the saints, that he deign to lend helping hands to my executors, lest my successor injure me or them or seek more than what is just for reparations,[15] by having pious and just consideration, if it please, for the condition in which I found the church, my manors, and my castle at Saltwood, and how subsequently, despite an earthquake,[16] I repaired as far as I could during my lifetime and not without heavy and excessive expenses, as my prior knows and the older and more responsible members of the chapter and the more worthy of the diocese, and as my executors will inform your highness, to whom may you deign to incline the ear of your excellency with the love of him who closes the bowels of compassion to no one in need. With confidence in your justice and equity, may your will be done.

I also recommend and leave to your most dread majesty your most devoted servant and suppliant, my dearest and only sister Dangayne (Catherine),[17] humbly and devoutly beseeching you that in your charity you deign to guard, favor, and protect her in this valley of misery under the wings of your most excellent protection. O my most dread lord, my most excellent, most trustworthy and loving lord, I ask you not to shut out the above from the hollow of your breast but to enclose her rather out of special friendship and kindness.

Next I leave my said sister 200 pounds and my moderate-sized missal bound with red satin cloth. I also leave her my altar of white striped silk, together with a table of my lord of Islip and my best chalice with the corporal of the angel's salutation which I received as a gift of the lord treasurer of England, and a table of peace given to me by my mother which John Glin knows well. I also leave to this my sister two silk cloths with woven popinjays that she may make therefrom ecclesiastical vestments. I also leave her my breviary that I have as a gift of my lord the bishop of Winchester, and my two best gilded silver cruets and two others. I also leave her 24 of my best silver dishes, six platters or chargers, 20 saucers, and three pair of the best spoons. I also leave her two silver basins with my arms engraved in the middle and two of the best matching ewers. I further leave her two other silver basins with the arms of Courtenay engraved which are at Slyndon. Next I leave her a round gold cup made to the likeness of feathers which I received as a gift from my lord the king, that she may drink from it in my memory.

Next I leave my brother Philip 40 pounds and my best gilded cup and cover and one ewer. Next I leave my brother Peter 40 pounds. To my sister Anna de Courtenay I leave 20 pounds and one gilded cup with cover according to the discretion of my executors. Next I leave my dearest child and foster son Richard Courtenay[18] 100 marks without any condition. I leave him also my best miter in case he becomes a bishop.[19] I wish the miter to remain in the custody of the dean and chapter of Exeter until Richard is promoted to an episcopacy, and, if it happens that he dies before he is raised to the office of prelate, I leave the miter to the use of the cathedral of Exeter with the provision and prohibition under pain of anathema that it ever be borrowed, transferred, or taken from that church or be given over to the use of another or in any way alienated. It shall remain there permanently for the use of any bishop who wishes to celebrate there to the honor of God and the church.

Next I leave Richard, in case he wishes to be a clerk and is ordained to the priesthood, my dictionary in three volumes together with its calendar. I also leave him the *milleloquium* of St. Augustine and my handsome book called the *lira* bound in two volumes, but with this condition, that if he should remain with sacred things, he shall have these books for his whole life; after his death or if, may this not happen, he should return to the world, I want all these books to remain the possession of the holy church of Canterbury and be wholly restored to it with my blessing and strict injunction that she protect those books from disfigurement. I want them to be given into his hands whenever he begins in the arts or is a bachelor in civil law or decrees.[20]

Next I leave my little child William Courtenay, the son of my brother Philip, 100 marks should he live to the age of

12 years. Next I leave 100 marks to be distributed among the remaining sons and daughters of my brother Philip according to the discretion of my executors and for their well-being.

Next I bequeath to my metropolitan church my best and most beautiful cope of red which is embroidered with pearls. I also leave to the same church my green vestment adorned with gold with the white deer interwoven, the gold fringe and the archangels that lend it the splendor of seven copes. I further leave to the same church my best white vestment of gold with diapered deers or red animals with seven copes of the same material.

Next I leave 200 pounds and somewhat more at the discretion of my executors and their instructions, for the new building or construction of a wall for the cloister extending from the door of the palace to the church along the right path.

Next I leave to the prior of my church of Canterbury, Thomas Chillenden, my most faithful friend, my silver cup or bowl which belonged to my most reverend lord and father, from which he and his ancestors were accustomed to drink and I as well while alive, asking him that in my memory he drink from that cup and his successors after his death use it in my memory. I also leave to the prior 40 pounds or something of that value. I also leave him and his successors the halling and entire hangings with embroidered bed and all the furnishings which remain in the care of the guard of my palace.

Next I leave to my subprior in the same church 100 shillings that he may pray for me; to each monk, my brother priests in said church, 20 shillings; to each monk in said church not a priest 13 shillings 4 pence, and I wish the monks in my college at Oxford to be included in this number.

Next I leave to Walter Causton, monk of said church, 10 marks.

Next I leave the cathedral of Rochester my white striped vestment with five copes of the same material.

Next I leave Hugo Lutterell,[21] my nephew, 100 marks and to his newly wedded wife one gilded silver cup with cover at the discretion of my executors. I also leave something to Hugo Stafford at the discretion of my executors. I leave to John Lutterell 20 marks and to William Lutterell, my little son, 20 marks.

Next I leave to Adam de Mottrum, my chancellor, 20 pounds or something of that value, my large decretals in which I used to study, and the handsome book of the sexts.

Next I leave to Guy Mone 100 marks which I once promised him for his residence which I want him to have or something of equal value whether the residence remains or not.

Next I leave to Walter Gibbes my law *speculum* and 20 marks or their equivalent. I leave to Robert Hall my decretals together with a sixth book in fine and 20 marks or the true value of those 20 marks. I leave to Henry Brony 20 marks or something of equal value.

Next I leave to each priest of my chapel, whether promoted or not, 20 marks or something of equal value.

Next I leave to John Wotton 20 marks and a gilded silver cup with cover. I leave to Richard Lentwardyn the same; to Laurence Hawkyn 20 marks, and to John Gline 20 marks; to Thomas Scodier 20 marks and the allowance I have had this year from my lord the king.

Next I leave the clerk of Salisbury in my chapel 10 pounds and to William Motte 10 pounds. I also leave each boy of my chapel five marks so that they pray for my soul, and to William of the almshouse who should be counted one of these and have five marks.

Next I leave Nicholas Weston my squire 40 marks and my best robe which he may select; to Robert Seymour, my relative, 20 pounds and my second best robe which he may select. I leave to John Frenyngham 20 marks and a gilded silver cup with cover suitable to his station; to John Culpeper one gilded cup with cover and a waterpot suited to his station or something else according to the discretion of my executors.

Next I leave William Hansom 20 pounds and my third best robe which he may select. Next I leave Richard Hidon 10 marks, Henry Casteleyn 10 marks, John Hope 10 marks, and Richard Trist and his wife 20 marks. Next I leave to John Boteler 20 pounds and my fourth best robe which he may select; to Gerard 10 marks, and to the children Brokhull and Waleys something at the discretion of my executors.

Next I leave William Barrok 10 marks, Walter Faukoner 10 marks, Rose Mounfort my pair of gold rosaries which were my mother's that she use them and pray for me; to Christina who lives with my sister Dangayne five marks to pray for me; to Julia, my sister's servant, four marks; to Thomas Burgh 20 pounds and a robe not bequeathed at the discretion of my executors; to John the valet in my room, 100 shillings; to William Pope 100 shillings; to William Seger five marks; and to Thomas

Porter of Lambeth 40 shillings. Next I leave each of my valets living with me in my house, if he is a member of my household at the time of my death, 100 shillings; to Henry of my room, 40 shillings; to John his companion two marks; and to each of my servant boys 40 shillings, and to each page 20 shillings.

Next I leave to John Barnet, official of my court of Canterbury, a gilded silver cup with cover; to Michael Sergeaux, my dean in the church of St. Mary of the Arches in London, a gilded silver cup with cover according to their status. Next I leave John Prophet 10 pounds and my best book of *Clementines*;[22] to John Lynton 10 pounds; to William Baunton 20 marks; to John Dodyngton 20 marks; to Robert Wilford, Oto Chambernoni and to his wife Agnes, to each of them one cup at the discretion of my executors. Next I leave William Trevellis 10 marks and one cup worth five marks; to Nicholas Hereford half of the money he owes me that he may pray for me.

Next I leave Richard Cicester, alias Gardiner, concerning the 20 books for which he is obligated to me on his pledge, 10 pounds; to Richard Broun one gilded cup with cover at the discretion of my executors and 10 pounds; to Brother Bartholomew of the Order of Minors 10 marks; to John Cateby a gilded cup with cover suitable to his state, and I want this to satisfy him for his expenses.

Next I want Robert Bradgar to be remunerated for his labor at the discretion of my executors because he has always been faithful to me and has never wished to accept anything from me. I also leave Thomas a suitably gilded cup at the discretion of my executors.

Next I leave to the cathedral church of Exeter my red vestment diapered with golden stars, five copes of the same kind, two censers with the arms of my lord the king and my arms, which I received as a gift of my lord the king, together with my best incense boat and spoon. I leave to the same church my russet vestment diapered with falcons of gold with five copes of the same material. I leave to the same church for use at the main altar two gilded silver fonts which I received as a gift from my lord of Winchester and I want my arms placed on the base of each.

Next I leave to the cathedral church of London my most special golden vestment with three copes of the same material with two white embroidered stoles and maniples and two gilded fonts which I have as a gift from Hilbrand, soldier and Knight

Hospitaler of Jerusalem who lives at Clerkenwell, for use at the high altar of said church of London, and I want my arms engraved on its base.

Next I leave the cathedral church of Hereford one white vestment diapered with dragons of gold with tunicle, dalmatic, and three copes of the same material, two white embroidered stoles and maniples, and two white copes diapered with gold. There are no more of that material because my brother Philip received the third from me. Next I leave the same church my service book which I bought from the executors of John de Grandisson. I also leave the same church two silver fonts for use at the main altar with the arms of my lord the king on its base, and I want my arms placed there as well.

Next I leave the church of St. Mary of Otery my black vestment with chasuble, tunicle, dalmatic, and one cope of the same material which belonged to John of Grandisson, once bishop of Exeter, and my best gilded chalice not yet bequeathed, together with the two best gilded cruets not yet bequeathed.

Next I leave my venerable brother Thomas, by the grace of God archbishop of York, primate of England, one gold cross with precious stones which has a pall on its back and beneath this a beautiful piece of the wood of the Lord, which cross I received as a gift of my lord the king. I also leave the same venerable brother my beautiful decretals bound with red leather.

Next I leave my venerable brother John, by the grace of God bishop of Salisbury, a gold cross with pearls and precious stones, which contains a beautiful piece of the black wood of the Lord; also, a beautiful missal which I received as a gift of my venerable brother Thomas, by the grace of God archbishop of York.

Next I leave my venerable brother Robert, by the grace of God bishop of London, a gold cross decorated with precious stones and pearls and having a piece of the cross of the Lord, which I received from the executors of my mistress, the mother of the king; and a new missal bound in golden cloth of damask which Gerard my squire copied.

Next I leave to my venerable brother John, by the grace of God bishop of Lincoln, my best golden jewel which has not been bequeathed.

Next I leave to my venerable brother William, bishop of Winchester, my second best golden jewel not yet bequeathed.

Next I leave my venerable brother Edmund, by the grace

of God bishop of Exeter, my large marked breviary which I received from my venerable brother the archbishop of York.

Next I leave Radulph, by the grace of God bishop of Bath and Wells, one ring with ruby which I received from the executors of Simon of good memory, my predecessor, and a beautiful psalter bound in golden cloth.

Next I leave the abbot and convent of Faversham of my diocese 10 pounds; to the abbot and convent of Boxle 10 pounds; to the abbot and convent of Langedon 100 shillings; to the abbot and convent of St. Radegund 100 shillings; to the prior and convent of Leeds 10 pounds and a beautiful gilded chalice; to the abbot and convent of St. Gregory, Canterbury, 10 pounds and a gilded chalice; to the prioress and convent of St. Sepulcher, Canterbury, 10 pounds; to the prior and convent of Dover 20 pounds and my red vestment of silk diapered with white lions, together with six copes of the same material; to the prior and convent of Bilsington 100 shillings; to the priory of Combewell 100 shillings; to the prioress and convent of Scapeia 20 pounds; to the prioress and convent of Davyngton near Faversham 10 pounds; to the prior and convent of Merton in the diocese of Winchester 20 pounds; to the prior and convent of Bermondesey 20 pounds. I leave to my kinswoman Elizabeth, nun of Canonle, 10 marks; to the prioress and convent of Polslo of the diocese of Exeter 10 pounds; to Thomas Palmer provincial of the Order of Preaching Friars 10 marks that he may pray for me. I leave five marks to each mendicant friar of that order in my diocese.

Next I leave to the poor of Northgate five marks; to the poor of Herbaldoune five marks; to the recluse in Crukern in the diocese of Wells five marks; to the recluse of Shirbourn 40 shillings; and 40 shillings to each recluse within my province.

Next I wish and direct that my debts be paid before anything and that everyone having a just complaint of injury from me receive satisfaction.

Should other goods remain, I ask my executors, by the bowels of mercy of our Lord Jesus Christ, that they expend these in the best possible way they can or know, for the salvation of my soul and the souls of all those named in my will.

I wish, furthermore, that my executors dispose of my demesne of Tunbrigg and the estate of my manor of Cherleton in the best way they know, for the salvation of my soul. Also concerning the advowsons of the two churches acquired by me, namely of Kemsing in the country of Kent and of Cornewood in the county of Devon, let them dispose of these in the best way they know and can.

I ask my executors noted below and beg and adjure them by the bowels of the Mother of Mercy and the shedding of the blood of our Lord Jesus Christ that, dismissing every voluntary excuse, they assume and apply themselves to the entire administration of my possessions and the execution of this my last will and testament, and faithfully carry out the provisions of the same to the best of their ability and at the expenditure of modest and not lavish costs, so that they may receive everlasting life from the retributor of all goods.

If moreover, hopefully not, any of the executors noted below should refuse to accept or respect the execution of this my last will and testament, I want him for that very reason to be deprived of what has been bequeathed to him.

I also wish and direct that each and every one of the above legatees, excepting only my sister and my relatives, receive and have in good measure the true value of the sums of money bequeathed to them if this is agreeable to my executors.

For the faithful execution and carrying out of this my last will, therefore, I appoint and designate as my executors the most beloved son in Christ Thomas Chillenden, prior of my church of Canterbury; and my most trustworthy sons in Christ, Adam de Mottrum, my archdeacon; Guy Mone, rector of the church of Maidstone; John Frenyngham, squire; William Baunton, rector of the church of Harrow; John Dodyngton, rector of the church of Crukern; Robert Hall, rector of the church of Northfleet; and John Wotton, rector of the church of Stapelhurst.

[There follows this codicil:]

What was written above was and is the true testament of William of pious and worshipful memory, recently while he lived archbishop of Canterbury by the grace of God, now deceased, except in so far as the will is modified by a subsequent codicil, namely that on July 28 just past, the same most reverend father, languishing in his last agony in an inner room of his manor of Maidstone in the diocese of Canterbury, willed and directed that since he did not consider himself worthy, as he said, to be buried in his metropolitan or any cathedral or collegiate church, wished and chose to be buried in the churchyard of the collegiate church of Maidstone at a place pointed out to John Boteler his squire.

Then the same most reverend father wished, said and ordered that his debts be paid and that legacies for the members of his household listed in the above testament be paid. The same most reverend father willed, however, and said that the legacies in the above testament that concerned legatees outside the household be defaulted at the discretion of his executors, and that what remained of his goods after the last debts and legacies had been paid be expended, at the discretion of his executors, on the construction of the collegiate church at Maidstone.

⟬NOTES⟭

CHAPTER ONE (Pages 1–15)

1. *Chronicon Angliae, 1328–1388*, T. *Walsingham*, p. 120. See below, p. 37.

2. See Burke, *A Genealogical and Heraldic Dictionary of the Peerage and Baronetage*, p. 430. Gibbon digresses on the family of Courtenay in the sixth volume of his *Decline and Fall*. See also Dugdale, *The Baronage of England*, I, 634, and *The Complete Peerage*, III, 465–467; IV, 323–325. Though the Courtenays were Devon's most distinguished family, they had neighbors who boasted Devonian ancestry reaching back beyond the Christian era and who dismissed the Courtenays as "mere parvenus and upstarts." See Hoskins and Finberg, *Devonshire Studies*, p. 106.

3. Philip Courtenay, William's younger brother by seven years, started out on a career similar to William's, for he was well beneficed already at the age of thirteen. See *Papal Registers, Petitions*, I, 374. He must have decided on a political or civil career, however, for he is referred to as "admiral of the king's fleet toward the west" in 1374 (*Patent Rolls, 1374–1377*, p. 62) and as keeper of Dartmoor forest in 1376. *Ibid.*, 308.

4. Somner, *The Antiquities of Canterbury*, p. 75. A dispensation dated August 17, 1369, authorized Courtenay's consecration as bishop of Hereford. See *Registrum Willelmi de Courtenay*, p. 1. Such a dispensation was necessary since Courtenay was but twenty-eight years old at the time. See Courtenay's will, Appendix p. 267, for reference to Exminster as birthplace. Baigent believes Courtenay was born on December 4, the festal day of St. Barbara, since the figure of St. Barbara appears on Courtenay's seal. See *Collectanea Archaeologica*, I, 237, n. 1.

5. Wood, *Appendix to the History and Antiquities of the Colleges and Halls in the University of Oxford*, p. 28. Stapledon Hall was founded in or soon after 1314. See Rashdall, *The Universities of Europe in the Middle Ages*, III, 202.

6. "Under Edward III the study of law was more and more regarded as an essential preliminary to a successful career." Highfield, "The English Hierarchy in the Reign of Edward III," *Transactions of the Royal Historical Society*, Fifth Series, VI, 127.

7. *Registrum Willelmi de Courtenay*, p. 2; *Fasciculi Zizaniorum Magistri Johannis Wyclif*, p. 286; *Papal Registers, Letters*, IV, 62. In Buckingham's register Courtenay is referred to as *iuris civilis professor*. See "Register of John Buckingham," Institutions, fol. 342, and *Snappe's Formulary and Other Records*, p. 85. The prior of Christ Church also referred to him in this way in 1381 when he asked Richard to approve Courtenay's election. "Register G," fol. 223.

8. Grandisson's register refers to him as a priest in that year. *Register of John de Grandisson*, III, 1260. Grandisson as bishop of Exeter was Courtenay's ordinary.

9. *Papal Registers, Petitions*, I, 284. For Courtenay's appointment to other benefices, see *Petitions*, I, 291, 320, 374.

10. *Grandisson*, III, 1260. The average annual income of a parish priest of the time was approximately five pounds. See Tierney, *Medieval Poor Law*, p. 92, and Richardson, "The Parish Clergy of the Thirteenth and Fourteenth Centuries," *Transactions of the Royal Historical Society*, Third Series, VI, 114–117.

11. "Register of John Buckingham," Institutions, fol. 342. See *Snappe's Formulary*, pp. 85–86.

12. The question was raised "whether John is of sufficient learning to rule so populous and noble a diocese." *Papal Registers, Letters*, IV, 1.

13. "Register of John Buckingham," Institutions, fol. 342. See *Snappe's Formulary*, p. 85, and Gibson, "Confirmations of Oxford Chancellors in the Lincoln Episcopal Registers," EHR, XXVI, 503. One can appreciate the university's position in its argument with the bishop, since the chancellor usually held office for but two years. See *Munimenta Academica*, I, 228–230. Oxford would, of course, have objected to the need for obtaining episcopal confirmation, however infrequent the occasion to do so.

14. See below, p. 140. Yet Courtenay bequeathed the bishop his best golden jewel in his will. See below, p. 273.

15. *Munimenta Academica*, I, 228–230; Wilkins, *Concilia Magnae Britanniae et Hiberniae*, III, 75. See *Papal Registers, Letters*, IV, 66, 83. The papal curia must have neglected to notify Buckingham of this action, for on May 13, 1369, he cited Adam Toneworth, Courtenay's successor as chancellor, for having failed to receive episcopal confirmation of his election. "Register of John Buckingham," Memoranda, fol. 70; *Snappe's Formulary*, p. 86. On June 23, Buckingham asked the official of the bishop of Lichfield to serve a citation on Adam Toneworth. "Register of John Buckingham," Memoranda, fol. 73; *Snappe's Formulary*, pp. 45, 86–89. See Rashdall (III, 124–125, n. 3) who says Urban's bull granting Oxford this exemption was not recorded in the Lincoln Register until the time of Bishop Repingdon. See also Gibson, "Confirmations of Oxford Chancellors in the Lincoln Episcopal Registers," EHR, XXVI, 502.

16. *Munimenta Academica*, I, 18, 226–227.

17. Courtenay's aristocratic background might today recommend his election as chancellor, since one of the criteria governing the selection of modern university chancellors and presidents is the ability to raise money.

18. Robson comments in his *Wyclif and the Oxford Schools* (pp. 112, 170) on the lag in scholastic life at Oxford in the decades of the 1350's and 1360's.

19. *Munimenta Academica*, I, 25, 206; II, 388–389. In 1365 the pope had summoned the chancellors, regents, and other officials, to show cause why the suspension of these statutes for one year should not be made permanent. *Papal Registers, Letters*, IV, 52–53.

20. *Rotuli Parliamentorum*, II, 290; Wood, *The History and Antiquities of the University of Oxford*, I, 480.

21. *Ibid.*

22. See below, p. 36. The paths of Courtenay and Wyclif which crossed several times in later years just missed one another here at Oxford in the decade of the 60's. Wyclif's removal as warden of Canterbury Hall by the archbishop of Canterbury had been ordered just three months before Courtenay's election to the chancellorship. See Workman, *John Wyclif*, I, 180, and Pantin, *Canterbury College Oxford*, III, 14.

23. *Munimenta Academica*, I, 230, 231.

24. *Ibid.*, 231–232.

25. Salter says Courtenay must have resigned about Easter, since Adam Toneworth was elected chancellor at some date before May 4 when he was installed. *Snappe's Formulary*, p. 329.

26. The king's *congé d'élire* is dated July 8. See *Patent Rolls*, 1367–1370, p. 282.

27. Boggis, *A History of the Diocese of Exeter*, p. 255, and Hingeston-Randolf, *Register of Thomas de Brantyngham*, II, vii. One wonders what arguments and pressures were advanced in the contest between Courtenay and Brantingham over Hereford. Brantingham as the royal treasurer was surely slated for a bishopric. Courtenay may have received the nod because he was "out of a job" and Brantingham in a better position to wait for a later vacancy.

28. McKisack, *The Fourteenth Century*, p. 275. See Pantin, *The English Church in the Fourteenth Century*, p. 55.

29. Upon Grandisson's death the cathedral chapter at Exeter elected Brantingham, only to encounter something like the same opposition at Westminster (or Avignon) as the Hereford chapter had experienced when they elected him. This time, however, there were no aristocratic candi-

dates like Courtenay or candidates with aristocratic advocates to interpose claims, so the pope at length confirmed Brantingham's election.
The pope explained that he had initially objected to Brantingham's
election only because he had reserved the right of provision to the
see to himself, and that he was now independently providing the
man whom they had selected. See Boggis, p. 255.

30. *Registrum Willelmi de Courtenay,* pp. 1–2. Courtenay was but 28
years of age and canon law required an episcopal candidate to be
30 years old when consecrated, wherefore the dispensation. Note might
be made here of an indult the pope granted Courtenay in 1367 when
the latter was still a priest, to have a portable altar. (*Papal Registers,
Letters,* IV, 62.) Why had Courtenay made this request? A sympathetic
observer would suggest piety, an unfriendly critic would construe
it as the action of an ambitious cleric anxious to make Rome aware
of his existence. Still such requests were not uncommon and were
even granted to laymen. Incidentally, as bishop-elect of Hereford,
Courtenay secured permission to have masses and divine offices celebrated privately in places under interdict (*ibid.* 82), which was also
not an unusual concession.

31. Stubbs, *Registrum Sacrum Anglicanum,* p. 79.

32. *Patent Rolls,* 1367–1370, p. 379.

33. *Registrum Willelmi de Courtenay,* pp. 4–5. See *Collectanea Archaeologica,* I, 232, 233.

34. See Boggis, p. 259.

35. See below, p. 117.

36. There is not even any record of papal provisions. These appear to
have halted abruptly in the case of the diocese of Hereford in 1369,
and Driver suggests the effectiveness of the statute of provisors. See
"The Papacy and the Diocese of Hereford, 1307–1377," *The Church
Quarterly Review,* CXLV, 41.

37. Pantin, *The English Church in the Fourteenth Century,* p. 11. Eighteen
of the eighty-five bishops who served during Edward's reign "may
be said to have passed an important part of their life before episcopal
promotion in a major government department." Highfield, "The English
Hierarchy in the Reign of Edward III," p. 85. "Altogether eleven
of Edward III's seventeen chancellors and fourteen of his twenty-one
treasurers were bishops." *Ibid.,* 119.

38. See Highfield, p. 120.

39. Highfield who appears to question this view, notes that only fifteen
bishops in the reign of Edward came from aristocratic families, and
that "Their numbers were by no means proportionate to the impression
they created on their contemporaries and have continued to exert
on modern historians." *Ibid.*

40. See Pantin, *The English Church in the Fourteenth Century*, p. 23.

41. McKisack notes that the number of magnates tended to decrease in the later Middle Ages, with correspondingly greater wealth and influence—and probably with greater anxiety to protect or expand this influence by means of episcopal appointments. *The Fourteenth Century*, p. 260. See Pantin, pp. 22–25, for a discussion of aristocrats among the hierarchy.

42. Stubbs, *The Constitutional History of England*, III, 351.

43. *Rot. Parl.*, II, 317.

44. *Matthaei Parker Cantuariensis Archiepiscopi De Antiquitate Britannicae Ecclesiae et Privilegiis Ecclesiae Cantuariensis*, p. 380. See Wilkins, *Concilia Magnae Britanniae et Hiberniae*, III, 97. Concerning the authenticity of the document, see Perroy, *L'Angleterre et le grand Schisme d'Occident*, p. 34. See also *Close Rolls*, 1374–1377, p. 37, and *The Register of the Diocese of Worcester During the Vacancy of the See*, p. 305.

45. That the pope's needs were, nonetheless, desperate is suggested by the demand made unsuccessfully by him in 1365 that the tribute promised by John and so many years in arrears be paid. See Perroy, p. 28.

46. *Papal Registers, Letters*, IV, 101. Less offensive to episcopal sensibilities, although illustrative of the manner the curia could bypass the bishop in purely diocesan matters, was a papal grant to the same nuncio at about this time to "grant dispensation to twelve men and as many women in France and England who have married in ignorance that they were related in the fourth degree of kindred or affinity, declaring past and future offspring legitimate." *Ibid.*, 104. Fees and offerings from the beneficiaries of such dispensations would help finance the legate's journey.

47. *Ibid.*, 93.

48. *Ibid.* Perroy says the papal envoys were held up for several weeks by the English. "The Anglo-French Negotiations at Bruges," *Camden Miscellany*, XIX, ix.

49. *Papal Registers, Letters*, IV, 115. See also pp. 106–107.

50. *Ibid.*, 115. The immediate necessity was the war with the Visconti of Milan, in which papal fortunes had been entrusted to that doughty warrior, John Hawkwood, but without much success. "The pope is surprised that, although John fights in battle like a champion of the church and mighty man of valour, yet the son of Belial, Barnabas, has hitherto lost no city, fortress, or territory. The pope exhorts him to arise in his strength against those sons of perdition, Barnabas and Galeatius, and to do something notable." *Ibid.*, 125. This he was eventually to do, and when the pope proved successful in enlisting the

aid of the emperor, the queen of Naples, and the king of Hungary, Milan sued for peace. See below, 286, n. 38.

51. *Ibid.*, 116.

52. This letter did not reach England, according to the pope's complaint. *Ibid.*, 117. See Perroy, *L'Angleterre et le grand Schisme d'Occident*, p. 30.

53. *Papal Registers, Letters*, IV, 117. See also pp. 106–107.

54. *Ibid.*, 123–124.

55. See above, p. 10.

56. *Papal Registers, Letters*, IV, 116–117.

57. *Matthaei Parker Cantuariensis Archiepiscopi De Antiquitate Britannicae Ecclesiae*, pp. 380–381; Wilkins, III, 97. The report in Witlesey's register has Courtenay protesting "that unless the burdens so frequently and unjustly placed upon him and his church of Hereford were made an end to by the king and his council, the king would not have one penny from him or the clergy of his diocese. . . ." "Register of William Witlesey," fol. 65.

58. This is what Perroy believes. *L'Angleterre et le grand Schisme d'Occident*, p. 34, n. 4. Actually the crown would normally have been the principal beneficiary of such taxation if past levies were any indication. See McKisack, pp. 283–285.

59. *Patent Rolls*, 1370–1374, p. 190.

60. Highfield implies the protest was made in the interest of the lower clergy upon whom fell the heaviest burden. He says Courtenay's protest "was quite exceptional," the only one made in their behalf in the second half of Edward's reign. "The English Hierarchy in the Reign of Edward III," *Transactions of the Royal Historical Society*, Fifth Series, VI, 138.

61. *Charters and Records of Hereford Cathedral*, tr. William W. Capes, p. 236. The exact amount due the curia is not revealed.

62. *Rot. Parl.*, II, 337. See McKisack, p. 236.

63. For a discussion of these negotiations, see Perroy, *L'Angleterre et le grand Schisme d'Occident*, pp. 32–33, 35–44, and "The Anglo-French Negotiations at Bruges," *Camden Miscellany*, XIX, xii, as well as Pantin, *The English Church in the Fourteenth Century*, pp. 88–91. As late as May 1376, the pope was complaining that the province of York had as yet paid nothing, while several bishops in the province of Canterbury were also delinquent. *Papal Registers, Letters*, IV, 154–155. See *Wykeham's Register*, II, 244–245.

64. *Papal Registers, Letters*, IV, 134.

65. Archbishop Witlesey had died in June 1374.

66. Did the pope consider Courtenay's outburst in convocation as aimed at himself or the king? Perroy believes Courtenay was exercised over royal demands. See above, p. 12, n. 58. If Courtenay did soften his position on the charitable subsidy, he did not bend to the extent of authorizing its collection in his diocese of Hereford. A year later, Sudbury as archbishop of Canterbury ordered John Gilbert, Courtenay's successor in Hereford, to proceed with its collection inasmuch as Courtenay had neglected to do so. "Register of Simon Sudbury," fols. 24v-25.

67. See below, p. 24.

CHAPTER TWO (Pages 16–30)

1. Despite the importance of London, Sudbury and Courtenay were the only bishops since Dunstan (d. 988) who moved from there to Canterbury.

2. Archbishop Sudbury reminded Bishop Wykeham that Winchester stood second only to London (*Wykeham's Register*, II, 240).

3. Lambeth was formally acquired in 1197. Canterbury was some 60 miles from London.

4. Official records, whether of church or state, are generally too impersonal for this period (any period?) to note anything so personal as an individual's qualifications or deficiencies. The papal query concerning John Buckingham's ability (see above, p. 12) is rare.

5. In the fourteenth century, "the general rule seems to have been provision by the pope, more or less at the king's nomination." Pantin, *The English Church in the Fourteenth Century*, p. 55. As McKisack writes, "the political importance of medieval bishops rendered a system of free elections impracticable." *The Fourteenth Century*, p. 275.

6. See above, p. 14. As suggested, the papal curia already recognized Courtenay as one of England's two most influential bishops.

7. "Register of Simon Sudbury," fols. 21v-22.

8. "Among the middle and lower classes, the dislike of lawyers was, at this time, only surpassed by their dislike of a Frenchman." Hook, *Lives of the Archbishops of Canterbury*, IV, 249. An echo of this hostility may be reflected in the act of parliament in 1372 in ruling such lawyers ineligible to serve as knights of the shire who used their position in parliament to transact the business of their clients. *Rot Parl.*, II, 310; *The Statutes of the Realm*, I, 394.

9. The Londoners would have applauded Courtenay's protest. Not only might English money find its way into French coffers, but the clergy's "depleted resources [would] make it impossible for them to contribute adequately to the needs of the State." McKisack, p. 286.

10. Philippa was one of medieval England's greatest queens. Had she lived the course of the seventies might have been different.

11. *Anonimalle Chronicle*, p. 94. Edward's hold over his baronage was based upon his military success. When this failed him, there was nothing left to enlist their support. See Wilkinson, *The Chancery under Edward III*, pp. 126–127.

12. "The last years of Edward III's reign form one of the most confused periods in fourteenth-century history." McFarlane, *John Wycliffe and the Beginnings of English Nonconformity*, p. 37.

13. See below, p. 92.

14. His "wealth and wide connections constituted a party in themselves. . . ." Steel, *Richard II*, p. 13.

15. Wilkinson (pp. 127, 135–136) believes Gaunt and his friends assumed direction of the government soon after 1371, if not before. In that year his associates, Robert Thorpe and Richard Scrope, replaced Wykeham and Brantingham, friends of the Black Prince, as chancellor and treasurer respectively. (See below, p. 21.) Although Gaunt was often out of the country, first pursuing ambitions in Castile and then fighting in France, his agents looked after his interests at home. See Steel, p. 20.

16. Gaunt's unpopularity sprang from several sources: his arrogant manner, his lack of military prowess, the military and diplomatic reverses suffered during this period and blamed on him (see McKisack, p. 386), and, above all, as Thompson suggests (*Chron. Angl.* p. xxxix), the realization that with the death of the Black Prince and the incapacity of Edward, Gaunt would assume the direction of the government. "It was but natural that this posture of affairs should cause him to be regarded by the people with jealousy—a jealousy that was changed by his own conduct into actual suspicion that he had formed designs upon the throne, to the prejudice of the young prince Richard."

17. See McFarlane, p. 74.

18. See McFarlane, p. 40, and Steel, p. 20.

19. Trevelyan, *England in the Age of Wycliffe*, p. 4.

20. Both men had succeeded bishops: Wykeham followed Bishop Langham of Ely, and Brantingham, Bishop Barnet of Worcester.

21. Accepting always Tout's warning about the "fierce individualism of a greedy bachelor," (see Steel, p. 15) which even at worst could not endanger a throne.

22. See Steel, pp. 15–16, for the advantages of a "clerical" government.

23. Unwin, *Finance and Trade under Edward III*, p. xiii.

24. Shirley, *Fas. Ziz.*, p. xxi. See V. H. Galbraith, "Articles Laid before the Parliament of 1371," *EHR*, XXXIV, 579–582.

25. *Rot. Parl.*, II, 304. The chroniclers see only hatred of the church in the dismissal of Wykeham and Brantingham. Walsingham speaks of the "hatred of the church" (*Historia Anglicana, T. Walsingham*, I, 313), while Capgrave comments on the petition of the lords that the chancellor and others be removed: "And so was it fulfillid in dede; and alle this was don for hate of the clergie." *The Chronicle of England by John Capgrave*, p. 228.

26. In terms of a movement affecting many people, it is almost an anachronism to speak of anticlericalism in the Middle Ages. Men like Marsiglio of Padua were fairly lonely figures. For a discussion of the anticlerical character of the attack on the government in 1371, see McKisack, pp. 289–291, Wilkinson, p. 125, the *Cambridge Medieval History*, VII, 454, and Healy, "John of Gaunt and John Wyclif," *Canadian Catholic Historical Report* (1962), pp. 41–42.

27. See Dahmus, *The Prosecution of John Wyclyf*, p. 14.

28. See Wilkinson, pp. 125, 135.

29. What made these the most prominent were the scandalous charges brought against them in 1376 in the Good Parliament and the hostility of the chroniclers.

30. See Steel, p. 21.

31. Workman, I, 217. See Clarke, *Fourteenth Century Studies*, pp. 37–39.

32. One of the unanswered questions of the early seventies concerns the exact relationship between the Black Prince and Gaunt. If they had become embittered toward one another, scholars would have less difficulty presenting a clear-cut analysis of the period. One is tempted to suspect some estrangement, partly because of occasional hostility between their associates, partly because Gaunt and his men gradually replaced the Black Prince and his friends in the government and in the prosecution of the war, a development which should normally have engendered some bitterness. This line of reasoning may be what prompts Wilkinson to speak of the "rapidly developing hostility" between the two brothers. *The Chancery Under Edward III*, p. 125. Since the chroniclers do not notice any friction before the meeting of the Good Parliament (see below, p. 25), it is perhaps dangerous to go beyond the suggestion that contemporaries were inclined to identify men in political life as being associates of either the prince or the duke. See Lewis, "The 'Continual Council' in the Early Years of Richard II, 1377–80," *EHR*, XLI, 249. Tout writes: "I can see no evidence of friction between Lancaster and the prince to the very day of the latter's death. But it is clear that the prince acted as a restraining influence upon him." *Chapters in the Administrative History of Mediaeval England*, III, 303, n. 1.

33. According to Walsingham (*Hist. Angl.*, I, 317), Edward granted the monks at Canterbury permission to hold an election, but was quite indignant when they agreed upon Simon Langham, the cardinal. Still the king had his way in the end, which was more than the pope could say. In a letter to Sudbury announcing his translation to Canterbury, the pope complained over the manner in which the papal envoys had been kept out of England and how his own letter had been held up, and he exhorted Sudbury meantime "to study to multiply the talent with which he was endowed." *Papal Registers, Letters,* IV, 147; Wilkins, III, 97. Reading between the lines of the pope's letter, one can detect a definite lack of enthusiasm for Sudbury. The pope probably had no voice in his elevation to Canterbury other than to approve it.

34. *Hist. Angl.,* I, 318.

35. Hennessy, *Novum Repertorium,* p. 2.

36. *Patent Rolls,* 1374–1377, p. 302; Rymer, *Foedera, Conventiones, Literae, et Cujuscunque Generis Acta Publica,* VII, 97. It is regrettable that here and throughout this chapter which deals with Courtenay as bishop of London reference cannot be made to Courtenay's London register. This has never been located. See *Historical Manuscripts Commission Report on Manuscripts in Various Collections,* VII, p. 2.

37. Hunt suggests that Courtenay "as a constitutional politician . . . probably was glad to forward the downfall of the Italian merchants, from whom the king had long derived the money wasted in extravagance. . . ." *Dictionary of National Biography,* p. 1268.

38. The pope's earlier war with the Visconti of Milan (see above, p. 281, n. 50) had ended more or less satisfactorily. But in 1375 Milan allied itself with Florence which feared any strengthening of papal power in central Italy, and both countries did what they could to induce rebellious elements in the papal territories to revolt. When Florence sent troops to aid insurgent Bologna in March (1376) and refused peace overtures, Gregory issued his anathema. See Gregorovius, *History of the City of Rome in the Middle Ages,* VI, Pt. II, 471–472.

39. *Hist. Angl.,* I, 322–323; *Chron. Angl.,* pp. 109–111; *Eulogium Historiarum sive Temporis (Continuatio),* III, 335.

40. Rymer, VII, 103–104; *Chron. Angl.,* p. 109; *Eulogium,* III, 335.

41. *Chron. Angl.,* p. 111; *Eulogium,* III, 335.

42. The English disliked all foreigners, particularly foreign merchants. Even in the expulsion of the Jews in 1290, "there could be no spice of religious bigotry." Capes, *The English Church in the Fourteenth and Fifteenth Centuries,* p. 22.

43. Rymer, VII, 135; *Eulogium,* III, 335; *Calendar of Letter-Books . . . of the City of London, Letter-Book H,* p. 55.

44. *Eulogium,* III, 335. Had the chancellor been anyone else but Brantingham, Courtenay's friend, the bishop might not have come off so easily.

45. See below, p. 66.

46. The identification "good" was given this parliament by contemporaries. Walsingham refers to it as the parliament "quod 'Bonum' merito vocabatur." *Hist. Angl.,* I, 324.

47. Edward the Black Prince, was physically unable to preside.

48. Peter de la Mare was the steward of the earl of March, a very wealthy, powerful lord, who had married the king's granddaughter (Lionel's only daughter). The chroniclers are loud in their praise of de la Mare's eloquence and courage. See *Hist. Angl.,* I, 321; *Chron. Angl.,* pp. 72, 392; *Anonimalle Chronicle,* p. 83.

49. According to Walsingham (*Chron. Angl.,* pp. 69–70), commons first sought the advice of four bishops, who in turn suggested the addition of four barons, and who in turn recommended the addition of four earls.

50. See Tout, III, 294–296.

51. Perrers was also meddling in the government. The chronicler laments: "This woman would sumtyme sitte be the Juges on the bench, and sumtyme be the Doctouris in the Consistory, and plete with the Treuth, and ageyn the treuth, be the Kyngis auctorite. . . ." *The Chronicle of England by John Capgrave,* p. 231. See *Hist. Angl.,* I, 320–321, and *Anonimalle Chronicle,* p. 87.

52. *Chron. Angl.,* p. 100. The work of the Good Parliament is well preserved in contemporary records. Tout (III, 290, n. 4) writes: "We are lucky in having fuller accounts of the Good Parliament than of any other parliament of the middle ages." For a discussion of this parliament, see Tout, III, 290–307; McKisack, pp. 387–393; Steel, pp. 23–31.

53. Parliament refused to vote a badly needed tenth and only conceded the collection of a wool subsidy for three months.

54. The duke may have had another reason to object to the Good Parliament, namely, the fact that it had not appointed him to the advisory council. The chronicler writes: "the duke of Lancaster was not well satisfyed, but sore grieved and vexed because himself was not chosen to be the kinges counsaile." *Chron. Angl.,* p. lxx.

55. It is dangerous to disregard completely the testimony of the chroniclers who looked upon the Black Prince as the patron of the insurgent group in the Good Parliament. Walsingham writes: "extincto Principe, extinctus est cum eo profecto Parliamenti praesentis effectus. Nam communes, cum quibus ipse tenebat, dicti Parliamenti sortiti non sunt talem exitum qualem pro meliori habuisse sperabant." *Hist. Angl.,* I, 321. See also *Chron. Angl.,* pp. xxxix, 74–75, 391–393.

56. *Chron. Angl.*, p. 104. Trevelyan has this comment: "Sudbury, whose special duty it was to denounce her, was not the man to take so bold a step on his own initiative; while Courtenay, whose conduct was never tinged with cowardice or irresolution, had probably not yet discovered how necessary it was to force the hand of his superior, if the Church was to take decided action." *England in the Age of Wycliffe*, p. 33. It is possible Gaunt had no fear of his father's reaction to his defiance of parliament, since Edward was seriously ill from September until February. See *Chron. Angl.*, p. 103. Walsingham says Edward did not wish to rule with the continual council and turned the government over to Gaunt "who acted as the governor and ruler of the realm until the death of the king." *Hist. Angl.*, I, 322; *Chron. Angl.*, p. 394.

57. *Ibid.*, pp. lxxiv–lxxix, 102–104. See Tout (III, 310) who writes: "An ingenious malice made both the articles of accusation and the method of his trial a parody of the impeachment of Latimer, and we may feel pretty sure that Latimer himself inspired this procedure." For Wykeham, see Tout, III, 235–239, 310–312; McKisack, pp. 225–228; Lowth, *The Life of William Wykeham*, pp. 131–134. Of Wykeham's guilt, Wilkinson writes: "The charges . . . brought against him by his enemies . . . are themselves sufficient to prove that he was both an honest and an able chancellor." *The Chancery Under Edward III*, p. 123. Bad blood may have existed between Wykeham and the duke. According to the chronicler, the duke charged the bishop with having slandered him as being illegitimate. *Chron. Angl.*, pp. 107, 398.

58. *Ibid.*, p. lxxviii.

59. As a bid for popularity and to reduce criticism, Wykeham's temporalities were assigned to young Prince Richard. Thompson, *Chron. Angl.*, p. li.

60. *Patent Rolls*, 1374–1377, p. 347. See Tout, III, 309.

61. For this parliament, see Steel, pp. 32–35; Tout, III, 312–318; McKisack, pp. 395–396; Wedgwood, "John of Gaunt and the Packing of Paliament," EHR, XLV, 623–625.

62. *Chron. Angl.*, lxxx. See *Anonimalle Chronicle*, p. 100.

63. *Chron. Angl.*, p. lxxxi. See *Anonimalle Chronicle*, p. 101.

64. *Chron. Angl.*, pp. 113–114.

65. The chronicler says the bishops were incensed at Sudbury because he appeared to be taking the duke's part. *Ibid.*, 114. But see Warren, "A Reappraisal of Simon Sudbury, Bishop of London (1361–1375) and Archbishop of Canterbury (1375–1381)," *The Journal of Ecclesiastical History*, X, 147–148, who attempts to defend Sudbury.

66. *Ibid.*

67. *Rot. Parl.*, II, 365; *Statutes of the Realm*, I, 397.

CHAPTER THREE (Pages 31–43)

1. See Tout, III, 319; Steel, p. 35; McKisack, p. 396; Shirley, *Fas. Ziz.*, p. xxvii.

2. See Dahmus, "John Wyclif and the English Government," *Speculum*, XXXV, 52–53.

3. *Polychronicon Ranulphi Higden Monachi Cistrensis*, VIII, 380. See Dahmus, *Prosecution*, pp. 4–5.

4. Hanrahan suggests that Wyclif was dropped from the deputation sent to Bruges in 1375 because the commission felt the presence of a theologian to be superfluous. "John Wyclif's Political Activity," *Mediaeval Studies*, XX, 155.

5. See above, p. 21.

6. See Dahmus, *Prosecution*, p. 15.

7. For a discussion of Gaunt's attitude toward Wyclif's theories, see Dahmus, "John Wyclif and the English Government," *Speculum*, XXXV, 66–67.

8. Tout, III, 346. See also Thompson, *Chron. Angl.*, p. xxxviii, and Galbraith, "Thomas Walsingham and the Saint Albans Chronicle, 1272–1422," EHR, XLVII, 12–29.

9. *Chron. Angl.*, p. 115.

10. See Dahmus, "John Wyclif and the English Government," *Speculum*, XXV, 53.

11. See below, p. 44.

12. *Transcript of a Chronicle*, p. 255. See *Chron. Angl.*, p. 117.

13. Interest in arraigning Wyclif may have come to a head at this time because of the appearance of the first volume of the Reformer's treatise on civil dominion.

14. See below, p. 57.

15. The first notice of Percy's new office as marshal appears in the summons to parliament dated December 1, 1376. *Close Rolls*, 1374–1377, p. 467.

16. Principally if not wholly within the halls of Oxford. See Dahmus, *Prosecution*, pp. 20–21.

17. Even today, when the maintenance of secrecy has become a fine art, it would be difficult to keep secret the appearance of men like Wyclif, Gaunt, and Percy, before a group of bishops.

18. *Chron. Angl.*, p. 120.

19. While the friars came upon the invitation of the duke, they may still have been in substantial agreement with Wyclif since up to this time the Reformer had concentrated his attack on the wealth of the church. The chroniclers note how Wyclif had been seeking to befriend the friars and how he commended them for their poverty which made them "Deo carissimos." *Eulogium*, III, 345. "Nor was it difficult to induce the willing friars to give assistance," says Walsingham. *Chron. Angl.*, p. 118.

20. A jibe at the duke.

21. *Chron. Angl.*, pp. 119–121.

22. Walsingham does not specifically say how the meeting ended, but he does indicate that, because of the dissension between the barons and the bishops, Wyclif escaped punishment. He writes: "Jam jamque tali occasione alumnum suum, multorum mortibus evasurum et praelatorum manibus, astute subtrahere diabolus viam invenerat; ut, primum facta dissensione inter magnatos et episcopos, ejus responsio dilationem acciperet." *Chron. Angl.*, p. 119. The shorter description of the encounter in Walsingham's *Historia Anglicana* (I, 325) is confused, as is that in the *Anonimalle Chronicle* (pp. 103–104). The latter has the duke ordering Percy to arrest any person in the church who might oppose Wyclif, and Courtenay protesting the marshal's exercise of his authority in the church. But the account ends with the statement that the duke's party "departed in great anger." For a closer consideration of Walsingham's account, see Galbraith, pp. 21–23, and Dahmus, *Prosecution*, p. 30.

23. See below, p. 57.

24. Workman (*John Wyclif*, I, 287) attributes the rioting of the crowd, not to the bitter words which passed between Gaunt and Courtenay, but to the morning's developments in parliament. When news of the bills there proposed by the duke's followers reached the people, crowded as they were in St. Paul's, he says they began to riot. This is not what the chronicler writes. He does insert mention of these bills between his description of the meeting in St. Paul's and its breaking up, but it is only to let the reader know that the people were *already* angry at Gaunt. Thomson (*Speculum*, XXVIII, 564), although stating his agreement with Workman on this point, actually endorses my interpretation, for he writes: "It will be remembered that the 'hearing' ended in an uproar, *precipitated* by an altercation between Gaunt and his partisans on the one hand, the Bishop of London on the other." (Italics mine.) Adam of Murimouth (*Chronica Sui Temporis*, p. 223) says the people rioted because of the insults cast at their bishop, which statement is corroborated in *Chronicon Angliae* (pp. 125, 397). Adam of Usk (*Chronicon Adae De Usk*, p. 141) says the Londoners "rose against the duke of Lancaster to slay him, because he favoured the said Master John [Wyclif]. . . ."

25. See below, p. 40.

26. *Letter-Book H*, pp. 116–117. Three such appeals were made to Urban within a period of six months. They are dated December 4, 1378, April 25 and May 16, 1379.

27. See Tout, III, 319. Fitzwalter obtained entrance to the meeting by reason of his office as banner-bearer of London. See Thompson, *Chron. Angl.*, p. liv.

28. The prisoner was John Prentig whom Percy had imprisoned for his criticism of Gaunt. *Anonimalle Chronicle*, p. 104. See McFarlane, *John Wycliffe and the Beginnings of English Nonconformity*, p. 77.

29. This was done to the arms of traitors.

30. "And had similar words of the bishop not been able to soothe their frenzied passions, without doubt both duke and Henry Percy would that day have lost either life or limbs." *Chron. Angl.*, p. 125. "thei of London wold a killid the forseid duk, had thei not be lettid be her bischop." *The Chronicle of England by John Capgrave*, p. 232. See *Anonimalle Chronicle*, p. 104.

31. See below, p. 57.

32. See below, p. 66.

33. *Rot. Parl.*, II, 375. See Tout, III, 317.

34. Slightly different accounts are provided by the various chroniclers that touch upon these efforts to reconcile Gaunt and the Londoners. See *Chron. Angl.*, pp. lxviii, 148–150, 398, and the *Anonimalle Chronicle*, pp. 105–106.

35. The principal source for the story of the duke's difficulties with London is the *Chronicon Angliae*, pp. 126–137. Tout (III, 320, n. 2) questions the chronicler's statement concerning Wykeham's appeal to Perrers and the extent of the latter's influence. He does say that Wykeham thought it judicious to buy lands from her for the use of his new college at Oxford. But that Alice still possessed powers over the king he insists was impossible in view of the king's increasing infirmities. Thompson (*Chron. Angl.*, p. lviii) is inclined to believe the chronicler knows what he is talking about since he was a friend of the bishop. Testimony of the great influence Perrers once enjoyed over Edward is seen in the appeal Pope Gregory XI made to her in 1371, urging her to use her favor with the king to secure the release of his brother, Roger de Belloforti, from prison. *Papal Registers, Letters*, IV, 96.

CHAPTER FOUR (Pages 44–63)

1. Sudbury may have taken a more vigorous stand on Wyclif than generally supposed. Hereford said he had been "justly" killed since he had wished to punish (*corripere*) "his master." *Fas. Ziz.*, p. 296. See also Warren, *The Journal of Ecclesiastical History*, X, 139–152.

2. Rashdall, *The Universities of Europe in the Middle Ages*, III, 124. See above, p. 4.

3. See H. J. Wilkins, *Westbury College*, p. 86.

4. See Dahmus, *Prosecution*, pp. 36–38.

5. Shirley, *Fas. Ziz.*, pp. xxvii–xxviii.

6. Gregory must have envisioned the possibility of inaction on Sudbury's part.

7. "Register of Simon Sudbury," fols. 45v–46; Wilkins, III, 116–117; *Chron. Angl.*, pp. 178–180; *Hist. Angl.*, I, 350–352. Why did Gregory insist upon secrecy in this matter when he was informing the king of what he had ordered them to do? Did he fear the intervention of others than the king? Or was his letter ever sent to Edward? It is not recorded in the *Papal Registers, Letters*.

8. "Register of Simon Sudbury," fol. 46; Wilkins, III, 117; *Chron. Angl.*, pp. 176–178; *Hist. Angl.*, I, 347–348.

9. "Register of Simon Sudbury," fol. 46; Wilkins, III, 118; *Chron. Angl.*, pp. 175–176; *Hist. Angl.*, I, 347–348.

10. *Chron. Angl.*, pp. 180–181; *Hist. Angl.*, I, 352–353.

11. *Chron. Angl.*, pp. 174–175; *Hist. Angl.*, I, 346–347; *Fas. Ziz.*, pp. 242–244.

12. "Register of Simon Sudbury," fols. 46–46v; Wilkins, III, 123; *Hist. Angl.* I, 353–355; *Chron. Angl.*, pp. 181–183. For a discussion of the number of propositions condemned, whether 18 or 19, see Dahmus, *Prosecution*, pp. 50–52.

13. *Hist. Angl.*, I, 345; *Chron. Angl.*, p. 173.

14. See above, p. 45.

15. This assumption may be valid concerning the bull directed to Edward which may never have been delivered. That to Oxford, on the other hand, was carried there by a papal emissary, although this emissary may have been delayed at Lambeth, for Sudbury's mandate to the university must have reached Oxford at the same time. See *Chron. Angl.*, p. 173; *Hist. Angl.*, I, 345.

16. The chronicler excoriates Sudbury and Courtenay for their tardiness in carrying out the pope's commission. See below, p. 53. This censure must apply, however, to the summons they issued pursuant to the receipt of the bulls, rather than to delay in publishing the bulls themselves.

17. Walsingham laments the fact that Wyclif had gained adherents among the nobility. *Chron. Angl.*, p. 116.

18. *Rot. Parl.*, II, 322.

19. See Trevelyan, *England in the Age of Wycliffe*, p. 81.

20. *Fas. Ziz.*, pp. 245–257.

21. See Workman, I, 311.

22. Knowles, *The Religious Orders in England*, II, 148.

23. For Netter and the *Libellus*, see Dahmus, "John Wyclif and the English Government," *Speculum*, XXXV, 60.

24. *Chron. Angl.*, pp. 173–174; *Hist. Angl.*, I, 345.

25. Wyclif probably entered the university in 1345.

26. See below, p. 53.

27. *Eulogium* III, 348.

28. *Ibid.*, III, 349.

29. *Chron. Angl.*, pp. 180–181; *Hist. Angl.*, I, 352–353.

30. One need not immediately suppose sympathy for Wyclif guided the crown's action. Bishop Brantingham proved as firm in dealing with Courtenay in the case of the Florentines. See above, p. 24.

31. Walsingham complains: "Qui quam indevote, quam segniter commissa sibi mandata compleverint, melius est silere quam loqui." *Chron. Angl.*, p. 183; *Hist. Angl.*, I, 356.

32. "Register of Simon Sudbury," fol. 46v; Wilkins, III, 123–124. Wilkins copied the date incorrectly from Sudbury's register.

33. *Eulogium* III, 348. One might conclude from the chronicler's language that the judgment in Wyclif's favor was unanimous. Incidentally, Wyclif is supposed to have had this incident in mind when he later wrote: "It is not proper for the church of Christ to condemn truth because it sounds poorly to sinners and the unlearned; for then the entire faith of scripture might be damnable." *Chron. Angl.*, p. 189; *Hist. Angl.*, I, 363.

34. For a discussion of the possibility that Wyclif refused to appear at St. Paul's and was then summoned a third time, see Dahmus, *Prosecution*, pp. 67–68.

35. *Hist. Angl.*, I, 357; *Chron. Angl.*, p. 184. Wyclif lived in the late fourteenth century when only a positive rebel in theological matters could have taken a different position. Wyclif never was a rebel; he never broke with either the church or the papacy. See below, p. 63.

36. *Hist. Angl.*, I, 361; *Chron. Angl.*, p. 188. See Dahmus, *Prosecution*, p. 69.

37. *Hist. Angl.*, I, 363; *Chron. Angl.*, p. 190.

38. *Hist. Angl.*, I, 356; *Chron. Angl.*, p. 183.

39. *Hist. Angl.*, I, 363; *Chron. Angl.*, p. 190. See also *Eulogium*, III, 348.

40. *Ibid.*, III, 348.

41. Even should Courtenay's London register ever turn up, it would probably have no reference to this trial since it took place at Lambeth.

42. Sudbury must have sent the pope a report of the Lambeth trial, although none has been discovered.

43. Wyclif does refer to the summons he received, but that is all. See *De Veritate Sacrae Scripturae*, I, 374, and Dahmus, *Prosecution*, pp. 67–68.

44. She did not attempt to reconcile Gaunt and the Londoners. See above, p. 41.

45. For a discussion of this point, see Dahmus, "John Wyclif and the English Government," *Speculum*, XXXV, pp. 55–56. The chronicler appears to think it was Clifford who warned the prelates, and no one else, which causes him to ridicule them all the more for their lack of courage. See *Hist. Angl.*, I, 356, and *Chron. Angl.*, p. 183.

46. See Steel, p. 44.

47. Gaunt was her "most intimate friend," says McKisack. *The Fourteenth Century*, p. 424.

48. Stubbs writes: "We must suppose that by using the influence of the princess in Wycliffe's favour, instead of interfering personally, the duke avoided provoking the hostile party which had risen to defend Courtenay in 1377." *The Constitutional History of England*, II, 446, n.1.

49. *Fas. Ziz.*, p. 258.

50. For this council, see below, p. 69.

51. See below, p. 78.

52. See Pantin, *The English Church in the Fourteenth Century*, pp. 162–163.

53. See Workman, I, 304, and Buddensieg, *John Wyclif's Polemical Works in Latin*, I, xlii, lvi.

54. *Fas. Ziz.*, pp. 258–271. For a discussion of the authenticity of the document, see Dahmus, *Speculum*, XXXV, 58–60. On the authorship of the *Fasciculi Zizaniorum*, see Crompton, "Fasciculi Zizaniorum II," *The Journal of Ecclesiastical History*, XII, 155–166.

55. See Rymer, VII, 172 and *Patent Rolls*, 1377–1381, p. 276.

56. See Dahmus, "John Wyclif and the English Government," *Speculum*, XXXV, 60–61.

57. If the "actual government was carried on by a 'continual council' of twelve persons" at this time, as Steel believes (*Richard II*, p. 44), episcopal influence would have been considerable. At least three of its members were bishops, one of them Courtenay.

58. See Pantin, "A Benedictine Opponent of John Wyclif," EHR, XLIII, 75–76, and Pantin, *The English Church in the Fourteenth Century*, p. 162.

59. Note the presence of the four friars in the group that accompanied Wyclif to St. Paul's in February 1377. See above, p. 35.

60. The rubric of the document which tells of Acley refers to him as the Benedictine order's opponent of Wyclif.

61. *Rot. Parl.* III, 6.

62. Courtenay may have commended the bishop of Lincoln some years later for his efforts against Wyclif. See Dahmus, *Prosecution*, pp. 138–139.

63. See below, p. 79.

64. The modern reader wonders why Wyclif appealed against Berton's order since he was not to "preach" even at Oxford. Had he simply proposed certain views on transubstantiation, Berton would probably have taken no action. This suggests that Wyclif's repute was so great at Oxford that even his ideas could not be tolerated.

65. "Register of Simon Sudbury," fol. 76v; Wilkins, III, 117; *Fas Ziz.*, p. 114. For a discussion of Gaunt's order to Wyclif and Wyclif's response, see Dahmus, pp. 132–133.

66. For this papal summons and Wyclif's response, see *Prosecution*, pp. 139–149.

CHAPTER FIVE (Pages 64–77)

1. The best account of this colorful incident is provided by Perroy, "L'Affaire du Comte de Denia," *Mélanges d'Histoire du Moyen Âge*, pp. 573–580.

2. *Hist. Angl.*, I, 377–378; *Chron. Angl.*, pp. 208–209. See *Anonimalle Chronicle*, p. 122.

3. "Register of Simon Sudbury," fols. 49v–50. Sudbury did order the excommunication proclaimed on Sundays and festivals "when many people were present," and continued denunciation of the act until further notice. Though Warren points out in defense of Sudbury that the archbishop was at the manor of Mayfield fifty miles from London when the incident took place and that, in any event, it was Courtenay's responsibility as bishop of London to take the initiative, his argument does not appear wholly convincing. See "A Reappraisal of Simon Sudbury, bishop of London (1361–1375) and archbishop of Canterbury (1375–1381)," *The Journal of Ecclesiastical History*, X, 143.

4. *Hist. Angl.*, I, 379; *Chron. Angl.*, p. 210. Walsingham says Sudbury and five of his suffragans also excluded Richard, his mother, and Gaunt from the force of the anathema, but the decree as recorded in Sudbury's register makes no such exception.

5. Almost all unpopular acts of the government were blamed on Gaunt. See Steel, p. 34.

6. *Chron. Angl.*, p. 210.

7. *Hist. Angl.*, I, 379; *Chron. Angl.*, p. 210.

8. Davies, *An English Chronicle*, p. 2.

9. *Hist. Angl.*, I, 380; *Chron. Angl.*, p. 211.

10. *Rot. Parl.*, III, 37.

11. *Anonimalle Chronicle*, p. 123. See also *Higden*, VIII, 398, which also speaks of Wyclif's presence.

12. See *De Ecclesia*, p. 266; *Fas. Ziz.*, pp. xxxvi–xxxvii; *Hist. Angl.*, I, 377; *Chron. Angl.*, p. 208.

13. *Rot. Parl.*, III, 37. For a description of the privilege of sanctuary, see Jusserand, *English Wayfaring Life in the Middle Ages*, pp. 77–86.

14. *Statutes of the Realm*, II, 12; *Hist. Angl.*, I, 391–392; *Chron. Angl.*, p. 223. Buxhill and the others implicated in the outrage made their submission to Courtenay. See Warren, pp. 143–144.

15. For the effect of the Peasants' Revolt upon Wyclif's popularity, see Dahmus, *Prosecution*, pp. 82–85.

16. See below, p. 283, n. 1.

17. Conversely, a vigorous archbishop such as Courtenay proved himself to be, left Braybroke, the new bishop of London, in deep shadow.

18. Courtenay was not one of the four bishops appointed to the committee of peers which was to advise commons in the parliament of January 1377. See Tout, III, 315.

19. See Tout, III, 326, for a description of these developments and McKisack, pp. 397–398. Steel (p. 44) speaks of the "continual council" as carrying on the "actual government."

20. See Tout, III, 334 and 336, n. 5, where he speaks of the difficulty of distinguishing between the different councils to which contemporary writers refer.

21. *Rot. Parl.*, III, 57.

22. *Ibid.*, III, 101. Courtenay was among those given crown jewels to hold as security of loans advanced to the crown by wealthy Londoners and members of the aristocracy. *Fine Rolls*, 1377–1383, p. 81.

23. See below, p. 162.

24. Steel (p. 65) believes few clerks could have become agitators for revolt. "It is for this reason that the Lollards, or rather Wyclif's Poor Preachers, were so freely accused of having fomented the rising. . . ."

25. *Hist. Angl.*, II, 32; *Chron. Angl.*, p. 321. To what extent, if at all, Ball was influenced by Wyclif is difficult to say. Still whether influenced or not, it is what contemporaries believed, and they were convinced Ball had drawn his inspiration from Wyclif. *Higden* (VIII, 459) refers to Ball as a "disciple of maister John Wyclif." See also *Chronicon Henrici Knighton*, II, 170. For a discussion of Wyclif's part in the uprising, see Dahmus, *Prosecution*, pp. 82–85.

26. *Fas. Ziz.*, pp. 273–274. Workman (*John Wyclif*, II, 237) questions the authenticity of this document.

27. *Hist. Angl.*, II, 11; *Chron. Angl.*, pp. 310–311.

28. The situation was similar to that of 1939 when the failure of appeasement brought forward Winston Churchill, the man most violently opposed to the policy.

29. See above, p. 39.

30. Richard was only fourteen at the time.

31. For all his deficiencies, Gaunt was no coward, however, and he would not have lost his head in the excitement. Had he been in London at the time of the revolt, he might have stopped it even before it got started.

32. All this information is contained in "Register G," fols. 221v–226. It is of interest to note that the prior, in his capacity as director of the see of Canterbury during its vacancy, instructed Courtenay as bishop of London to excommunicate the persons who had been implicated in the death of Sudbury. *Ibid.*, fol. 227.

33. "a priore et capitulo ecclesie Cantuariensis unanimiter postulati et ante presentacionem postulacionis sue sanctissimo in Christo patri domino Urbano divina providencia pape sexto factam, per eundem dominum Urbanum translati. . . ." "Reg. Courtenay," fol. 1. In Urban's letter to the bishops of London and Rochester, he does refer to Courtenay, however, as the one who had been "elected." And if Urban did not know of the chapter's action, as is probable, he must surely have known the mind of the crown.

34. *Ibid.*, fols. 1–1v.

35. *Ibid.*, fols. 1v–2; Wilkins, III, 154–155. On the same day the pope sent bulls to the suffragan bishops, the chapter at Canterbury, the clergy and people of the diocese, and the vassals of the archbishop, ordering them to accept Courtenay as archbishop. "Reg. Courtenay," fols. 2–2v. For Courtenay's oath, see Appendix, pp. 239–240.

36. *Ibid.*, fol. 2v.

37. *Ibid.*, fol. 3.

38. See Churchill, *Canterbury Administration*, I, 158.

39. "Reg. Courtenay," fol. 9. Urban informed Courtenay that the pallium was to be conferred by the bishops of London and Rochester after they had received his oath of obedience. He sent a separate bull to these bishops at the same time with these instructions. *Ibid.*

40. *Ibid.*, fol. 5. One of the proctors was John Trefnant, later bishop of Hereford, with whom Courtenay clashed over the right of visitation. See below, p. 159.

41. *Patent Rolls*, 1381–1385, p. 33.

42. "Reg. Courtenay," fol. 3.

43. *Ibid.*

44. *Ibid.*

45. *Ibid.*

46. *Higden*, IX, 12. See *Chron. Angl.*, p. 332.

47. See *Close Rolls*, 1381–1385, p. 88, and "Reg. Courtenay," fol. 35v.

48. *Ibid.*, fol. 10. The pallium was issued by the pope on February 12. One explanation for the pallium's delay may have been Courtenay's failure to send a "gift." Did Cheyne take this "gift" to Rome?

CHAPTER SIX (Pages 78–106)

1. *Knighton*, II, 191. Knighton may have had only the region about Leicester in mind. See also *Chronicon Adae De Usk*, p. 4.

2. See below, p. 225.

3. *Hist. Angl.*, II, 12; *Chron. Angl.*, p. 311.

4. *Rot. Parl.*, III, 124–125. See *Fas. Ziz.*, p. 272.

5. See above, p. 62.

6. "Reg. Courtenay," fol. 25; Wilkins, III, 157; *Fas. Ziz.*, p. 272.

7. The *Fasciculi* includes the names of the bishops of London and Lincoln. On this point, see Dahmus, *Prosecution*, p. 90, n. 6.

8. Arnold, *Select English Works of John Wyclif*, III, 503. *Joannis Wyclif Trialogus*, p. 374; *Fas. Ziz.*, pp. 283–284. Courtenay referred to the members of this council as "the most distinguished and expert in the kingdom," a statement which may or may not have any significance. See Dahmus, *Prosecution*, p. 91.

9. "Reg. Courtenay," fol. 25; Wilkins, III, 157.

10. *Fas. Ziz.*, pp. 272–273. Wyclif interpreted the earthquake as a sign of God's displeasure with the action of the council. *Trialogus*, pp. 376–377.

11. See above, p. 53.

12. The Latin word here translated as "foreknown" is *praescitus*, that is, one predestined for hell, a reprobate.

13. The Lambeth scribe added the marginal comment, "A pernicious error."

14. What the scribe meant by "friars" is not clear. He may have had Franciscans in mind. A "preaching friar" was a member of the Dominican order.

15. "Reg. Courtenay," fols. 25–25v; Wilkins, III, 157–158. The same lists appear with some variation in *Hist. Angl.*, II, 58–59; *Chron. Angl.*, pp. 342–344; *Fas. Ziz.*, pp. 277–282, 493–497; *Knighton*, II, 158–160.

16. See Dahmus, *Prosecution*, p. 96, for an elaboration of this point.

17. *Fas. Ziz.*, pp. 283–285.

18. Yet Wyclif did accept in theory the right of the clergy to confiscate the goods of delinquent lords. *De Civili Dominio*, II, 34. See Daly, *The Political Theory of John Wyclif*, pp. 143–145.

19. Surely a reference to Wyclif's Poor Priests.

20. *Rot. Parl.*, III, 124–125.

21. "Reg. Courtenay," fols. 25v–26; Wilkins, III, 158–159.

22. *Register of Thomas de Brantyngham*, I, 464–465.

23. *Knighton*, II, 162–163. Cunningham had disputed with Wyclif at Oxford during the seventies.

24. "Reg. Courtenay," fol. 31; Wilkins, III, 156. See *Patent Rolls*, 1381–1385, p. 150.

25. *Fas. Ziz.*, pp. 275, 297.

26. "etiam antequam fuit doctor; et aliis doctoribus [Rigg]negavit." *Ibid.*, 306.

27. Concerning Rigg's undependability, see below, p. 86. The *Fasciculi* says of Stokes: "quem novit [Courtenay] prae ceteris laborasse contra Lollardos. . . ." *Ibid.*, 297.

28. *Ibid.*, 296. Since the sermon was in English, the people might have been aroused.

29. Courtenay may have heard with what hostility Oxford had received Pope Gregory's reprimand concerning Wyclif back in 1377. See above, p. 51.

30. *Fas. Ziz.*, pp. 298-299.

31. *Ibid.*, 299.

32. *Ibid.*, 299–300.

33. *Ibid.*, 307.

34. *Ibid.*, 300.

35. *Ibid.*, 300–301.

36. *Ibid.*, 302.

37. Stokes must have been a timid soul. The presence of all these half-concealed weapons suggests a maneuver to frighten him, hardly anything more.

38. *Ibid.*, 302.

39. It is impossible to determine exactly who was present at this meeting. The register notes that the bishop of Winchester was present, but fails to list any others. The *Fasciculi* says all were present who had taken part in the first session, plus eleven more doctors of theology, doctors of laws, and bachelors of theology. But among these eleven appear the names of Rigg, Brightwell, and Stokes.

40. *Ibid.*, 304–308.

41. "Reg. Courtenay," fol. 26v; Wilkins, III, 159. This third scholar might have been the John Balton who is listed by the *Fasciculi* as one of the two bachelors at the meeting. *Fas. Ziz.*, p. 289. It could not have been Stephen Patrington, the other bachelor mentioned, for Patrington was an outspoken critic of Wyclif. For Patrington, see Workman, II, 247.

42. "Reg. Courtenay," fols. 26v–27; Wilkins, III, 159–160.

43. "Reg. Courtenay," fol. 27v; Wilkins, III, 160; *Fas. Ziz.*, pp. 309–311. For certain inaccuracies concerning this incident, see Dahmus, *Prosecution*, p. 112, n. 4.

44. *Fas. Ziz.*, p. 311. The sympathies of Netter are manifestly with the opponents of Wycliffitism at the university. It is doubtful whether their safety was in as much danger as he suggests.

45. Hereford and Repingdon had reason to consider the duke a friend. Five months before the four mendicant orders at Oxford had appealed to him against the Lollards and against Hereford in particular but he had done nothing. *Ibid.*, 292–295. According to Knighton (II, 193), the duke had shortly before saved the Lollard Swinderby from the stake, and it was common knowledge, no doubt, that Wyclif owed his immunity to Gaunt.

46. *Fas. Ziz.*, p. 318.

47. The duke used the term *laicos* in the sense of uneducated commoners.

48. *Ibid.* For some discrepancy in the sources concerning the movements of Repingdon and Hereford after leaving Oxford, see Dahmus, *Prosecution,* p. 114, n. 4.

49. "Reg. Courtenay," fol. 28; Wilkins, III, 161.

50. Concerning the membership of the council at this meeting, see Dahmus, *Prosecution,* p. 115, n. 6.

51. See above, p. 82.

52. *Fas. Ziz.,* p. 319; "Reg. Courtenay," fol. 29; Wilkins, III, 162.

53. There is some inaccuracy in the listing of the twenty-four propositions as they appear in this section of the register.

54. "Reg. Courtenay," fol. 29v; Wilkins, III, 163; *Fas. Ziz.,* p. 329.

55. "Poison" in the figurative sense of heresy.

56. *Knighton,* II, 176.

57. *Ibid.,* 176-178.

58. *Hist. Angl.,* II, 65-66; *Chron. Angl., p.* 350.

59. Aston admitted in his "Confession" (see below) that he was a priest. He may have denied that fact here in order to gain greater sympathy with the laymen present.

60. "Reg. Courtenay," fol. 29v; Wilkins, III, 164; *Fas. Ziz.,* pp. 290, 329. Only the *Fasciculi* says he was turned over to the civil authorities. He was lodged in the jail at St. Albans. *Higden,* VIII, 462.

61. The *Fasciculi* (p. 290) indicates the place they were to appear.

62. "Reg. Courtenay," fol. 30; Wilkins, III, 164.

63. "Reg. Courtenay," fol. 30; Wilkins, III, 164-165. See *Fas. Ziz.,* p. 290.

64. For *apostoli,* see below, p. 305, n. 37.

65. "Reg. Courtenay," fol. 30v; Wilkins, III, 165.

66. "Reg. Courtenay," fol. 32; Wilkins, III, 168-169.

67. "Reg. Courtenay," fol. 32; Wilkins, III, 168-169.

68. Rigg's exact movements on July 14 are difficult to trace. The second patent, dated July 14, refers to a day appointed Rigg when he was to have appeared as "now past." Since Rigg would hardly have dared delay his appearance for more than a day or two, one may assume he presented himself at Westminster on July 14 or 15. What probably happened is that Rigg left London on July 14 after having been handed the two royal briefs, then found Courtenay's mandate at Oxford when he returned that night or the following morning.

69. For a discussion of this incident, see Dahmus, *Prosecution,* pp. 129-133.

70. *Fas. Ziz.*, pp. 311–312, 315.

71. "Reg. Courtenay," fols. 31–31v; Wilkins, III, 166–167; *Fas. Ziz.*, pp. 312–314.

72. "Reg. Courtenay," fol. 31v; Wilkins, III, 167; *Fas. Ziz.*, pp. 314–317. For a translation of this patent and the preceding, see Dahmus, *Prosecution*, pp. 122–125.

73. Workman gives the chapter in which he discusses the submission of Repingdon and Aston the apt caption, "Broken Reeds." *John Wyclif*, II, 325.

74. "Reg. Courtenay," fol. 32; Wilkins, III, 168. Bedeman was among those who had been barred from teaching at Oxford. See above, p. 90.

75. "Reg. Courtenay," fol. 32; Wilkins, III, 168.

76. *Wykeham's Register*, II, 342–343.

77. "Reg. Courtenay," fol. 32v; Wilkins, III, 169.

78. "Reg. Courtenay," fol. 33v.

79. Aston had just made his peace with the archbishop. See below, p. 102.

80. "Reg. Courtenay," fols. 33–34.

81. "Reg. Courtenay," fol. 33.

82. *Ibid.*, fol. 34.

83. *Ibid.*, fol. 34v; Wilkins, III, 172.

84. *Fas. Ziz.*, pp. 329–330. See also *Knighton*, II, 171–172.

85. The omission of the *non* is manifestly an editorial error.

86. *Fas. Ziz.*, p. 331.

87. *Ibid.*, 331–333.

88. "Reg. Courtenay," fol. 32v; Wilkins, III, 169.

89. The view that Wyclif appeared at Oxford before convocation at this time is based on Knighton's mistaken evidence. See Dahmus, *Prosecution*, pp. 136–137.

90. Hereford became a staunch opponent of Lollardy, Repingdon a bishop.

91. "Reg. Courtenay," fols. 34v–35.

92. Convocation resumed its work in London after Epiphany. *Ibid.*, fol. 35.

93. "Register of Robert Braybroke," fol. 237. See also "Reg. Courtenay." fol. 65v. Walsingham tells of a Lollard priest who had repented on his deathbed and had asked for a priest to hear his confession. Hereford who happened to be in the neighborhood was brought in, but instead

of shriving the dying man argued with him over the necessity of confession. The priest died without confessing. See *Hist. Angl.*, II, 159–160.

94. "Reg. Courtenay," fol. 69.

95. *Patent Rolls*, 1385–1389, p. 316.

96. See Workman, II, 336–339.

CHAPTER SEVEN (Pages 107–160)

1. Churchill, *Canterbury Administration*, I, 290.

2. No complaint over the collection of such fees is recorded in Courtenay's register.

3. See *Canterbury Administration*, I, 290.

4. "It is clear that the objection to metropolitan visitation had its origin in the burden of procuration." Rose Graham, *The Metropolitan Visitation of the Diocese of Worcester by Archbishop Winchelsey in 1301, Transactions of the Royal Historical Society*, Fourth Series (1919), II, 61.

5. *Matthaei Parisiensis Chronica Majora*, V, 120.

6. Wilkins, I, 505.

7. *Matthaei Parisiensis Chronica Majora*, VI, 289–290. See Churchill, I, 290.

8. *Ibid.*, I, 292.

9. *Matthaei Parisiensis*, V, 225. The sharp-tongued chronicler says Archbishop Boniface's motive for making this visitation was greed, "for he was as ignorant of monastic life as he was of letters." See Graham, p. 59. To express the value of 4000 marks in modern terms would require the cooperative efforts of the economist, sociologist, and historian. In any case, it was an enormous sum, surely exceeding $500,000. See below, p. 324, n. 10, for a discussion of this problem.

10. See below, p. 118.

11. Only the Protestant Reformation and the council of Trent brought a halt to the appalling amount of time and money expended in these and similar jurisdictional disputes between bishop and archbishop and between bishop and dean, to say nothing of the bitterness they engendered among members of the clergy and the scandal they created among the laity. It would be hard to find one area where the medieval papacy failed more tragically than in keeping peace among its bishops, a failure for which it had almost no one but itself to blame. There

were canons that might have prevented such confusion and controversy, but few gave them thought, including apparently none in the
papal curia.

12. This is true of most registers. Perhaps the explanation why these
registers do not provide more complete accounts of visitations is
found in the lack of success many visitations suffered.

13. See Churchill, I, 291, 295–304.

14. *Register of John de Grandisson*, III, xxxii.

15. For Sudbury's visitations, see "Register of Simon Sudbury," fols.
31v–32, 35v–36; Wilkins, III, 109–112.

16. "Reg. Courtenay," fol. 86; Wilkins, III, 183. See Appendix, pp. 240–241.
Innocent IV had decreed that the "archbishop must visit all the
churches of his diocese before he visited those of his suffragans.
In the circuit of his province he must neither omit to visit a diocese
nor go back on his steps." Cheyney, *Episcopal Visitation of Monasteries in the Thirteenth Century*, p. 136. See Graham, p. 59.

17. In his request of late 1385 or early 1386 to Pope Urban for an
extension of these privileges, Courtenay pointed out that the papal
bull issued in November 1382 was more than a year in reaching
Lambeth. See below, p. 136. The bull, despite its generous provisions,
did not extend to Courtenay the right to visit exempt monasteries.
The chronicler says Courtenay received many new privileges, including that of visiting exempt Cluniac houses. *Gesta Abbatum Monasterii
Sancti Albani*, III, 279. This statement is probably not correct. The
pope appointed Courtenay vicar general of the order in 1386 (see
below, p. 193) and it was by virtue of that appointment that he
visited their houses.

18. "Reg. Courtenay," fols. 86–86v; Wilkins, III, 183–184. See Appendix,
pp. 241–243.

19. *Register of Thomas de Brantyngham*, I, 513–518.

20. "Reg. Courtenay," fol. 87. For the certification of the president of
the chapter and those of the archdeacons of the diocese to the bishop,
see *Register of Thomas de Brantyngham*, I, 515–517.

21. Priests in charge of anniversaries.

22. "Reg. Courtenay," fol. 87v.

23. *Ibid.*, fol. 88.

24. *Ibid.*, fols. 102v–103.

25. *Ibid.*, fol. 111.

26. In an order issued a month later, Courtenay spoke of his "serious
illness" as slowing his progress. See below, p. 123.

27. "Reg. Courtenay," fol. 88v.

28. *Ibid.*, fols. 88v, 117v.

29. *Ibid.*, fols. 123–123v.

30. *Ibid.*

31. *Ibid.*, fols. 118–119.

32. "The 'detecta' were probably the actual answers to the articles given by those being visited and these were not published, while the 'comperta' are the answers as worked up by the visitor; their source was always a subject of interest." Churchill, I, 293, n. 2. See also Cheyney, p. 95.

33. "Reg. Courtenay," fols. 88v–89.

34. *Ibid.*, fols. 91–91v. See Hingeston-Randolf, *Register of Thomas de Brantyngham*, II, xvii.

35. "Reg. Courtenay," fols. 89–90.

36. *Ibid.*, fol. 90.

37. *Ibid.*, fols. 91v–92v. The word *apostoli* referred to a short statement of the case sent up by a lower to a higher court in an appeal. The appellant had the right to ask for this. When the court in question did not accept the appeal, it could issue *apostoli refutatorii* instead, a formal instrument which dismissed the appeal as invalid. See Churchill, I, 319, n. 2, and Dahmus, *The Metropolitan Visitations of William Courteney*, p. 19.

38. There was no great difference between an *appellacio* and a *provocacio*. The latter is shorter and more legal in tone and, in contrast to the *appellacio*, was issued directly by the bishop and not by a proctor.

39. These documents appear on folios 93–95 of the archbishop's register. They are not recorded in Brantingham's register, although Courtenay's reply is. See Dahmus, *Visitations*, p. 18.

40. See above, p. 117.

41. "Reg. Courtenay," fols. 90–91; *Register of Thomas de Brantyngham*, I, 530–532. See Appendix, pp. 243–247. There is some discrepancy between the two documents as recorded in the two registers. See Dahmus, *Visitations*, p. 18, n. 46. Churchill (I, 318, n. 4) suggests the possibility that the bishop issued two separate protests on this subject.

42. "Reg. Courtenay," fol. 95.

43. *Ibid.*, fol. 95v. See Appendix, p. 247.

44. *Ibid.*, fols. 95v–98; *Register of Thomas de Brantyngham*, I, 535–540.

45. "Reg. Courtenay," fol. 98.

46. *Higden*, IX, 42. See Dahmus, *Visitations*, p. 21, n. 58.

47. Boggis (p. 270) says the three emissaries fled "altogether out of their proper course" back to Exeter.

48. "Reg. Courtenay," fol. 98v. See Hingeston-Randolf, *Register of Thomas de Brantyngham*, II, xiii–xxxv.

49. "Reg. Courtenay," fols. 98v–99v. Courtenay was convinced the bishop was partner to this defiance. In the mandate he issued on June 6 summoning Brantingham *viis et modis*, he described how very many members of the bishop's household had assembled, bearing a variety of weapons, "with the consent, approval, and connivance of said bishop, as we truthfully suppose. . . ." *Ibid.*, fol. 100v. The crown ordered the arrest of the culprits. *Ibid.*

50. Parliament sat from April 29 to May 27.

51. Since a formal summons was impossible, the bishop was to be cited *viis et modis,* that is, by whatever means appeared feasible.

52. *Ibid.*, fols. 100v–101.

53. *Ibid.*, fols. 99v–100.

54. *Ibid.*, fol. 101.

55. *Higden*, IX, 42–43.

56. "Reg. Courtenay," fol. 112v.

57. *Ibid.*, fol. 100.

58. At the meeting on June 6 at the chapter house, Courtenay had blamed the delay on several factors, among them the refusal of the chapter to cooperate. See above, p. 121.

59. *Ibid.*, fol. 100.

60. *Ibid.*, fol. 101. The form of the oath was that taken by the bishop upon his profession of obedience to the archbishop on his appointment as bishop. See Churchill, II, 320, n. 5.

61. The scribe may have intended to write Nicholas Braybroke. See above, p. 122.

62. "Reg. Courtenay," fols. 101–101v.

63. Hingeston-Randolf (*Register of Thomas de Brantyngham*, II, xx–xxi) doubts prospects for an early settlement had materially brightened, Churchill (I, 321, n. 1) believes they had.

64. Probably Adam Easton of Norwich whom Urban raised to the cardinalate when discouraged by the Londoners from so honoring Courtenay. See above, p. 39.

65. See Hingeston-Randolf, *Register of Thomas de Brantyngham*, II, xxi, n. 1, on this point, and Dahmus, *Visitations*, p. 28.

66. "Reg. Courtenay," fol. 112v.

67. *Ibid.*

68. The Lambeth clerk speaks of a *concordia* between the archbishop and bishop, rather than the *submissio* of the latter.

69. *Ibid.*, fols. 113v–114.

70. *Ibid.*, fols. 110v–111. In the case of the outrages perpetrated in the collegiate church of the Holy Cross at Crediton, however, when Brantingham excommunicated some 140 persons, Courtenay was on surer ground in denouncing the bishop's action as a flagrant usurpation of his own rights as based upon common law. See "Reg. Courtenay," fol. 102, and Dahmus, *Visitations*, p. 21.

71. "Reg. Courtenay," fol. 114.

72. *Ibid.*, fols. 112v–113.

73. *Ibid.*, fol. 115. See Appendix, pp. 248–249.

74. *Ibid.*, fols. 104, 106v, 109–109v.

75. *Register of Thomas de Brantyngham*, I, 526–527.

76. *Ibid.*, I, 88.

77. See "Reg. Courtenay," fol. 119, and *Register of Thomas de Brantyngham*, I, 88–89.

78. *Ibid.*, I, 88, 175; "Reg. Courtenay," fols. 107–107v.

79. *Ibid.*, fols. 110–110v.

80. For a discussion of this case, see Hingeston-Randolf, *Register of Thomas de Brantyngham*, II, xxxi, and Dahmus, *Visitations*, pp. 31–32.

81. "Reg. Courtenay," fols. 122v–123.

82. *Ibid.*, fol. 123.

83. *Ibid.*, fol. 124v.

84. *Ibid.*, fol. 170–171.

85. A document dated August 28 from Crediton reveals the archbishop still visiting on that day. Two documents dated from Exminster on September 9 suggest that he had completed his visitation by that time. *Ibid.*, fol. 122–122v.

86. The three names appear as John Hughlot, William Usflet, and John Maundwvyl on folio 114, but on folios 98v and 114, as they are given in the text.

87. *Ibid.*, fols. 114–114v.

88. *Ibid.*, fols. 125–125v. Courtenay's first letter to Harewell concerning his projected visitation is dated May 30. His second letter is dated June 17.

89. *Ibid.*, fols. 126–126v.

90. *Ibid.,* fol. 127. Stratford-on-Avon was located in the diocese of Worcester. The Fourth Lateran Council prohibited summoning anyone to a judicial hearing more than a journey of two days outside the diocese in which that person resided. See Churchill, I, 322, n. 4.

91. "Reg. Courtenay," fol. 126.

92. *Ibid.,* fol. 62; Wilkins, III, 193.

93. "Reg. Courtenay," fol. 64v.

94. *Ibid.,* fols. 127–127v. Although earlier archbishops ran into opposition in visiting one or the other of these houses, Courtenay appears to have encountered none. See Churchill, II, 323.

95. "Reg. Courtenay," fols. 60–60v.

96. *Ibid.,* fols. 57v–58.

97. *Historia Vitae et Regni Ricardi II Angliae Regis,* pp. 53ff. One is inclined to accept the substantial accuracy of this chronicler's accounts. His tone is sober and the date he assigns for the archbishop's visit corresponds with the date given in the Lambeth register for the visitation of Fladbury (whence the archbishop rode over to Evesham). Evesham's own chronicler comments bitterly and briefly: "expulit gratiose (gloriose) et viriliter et magnis expensis Willielmum Cowrteney . . . qui, ut dicebatur, voluit tunc attentare contra privilegia nostra et visitare nos." *Chronicon Abbatiae de Evesham,* p. 306. See *Higden,* VIII, 467–468.

98. The last place Courtenay visited in the diocese of Worcester was Lechlade on November 9. "Reg. Courtenay," fol. 127v. See above, p. 135.

99. See below, p. 157.

100. *Ibid.,* fols. 128v–129.

101. Courtenay's letter to Urban is undated; the pope's reply is dated April 23, 1386.

102. *Ibid.,* fols. 128v–129, 185v–186.

103. Bishop Rushook was judged guilty of treason in 1388—he had supported Richard—and was banished to Ireland. For the political struggle in which he had become involved, see below, p. 172.

104. *Ibid.,* fol. 160.

105. *Ibid.,* fol. 130.

106. *Ibid.,* fol. 131.

107. A full report of the visitation of Bradegar is recorded in the register. *Ibid.,* fols. 354–362.

108. *Ibid.,* fols. 132–132v.

109. The rector, John Wellyngborne, made his peace with the archbishop some time later. Upon payment of the procuration fee, the sequestration order was rescinded. *Ibid.*, fol. 133v.

110. *Ibid.*, fol. 134v.

111. *Ibid.*, fol. 135.

112. *Ibid.*, fols. 135–135v.

113. *Ibid.*, fol. 135v. Some time later the abbot sent Courtenay a favorable report on Brother William's spiritual progress. *Ibid.*

114. *Ibid.*, fols. 135v–136.

115. Chyllenden was well known for his knowledge of ecclesiastical architecture. See Thompson, *Visitations of Religious Houses*, I, xxviii.

116. "Reg. Courtenay," fols. 136v–137. See Appendix, pp. 249–251. The *minuti* were allowed several days for convalescence. They spent this time either in the monastic infirmary or more often in a grange belonging to the monastery. See Thompson, *Visitations of Religious Houses*, I, 237–238.

117. "Reg. Courtenay," fol. 137.

118. Courtenay had notified the dean of the college from Lincoln on October 10 to expect him on October 29, the day he appeared.

119. *Ibid.*, fols. 138v–139.

120. The eight persons identified as Lollards were Roger Dexter, Nicholas Taylor, Richard Waystathe (chaplain), Michael Scriviner, William Smyth, John Harry, William Perchemener, and Roger Goldsmyth. According to Knighton (II, 182–183) Waystathe and Smyth had desecrated the chapel of St. John the Baptist near Leicester, had taken an image of St. Catherine from the church to make a fire for their vegetables, and had even composed verses commemorating this profanation. Knighton also offers the information that William Smyth was a malformed, homely person who had been spurned by the girl he loved, had thereupon given up his wealth, taken a vow of chastity, ate no meat, and had learned to read the *abcdarium*.

121. "Reg. Courtenay," fol. 139.

122. *Ibid.*, fol. 139v.

123. *Ibid.*, fol. 142.

124. *Ibid.*, fols. 139v, 142v–143. See *Knighton*, II, 312.

125. "Reg. Courtenay," fol. 143v.

126. *Ibid.*, fol. 143v.

127. The abbot of St. Albans, Thomas de la Mare, was a truly remarkable man. See Knowles, *The Religious Orders in England*, II, 39–48.

128. *Hist. Angl.*, II, 189–192.

129. One can not be certain the chronicler's account of Courtenay's decision not to visit St. Frideswide is correct. He might actually have
visited the college. In 1397, spokesmen for Archbishop Arundel, Courtenay's successor in Canterbury, insisted Arundel had the right to
visit the college since Courtenay had done so *tam in capite quam
in membris,* had corrected various abuses, and had suspended several
of the monks. "Register of Thomas Arundel," fol. 46. See *Snappe's
Formulary,* pp. 148–149.

130. *Gesta Abbatum Monasterii Sancti Albani a Thoma Walsingham,* III,
279–281.

131. William had used an image of St. Catherine to cook his vegetables.
See above, p. 141, n. 120, and *Knighton,* II, 313.

132. "Reg. Courtenay," fol. 144v.

133. *Knighton,* II, 313.

134. "Reg. Courtenay, fol. 140.

135. *Ibid.,* fol. 143.

136. "Reg. Courtenay," fols. 335v–336v. See Appendix pp. 251–255. Bishop
Buckingham also had occasion to reprimand the nuns of Elstow.
He found them "arranging their veils as to enhance rather than conceal
their charms." See Johnstone, "The Nuns of Elstow," *The Church
Quarterly Review,* CXXXIII, 47.

137. "Reg. Courtenay," fol. 339. See Appendix, pp. 255–257.

138. Courtenay's register records a series of injunctions for only monasteries
and cathedral chapters in the diocese of Lincoln.

139. *Ibid.,* fol. 335.

140. *Ibid.,* fols. 335–335v.

141. "Reg. Courtenay," fols. 334–334v; Bradshaw, *Statutes of Lincoln Cathedral,* pp. 245–248. See Appendix, pp. 257–259. Some variation exists
in the statutes as recorded in these two sources. It is a curious fact
that Grosseteste had occasion to condemn the same improprieties
at Lincoln more than a hundred years before. Bradshaw, p. 247.

142. Boniface's bull is dated February 20, 1390, less than four months
after his elevation to the pontificate. Waltham must have gotten off
his appeal the minute he learned of Boniface's election.

143. "Reg. Courtenay," fols. 146–146v.

144. There is the possibility that Waltham had learned months before
of Courtenay's plan to visit his diocese and had appealed to the
pope to prevent this. That Waltham was but eighteen months a
bishop made his defiance of the archbishop all the more galling.

145. *Ibid.*, fol. 146v.

146. The document bears no date, but the archbishop must have issued it the same day he sent the dean his mandate. This last is dated May 18.

147. *Ibid.*, fols. 147–147v.

148. *Ibid.*, fols. 148–148v.

149. *Ibid.*, fols. 148v–149.

150. *Ibid.*, fol. 149v.

151. When the Lambeth scribe speaks of *prandium* or dinner, he refers to the main meal which was taken at noon or shortly after.

152. *Ibid.*, fols. 149v–150v. The certificate of the dean enumerated the names of the dean, precentor, chancellor, treasurer, the four archdeacons of the diocese, twenty-one priestly prebendaries, eighteen diaconal prebendaries, eleven subdiaconal prebendaries, the confessor (*penitenciarius generalis*), the succentor, the master of the grammar schools, twenty-one priestly vicars, seventeen diaconal vicars, eleven subdiaconal vicars, seven chaplains having chantries in the church at Salisbury, two sacristans, nine acolytes, and two minor sacristans.

153. Letter of proxy.

154. *Ibid.*, fols. 151v–153v. The date of this *provocacio* is May 23.

155. One may wonder how "diligent" the examination of the dean, chapter, other ministers, and other matters could have been if the task consumed no more than one hour.

156. *Ibid.*, fols. 154–155.

157. *Ibid.*, fol. 155.

158. *Ibid.*, fol. 157.

159. *Close Rolls*, 1389–1392, pp. 195–196. See *Higden*, IX, 237.

160. "Reg. Courtenay," fol. 157v.

161. *Ibid.*, fol. 158. Courtenay appointed a third deputy to help with the work of visitation at the cathedral.

162. *Ibid.*, fol. 159v.

163. *Ibid.*, fol. 187 (Ex Reg. Morton).

164. *Ibid.*, fol. 66. The commission is dated September 25, 1386.

165. Courtenay empowered his commissaries to correct and punish irregularities, to probate wills, examine accounts, order and relax sequestrations, institute to benefices, authorize the augmentation of portions, and examine all titles, even those of persons who claimed exemption. *Ibid.*, fols. 68–68v.

166. Churchill (I, 323) says this was not a visitation since Courtenay
in his mandate to the bishop of Chichester issued in 1388, quoted
Pope Urban's indult. This indult, it will be recalled, permitted the
archbishop to visit the dioceses of his province without first visiting
his own. But Urban issued this indult in response to a request Courtenay had made in 1385 or early 1386 (see above, p. 136), that is,
before the diocese of Canterbury had been visited. Furthermore, Urban's indult extended to Courtenay additional privileges beyond that
of visiting his province before visiting his own diocese. It was about
these additional privileges that the archbishop was concerned after
1386, for he was still quoting Urban's bull in 1396 when he notified
Trefnant, the bishop of Hereford, of his intention to visit his diocese.
See below p. 159.

167. Since the archbishop conducted this second visitation of Canterbury
in person, a full description of his activities is entered in the register.
See "Reg. Courtenay," fols. 191–194v (Ex Reg. Morton).

168. All the churches of Romney had been placed under an interdict
several years before. See below, p. 183. The scribe notes in his description of Courtenay's visitation of Romney in 1393 that he "fuit valde
honorifice susceptus. . . ."

169. The scribe made a slip here in his chronology.

170. One of Courtenay's first acts as archbishop had been to send the
prior of Leeds to the monastery of St. Gregory to investigate "non-
nulla crimina et excessus enormia." *Ibid.*, fol. 39.

171. *Ibid.*, fol. 193 (Ex Reg. Morton).

172. *Ibid.*, fol. 194 (Ex Reg. Morton).

173. *Registrum Johannis Trefnant*, pp. 120–122.

174. See below, p. 197.

175. See below, p. 197.

176. It is possible that Courtenay decided to visit the diocese of Hereford
simply because that diocese had never been visited. See Churchill,
II, 329.

177. *Registrum Johannis Trefnant*, p. 123. No date is given beyond the
year 1396.

178. *Ibid.*, 123–125.

179. "Trefnant's official work at the papal court had brought with it
a remarkable familiarity with both civil and canon law which it
was afterwards apparently his pleasure to display." Capes, *ibid.*, i.

180. Courtenay's death terminated another dispute he had with Trefnant,
this one over the fruits of the parish of Newland in the diocese
of Hereford. The income of the parish had been going to the bishop
of Llandaff, but he had just died. Both archbishop and bishop laid
claim to this revenue during the vacancy of the see. *Ibid.*, 125.

CHAPTER EIGHT (Pages 161–186)

1. The archbishop of York was "primate of England."

2. These statements are based on Rymer, VII, 310, and *Close Rolls,* 1381–1385, pp. 84–85.

3. *Rot. Parl.,* III, 101.

4. He may have re-entered politics to protect himself from plots against his person. See Tout, III, 378.

5. *Ibid.,* 380. Stubbs suggests Courtenay resigned because, with the king, he had "wished so far to observe the agreement with the rustics as to introduce some amelioration into their condition." *The Constitutional History of England,* II, 461.

6. The archbishop normally enjoyed this privilege.

7. *Rot. Parl.,* III, 98–121; *Anonimalle Chronicle,* p. 155. See Cobbett, *The Parliamentary History of England,* p. 172.

8. Although no longer chancellor, Courtenay was not permitted to turn his back on politics. He was appointed to a committee of sixteen, headed by the duke, with responsibility for reforming the administrative machinery of the government. See Tout, III, 380–381.

9. There is record of fifteen convocations during Courtenay's tenure as archbishop. See Weske, *Convocation of the Clergy,* p. 140.

10. See above, p. 9. For a discussion of convocation, see Eric Kemp, "The Origins of the Canterbury Convocation," *The Journal of Ecclesiastical History,* III, 132–143, and J. A. Robinson, "Convocation of Canterbury: Its Early History," *The Church Quarterly Review,* LXXXI, 81–137.

11. The crown might send its own officials to add their arguments to those of the archbishop. See McKisack, pp. 288–289; Weske, p. 141.

12. See Highfield, "The English Hierarchy in the Reign of Edward III," *Transactions of the Royal Historical Society,* Fifth Series, VI, 137–138.

13. "Courtenay's courage and determination provided convocation with the leadership which had been lacking and served to avert the worst dangers threatening the church." McKisack, p. 291. For Archbishop Stratford, see McKisack, 160–165.

14. *Chron. Angl.,* pp. lxxx–lxxxi. See *Anonimalle Chronicle,* p. 101.

15. *Rot. Parl.,* II, 185. The rolls actually make no mention of this condition, but this is what one would expect should the king's order have been respected. For he directed that "the condition to be taken out or altogether erased from the roll. . . ." See below, p. 167.

16. Wake says this occasion in the fall of 1384 was the third time commons had made a grant conditional on similar action by the clergy. *The State of the Church in the Fourteenth and Fifteenth Centuries*, p. 317. See also Weske, p. 73.

17. "Reg. Courtenay," fol. 82; Wilkins, III, 193.

18. *Hist. Angl.*, II, 140.

19. *Ibid.* See also "Reg. Courtenay," fol. 82; Wilkins, III, 193.

20. "Reg. Courtenay," fol. 82; Wilkins, III, 193.

21. Richard's brief, dated January 15, reached Courtenay on February 3. He was at Exminster preparing to begin the visitation of the diocese of Exeter.

22. In December 1383 the clergy had agreed to give the crown a subsidy but under protest since, because of their poverty, they had not yet paid the subsidy granted previously at Salisbury. "Reg. Courtenay," fol. 80.

23. *Ibid.*, fols. 82–82v; Wilkins, III, 185–186.

24. "Reg. Courtenay," fol. 83; Wilkins, III, 187.

25. *Close Rolls*, 1381–1386, p. 609.

26. *Wykeham's Register*, II, 365. In the fall of 1383 Richard had specified the day convocation was to convene. Courtenay had denounced his action as unprecedented and in order not to cooperate in breaking a tradition, summoned the clergy to meet on December 2 rather than November 12 as the king had directed. *Reg. of Thomas de Brantyngham*, I, 502.

27. The register simply states the archbishop appointed the bishops of London and Winchester to take his place. There is no suggestion of any illness or similar cause which might have excused him from presiding. This was unusual.

28. "Reg. Courtenay," fol. 83; Wilkins, III, 187.

29. *Fine Rolls*, 1383–1391, p. 97.

30. *Ibid.* Parliament and convocation had both voted the grant for an expedition the king was to lead against the French. In the meantime, however, the French had landed troops in Scotland to aid the Scots.

31. "Reg. Courtenay," fols. 83–83v; Wilkins, III, 187.

32. *Close Rolls*, 1385–1389, p. 21.

33. "Reg. Courtenay," fols. 84v–85; Wilkins, III, 200.

34. *Ibid.*

35. *Hist. Angl.*, II, 165–167.

36. The supporters of the Avignonese pope, Clement VII. See below, p. 188.

37. *Higden*, IX, 18.

38. "Reg. Courtenay," fols. 36–36v, 44–44v; Wilkins, III, 176–178.

39. See below, p. 190.

40. *Higden*, IX, 33–40; *Hist. Angl.*, II, 112–115; *Chron. Angl.*, p. 359.

41. *Higden*, IX, 56–57.

42. "And after that in Lente maister William Courteney, archebischop of Cawnterbery, rebukede the kynge for his insolent lyfe and ylle governaunce in the realm longe contynuede, as hit longede to the seide metropolitan to do. . . ." *Ibid.*, VIII, 469.

43. *Ibid.*, IX, 58–59.

44. *Hist. Angl.*, II, 128.

45. *Chronicon Adae de Usk*, pp. 149–150. Usk confused the cause of Courtenay's disgrace with the archbishop's protest against a tax on the clergy, possibly the one Richard demanded on January 13, 1385. See above, p. 167. Walsingham attributes the quarrel "ad leves occasiones." *Hist. Angl.*, II, 128. See *Higden*, VIII, 469.

46. *Ibid.*, IX, 69–70.

47. *Patent Rolls*, 1385–1389, p. 76.

48. *Ibid.*, 186.

49. *Rot. Parl.*, III, 213.

50. *Knighton*, II, 215.

51. The chronicler says Courtenay implored Richard to receive the two men and to do them no harm. *Eulogium*, III, 364.

52. *Rot. Parl.*, III, 223–224; "Reg. Courtenay," fols. 69v–70; Wilkins, III, 195–196.

53. *Rot. Parl.*, III, 224.

54. See Tout, III, 423–438, for a detailed account of this crisis.

55. Richard's action and those of Robert de Vere led the king's enemies and their forces to converge on London. Courtenay and the earl of Northumberland were able to arrange a parley between them and the king at which Richard capitulated. *Knighton*, II, 243–245. See *Chron. Angl.*, p. 387, and McKisack, p. 453.

56. *Rot. Parl.*, III, 236–237; "Reg. Courtenay," fol. 174; Wilkins, III, 203–204.

57. See Steel, pp. 235–236, and Dahmus, "Richard II and the Church," *The Catholic Historical Review*, XXXIX, 418.

58. Arundel replaced Neville as archbishop of York in 1388 and succeeded Courtenay as archbishop of Canterbury in 1396. Both appointments were "political."

59. For a general treatment of the practice, see Barraclough, *Papal Provisions*.

60. The practice of exchanging benefices was common, and the motive behind such exchanges was generally financial. See below, p. 214.

61. This may sound more reprehensible that it should. An analagous situation today might be that of a teacher who is in a position to choose one of three positions. He will normally let salary and advancement possibilities guide him in his choice, a fact that does not make him any the less competent as a teacher. Not all benefices, of course, involved the cure of souls.

62. *Rot. Parl.*, III, 274. Had parliament simply confirmed the provisions of the statute of provisors, the pope could have ignored its actions, for, as Higden observes, "the said parliamentary statute was never enforced. . . ." IX, 205. Walsingham says the same, *Hist. Angl.*, II, 177.

63. *Rot. Parl.*, III, 405; Rymer, VII, 644–645.

64. *Papal Registers, Letters*, IV, 272–273; "Reg. Courtenay," fol. 331v; Wilkins, III, 207–208.

65. Richard sent Courtenay a sharp note ordering him to stop the raising of this subsidy. He said he found the archbishop's action surprising since he "is not ignorant how that the king is bound by oath to preserve the laws and customs of the realm. . . ." *Close Rolls, 1389–1392*, pp. 26–27.

66. Their destination was believed to be Rome, where their objective was that of securing benefices.

67. *Rot. Parl.*, III, 266–267; *Statutes of the Realm*, II, 73–74.

68. *Rot. Parl.*, III, 266–267; "Reg. Courtenay," fol. 332; Wilkins, III, 208.

69. *Papal Registers, Letters*, IV, 274.

70. Rymer, VII, 698. "In these dayes was proclamacion, be consent of the Kyng, that everi benefised man that was in the Cort of Rome schuld be at hom on the fest of Seynt Nicholace. This cry stoyned gretly the Court, and caused that the Pope sent an abbot to the Kyng brynging swech message." *The Chronicle of England by John Capgrave*, p. 255. See *Hist. Angl.*, II, 199–200.

71. *The Diplomatic Correspondence of Richard II*, p. 230.

72. *Ibid.*, pp. 89–90; Higden, IX, 254–258.

73. *Rot. Parl.*, III, 285; *Hist. Angl.*, II, 203; Higden, IX, 262.

74. Perroy, *L'Angleterre et le grand Schisme d'Occident*, p. 331, and *The Diplomatic Correspondence of Richard II*, pp. 108–109.

75. *Statutes of the Realm*, II, 84–85.

76. *Rot. Parl.*, III, 304.

77. See Waugh, "The Great Statute of Praemunire," EHR, XXXVII, 173–205, and "The Great Statute of Praemunire," *History*, VIII, 289–292.

78. "Reg. Courtenay," fol. 11. See also *ibid.*, fols. 52v–53, 64v, 188 (Ex Reg. Morton).

79. *Higden*, IX, 175.

80. *Patent Rolls*, 1388–1392, p. 415.

81. "Reg. Courtenay," fols. 330v–331.

82. *Ibid.*, fols. 116–116v.

83. *Ibid.*, fol. 14.

84. *Ibid.*, fol. 286. The scribe, possibly to break the tedium of his job, has left a drawing of two bells on the margin of the folio telling of this interdict. As noted above, the bells were rung to call the people together for the announcement of the interdict. The bells are suspended from a bar on which are inscribed the words, "Sentencia interdicti," while at the top of each bell appears the word "Romeney."

85. *Ibid.*, fols. 285–286.

86. *Ibid.*, fol. 11. See also "Reg. Courtenay," fols. 32–33.

87. *Ibid.*, fols. 107–107v.

88. *Ibid.*, fol. 107v; *Register of Thomas de Brantyngham*, I, 88. See also *Brantyngham*, I, 75.

89. *Patent Rolls*, 1388–1392, pp. 34–35.

90. "Reg. Courtenay," fol. 331.

CHAPTER NINE (Pages 187–227)

1. See above, chapter 8.

2. Pope Urban probably summoned Wyclif on his own responsibility in 1384. See Dahmus, *Prosecution*, pp. 139–149.

3. The one mandate of a spiritual nature to come from Rome was the papal bull introducing the feast of St. Anne, the mother of Mary. "Reg. Courtenay," fols. 38–38v; Wilkins, III, 178–179. Lyndwood (*Provinciale seu Constitutiones Angliae*, p. 60) says this mandate concerning St. Anne was the only one of a spiritual character Courtenay received from Rome. The pope did direct Courtenay and the bishops of London and Rochester to investigate the cause of Brother Thomas de la Hale, a monk of the monastery of Dover. See "Reg. Courtenay,"

fols. 50, 175; Wilkins, III, 174. But "the canonization unfortunately did not go through," writes Haines, because "the monks of Canterbury did not want a rival to their own Thomas. . . . *Dover Priory*, p. 478.

4. For England's reaction to the schism, see Ullmann, *The Origin of the Great Schism*, Ch. VII.

5. See above, p. 66.

6. *Register of Thomas de Brantyngham*, I, 395.

7. *Hist. Angl.*, I, 382.

8. See above, p. 39.

9. "Reg. Courtenay," fols. 80v–81; Wilkins, III, 191.

10. Froissart, *The Chronicles of England, France, and Spain*, p. 260.

11. "Reg. Courtenay," fols. 36–36v, 44, 64.

12. Rymer, VII, 479–480. See above, p. 172.

13. "Reg. Courtenay," fols. 58v–59. Courtenay's letter to the bishop of Rochester is dated September 9, 1384. He had just completed his visitation of Exeter.

14. *Ibid.*, fol. 59v.

15. *Ibid.*, fols. 60–60v.

16. *Ibid.*, fol. 66v.

17. See above, p. 181.

18. In 1394 Courtenay ordered the clergy of his province to receive the papal legate, Bartholomew de Navarre, with courtesy, and arranged to have a half-penny collected to provide for the legate's necessities. *Ibid.*, fol. 196v (Ex Reg. Morton).

19. *Ibid.*, fol. 183; Wilkins, III, 179–181.

20. *Ibid.*, fol. 186.

21. *Ibid.*, fol. 186; *Papal Registers, Letters*, IV, 454.

22. "Reg. Courtenay," fols. 187v–188.

23. *Ibid.*, fol. 187.

24. See below, p. 197.

25. "Reg. Courtenay," fol. 112; Wilkins, III, 188–189. See above, p. 126.

26. For a discussion of the rights of the archbishop of Canterbury in testamentary matters, see Churchill, I, Chapter IX.

27. See Churchill, I, 397, and Appendix H (II), p. 177.

28. "Register of Simon Sudbury," fol. 23v. See Churchill, I, 397, n. 2.

29. Smith, *Index of Wills Proved in the Prerogative Court of Canterbury*, ix. See also Churchill, I, 396–397.

30. *Index of Wills Proved in the Prerogative Court of Canterbury*, vii. See Churchill, I, 397, n. 2.

31. "Reg. Courtenay," fols. 288–288v.

32. *Registrum Johannis Trefnant*, p. 102.

33. *Ibid.*, 103.

34. One argument Trefnant advanced was that the books were only loaned, that they had never been "separated from the patrimony of Richard he held in the diocese of Hereford. . . ." *Ibid.*, 107.

35. *Ibid.*, 114. As soon as Courtenay withdrew his claim, Trefnant notified Rome to dismiss his appeal. *Ibid.*, 115.

36. "Reg. Courtenay," fol. 288.

37. *Hist. Angl.*, II, 217–218. See *Ypodigma Neustriae*, p. 369. Courtenay may have planned to use the money for the expansion of the church at Maidstone. See below, p. 231.

38. *The Chronicle of England by John Capgrave*, p. 261. The bishop of Lincoln also protested against the tax. See *Hist. Angl.*, II, 217–218.

39. *Registrum Johannis Trefnant*, p. 114. The pope appointed the bishop of London and the archbishop of York to execute the order. See also *Wykeham's Register*, II, 459–460.

40. *Registrum Johannis Trefnant*, p. 119.

41. The appeal over the books Courtenay had conceded. That over Courtenay's right to visit the diocese of Hereford was still pending. See above, p. 159.

42. How distorted a view of the church emerges, for instance, from a study based purely upon episcopal registers!

43. "Reg. Courtenay," fols. 11v–12; Wilkins, III, 155–156. See Appendix, pp. 259–261. This mandate was issued on June 8, 1382.

44. "Reg. Courtenay," fols. 21v–22.

45. *Ibid.*, fol. 337.

46. This suggests that the archbishop enjoyed the right to approve or disapprove the vote cast by the chapter.

47. *Ibid.*, fols. 336v–337.

48. *Canterbury College*, III, 12–13. Islip appointed John Wyclif warden in 1365.

49. *Ibid.*, 15–16.

50. *Ibid.*, pp. 36–37; "Register of Simon Sudbury," fol. 22v.

51. *Canterbury College*, III, 39; "Reg. Courtenay," fol. 22v.

52. *Canterbury College*, III, 39–40; "Reg. Courtenay," fol. 23v.

53. The living of Pagham had been appropriated for use of the college. See above, p. 200.

54. *Canterbury College*, III, 43–45; "Reg. Courtenay," fol. 42v.

55. See above, p. 200.

56. *Canterbury College*, III, 45–46; "Reg. Courtenay," fol. 43. That the names follow in alphabetical sequence is a coincidence. After these three names in the prior's letter appear those of the three monks recommended for fellows. These are not in alphabetical order.

57. See *Canterbury College*, III, 158.

58. See Pantin, *Canterbury College*, III, 158.

59. According to statutes issued subsequent to Islip's, the archbishop gained a voice in the selection of one of the fellows. See above, p. 202. Was Courtenay giving the monks a free hand here so that he might the easier declare Dovor a permanent warden, which he did two weeks later?

60. *Canterbury College*, III, 172–183.

61. *Ibid.*, 183.

62. *Ibid.*, 48.

63. *Ibid.*

64. *Charter Rolls*, V, 287. See Smith, *Canterbury Cathedral Priory*, p. 142.

65. See below, p. 232.

66. See Churchill, I, 148.

67. *William Thorne's Chronicle of Saint Augustine's Abbey Canterbury*, pp. 612–614. Canon law actually extended the archbishop the right to make such visits. See Churchill, I, 148, n. 4.

68. *Historiae Anglicanae Scriptores X*, 2157. See *William Thorne's Chronicle of Saint Augustine's Abbey Canterbury*, p. 616, and "Reg. Courtenay," fol. 256.

69. *Historiae Anglicanae Scriptores X*, pp. 2158–2159. See *William Thorne's Chronicle of Saint Augustine's Abbey Canterbury*, pp. 617–620.

70. *Ibid.*, 670; *Historiae Anglicanae Scriptores X*, p. 2194.

71. *Historiae Anglicanae Scriptores X*, p. 2194.

72. St. Augustine was buried there.

73. "Reg. Courtenay," fols. 288v–289v, 337v. This incident probably took place in March 1389. Two of the pertinent documents carry that year, a third 1390.

74. *Historiae Anglicanae Scriptores* X, p. 2194. Mr. Davis writes of Thorne: "The most marked characteristic of Thorne is his 'zeal for his house,' a quality he blames his predecessors for though he excels them in it." *William Thorne's Chronicle of Saint Augustine's Abbey Canterbury*, p. xxxvi.

75. See above, p. 147.

76. "Reg. Courtenay," fols. 168–169.

77. See Wilkins, *Was John Wycliffe a Negligent Pluralist?* and Dahmus, "Wyclyf Was a Negligent Pluralist," *Speculum*, XXVIII, 378–381. Courtenay's predecessor, Sudbury, also issued a mandate against nonresidence. See "Register of Simon Sudbury," fol. 40v; Wilkins, III, 120–121.

78. See above, p. 193.

79. "Reg. Courtenay," fol. 190 (Ex Reg. Morton).

80. *Ibid.*, fol. 21v.

81. *Ibid.*, fol. 140. See also fols. 140v, 143v. Otho and Othobon were papal legates who issued a decree against nonresidence in 1268.

82. *Ibid.*, fol. 21.

83. See below, p. 216.

84. For a discussion of such practices, see Thompson, *The English Clergy*, pp. 107–109.

85. "Reg. Courtenay," fols. 225–226v (Ex Reg. Morton); Wilkins, III, 215–217. See Appendix, pp. 261–265.

86. "Register of Simon Sudbury," fols. 27v–28.

87. "Register of Thomas Arundel," fol. 149; Wilkins, III, 213–214. For Winchelsey's statutes, see Wilkins, II, 28. On the same subject of clerical avarice, Courtenay threatened to excommunicate priests who accepted almost a penny for the performance of marriages, burials, and other religious services. "Register of Thomas Arundel," fol. 149; Wilkins, III, 207.

88. "Reg. Courtenay," fol. 51v.

89. *Ibid.*, fol. 65v.

90. "Register of Thomas Arundel," fol. 149; Wilkins, III, 205–207.

91. "Reg. Courtenay," fols. 194–194v (Ex Reg. Morton); Wilkins, III, 219–220.

92. *Hist. Angl.*, II, 65–66; *Chron. Angl.*, pp. 349–350.

93. "Reg. Courtenay," fols. 19v–21.

94. *Ibid.*, fol. 21.

95. *Ibid.*, fol. 190 (Ex Reg. Morton).

96. *Ibid.*, fol. 51v.

97. *Ibid.*, fol. 52v.

98. *Ibid.*, fol. 337v. The archbishop's scribe has sketched a strikingly clear picture of one of these tenants on the left margin of this folio. The figure, approximately five inches tall, is that of a man, presumably a peasant, carrying a large sack of straw over his left shoulder. A staff some five feet long supports the sack. The man is dressed in a long cloak that reaches below his knees, with short pants just showing through the opening in the cloak. The cloak is secured by a broad belt from which a gourdlike bottle is suspended. The man is bearded, with short cropped hair, barefooted, and apparently in his sixties.

99. *Ibid.*, fols. 40–41. The order was issued July 3, 1383.

100. *Ibid.*, fol. 40v. The report of the commissary general is dated July 19.

101. *Ibid.*

102. *Ibid.*, fols. 41–41v.

103. *Ibid.*, fols. 12–12v.

104. *Ibid.*, fol. 12v.

105. *Ibid.*, fol. 45.

106. *Ibid.* Several years later Courtenay directed the vicar general of Chichester to excommunicate those persons who had hunted on Canterbury property at Warren. *Ibid.*, fol. 63.

107. *Ibid.*, fol. 38v.

108. How much support Lollardy received from such Wycliffites as Hereford and Repingdon, or even from Wyclif himself, has not been established. Until documented evidence to the contrary is provided, one may assume that the connection between Wycliffitism at Oxford and Lollardy was hardly more than accidental.

109. *Knighton*, II, 260–264.

110. Wilkins, III, 204.

111. *Hist. Angl.*, II, 189. The bishop of Norwich may have attacked Lollardy with more vigor than his colleagues because of Wyclif's bitter attack on his crusade.

112. See above, p. 138.

113. "Reg. Courtenay," fol. 338; Wilkins, II, 215.

114. *Ibid.*, fol. 196v (Ex Reg. Morton).

115. *Hist. Angl.*, II, 215–217.

116. Rymer, VII, 805–806.

117. *The Chronicle of England by John Capgrave*, p. 260.

118. *Papal Registers, Letters*, IV, 515–516.

CHAPTER TEN (Pages 228–237)

1. *William Thorne's Chronicle of Saint Augustine's Abbey Canterbury*, p. 675.

2. This information is from Courtenay's will ("Register G," fols. 258–258v, 264) and from *Archaeologia: Or Miscellaneous Tracts Relating to Antiquity*, X, 273. It appears that Courtenay was planning in 1381 to be buried with his father and mother within the close of Exeter cathedral, for on November 15 of that year the king granted him permission to erect a chantry there for that purpose. *Patent Rolls, 1381–1385*, p. 61.

3. Somner, *The Antiquities of Canterbury*, p. 135. Noncontemporary writers speak of "many," a "thousand," "eight or ten thousand" people attending the obsequies. The chronicler does not specify. Maidstone was thirty miles from Canterbury.

4. As specified in the codicil. "Register G," fol. 264. The marble slab was raised in 1794 and some bones discovered underneath, although no supporting evidence that established them as Courtenay's. See Beazeley, "The Burial-Place of Archbishop Courtenay," *Archaeologia Cantiana*, XXIII, 41, 45.

5. Weever, *Antient Funeral Monuments*, pp. 31, 81–82. The epitaph in hexameter verse read:

   Nomine Willelmus en Courtneius reverendus,
   Qui se post obitum legaveret hic tumulandum,
   In presenti loco quem iam fundarat ab imo;
   Omnibus et sanctis titulo sacravit honoris.
   Ultima lux Iulii sit vite terminus illi;
   M. ter C. quinto decies nonoque sub anno,
   Respice mortalis quis quondam, sed modo talis,
   Quantus et iste fuit dum membra calentia gessit.
   Hic primas patrum, cleri dux et genus altum,
   Corpore valde decens, sensus et acumine clarens.
   Filius hic comitis generosi Devoniensis.
   Legum doctor erat celebris quem fama serenat.
   Urbs Herefordensis, polis inclita Londoniensis.
   Ac Dorobernensis, sibi trine gloria sedis
   Detur honor digno, sit cancellarius ergo.
   Sanctus ubique pater, prudens fuit ipse minister

Nam largus, letus, castus, pius atque pudicus,
Magnanimus, iustus, et egenis totus amicus.
Et quia rex Christe pastor bonus extitit iste,
Sumat solamen nunc tecum quesumus. Amen.

6. For a summary of these arguments, see Beazeley, pp. 31–50.

7. The scholar was M. Beazeley. See *Archaeologia Cantiana*, XXIII, 49. Mr. Beazeley may be commended for the thoroughness with which he examined this register. One wonders, however, about the validity of his speculations concerning Richard's motives in having Courtenay buried in Canterbury cathedral. He believes the king ordered his burial there in order to atone for the "indecent haste" with which he had authorized the election of a successor to Courtenay, "before the latter was yet cold in his coffin, and still unburied. . . ." Another reason, according to Mr. Beazeley, was Richard's vanity. Having Courtenay's obsequies in the cathedral would provide the king "an opportunity for a display of himself. . . ." *Ibid.*, 52–54. Whatever the depth of Richard's vanity, he scarcely deserves censure for granting the monks his *congé d'élire* just three days after Courtenay's death. He was on his way to France to marry the daughter of the king, and it might be some weeks before he returned. The monastery would have preferred not to wait so long to proceed with the election of a successor. It will be recalled that the prior in 1381 had requested the king's *congé d'élire* just three days after Sudbury's death. See above, p. 73.

8. Friends of Canterbury Cathedral. *Eleventh Annual Report*, p. 38. "It was a position of the greatest honour, there by the shrine where, in 1396, Prince Edward's was the only monument and where that of the king's cousin (who in three years' time would take the crown of England from his hands) was to be the third. *Ibid.*

9. "Register G," fols. 258–261v, 264. See Appendix, pp. 265–276.

10. In arriving at the figure of $350,000, I have used the ratio of one fourteenth-century pound to 20 pre-World War I pounds, and have multiplied this by three to cover inflation since 1914. The ratio of one medieval pound to 20 1914 pounds was employed by a writer in 1938 in estimating the modern equivalent of the 200 pounds Courtenay gave to Christ Church monastery for the building of the south walk of the Great Cloister. See Friends of Canterbury Cathedral. *Eleventh Annual Report*, p. 38.

11. Catherine may have been both the dearest and poorest of his sisters or, as Battely affirms, not his sister but his sister-in-law, the widow of his brother Edward. See *Cantuaria Sacra (The Antiquities of Canterbury)*, p. 44.

12. See above, p. 3.

13. Waltham was royal treasurer from 1391 until his death in September 1395. This means, incidentally, that Waltham was dead when Courtenay's will was proved. Courtenay's will bears no date, but the fact that the archbishop left a legacy to Edmund Stafford who became

bishop of Exeter in June 1395 and another to Waltham who died in September limits its preparation to the summer of that year.

14. See above, p. 231, n. 13.

15. In 1395 Pope Boniface approved Courtenay's request to convert the parish church of Maidstone into a collegiate church and to endow it with revenues sufficient to support 24 members. *Literae Cantuarienses*, III, 45–48; *Papal Registers, Letters*, IV, 505. On August 2, 1395, the king gave Courtenay permission to found the college, and on June 14, 1396, authorized him to take 48 masons "for executing certain works of a college to be by him erected at Madenston, and to pay them from his own moneys until the works are completed, and meanwhile they are not to be taken by the king's officers or ministers for his works." *Patent Letters*, 1391–1396, pp. 635, 719.

16. The church, known as All Hallows College and credited to Courtenay, was a "large and handsome stone building in the fine perpendicular of Wykeham's time and fortified with three towers." Parts of the structure are still used for educational purposes. See *Collectanea, Oxford Historical Society Publications*, XVI, 362, and Somner, pp. 256–266. For a description of Courtenay's coat of arms which appears at several places in the cloisters of Christ Church cathedral, see Griffin, "The Heraldry in the Cloisters of the Cathedral Church of Christ at Canterbury," *Archaeologia*, LXVI, 460, 463–465, 469, 476, and Denne, "Remarks on the Stalls near the Communion Table in Maidstone Church, with an Enquiry into the Place of Burial of Archbishop Courtney," *Archaeologia*, X, 269. For a description of Courtenay's seal which is in the British Museum, see Baigent, "On The Prelates Of The Courtenay Family," *Collectanea Archaeologica*, I, 236–262.

17. "Register S," fols. 23–23v. See *Ninth Report of the Royal Commission on Historical Manuscripts*, Pt. I, III, and *Literae Cantuarienses*, III, 41–45.

18. "idem reverendissimus et pius pater nobis et ecclesie sue Cantuariensi benignus et toto tempore suo benevolus fuerat devotus et modestus." "Register S," fol. 23.

19. "Reg. Courtenay," fol. 57.

20. *Ibid.*, fol. 57.

21. *Ibid.*, fols. 53–53v.

22. See above, p. 139.

23. See above, p. 71.

24. See above, p. 104.

25. See above, p. 190.

26. See above, p. 146.

27. See above, p. 185 and p. 224.

28. See above, p. 211.

APPENDIX (Pages 239–276)

1. "Reg. Courtenay," fols. 1v–2; Wilkins, III, 154–155.

2. "Reg. Courtenay," fol. 86; Wilkins, III, 183.

3. "Reg. Courtenay," fols. 86–86v; Wilkins, III, 183–184.

4. "Reg. Courtenay," fols. 90–91; *Register of Thomas de Brantyngham*, I, 530–532.

5. This same order was sent to the other archdeacons of the diocese. "Reg. Courtenay," fol. 101v.

6. "Reg. Courtenay," fol. 95v.

7. *Ibid.*, fol. 115.

8. "Reg. Courtenay," fols. 136v–137.

9. "Reg. Courtenay," fols. 335v–336v.

10. "Reg. Courtenay," fol. 339.

11. "Reg. Courtenay," fols. 334–334v. See Bradshaw, *Statutes of Lincoln Cathedral*, pp. 245–248.

12. "Reg. Courtenay," fols. 11v–12; Wilkins, III, 155–156.

13. *Ibid.*, fols. 225–226v (Ex Reg. Morton); Wilkins, III, 215–217.

14. "Register G," fols. 258–261v, 264. A copy of the will appears in *Archaeologia Cantiana*, XXIII, 58–67.

15. Since his successor was his close friend Thomas Arundel, archbishop of York, his fear in the matter of dilapidations was unfounded.

16. This must be reference to the earthquake that threw the council at Blackfriars into turmoil in May 1382. See above, p. 80.

17. An expression of endearment.

18. Son of Courtenay's brother Philip.

19. Richard became bishop of Norwich in 1413.

20. These books were valued at 300 pounds according to the entry in the obituary of Christ Church. See *The Church Historians of England*, IV, Pt. I, p. 309.

21. Son of his sister Elizabeth, wife of Sir Andrew Luttrell.

22. A section of canon law.

⟨BIBLIOGRAPHY⟩

(The following lists include manuscripts, books, and articles that have been used and quoted in the text or footnotes of this book. Books of only minor significance for the subject have not been listed.)

EPISCOPAL REGISTERS

Manuscripts

"Register G" (Canterbury)

"Register S" (Canterbury)

"Register of Thomas Arundel," Archbishop of Canterbury, 1396–1414 (Lambeth)

"Register of Robert Braybroke," Bishop of London, 1382–1398 (Guildhall)

"Register of John Buckingham," Bishop of Lincoln, 1362-1398 (Lincoln)

"Register of William Courtenay," Archbishop of Canterbury, 1381–1396 (Lambeth). (Folios in that part of Courtenay's register which is assembled with acts of Bouchier, Morton, and Dean are identified as Ex Reg. Morton.)

"Register of Simon Sudbury," Archbishop of Canterbury, 1375–1381 (Lambeth)

"Register of John Waltham," Bishop of Salisbury, 1388–1395 (Salisbury)

"Register of William Witlesey," Archbishop of Canterbury, 1368–1374 (Lambeth)

Printed

Register of Thomas de Brantyngham, Bishop of Exeter, 1370–1394. Ed. F. C. Hingeston-Randolf, I, II. London, 1901, 1906.

Registrum Willelmi de Courtenay, Episcopi Herefordensis, 1370–1375. Ed. W. W. Capes. Canterbury and York Society Publications. London, 1914.

Register of John de Grandisson, Bishop of Exeter, 1327–1369. Ed. F. C. Hingeston-Randolf, III. Exeter, 1899.

Registrum Johannis Trefnant. Ed. W. W. Capes. Canterbury and York Society Publications. London, 1916.

Register of the Diocese of Worcester During the Vacancy of the See, usually called *"Registrum Sede Vacante."* Ed. J. W. Willis Bund. Worcestershire Historical Society, III. Oxford, 1895.

Wykeham's Register. Ed. T. F. Kirby. Hampshire Record Society Publications, II. London, 1899.

CHRONICLES

Adami Murimuthensis Chronica Sui Temporis. Ed. E. Hog. English Historical Society Publications, I. London, 1846.

The Anonimalle Chronicle, 1333 to 1381. Ed. V. H. Galbraith. Manchester, 1927.

Chronicle of England by John Capgrave, The. Ed. F. C. Hingeston. Rolls Series. London, 1858.

Chronicon Abbatiae de Evesham. Ed. W. Dunn Macray. Rolls Series. London, 1863.

Chronicon Adae de Usk. Ed. E. M. Thompson. London, 1904.

Chronicon Angliae, 1328–1388, T. Walsingham. Ed. E. M. Thompson. Rolls Series. London, 1874.

Chronicon Henrici Knighton, II. Ed. J. R. Lumby. Rolls Series. London, 1895.

English Chronicle of the Reigns of Richard II, Henry IV, Henry V, and Henry VI, An. Ed. J. S. Davies. Camden Society, LXIV. 1856.

Eulogium Historiarum sive Temporis (Continuatio), III. Ed. F. S. Haydon. Rolls Series. London, 1863.

Fasciculi Zizaniorum Magistri Johannis Wyclif. Ed. W. W. Shirley. Rolls Series. London, 1858.

Froissart, John, *The Chronicles of England, France and Spain.* New York, 1961.

Gesta Abbatum Monasterii Sancti Albani a Thoma Walsingham, III. Ed. H. T. Riley. Rolls Series. London, 1869.

Historia Anglicana, T. Walsingham, I, II. Ed. H. T. Riley. Rolls Series. London, 1863, 1864.

Historiae Anglicanae Scriptores X. London, 1652.

Historia Vitae et Regni Ricardi II Angliae Regis. Ed. T. Hearne. Oxford, 1729.

Matthaei Parisiensis Chronica Majora, V, VI. Ed. H. R. Luard. Rolls Series. London, 1880, 1882.

Polychronicon Ranulphi Higden Monachi Cistrensis, VIII, IX. Ed. J. R. Lumby. Rolls Series. London, 1886.

William Thorne's Chronicle of Saint Augustine's Abbey Canterbury. Ed. A. H. Davis. Oxford, 1934.

Transcript of a Chronicle in the Harleian Library of MSS. No. 6217, entitled "An Historical Relation of Certain Passages about the End of King Edward the Third, and His Death." *Archaeologia,* XXII. London, 1828.

Ypodigma Neustriae, Thoma Walsingham. Ed. H. T. Riley. Rolls Series. London, 1876.

OTHER PRIMARY SOURCES

Calendar of the Charter Rolls Preserved in the Public Record Office, V, 1341-1417. Rolls Series.

Calendar of the Close Rolls Preserved in the Public Record Office, 1374-1392. Five volumes. Rolls Series.

Calendar of the Fine Rolls Preserved in the Public Record Office, 1377-1383, 1383-1391. Rolls Series.

Calendar of Letter-Books . . . of the City of London, Letter-Book H, ca. 1375-1399. Ed. R. R. Sharpe. London, 1907.

Calendar of Entries in the Papal Registers Relating to Great Britain and Ireland, Papal Letters, IV. Rolls Series.

Calendar of Entries in the Papal Registers Relating to Great Britain and Ireland, Petitions to the Pope, I. Rolls Series.

Calendar of the Patent Rolls Preserved in the Public Record Office, 1367-1392. Seven volumes. Rolls Series.

Canterbury College Oxford, III. Ed. W. A. Pantin. Oxford Historical Society. New Series, VIII. Oxford, 1950.

Charters and Records of Hereford Cathedral. Ed. W. W. Capes. Hereford, 1908.

Diplomatic Correspondence of Richard II, The. Ed. E. Perroy. Camden Third Series, XLVIII. London, 1933.

Literae Cantuarienses, III. Ed. J. B. Sheppard. Rolls Series. London, 1889.

Lyndwood, William, *Provinciale seu Constitutiones Angliae.* Oxford, 1679.

Matthaei Parker Cantuariensis Archiepiscopi De Antiquitate Britannicae Ecclesiae et Privilegiis Ecclesiae Cantuariensis. Ed. S. Drake. London, 1729.

Munimenta Academica, I. Ed. H. Anstey. Rolls Series. London, 1868.

Rotuli Parliamentorum; ut et Petitiones, et Placita in Parliamento Tempore Edwardi R. III, Vol. II; *et in Parliamento Tempore Richardi R. II,* Vol. III. Ed. J. Strachey, 1767.

Rymer, Thomas. *Foedera, Conventiones, Literae, et Cujuscunque Generis Acta Publica,* VII. London, 1709.

Snappe's Formulary and other Records. Ed. H. E. Salter. Oxford Historical Society, LXXX. Oxford, 1924.

Statutes of Lincoln Cathedral. Arranged by H. Bradshaw. Ed. C. Wordsworth. Pt. II. Cambridge, 1897.

Statutes of the Realm, I, II. Record Commission. London, 1810, 1816.

Visitations of Religious Houses in the Diocese of Lincoln, I. Ed. A. H. Thompson. London, 1915.

Wilkins, David. *Concilia Magnae Britanniae et Hiberniae,* III. London, 1737.

(WYCLIF'S WRITINGS)

De Civili Dominio, II. Ed. J. Loserth. London, 1900.

De Ecclesia. Ed. J. Loserth. London, 1886.

De Veritate Sacrae Scripturae, I. Ed. R. Buddensieg. London, 1905.

John Wiclif's Polemical Works in Latin, I. Ed. R. Buddensieg. London, 1883.

Select English Works of John Wyclif, III. Ed. T. Arnold. Oxford, 1871.

Joannis Wyclif Trialogus. Ed. G. Lechler. Oxford, 1869.

ARTICLES

Beazeley, M. "The Burial-Place of Archbishop Courtenay," *Archaeologia Cantiana,* XXIII (1898), 31–54.

Baigent, Francis Joseph. "On the Prelates of the Courtenay Family," *Collectanea Archaeologica*, I (1862), 232–262.

Crompton, James. "Fasciculi Zizaniorum II," *The Journal of Ecclesiastical History*, XII (1961), 155–166.

Dahmus, Joseph. "John Wyclif and the English Government," *Speculum*, XXXV (1960), 51–68.

Dahmus, Joseph. "Richard II and the Church," *Catholic Historical Review*, XXXIX (1954), 408–433.

Dahmus, Joseph. "Wyclyf Was a Negligent Pluralist," *Speculum*, XXVIII (1953), 378–381.

Denne, Samuel. "Remarks on the Stalls near the Communion Table in Maidstone Church, with an Enquiry into the Place of Burial of Archbishop Courtney," *Archaeologia*, X (1792), 261–297.

Driver, J. T. "The Papacy and the Diocese of Hereford, 1307–1377," *The Church Quarterly Review*, CXLV (1947–1948), 31–47.

Duncan, Leland L. "The Will of William Courtenay, Archbishop of Canterbury, 1396," *Archaeologia Cantiana*, XXIII (1898), 55–67.

Anonymous. "The Bequest of William Courtenay Archbishop of Canterbury," Friends of Canterbury Cathedral. *Eleventh Annual Report* (1938), 33–38.

Galbraith, V. H. "Articles Laid before the Parliament of 1371," *English Historical Review*, XXXIV (1919), 579–582.

Galbraith, V. H. "Thomas Walsingham and the Saint Albans Chronicle, 1272–1422," *English Historical Review*, XLVII (1932), 12–29.

Gibson, S. "Confirmations of Oxford Chancellors in the Lincoln Episcopal Registers," *English Historical Review*, XXVI (1911), 501–512.

Griffin, Ralph. "The Heraldry in the Cloisters of the Cathedral Church at Canterbury," *Archaeologia*, LXVI (Second Series, XVI) (1915), 447–568.

Hanrahan, T. J. "John Wyclif's Political Activity," *Mediaeval Studies*, XX (1958), 154–165.

Healey, J. E. "John of Gaunt and John Wyclif," *Canadian Catholic Historical Report* (1962), 41–57.

Highfield, J. R. L. "The English Hierarchy in the Reign of Edward III," *Transactions of the Royal Historical Society*, Fifth Series, VI (1956), 115–138.

Johnstone, Hilda. "The Nuns of Elstow," *The Church Quarterly Review*, CXXXIII (1941), 46–54.

Kemp, Eric. "The Origins of the Canterbury Convocation," *The Journal of Ecclesiastical History*, III (1952), 132–143.

Lewis, N. B. "The 'Continual Council' in the Early Years of Richard
    II, 1377–1380," *English Historical Review*, XLI (1926), 246–251.

Pantin, W. A. "A Benedictine Opponent of John Wyclif," *English Histori-
    cal Review*, XLIII (1928), 74–77.

Perroy, Edouard. "The Anglo-French Negotiations at Bruges, 1374–1377,"
    Camden Miscellany, XIX (Camden Third Series, LXXX) (1952),
    i–xix, 1–95.

Richardson, H. G. "The Parish Clergy of the Thirteenth and Fourteenth
    Centuries," *Transactions of the Royal Historical Society*, Third
    Series, VI (1912), 89–128.

Robinson, J. A. "Convocation of Canterbury: Its Early History," *The
    Church Quarterly Review*, LXXXI (1915–1916), 81–137.

Thomson, S. Harrison. Book Review. *Speculum*, XXVIII (1953), 563–566.

Warren, W. L. "A Reappraisal of Simon Sudbury, Bishop of London
    (1361–1375) and Archbishop of Canterbury (1375–1381)," *The Jour-
    nal of Ecclesiastical History*, X (1959), 139–152.

Waugh, W. T. "The Great Statute of Praemunire," *English Historical
    Review*, XXXVII (1922), 173–205.

Waugh, W. T. "The Great Statute of Praemunire," *History*, VIII (1924),
    289–292.

Wedgwood, J. C. "John of Gaunt and the Packing of Parliament," *English
    Historical Review*, VL (1930), 623–625.

MODERN WORKS

Barraclough, Geoffrey. *Papal Provisions*. Oxford, 1935.

Boggis, R. J. E. *A History of the Diocese of Exeter*. Exeter, 1922.

Burke, Bernard. *A Genealogical and Heraldic Dictionary of the Peerage
    and Baronetage*. London, 1898.

Capes, W. W. *The English Church in the Fourteenth and Fifteenth Cen-
    turies*. London, 1903.

Cheney, C. R. *Episcopal Visitation of Monasteries in the Thirteenth Cen-
    tury*. Manchester, 1931.

Churchill, Irene Josephine. *Canterbury Administration*, I, II. London, 1933.

Clarke, Maude Violet. *Fourteenth Century Studies*. Oxford, 1937.

Cobbet, William. *The Parliamentary History of England*, I. London, 1806.

Complete Peerage, The, III, IV. London, 1913.

Dahmus, Joseph. *The Metropolitan Visitations of William Courteney*. Urbana, 1950.

Dahmus, Joseph. *The Prosecution of John Wyclyf*. New Haven, 1952.

Daly, L. J. *The Political Theory of John Wyclif*. Chicago, 1962.

Dugdale, William. *The Baronage of England*, I. London, 1675.

Edwards, Kathleen. *The English Secular Cathedrals in the Middle Ages*. Manchester, 1949.

Emden, A. B. *A Biographical Register of the University of Oxford to A.D. 1500*, I. Oxford, 1957.

Graham, Rose. *The Metropolitan Visitation of the Diocese of Worcester by Archbishop Winchelsey in 1301. Transactions of the Royal Historical Society*, Fourth Series, II, 1919.

Gregorovius, Ferdinand. *History of the City of Rome in the Middle Ages*, VI, Pt. II. London, 1898.

Haines, Charles Reginald. *Dover Priory*. Cambridge, 1930.

Hennessy, George. *Novum Repertorium Ecclesiasticum Parochiale Londoniensis*. London, 1898.

Historical Manuscripts Commission Report on Manuscripts in Various Collections, VII, 1914.

Hook, Walter Farquar. *The Lives of the Archbishops of Canterbury*, IV. London, 1875.

Hoskins, W. G. and Finberg, H. P. R. *Devonshire Studies*. London, 1952.

Jusserand, J. J. *English Wayfaring Life in the Middle Ages*. London, 1961.

Knowles, Dom David. *The Religious Orders in England*, II. Cambridge, 1955.

Lowth, Robert. *The Life of William of Wykeham*. London, 1758.

Manning, B. L. "Wyclif," *Cambridge Medieval History*, VII. Cambridge, 1932.

McFarlane, K. B. *John Wycliffe and the Beginnings of English Nonconformity*. New York, 1953.

McKisack, May. *The Fourteenth Century*. Oxford, 1959.

Ninth Report of the Royal Commission on Historical Manuscripts. London, 1883.

Pantin, W. A. *The English Church in the Fourteenth Century*. Cambridge, 1955.

Perroy, Edouard. *L'Angleterre et le grand Schisme d'Occident*. Paris, 1933.

Perroy, Edouard. "L'Affaire du Comte de Denia," *Mélanges d'Histoire du Moyen Age.* Paris, 1951.

Rashdall, Hastings. *The Universities of Europe in the Middle Ages,* III. Oxford, 1936.

Robson, J. A. *Wyclif and the Oxford Schools.* Cambridge, 1961.

Smith, John Challenor. *Index of Wills Proved in the Prerogative Court of Canterbury,* 1383-1558. *The British Record Society,* X. London, 1893.

Smith, Reginald Anthony. *Canterbury Cathedral Priory.* Cambridge, 1943.

Somner, William. *The Antiquities of Canterbury.* London, 1640. The Antiquities of Canterbury in Two Parts. The First Part, *The Antiquities of Canterbury* by William Somner; the Second Part, *Cantuaria Sacra* by Nicholas Battely. London, 1703.

Steel, Anthony. *Richard II.* Cambridge, 1941.

Stubbs, William. *The Constitutional History of England,* II, III. Oxford, 1875, 1878.

Stubbs, William. *Registrum Sacrum Anglicanum.* Oxford, 1897.

Thompson, A. Hamilton. *The English Clergy.* Oxford, 1947.

Tierney, Brian. *Medieval Poor Law.* Berkeley, 1959.

Tout, Thomas F. *Chapters in the Administrative History of Mediaeval England,* III. Manchester, 1928.

Trevelyan, George M. *England in the Age of Wycliffe.* London, 1900.

Ullmann, Walter. *The Origins of the Great Schism.* London, 1948.

Unwin, George. *Finance and Trade under Edward III.* London, 1962.

Wake, William. *The State of the Church and Clergy of England.* London, 1703.

Weever, John. *Antient Funeral Monuments.* London, 1767.

Weske, Dorothy B. *Convocation of the Clergy.* London, 1937.

Wilkins, H. J. *Was John Wycliffe a Negligent Pluralist?* London, 1915.

Wilkins, H. J. *Westbury College.* Bristol, 1917.

Wilkinson, B. *The Chancery under Edward III.* Manchester, 1929.

Wood, Anthony. *The History and Antiquities of the University of Oxford.* Ed. John Gutch. I. Oxford, 1792.

Wood, Anthony. *Appendix to the History and Antiquities of the Colleges and Halls in the University of Oxford.* Ed. John Gutch. Oxford, 1790.

Workman, Herbert B. *John Wyclif,* I, II. Oxford, 1926.

{INDEX}